Thinking with Deleuze

Thinking with Deleuze

Ronald Bogue

EDINBURGH
University Press

Edinburgh University Press is one of the leading university presses in the UK. We publish academic books and journals in our selected subject areas across the humanities and social sciences, combining cutting-edge scholarship with high editorial and production values to produce academic works of lasting importance. For more information visit our website: edinburghuniversitypress.com

Edinburgh University Press Ltd
The Tun – Holyrood Road
12(2f) Jackson's Entry
Edinburgh EH8 8PJ

Typeset in 10/12 Goudy Old Style by
Servis Filmsetting Ltd, Stockport, Cheshire,
and printed and bound in Great Britain.

A CIP record for this book is available from the British Library

ISBN 978 1 4744 4728 7 (hardback)
ISBN 978 1 4744 4730 0 (webready PDF)
ISBN 978 1 4744 4729 4 (paperback)
ISBN 978 1 4744 4731 7 (epub)

Contents

IV. Literature and Philosophy

V. Sight, Sound and Language

VI. Nature

Preface

The essays of this collection represent a decade-long attempt to think with Deleuze, both alongside him and through him, following diverse lines of his thought and deploying certain concepts to extend that thought into areas he did not explore. Each essay offers a separate point of entry into Deleuze's thought, but all focus ultimately on Deleuze's effort to 'think otherwise' and thereby invent possibilities for life, in the hope that such possibilities eventuate in a people to come and a new earth.

In a broad sense, the present effort to think with Deleuze is a continuation of my work since 2004. When my first book, *Deleuze and Guattari*, appeared in 1989, there was very little on Deleuze available in English. The book was commissioned as a contribution to the series Critics of the Twentieth Century, and hence it provided analyses of Deleuze's literary studies of Proust and Sacher-Masoch and Deleuze and Guattari's volume on Kafka. But the absence of secondary literature on Deleuze and Guattari and their marginal status in what was then referred to as critical theory meant that any consideration of Deleuze and Guattari as literary critics would have to be situated within a broad introduction to their thought in general – and, in fact, well over two-thirds of the book was devoted to that purpose. The publisher's page limit, however, precluded a consideration of the full Deleuzian corpus, and I chose to trace the outlines of Deleuze's thought by discussing only *Nietzsche and Philosophy*, *Difference and Repetition*, *The Logic of Sense*, *Anti-Oedipus* and *A Thousand Plateaus*.

Upon completing that project, I saw the need for a more

comprehensive exposition of Deleuze's thought as well as a thorough engagement with his approach to the arts as a whole. I therefore embarked on an examination of Deleuze's writings on literature, cinema, music and art, with the goal of providing discussions of each art sufficiently sophisticated to address the concerns of students and practitioners of the art in question, yet accessible enough to be understood by those engaged in other artistic fields and by philosophers interested in Deleuze's aesthetics and its relationship to his thought in general. This effort resulted in a 2003 trilogy on Deleuze and the arts: *Deleuze on Literature*, *Deleuze on Cinema* and *Deleuze on Music, Painting, and the Arts*.

Although I conceived of this trilogy as an exercise in 'reading along with' Deleuze, the emphasis was more on 'reading' than 'along with', in that most of my attention was directed towards an explication of Deleuze's difficult texts and an exposition of the broad tenets of his aesthetics. In this sense, the trilogy was largely a continuation of my initial project of offering an introduction to Deleuze for the uninitiated. It was only in the essays of *Deleuze's Wake: Tributes and Tributaries* (2004) and *Deleuze's Way: Essays in Transverse Ethics and Aesthetics* (2007) that I adopted as a primary goal that of thinking with Deleuze – untangling strands of motifs enmeshed in diverse arguments and using Deleuzian concepts to test their viability in the analysis of subjects Deleuze did not address, such as Nō drama and death metal music. Decisive in these efforts was my encounter with the concept of fabulation, a minor theme in Deleuze's work that had gone largely unnoticed by commentators. This encounter led me to develop an approach to narrative in terms of fabulation and to argue for its use in reading modern fiction. In *Deleuzian Fabulation and the Scars of History* (2010), I detailed the features of such Deleuzian fabulation and utilised them in extended analyses of five contemporary novels.

Central to the concept of fabulation is the goal of inventing a people to come. In the essays presented in this volume, I continue to meditate on the idea of inventing a people to come and all that such invention entails. What I have added to this meditation is a consideration of Deleuze and Guattari's call for the creation of a new earth. The term 'new earth' ('terre nouvelle' or 'nouvelle terre') occurs eight times in *Anti-Oedipus*, in each case as an indicator that the schizo's deterritorialisation discloses a new, deterritorialised 'terre'. (The English translation masks this repetition, rendering 'nouvelle terre' or 'terre nouvelle' as 'new earth' [AO 131, 299, 321], 'new land' [AO 318, 322] and 'new world' [AO 322].) In *A Thousand Plateaus*, Deleuze and Guattari refer to a 'nouvelle terre' five times (rendered as 'new earth' [ATP 423, 510] and 'new land' [ATP 149, 472, 509]), and they also speak of a 'people to come' ('peuple à venir') – a phrase that does not occur in *Anti-Oedipus* – three times (twice on page 345, translated first as 'people yet to come' and then as 'people to come', once on page 467). But it is only in *What is Philosophy?* that the notions of a new earth and a people to come are brought together. In the concluding paragraph of *What is Philosophy?*, Deleuze and Guattari state that what unites philosophy, the sciences and the arts is the creation of a 'people to come' (WP 218), but in Chapter 4, 'Geophilosophy', they connect that effort to the 'creation of a future new earth' ('la création d'une nouvelle terre à venir') (WP 88). Philosophy must '*summon forth a new earth, a new people*' (WP 99). It must induce absolute deterritorialisation 'even to the point where this calls for a new earth, a new people' (WP 101). The creation of concepts 'in itself calls for a future form, for a new earth and people that do not yet exist' (WP 108), for 'the people to come and the new earth' (WP 109).

Adding a call for a new earth to a call for a new people might seem a mere rhetorical flourish, a means of emphasising the all-encompassing transformations attendant on a truly revolutionary philosophy. In such case, it would make no difference whether 'terre' were translated as 'earth', 'world' or 'land'. But as Deleuze and Guattari suggest in *A Thousand Plateaus*, the concept of a new earth is inseparable from their ontology, which is that of a perpetually self-organising, disorganising and reorganising, metamorphic 'chaosmos'. In Plateau Three, 'The Geology of Morals', they present the earth both as the locus of strata encompassing the physico-chemical, organic and anthropic (or 'alloplastic') domains of an anorganic life, and as 'the Deterritorialized, the Glacial, the giant Molecule [. . .] a body without organs' (ATP 40). In Plateau Eleven, 'The Refrain', they elaborate on the ethological ramifications of Plateau Three's ontology of strata, and in Plateau Ten,

'Becoming-Intense, Becoming-Animal, Becoming-Imperceptible . . .', they detail processes of metamorphosis that traverse all the strata of the natural world. Hence, the call for a new earth is more than a vague utopian slogan. Rather, it is an invocation of absolute deterritorialisation as a cosmic force that plays through rocks, plants, animals and humans. 'We could say that the earth, as deterritorialized, is itself the strict correlate of D [deterritorialisation]. To the point that D can be called the creator of the earth – of a new earth, a universe, not just a reterritorialization' (ATP 509; trans. modified). Deterritorialisation is relative when it induces stratification, but it is absolute when it 'brings about the creation of a new earth, in other words, when it connects lines of flight, raises them to the power of an abstract vital line, or draws a plane of consistency' (ATP 510).

A central concern of the essays in this volume, then, is to connect this view of nature to the political goal of inventing a people to come and to situate the arts in relation to the project of creating a new earth and a new people. The key, I argue here, is to 'think otherwise', and thereby to open possibilities for new modes of existence, to adopt 'protocols of experience' as guides for experimentation in politics and the arts, and to embrace a 'chaosmopolitanism', in which a viable collectivity invents new ways of living in resonance with the chaosmos of nature.

Since the publication of my first book, the secondary literature on Deleuze has increased dramatically, especially over the last decade. Interest in Deleuze and Guattari has spread well beyond the confines of Europe, North America and Australia, with extremely rich uses of their thought being developed in East and South Asia, the Middle East, Africa and Latin America. That expansion is represented in a very small way in this collection by the essay on Chinese-American literature (Chapter 11), delivered at the first Deleuze conference held in the People's Republic of China (Henan University, 2012), and the study of Deleuze and Asian drama (Chapter 12), presented at the First International Deleuze Studies in Asia Conference in Taiwan (2013). In both cases, my effort was to redress the asymmetry so often evident in East–West engagements with philosophy and the arts, in which Asian scholars devote serious study to Western texts while

Occidental scholars largely ignore Asian traditions and practices. The thought of Deleuze has also generated considerable activity in numerous disciplines outside philosophy. This expansion of Deleuze studies is indicated only partially in this volume's chapters touching on issues in film (2, 14), music (4, 5, 6), the visual arts (13), literature (3, 5, 10, 11, 12, 13), law (17), ecology (14), ethology (18) and education (1).

It would take a taxonomic genius – or, more likely, a delusional system builder – to discern a clear pattern in the myriad publications on Deleuze and Guattari that have appeared in the last few decades and that continue to proliferate. Situating this volume within the expanding, heterogeneous, and perhaps incompossible areas of Deleuze studies must be limited and incomplete, but a few coordinates may help relate these essays to certain positions that have been staked out in the field. There has long been a tendency to minimise the role of Guattari in the development of Deleuze's thought, and in some cases to argue that Deleuze's collaboration with Guattari in *Anti-Oedipus* signalled the end of his work as a serious philosopher. The best-known expressions of this extreme view are Alain Badiou's *Deleuze: The Clamour of Being* (Badiou 2000), which treats *Difference and Repetition* (1968) as Deleuze's last significant book, and Slavoj Žižek's *Organs without Bodies: Deleuze and Consequences* (2003), which locates the apogee of Deleuze's philosophy in *The Logic of Sense* (1969). I agree with Badiou and Žižek that *Anti-Oedipus* marks a major divide in Deleuze's work, but one that is positive, not negative. What I find most interesting are Deleuze's writings from *Anti-Oedipus* on, a predilection reflected in this collection of essays, which focuses almost exclusively on the publications that appeared during the last two decades of Deleuze's life.

Indeed, far from representing an abandonment of serious philosophising, Deleuze's writings with Guattari, I believe, stand as his greatest achievements in philosophy. Evidence suggests that I am not alone in this judgement. Early studies of Deleuze and Guattari, including Brian Massumi's *A User's Guide to Capitalism and Schizophrenia* (1992), Eugene Holland's *Deleuze and Guattari's Anti-Oedipus* (1999) and Ian Buchanan's *Deleuzism* (2000), have paved the way for hundreds of books and articles on the jointly authored works – testimony to the significance others have found in these texts. Essential for my purposes here is the political dimension of these books, especially as it is laid out in *Anti-Oedipus*'s third chapter, 'Savages, Barbarians and Civilized Men', the Nomadology and Apparatus of Capture Plateaus of *A Thousand Plateaus*, and the Geophilosophy chapter of *What Is Philosophy?*, since the concepts of fabulation and the people to come only gain full coherence within this context. Eugene Holland and Paul Patton have provided invaluable analyses in this area (Holland 1999, 2006, 2013; Patton 2000 and 2010), and those studies have guided my response in Chapter 3 to Peter Hallward's charges of political inefficacy in Deleuze (Hallward 2006) and in Chapter 5 to Philippe Mengue's claims of an anti-democratic bias in Deleuze's thought (Mengue 2003).

Of the four jointly authored works, I regard *A Thousand Plateaus* as the most important, since it provides the basic ontological framework in which to understand the schizoanalysis of *Anti-Oedipus* and the minor literature of *Kafka*, as well as the themes of fabulation, the possible and vitalism that recur in later volumes, especially in *What is Philosophy?* and *Essays Critical and Clinical*. It has taken some time for philosophers to engage *A Thousand Plateaus* seriously, but the recent collection *A Thousand Plateaus and Philosophy* (2018), edited by Somers-Hall, Bell and Williams, perhaps testifies to a shift among philosophers towards a fuller appreciation of the significance of this great work. My reading of *A Thousand Plateaus* follows the lines laid out by those who approach Deleuze and Guattari via chaos and emergence theory, including, among many others, Manuel DeLanda (especially DeLanda's early essay 'Nonorganic Life' [DeLanda 1992]), Jeffrey Bell (*Philosophy at the Edge of Chaos: Gilles Deleuze and the Philosophy of Difference* [2006]), and. above all, John Protevi, whose essays 'Deleuze, Guattari and Emergence' (2006) and 'Deleuze and Life' (2012) aptly summarise his views.

In a very loose sense, this reading is in accord with elements of what has been called the New Materialism (see Coole and Frost [2010] and Dolphjin and van der Tuin [2012]), which has often taken tacit, if not explicit, inspiration from Deleuze. It is also compatible with the work of those who have brought Deleuze and

Guattari into discussions of ecology, animals and the non-human. As Eduardo Viveiros de Castro observes, *A Thousand Plateaus* marks a significant change from *Anti-Oedipus*, one that

> reflects a major shift of focus from an intraspecific to an interspecific horizon: from a human economy of desire – a world-historical desire, no doubt, that was racial and socio-political and not familial, personological, and Oedipal, but a human desire all the same – to an economy of trans-specific affects ignorant of the natural order of species and their limiting synthesis, connecting us, through inclusive disjunction, to the plane of immanence. (Viveiros de Castro 2014: 162)

A Thousand Plateaus's 'economy of trans-specific affects' provides the central theoretical framework for Viveiros's approach to anthropology, which in turn has inspired others to pursue an 'ontological anthropology' beyond the human (see, for example, Kohn 2013 and Holbraad and Pedersen 2017). *A Thousand Plateaus* also plays a major role in the contributions to three recent collective volumes that explore the implications of Deleuze and Guattari's ontology of anorganic life: *Deleuze/Guattari and Ecology* (Herzogenrath 2008), *Deleuze and the Non/Human* (Roffe and Stark 2015) and *Deleuze and the Animal* (Gardner and MacCormack 2017). Although my ends are very different from many of the contributors to these volumes, as well as those of ontological anthropologists, I share their interest in *A Thousand Plateaus*' conception of nature as a chaosmos of mutative forms, forces and processes that traverse the domains commonly designated as physical-chemical, organic, human, technological and so on.

One essential area remains to be explored in these essays – that of the contributions of Guattari's late writings to the chaosmopolitan project initiated in *A Thousand Plateaus*. In Chapter 16, I argue that *A Thousand Plateaus* may be judged 'ecosophic', in the sense given the term by Arne Naess, but I leave unexamined *A Thousand Plateaus*' relationship to the ecosophy of Guattari's *Three Ecologies* (1989), *Chaosmosis* (1992) and the posthumous *Qu'est-ce que l'écosophie?* (2013). Guattari subtitles *Chaosmosis* 'an ethico-aesthetic paradigm', and in *Chaosmosis* he asserts that 'the aesthetic power of feeling, although equal in principle with the other powers of thinking philosophically, knowing scientifically, acting politically, seems on the verge of occupying a privileged position within the collective Assemblages of enunciation of our era' (Guattari 1995: 101). Exactly how this primacy of the aesthetic might play out in the theoretical context of Guattari's late work is an area that holds great promise for future research.

I have organised the essays in six sections. Although each essay is self-contained, reiterated themes and concerns across the essays are meant to reinforce the broad argument that Deleuze's work from *Anti-Oedipus* on is dedicated to the search for new possibilities for life with the goal of fostering a new earth and a people to come. This is how I see the essays working together to support that argument.

I. Introduction: Thinking Otherwise. In *Foucault* (1986), Deleuze says that for Foucault, 'Thought thinks its own history (the past), but in order to free itself from what it thinks (the present) and be able finally to "think otherwise"' (F 119). The same may be said of Deleuze. 'The Master Apprentice', the first chapter in this volume, offers an introduction to Deleuze's 'thinking otherwise' by examining his conception and practice of teaching. In his seminars, he tried to model thought-in-process, to combine rigorous preparation with improvisation in an effort to transcend that preparation in moments of inspiration. He approached the history of philosophy in his courses as a discipline necessary for thought 'to free itself from what it thinks'. This apprenticeship in philosophy he expected of his students, and he himself practised it throughout his career. As master to his apprentices, he taught by inviting his students to think alongside him, for as he says in *Difference and Repetition*, 'we learn nothing from those who say: "Do as I do". Our only teachers [*maîtres*] are those who tell us to "do with me"' (DR 23). What he showed is that to think otherwise one must be a master apprentice, perpetually encountering signs and learning from the world.

II. The Possible and the People to Come. In his later works, Deleuze stressed repeatedly that the goal of philosophy and the arts is to create new possibilities for life and thereby enable the invention of a 'people to come', by which he meant a viable collectivity that does not yet exist. The essays of this section address various aspects of this general goal. Chapter 2 focuses on the ethics of 'choosing to choose', which Deleuze finds exemplified in the philosophy of Kierkegaard and the cinema of Robert Bresson. Deleuze argues that the way of living involved in choosing to choose, that of committing oneself to the perpetual responsibility of choosing, affords a means of restoring belief in this world and its power to open alternatives to the clichéd thought of the present. Chapter 3 looks at the theme of the possible in Deleuze's essay on Michel Tournier's novel *Friday*, and Chapter 4 expands on this notion of the possible, tracing its development throughout Deleuze's career. Chapter 5 directly addresses the topic of the people to come, its relation to utopian thought, and the practical methods that might guide the invention of such a people. Chapter 6 elaborates on these methods of fostering a new people by teasing out the implications of Deleuze's concept of 'protocols of experience' for creative aesthetic and political experimentation.

III. Music and Philosophy. Thinking otherwise for Deleuze often involves a dialogue between philosophy and the arts. Though philosophy and the arts occupy different domains, they share the goal of inventing possibilities for life, and they enrich one another when their differing modes of thought are juxtaposed. The essays of this section detail three encounters between music and philosophy. Chapter 7 fleshes out Deleuze's discussion in *The Fold* of Renaissance and Baroque music and what he sees as their philosophical corollaries – the occasionalism of Malebranche and the monadology of Leibniz. Leibniz's philosophy, Deleuze argues, provides a philosophical counterpart to the Baroque's 'new harmony', while also serving as a means for contemporary thought to go beyond Leibniz in the creation of a 'new new harmony', the harmony of a pluriverse of co-existing incompossible worlds. Chapter 8 takes as its starting point a passing reference in *A Thousand Plateaus* to Thomas Mann's novel *Doctor Faustus*, perhaps the greatest literary work ever written about music. Mann describes at length two fictional musical compositions and treats them as symptoms of the failures of modernity and the rise of fascism, but when placed in the context of Deleuze and Guattari's thought, the compositions signal a different conception not only of modernity and fascism but also of the powers of music to promote new modes of existence. Chapter 9 is dedicated to the opening image of *A Thousand Plateaus*, the score of Piece Four of Sylvano Bussotti's *Five Piano Pieces for David Tudor* (1959). Although Deleuze and Guattari say nothing about this image, I argue that the conception of music inherent in Bussotti's composition reinforces several themes of *A Thousand Plateaus*, and that the score provides guidelines for the reader's performance of the text.

IV. Literature and Philosophy. The first essay in this section concerns Kafka, a writer to whom Deleuze and Guattari devote an entire book and whom Deleuze cites frequently in various works. In this study, I examine the relationship Deleuze establishes between Kafka and Heinrich von Kleist, each of whom is a practitioner of 'minor literature', the one engaging a bureaucratic machine, the other a war machine, in an effort to invent a people to come. Kafka's object is to disclose in his fiction both the 'diabolical powers of the future' and the revolutionary possibilities inherent in his world, whereas Kleist's project is to invent a war machine that does not self-destruct but offers creative means for aesthetic and social transformation. The section's last two essays attempt to extend Deleuze's thought on literature by incorporating it into a discussion of two Chinese-American writers and three forms of Asian drama. In *Dialogues*, Deleuze speaks of the 'superiority of Anglo-American literature', citing that body of literature as one that engages a creative line of flight. In Chapter 11 I first determine the specificity of American as opposed to English literature and then show how the works of Maxine Hong Kingston and Tao Lin fulfil the promise of American literature as a minor literature that generates possibilities for a people to come. In Chapter 12, I review Deleuze's remarks on thought as theatre in *Difference and Repetition* and his thought about theatre in 'One Manifesto Less', and then reflect on the affinities his conceptions of theatre and thought have with the theories and practices of Beijing opera, Kathakali dance drama and Nō drama, concluding that the Asian theatrical traditions hold great promise for expanding the uses to which Deleuze's theory of affect may be put in our understanding of drama and the arts as a whole.

V. Sight, Sound and Language. For Deleuze, thinking otherwise in the arts involves an engagement with sight and sound at the limits of or beyond language. The complexities of the interrelationship of the visual, aural and linguistic are especially evident in the conceptual motif of the landscape, the subject of Chapter 13. Deleuze and Guattari identify painting as the deterritorialisation of the landscape, but they also speak of musical landscapes, and in his cinema books Deleuze makes the landscape an important element of the audiovisual configurations of what he calls the action-image and the reflection-image. In Deleuze's remarks about the landscape in literature, the tensions between language and sight–sound reach the breaking point, as he posits a seeing and a hearing that are not outside language, but that constitute the outside *of* language. Those tensions are explored further in Chapter 14, which offers a Deleuzian analysis of Jean-Luc Godard's 2014 3D film *Adieu au langage*. As Godard's title suggests, the film is a meditation on language and the need to bid it farewell in order to attain new modes of seeing and hearing. What Godard's images provide, I argue, is a visual and sonic world beyond our common-sense senses, one that restores our belief in the creative possibilities of this world. The same issues arise in Chapter 15, where I address the question of what Deleuze means when he says in a late essay that literature aspires to create Visions and Auditions, which are like a painting and a music that constitute the outside of language. Deleuze did not live long enough to elaborate on these concepts, but I conclude that they are closely tied to his thought about the image and its function in what he calls 'fabulation', which he sees as central in the effort to invent a people to come.

VI. Nature. In *What is Philosophy?*, Deleuze and Guattari say 'We lack creation. *We lack resistance to the present.* The creation of concepts in itself calls for a future form, for a new earth and people that do not yet exist' (WP 108). The five essays in this section investigate the relationship between Deleuze and Guattari's philosophy of nature and their project of creating a new earth. In the first chapter, 'A Thousand Ecologies', I show that *Anti-Oedipus* and *A Thousand Plateaus* articulate an ecological view of nature, but one that is at odds with 'deep ecology' and its efforts to escape 'speciesism'. Their aim, I argue, is not to approach nature from a non-human perspective, but instead to transform the category of the human through a process of becoming-other in interaction with the natural world. Chapter 17 proposes that Deleuze and Guattari's philosophy of nature be considered a 'chaosmopolitanism', a contemporary counterpart of Cynic and Stoic cosmopolitanism that conceives of philosophy as a way of living in resonance with the chaosmos of a dynamic, emergent and metamorphic nature. This chaosmopolitan view of nature, I claim, entails a normativity that supports a politics of liberation. In Chapter 18, I address Donna Haraway's critique of Deleuze and Guattari's concept of 'becoming-animal'. After identifying her misconceptions about the concept, I suggest that her notions of the cyborg and companion species may prove useful in delineating the roles domestication and technology might play in an expanded articulation of Deleuze and Guattari's philosophy of nature. Chapter 19 focuses on Deleuze's vitalism and his identification of Raymond Ruyer's philosophy of biology as a modern version of Leibniz's monadology. Deleuze claims that both Ruyer and Leibniz embrace the vitalism of a 'force that is but does not act', but I conclude that Ruyer differs from Leibniz in his conception of force, and that this difference is symptomatic of divergent orientations in Ruyer's and Deleuze's philosophy of nature. The final chapter offers an exegesis of Plateau Three of *A Thousand Plateaus*. Titled 'The Geology of Morals (Who Does the Earth Think It Is?)', this plateau provides a comprehensive account of nature in terms of strata and stratification. In this account, the domains of the inorganic, the organic and the human constitute strata within which there is a constant play of forces of coding and decoding, territorialisation and deterritorialisation. This plateau helps clarify the relation Deleuze and Guattari's philosophy of nature has to their project of inventing a new earth and thereby allows us to conceive of their geophilosophy as a central component of their chaosmopolitanism.

My hope, above all, is that the essays of this volume may help elucidate the pivotal role the arts play in the political project of inventing a people to come and the broader chaosmopolitan project of promoting an ecologically viable new earth. That role is complex and variable from art to art. In cinema, it may be that of instilling belief in this world or making visible all that is intolerable; in literature, that of imagining alternative mentalities and polities; in music, that of inventing a new harmony of incompossibilities. But, in all cases, the arts function as means of thinking otherwise, as ways of seeing, hearing, speaking and feeling differently, and thereby engendering new modes of existence.

Acknowledgements

I would like to thank the publishers for permission to reprint material from the following articles and chapters:

'The Master Apprentice', in *Deleuze and Education*, ed. Diana Masny and Inna Semetsky, Edinburgh: Edinburgh University Press, 2013, pp. 21–36.

'To Choose to Choose – To Believe in This World', in *Afterimages of Gilles Deleuze's Film Philosophy*, ed. D. N. Rodowick, Minneapolis: University of Minnesota Press, 2010, pp. 115–34.

'Speranza, the Wandering Island', *Deleuze Studies* 3:1 (2009), 124–34.

'The Art of the Possible', *Revue internationale de philosophie*, 61:241 (September 2007), 273–86.

'Deleuze and Guattari and the Future of Politics: Science Fiction, Protocols and the People to Come', *Deleuze Studies*, 5 supplement (2011), 77–97.

'The New Harmony', in *Gilles Deleuze: The Intensive Reduction*, ed. Constantin V. Boundas. London: Continuum, 2009, pp. 31–44.

'Deleuze, Mann and Modernism: Musical Becoming in *Doctor Faustus*', *Deleuze Studies*, 4:3 (2010), 412–31.

'Scoring the Rhizome: Bussotti's Musical Diagram', *Deleuze Studies*, 8:4 (2014), 470–90.

'Deleuze, Guattari, and the Kafka–Kleist Connection: Toward a Literature of War', in *Franz Kafka: Minority Report*, ed. Petr Kouba and Tomáš Pivoda, Prague: Litteraria Pragensia Books, 2011, pp. 62–86.

'On the Superiority of Anglo-American Literature', in *Deleuze Studies* 7:3 (2013), pp. 302–18.

'Theatrum Philosophicum Asiaticum', in *Deleuze and Asia*, ed. Bogue, Hanping Chiu and Yulin Lee, Newcastle upon Tyne: Cambridge Scholars Publishing, 2014, pp. 60–72.

'The Landscape of Sensation', in *Gilles Deleuze: Text and Image*, ed. Eugene W. Holland, Daniel W. Smith and Charles J. Stivale, London: Continuum, 2009, pp. 9–26.

'Deleuze and Roxy: The Time of the Intolerable in Godard's *Adieu au langage*', in *Deleuze and the Animal*, ed. Colin Gardner and Patricia MacCormack, Edinburgh: Edinburgh University Press, 2017, pp. 275–92.

'A Thousand Ecologies', in *Deleuze/Guattari and Ecology*, ed. Bernd Herzogenrath, London: Palgrave, 2008, pp. 42–56.

'Nature, Law and Chaosmopolitanism', in *Revisiting Normativity with Deleuze*, ed. Rosi Braidotti and Patricia Pisters, London: Continuum, 2012, pp. 98–112.

'The Companion Cyborg: Technics and Domestication', in *Deleuze and the Non/Human*, ed. Jon Roffe and Hannah Stark, London: Palgrave, 2015, pp. 163–79.

'The Force That Is But Does Not Act: Ruyer, Leibniz and Deleuze', *Deleuze Studies*, 11:4 (2017), 518–37.

'Plateau Three: Who the Earth Thinks It Is', in *A Thousand Plateaus and Philosophy*, ed. Henry Somers-Hall, Edinburgh: Edinburgh University Press, 2017, pp. 46–63.

Over the years, I have benefited greatly from exchanges with a number of individuals, who have enriched my understanding of Deleuze and Guattari and offered encouragement at various stages of this project, including Brent Adkins, Frida Beckman, Jeffrey Bell, Constantin V. Boundas, Rosi Braidotti, Ian Buchanan, Elizabeth Grosz, Eugene Holland, Davina Marques, David Martin-Jones, Catarina Pombo Nabais, Paul Patton, Teresa Rizzo, Jon Roffe, Anne Sauvagnargues, David Savat, Daniel W. Smith, Henry Somers-Hall, Charles J. Stivale, Elizabeth St. Pierre and Janell Watson. I am especially grateful to Gregg Lambert, who came up with the idea for this book, and to Carol Macdonald at Edinburgh University Press for providing invaluable assistance at every stage of this endeavour.

Abbreviations

AO Deleuze and Guattari, *Anti-Oedipus*, trans. Robert Hurley, Mark Seem and Helen R. Lane, Minneapolis: University of Minnesota Press, 1977.

ATP Deleuze and Guattari, *A Thousand Plateaus*, trans. Brian Massumi, Minneapolis: University of Minnesota Press, 1987.

B Deleuze, *Bergsonism*, trans. Hugh Tomlinson and Barbara Habberjam, New York: Zone Books, 1981.

C1 Deleuze, *Cinema 1: The Movement-Image*, trans. Hugh Tomlinson and Barbara Habberjam, Minneapolis: University of Minnesota Press, 1986.

C2 Deleuze, *Cinema 2: The Time-Image*, trans. Hugh Tomlinson and Robert Galeta, Minneapolis: University of Minnesota Press, 1989.

CC Deleuze, *Essays Critical and Clinical*, trans. Daniel W. Smith and Michael A. Greco, Minneapolis: University of Minnesota Press, 1997.

D Deleuze and Claire Parnet, *Dialogues II*, trans. Hugh Tomlinson and Barbara Habberjam, New York: Columbia University Press, 2000.

DI Deleuze, *Desert Islands and Other Texts, 1953–1974*, trans. Michael Taormina, New York: Semiotext(e), 2004.

DR Deleuze, *Difference and Repetition*, trans. Paul Patton, New York: Columbia University Press, 1994.

ES Deleuze, *Empiricism and Subjectivity*, trans. Constantin V. Boundas, New York: Columbia University Press, 1991.

F Deleuze, *Foucault*, trans. Seán Hand, Minneapolis: University of Minnesota Press, 1988.

FB Deleuze, *Francis Bacon: The Logic of Sensation*, trans. Daniel W. Smith, Minneapolis: University of Minnesota Press, 2003.

K Deleuze and Guattari, *Kafka: Toward a Minor Literature*, trans. Dana Polan, Minneapolis: University of Minnesota Press, 1986.

LET Deleuze, *Lettres et autres textes*, Paris: Minuit, 2015.

LS Deleuze, *The Logic of Sense*, trans. Mark Lester, with Charles Stivale, ed. Constantin V. Boundas, New York: Columbia University Press, 1990.

M Deleuze, *Masochism: An Interpretation of Coldness and Cruelty*, trans. Jean McNeil. New York: G. Braziller, 1971.

N Deleuze, *Negotiations: 1972–1990*, trans. Martin Joughin, New York: Columbia University Press, 1995.

NP Deleuze, *Nietzsche and Philosophy*, trans. Hugh Tomlinson, Minneapolis: University of Minnesota Press, 1983.

OML Deleuze 'One Manifesto Less', trans. Alan Orenstein, in *The Deleuze Reader*, ed. Constantin V. Boundas, New York: Columbia University Press, 1993, pp. 204–22.

PI Deleuze, *Pure Immanence: Essays on A Life*, trans. Anne Boyman, New York: Zone Books, 2001.

PS Deleuze, *Proust and Signs: The Complete Text*, trans. Richard Howard, Minneapolis: University of Minnesota Press, 2000.

SPP Deleuze, *Spinoza: Practical Philosophy*, trans. Robert Hurley, San Francisco: City Lights, 1988.

SZ Deleuze, 'Schizologie', Preface to Louis Wolfson, *Le Schizo et les langues*, Paris: Gallimard, 1970, pp. 5–23.

TF Deleuze, *The Fold: Leibniz and the Baroque*, trans. Tom Conley, Minneapolis: University of Minnesota Press, 1993.

WP Deleuze and Guattari, *What is Philosophy?*, trans. Hugh Tomlinson and Graham Burchell, New York: Columbia University Press, 1994.

2R Deleuze, *Two Regimes of Madness: Texts and Interviews, 1975–1995*, trans. Ames Hodges and Mike Taormina, New York: Semiotext(e), 2006.

I. Thinking Otherwise

1

The Master Apprentice

Deleuze describes Proust's *À la recherche du temps perdu* as 'the narrative of an apprenticeship' (PS 3). In Deleuze's reading, the narrator, Marcel, is engaged in an apprenticeship in signs, whereby he comes to understand first the signs of the world, then the signs of love and the signs of involuntary memory, and finally the signs of art. At times Marcel looks to others, like Swann or Charlus, to guide him in this apprenticeship, but they prove to be unreliable teachers. If Marcel has any teachers at all, they are the signs themselves.

Deleuze expands a bit further on the relation between signs and learning in *Difference and Repetition*, saying that 'learning [*l'apprentissage*] takes place [. . .] in the relation between a sign and a response (encounter with the Other)' (DR 22). To learn, says Deleuze, is 'to enter into the universal of the relations which constitute the Idea, and into their corresponding singularities' (DR 165). As an example of this engagement with the Idea and its corresponding singularities, Deleuze considers the process of learning to swim in the sea. Following Leibniz, Deleuze states that the Idea of the sea 'is a system of liaisons or differential relations between particles and singularities corresponding to the degrees of variation among these relations – the totality of the system being incarnated in the real movement of the waves' (DR 165; trans. modified). To learn to swim is create an interface between the 'distinctive [*remarquable*] points of our bodies' and the singular points of the sea. The physical sea is the object emitting signs, and it is a multiplicity of wave movements; the signs emitted constitute a system of connections or differential relations between particles (the Idea) and corresponding singular points, or degrees of variation among the differential relations; and the response to the signs involves the physical body of the swimmer, which engages the complex of the sea's system and its singular points via the body's own 'distinctive points' ('distinctive points', in my reading, being simply a synonym for 'singular points'). The body's movements do not resemble the sea's movements, but instead form a heterogeneous multiplicity responsive to an encounter with the sea as an 'other' heterogeneity.

It is within this complex relation between the multiplicities of the body and the sea that the teacher attempts to intervene. The 'swimming instructor [*maître-nageur*]' (DR 23) perhaps initiates instruction by demonstrating strokes while standing on the shore, and then having the learner imitate the strokes. But such instruction is useless, since there is no relation between the mock-swimming on land and actual swimming in the sea. Only when the swimmer's body interacts with the waves of the sea can swimming begin, and it is the encounter between wave-signs and the responding body movements that does the teaching. Hence, 'we learn nothing from those who say: "Do as I do". Our only teachers [*maîtres*] are those who tell us to "do with me", and are able to emit signs to be developed in heterogeneity rather than propose gestures for us to reproduce' (DR 23). Genuine teachers, it turns out, are simply emitters of heterogeneous signs who help students encounter other heterogeneous signs. In learning to swim, then, whether the signs are emitted by the sea or by the genuine *maître*, the signs themselves are the teachers.

At first glance, this characterisation of teaching seems to minimise the role of the teacher. Basically, the *maître-nageur* says, 'let's jump in the sea and start swimming', at which point the sea does the teaching. One might ask whether there is really any need for a *maître-nageur* at all, and whether the apprentice, like Marcel, might as well learn on her own. In part this portrait of the teacher as humble assistant is strategic, in that Deleuze is countering the orthodox image of the teacher as all-powerful master, the one who knows, the one who poses the questions and already possesses all the answers. 'According to this infantile prejudice, the master sets a problem, our task is to solve it, and the result is accredited true or false by a powerful authority'. Such is the 'grotesque image of culture that we find in examinations and government referenda as well as in newspaper competitions' (DR 158). But in the final analysis, the true master as emitter of signs indeed has an important role in education, one that Deleuze does not specify in an explicit fashion, but which can be extrapolated from Deleuze's own practice as a teacher and his occasional remarks about the process of giving courses. The Deleuzian teacher, I hope to show, is both master and apprentice, a master apprentice engaged with the apprentice in their mutual apprenticeship in and through signs.

The Teacher

Deleuze spent most of his adult life teaching, with the exception of a four-year CNRS fellowship (1960–4) and one year of sick leave (1969–70). He began teaching at age twenty-three at the lycée d'Amiens (1948–52), followed by posts at the lycée d'Orléans (1953–5), the lycée Louis-le-Grand in Paris (1955–7), the Sorbonne (1957–60), the University of Lyon (1964–9), the University of Paris VIII at Vincennes (1970–80), and Paris VIII at Saint Denis, following the government's destruction of the Vincennes site and relocation of the campus (1980–7). From the beginning, his students found in him an exceptional teacher, whose primary pedagogical tool was the venerable lecture (and remained so throughout his career). Michel Marié, one of Deleuze's Amiens students, recalls that

> With him, philosophy wasn't the severe discipline that I feared but an encounter, a fusion between a conceptual apparatus, a culture and its languages and learning techniques, its commentaries and links that you learn by reading generations of thinkers on one hand, and on the other hand, a sort of secret thrust, a mental attitude to perceive, to conceive of the simplest, most ordinary and yet most basic elements of existence. (cited in Dosse 2010: 101)

This notion of an encounter, and the dual focus on the history of philosophy and a prevailing mental attitude, are repeated time and again in accounts of Deleuze's teaching, whether conducted in the humblest lycée or the most exalted university. In the video *Deleuze's ABC Primer* (*L'Abécédaire de Gilles Deleuze*), Deleuze claims that his teaching never changed from the lycée to the university (Deleuze and Parnet 2004: 'P as in Professor'),[1] but it does seem that his sense of humour was more overtly displayed in the lycée context.[2] Alain Roger, a student at the lycée d'Orléans, says that although 'his courses were very arduous, based on a rigorous conception of philosophy and its history', at the same time 'he was hilarious, and this joking earned him the adoration of his students' (Roger 2000: 36). Generally, Deleuze would enter the classroom, impeccably dressed, briefcase in hand, take a sheet of paper from his coat pocket, and then launch into an amusing story. Misadventures constantly befell him in the commute from his Paris home to Orléans, and they often provided material for his anecdotes. Roger recalls one such account, in which Deleuze and a travelling salesman inadvertently picked up each other's briefcases. Deleuze described his own puzzlement at discovering a plethora 'of Colgates and Palmolives' (Roger 2000: 36) in his bag, and speculated on the panic the salesman would no doubt experience when presenting clients with *The Critique of Pure Reason*. At the close of the anecdote, Deleuze lamented that he had thus lost his lecture notes, but concluded that he would proceed anyway – and then did so in a flawless, magisterial performance.

This strategy of appearing to be unprepared was one Deleuze used often at Orléans, and in all his other positions. Roger recalls that Deleuze 'frequently gave the impression of having prepared nothing, expressing himself in a hesitant, uncertain fashion, as if unsure of himself'. He might begin '"Ah, there, you see . . . the transcendental . . . what is the transcendental . . . Well, obviously, Kant tells us that it's the conditions of possibility of knowledge . . . Yes . . . Yes . . . But why call this transcendental, why? . . . I don't know . . . I don't know . . ."' And then, following this stuttering introduction, Deleuze would gradually put everything in place, such that 'at the end of an hour of what had seemed useless and blank gropings, Deleuze's thought would rise, luminous . . .' (Roger 2000: 37).

The Lecturer

When Deleuze advanced to a university position, he soon gained a large following of enthusiastic students. His Sorbonne lectures were filled to overflowing, and his popularity was sufficient to arouse the jealousy of colleagues. Olivier Revault d'Allonnes reports that 'At three o'clock, when the course was over, everyone left, and the next professor, Raymond Polin, who taught in the same room, had six students. Utterly furious, he hated Deleuze' (cited in Dosse 2010: 116). Similar crowds jammed his Tuesday morning seminars at Vincennes, 'where the ritual was always the same. Deleuze arrived at a room already so packed with students that it was hard to get in the door. The place where Deleuze was supposed to sit was already filled with a forest of tape recorders' (Dosse 2010: 356–7).

The Vincennes seminars seem to have been especially memorable, and several former students have attempted to capture the atmosphere of those courses. Pierre Blanchaud speaks of the 'party atmosphere' (Dosse 2010: 358) of the courses, which Philippe Mengue confirms, noting that at Vincennes in general there was 'a climate of mad effervescence, a breath of total contestation, a wind of intellectual creation, of a liberation of mores and the imagination' (Mengue 2000: 49). Pascal Criton remembers vividly the 'encounter' presented by the 'peculiar climate of the seminars':

> the presence of the regulars, a mixture of all generations, the curious, those with a passion for philosophy, art, or those with a vaguer disposition – all this coalesced as a disparate, improbable composition. Were certain audience members students, philosophers, writers, actors, musicians? Yes, no doubt, but their presence was circumspect, because they came to be fused with that thought of the imperceptible, which embodies the vital impulses of thought rather than brandishing it, which proceeds by hesitations, interrogations [. . .] A shared experience, almost a *sotto voce* island, adjacent to the intimacy of the work of thinking, the elaboration of thought in 'real time', distant from stupidity and sad passions; and then, beyond the silence created by this island, sinuously would become manifest Deleuze's

> special craving to make things operational, to bestow on them the grace and necessity requisite for possible explorations of thought. (Criton 2007: 57)

Here again, the themes articulated by Deleuze's first students – hesitations, interrogations, encounters with the thrust of thought, the action of thinking 'in real time'.

For Philippe Mengue, the essence of Deleuze's teaching was distilled in his voice, a voice that Mengue continues to discern faintly in Deleuze's writings. The *ABC Primer*, says Mengue, conveys only weak hints of the charm and intensity of Deleuze's voice, which were made fully present in the seminars alone.

> A voice full of softness, but devoid of any flaccidity or pity, as is so often the case, free as well of that false amenity that poses as modesty the more easily to seize the opportunity of biting or stinging [. . .] One sensed, in that softness, a great firmness of thought, without a trace of rigidity, as if, in the tone of this flexible voice, were expressed the agility and subtlety of his mind, characteristics that allowed him to reject ready-made problems and to slip past static, obstructive contradictions. (Mengue 2000: 52)

In his work on Nietzsche, Deleuze stressed that affirmation does not mean blanket acceptance of everything, but must also include critique of the negative Will to Power, but that critical dimension, says Mengue, was scarcely evident in the seminars. Rather, Deleuze gave voice to the Nietzschean Yes 'that precedes all negation, the affirmative yes', leaving to others the critique of the philosophical priests of *ressentiment*. Deleuze's 'Yes' took a particular form, one that for Mengue made incarnate the spirit of Deleuze's thought.

> When he began a seminar, or in the first moments of an encounter, when dealing with a question, Gilles Deleuze would respond with a Yes whose sound was an exaggerated suspension, prolonged, and then slowly, indefinitely diminished [. . .] And, in that moment of suspension, you suddenly saw all the possibilities of thought surge forth, light and free like birds,

> liberated from ponderous habits and mediocre objections. How welcomed you felt! How intelligent you felt! The marvellous sensation of a sudden expansion of the space of thought, an opening to everything [*une ouverture à tout*], an open whole [*un tout ouvert*]. (Mengue 2000: 54)

In this suspended time, 'everything could be said, and even nonsense became a weapon for thinking' (Mengue 2000: 54).

Clearly, Deleuze put the standard lecture format to new use, imbuing it with a purpose beyond that of conveying information. The lecture functioned as an enactment of thought – fluid, halting, soft, yet thoroughly firm, intense and passionate. That intensity was not without humour, but its spirit resembled the playfulness of Lewis Carroll, rather than the biting satire and savage irony of Juvenal or Swift. And both the spontaneity and humour of the seminars were evident in the ludic pretence that Deleuze often offered of being thoroughly unprepared.

In fact, Deleuze put forth considerable effort in preparing his courses. François Dosse tells us that Deleuze

> attached enormous importance to his Tuesday seminar and spent most of the week preparing his class. Pierre Chevalier, a family friend who lived with the Deleuzes on rue Bizerte between 1973 and 1983, remembers the care Deleuze took in preparing the seminar for Vincennes. 'I saw Gilles set to work on Sunday morning, sometimes on Saturday, polishing the seminar for three days and before he left to teach, there was a physical preparation, as if he were going to take part in a race. He would turn up on Tuesday mornings, no longer needing the little page of notes in his hand because he knew by heart what he was going to say. Yet he gave the impression of thinking on his feet, that his class was a pure improvisation of mental development in harmony with his public.' (Dosse 2010: 354)

The Lecture Performer

Given the thoroughness of Deleuze's preparation, one might ask whether the seminars were genuine enactments of thought 'in real time', or mere performances, re-presentations of the act of thinking. A preliminary, hopelessly Platonic defence would be that, even if simple re-enactments, the seminars must have had as their models previous, original actions. But Deleuze himself indicates that the seminars were so carefully rehearsed in order to exceed the limits of preparation. In a 1988 interview, shortly after his retirement, Deleuze offered a rare glimpse into his conception of the seminars to which he devoted much of his life. 'Giving courses has been a major part of my life, in which I've been passionately involved. [. . .] It takes a lot of preparatory work to get a few minutes of inspiration. I was ready to stop when I saw it was taking more and more preparation to get a more taxing inspiration' (N 139). Deleuze's goal, then, was to make present, within the prepared performance of thought, unpredictable and spontaneous moments of inspiration. In this regard, Deleuze's object was that of such performing arts as theatre, dance and music. In these arts, performers succeed only to the extent that they attain a zone of indiscernibility, in which performer, audience and performance become indistinguishable elements of an a-personal event. This essential dimension of the seminars is what Deleuze signals in the same interview when he says that 'a course is a kind of *Sprechgesang*, closer to music than to theatre' (N 139). The positions of performer and audience in music are not those of emitter and receiver of messages, but co-participants in a sonic event. In another interview, while paying tribute to Foucault, Deleuze says that 'good lectures, after all, are more like a concert than a sermon, like a soloist "accompanied" by everyone else. And Foucault gave wonderful lectures.' Audiences 'accompany' Foucault 'because they're doing something with him, in their own work, in their own independent lives. It's not just a question of intellectual understanding or agreement, but of intensity, resonance, musical harmony' (N 86). As Deleuze argues in *Difference and Repetition*, the genuine teacher says, 'do with me', not 'do as I do'.

The seminar is also like a musical performance in another important sense. After describing the seminar as a kind of *Sprechgesang*, Deleuze reflects on the diverse audience he addressed at Vincennes. 'It was there that I realized how much philosophy needs not only philosophical understanding, through concepts, but a nonphilosophical understanding, rooted in percepts and affects' (N 139). In *What is Philosophy?*, Deleuze and Guattari associate percepts and affects most closely with the arts, arguing that, just as philosophers invent concepts, so artists invent percepts and affects. Such percepts and affects are not personal perceptions and emotions, but anonymous, autonomous manifestations of the 'being of sensation' (WP 164), elements that permeate and pass through the individuals who serve as their vehicles. As *Sprechgesang*, the Deleuzian seminar aims to infuse concepts with percepts and affects, giving them a necessary intensity, resonance and harmony. It is this musical and philosophical essence that Mengue felt in the voice of Deleuze, a sonic materialisation of concepts, percepts and affects belonging no longer to Deleuze the individual, but to thought itself. In the language of *Difference and Repetition*, the voice had become an emission of signs, a trajectory passing through the singular points of the cadences and rhythms of performance.

Deleuze's conception of the seminar as *Sprechgesang* has further implications concerning time and audience response, which he sketches in his 1988 interview. Here Deleuze contrasts seminars and professional conferences, finding in the latter a time and atmosphere that inhibit genuine thought. Conferences consist of discrete, short lectures, followed by 'discussion', by which Deleuze means fractious debate. 'Philosophy has nothing to do with discussing things, it's difficult enough just understanding the problem someone's framing and how they're framing it' (N 139). The short duration of the conference paper is insufficient for understanding the specific problem under consideration, for which reason conferences give rise to battles over pre-established territories, forensic skirmishes that in no way foster co-participation in thought. By contrast, seminars 'have to be carried on over a long period with a relatively fixed audience, sometimes for a number of years. It's like a research laboratory [*un laboratoire de recherche*]: you give courses on what you're investigating [*sur ce qu'on cherche*], not on what you know' (N 139). Understanding problems proceeds in a slow rhythm, stretching well beyond the limits of a given seminar. At Vincennes, says Deleuze, there were 'long sessions [two and a half hours], nobody took in everything, but everyone took what they needed or wanted, what they could use, even if it was far removed from their discipline' (N 139). Only in this time of 'a long period of time [*une longue durée*]' could comprehension take the form of a musical accompaniment, in which intellectual understanding would become a matter of 'intensity, resonance, musical harmony' (N 86).

In the *ABC Primer* ('P as in Professor'), Deleuze distinguishes two basic conceptions of the seminar: one which aims at provoking immediate audience response, soliciting questions, establishing a dialogue among the students and the teacher; and the model Deleuze followed, the traditional lecture, known in French as the *cours magistral*, the magisterial course, the course of the *magister*, the master (a name, Deleuze tells Parnet, with which he is not particularly happy). Deleuze claims that he used the *cours magistral* because that was what he had always done, but it was obviously a method well suited to his talents. Essential to the *cours magistral*, as Deleuze conceived it, was an uninterrupted delivery and, in this sense, very much like a musical performance, during which the audience is expected to remain silent. Since the courses were so long and comprehension occurred only slowly, there necessarily would be stretches of time when students would be baffled, or lose their concentration, but questions at every juncture of confusion would only impede understanding. The point of the lecture was to allow students to drop out of the flow of words, to give them opportunities to rejoin the flow, and to encourage them to wait for illumination. As in a musical performance, says Deleuze, a phrase or motif may become coherent only later in the piece, so the elements of the seminar often coalesce only towards the end of the presentation, or perhaps days later. Deleuze notes that his best students asked their questions the week following the lecture, when they had allowed the temporality of the seminar experience to exercise to the full the power of its *longue durée*.

The History of Philosophy

Clearly, one of Deleuze's goals in his seminars, and one that he met with considerable success, was that of performing the action of thinking and creating moments of inspiration during which the rehearsal of thought became thought 'in real time'. The pursuit of that goal suited a particular format, with its own temporality and mode of audience participation. But what of the content of his courses? What did he talk about? Deleuze gave lectures on the material in *Anti-Oedipus*, *A Thousand Plateaus*, *Cinéma 1*, *Cinéma 2* and *Francis Bacon*, but he also devoted several seminars to other philosophers, notably Kant (1978), Spinoza (1978, 1980, 1981) and Leibniz (1980 and 1986–7). These courses in the history of philosophy are especially important in considering the Deleuzian teacher as master apprentice.

In *Dialogues*, Deleuze speaks disparagingly of the traditional function of the history of philosophy:

> The history of philosophy has always been the agent of power in philosophy, and even in thought. It has played the repressor's role: how can you think without having read Plato, Descartes, Kant and Heidegger, and so-and-so's book about them? A formidable school of intimidation which manufactures specialists in thought – but which also makes those who stay outside conform all the more to this specialism which they despise. An image of thought called philosophy has been formed historically and it effectively stops people from thinking. (D 13)

One might assume from this critique that Deleuze had no use for the history of philosophy, but a few pages later Deleuze explains that he found his way out of this repressive regime via philosophers who had escaped from philosophy's orthodox history 'in one respect, or altogether: Lucretius, Spinoza, Hume, Nietzsche, Bergson' (D 14–15). In fact, as Deleuze explains in the *ABC Primer* ('H as in History of Philosophy'), the history of philosophy played an essential role in his own education.

For Deleuze, the history of philosophy is a form of portraiture in thought. The object of a historical study is to paint a philosopher's portrait by delineating the concepts he or she invented and to uncover the problem that gave rise to those concepts and to which they responded. Throughout his life, Deleuze defined philosophy as the invention of concepts, an activity parallel to that of the painter, who creates with colour, the musician, who creates with sound, and the writer, who creates with words. But he insists in the *ABC Primer* that the invention of concepts is extremely difficult and requires considerable training if one is to succeed in that endeavour. Deleuze speaks of the great respect, awe, hesitation, and even fear and panic that Van Gogh and Gauguin felt when approaching colour. They were great colourists, but it took them years to feel capable of exploiting colour to the full, of being 'worthy' (*digne*) of creating with colour. Deleuze expresses a similar respect towards concepts, and in his books on Hume, Nietzsche, Bergson and Spinoza, he was gradually learning to master the art of concept creation by working with and through these master concept-creators. This 'research into the concepts of others', he says, constituted an 'indispensable apprenticeship' that allowed him eventually, in *Difference and Repetition* and *The Logic of Sense*, to attempt the invention of concepts himself, to feel worthy of such an enterprise. He regards as absurd the idea that one can simply start 'doing philosophy' without training in the history of philosophy, an absurdity equal to that of a writer who claims to have no time to read other writers and hence simply creates *ex nihilo*.

Thus, Deleuze's own development involved an extended apprenticeship, well beyond his years as a student, and in his seminars on Kant, Spinoza and Leibniz, he re-enacted that apprenticeship, and in the process led his students in their own training. Before creating concepts, one must know what concepts are, and one can understand them only by studying the concepts of the great masters. One must also comprehend the relationship between concepts and problems, a task even more difficult since problems are only hinted at, partially articulated, or at times completely tacit and hidden. Without an understanding of the problem, the concepts remain abstract; once situated in relation to the problem, however, everything becomes concrete. Plato's 'Idea' is a genuine concept, Deleuze explains, which one may define as 'something that is only what it is'. An actual mother, for example, is a wife, a sister, a friend and so on, but the Idea of 'mother' is nothing more than mother, a pure mother. But this concept remains vague and seems unmotivated until one understands the problem that led

Plato to invent the concept of the Idea. The problem arose in the democratic city-state of Athens, and concerned the determination of the rights of claimants [*prétendants*] before various tribunals, legislative bodies or other venues for public decisions. Who is the genuine claimant? Who possesses the right to a given role, a given title, a given property? This problem, claims Deleuze, forces Plato to invent the Idea of pure things – the Idea of Justice, Truth, the Good and so on, as pure things that are nothing more than what they are – in order to address the very concrete situation of adjudicating claimants and their petitions, of ranking the claimants according to the extent to which their claims approach the purity of a given standard.

Hence, when Deleuze says in *Difference and Repetition* that teachers only teach by saying 'do with me', he is not downplaying the role of the teacher, but simply clarifying it. The teacher as emitter of signs does not provide apprentices with answers, but guides them in the art of discovering problems, an art that can be mastered only by practising it. Such practice is mysterious in its inner workings, and unpredictable in its effects. As Deleuze remarks in *Difference and Repetition*, 'We never know in advance how someone will learn: by means of what loves someone becomes good at Latin, what encounters make them a philosopher, or in what dictionaries they learn to think.' As a result, 'There is no more a method for learning that there is for finding treasures.' Nevertheless, learning involves 'a violent training, a culture or *paideïa* which affects the entire individual' (DR 165). The violent training, culture and *paideïa* of philosophy take place in the workshop of the history of philosophy. There, the master apprentice offers apprentices encounters with the concepts and problems of great philosophers, as well as the processes of thought involved in their disclosure. Not a method, but an art, not a programme of study, but a rigorous discipline.

The Master

The seminar played a central role in Deleuze's life as a teacher, but he also paid attention to individual students, fostering their development in accordance with the traditional master–apprentice relationship. In the *ABC Primer* ('E is for *Enfance*' [Childhood]), Deleuze himself singles out a certain Pierre Halwachs, a young teacher whom Deleuze met at age fourteen during an extended beach vacation at Deauville, as his first '*maître*'. Before meeting Halwachs, Deleuze was an indifferent student, but Halwachs introduced him to Gide, Anatole France, Baudelaire and other writers, and these encounters with Halwachs and great writers 'completely transformed' him. He grew passionate about learning, and during the ensuing fall term, when he studied philosophy, he discovered something important that he knew he would do the rest of his life.

Deleuze himself assumed the role of *maître* early in his career. At Amiens, when still in his twenties, Deleuze discovered that a student, Michel Marié, intended to become a worker-priest, but Deleuze insisted that he study philosophy. Marié persisted and did become a priest, but later followed Deleuze's advice and studied at the Sorbonne (Dosse 2010: 101). Another Amiens student, Claude Lemoine, developed a love of philosophy while in Deleuze's course, but Lemoine's parents wanted him to follow in his father's footsteps and become a lawyer. Deleuze told Lemoine that he would not allow that to happen, and then asked to meet Lemoine's father, 'who agreed, unenthusiastically, and was finally persuaded that his son would study philosophy' (Dosse 2010: 102). At Orléans, Deleuze assumed an especially important role in the life of Alain Roger. Transformed by Deleuze's courses, Roger planned to pursue advanced study in philosophy, but disastrous year-end examinations in other subjects led him to question the viability of that career, and he contemplated instead pursuing his other passion and becoming a professional cyclist. He spoke with Deleuze about his decision, and Deleuze responded by taking Roger to the lycée library and removing three books: Epictetus' *Discussions*, Spinoza's *Ethics* and Nietzsche's *Genealogy of Morals*. He then told Roger to prepare a class presentation according to these instructions: '"You are going to look for the centre of gravity in this triangle, the intersection of the three medians, it's easy"' (Dosse 2010: 104). Roger did not dare say no, and he spent the next few days feverishly reading and formulating his preparation. The exercise helped dislodge Roger from his cyclist plan. Later he wondered '"how

Deleuze was able to foresee that those three names were going to become my preferred authors for half a century"' (Dosse 2010: 104). During the ensuing four academic years, Deleuze drew up a rigorous programme of study for Roger and tutored him through regular discussions of his various assigned expositions of philosophical texts. Later, when Roger moved to Paris to study, he became friends with Deleuze, who, aware of Roger's lack of money, frequently took him out to eat. The winter of 1956, Roger was stricken with pleurisy 'and stuck in the lycée infirmary for several weeks, where, despite everything, I continued to work. Gilles came to see me and I don't know whether, without him, I would not have surrendered to that adversity' (Roger 2000: 40).

Such stories are touching, and one might view Deleuze's action simply as the caring attention of a decent human being, but there is more one may draw from this intense commitment to the master–apprentice relationship. These anecdotes provide evidence of Deleuze's conception of philosophy as more than mere thought, as a way of living that extends beyond the classroom. It is important, however, to recognise that in serving as a master to apprentices Deleuze was not recruiting disciples. Even when he had become a prominent philosopher, he always scorned the cultivation of acolytes and the project of building a Deleuzian 'school of thought'. In the *ABC Primer* ('P as in Professor'), Deleuze tells Parnet with a smile that he never had disciples because no one wanted to follow him, and then speaks of the 'awful', 'terrible' notion of a 'school'. A school, he says, should be contrasted with a 'movement'. Surrealism, for example, was a school, with a leader, tribunals, grudges, expulsions and so on, whereas Dada was a 'movement', with no orthodoxy, no structure, no collective purpose other than the pursuit of art in heterogeneous directions. If anything, he would have liked to have engendered a movement through his teaching. The ideal of such a movement would disperse its participants, not bring them together, since, for Deleuze, the ultimate aims of his teaching, he says, are (1) to help students 'be happy with their solitude' and (2) to provide students with pliable concepts, applicable in diverse spheres, such that each student, in his or her solitude, may encounter something that stimulates genuine thought.

The Master Apprentice

The master–apprentice relationship in philosophy is part of a mode of existence, and, I would argue, understandable in terms of Deleuze's ethics. In *The Logic of Sense*, Deleuze expounds on the Stoic notion of being worthy of the event, a concept that he himself embraces. He offers as an example of such worthiness Joë Bousquet, who had been paralysed by a bullet and yet refused to lament his misfortune. This Stoic ethics has a single goal: 'to become worthy of what happens to us, and thus to will and release the event' (LS 149). Deleuze identifies this worthiness with Nietzsche's *amor fati* and the rejection of all forms of *ressentiment*, and, given the example of Bousquet, one might conceive of this ethics primarily in terms of a reaction to what befalls us. But being worthy of the event is more than this. An event is an encounter, and the essence of learning, as well as thinking, resides in encounters. True, Deleuze says that thought only begins with a violence external to thought, but it is also important to do something with such violence, actively to become worthy of the encounters that occur. And one may also work to create encounters, to seek others with whom we may build ongoing encounters, to find what Deleuze calls 'intercesseurs' (translated as 'mediators' in N 121), such as he found in Guattari. In his courses, Deleuze provides encounters for his students, events of which they then must become worthy. And, as a master to individual apprentices, Deleuze again is being worthy of the event, not seeking affection, loyalty or adulation, but endeavouring to create individual encounters and thereby help his apprentices themselves become intercessors who actively fashion their own encounters.

In some ways, Deleuze's practice as a teacher resembles that of the master of a Japanese martial art. For example, in *kyudo*, the Zen art of archery, when the *sensei*, or master, accepts students, the apprentices enter into a bond that should last for a lifetime. The *sensei*'s concerns for the students extend to all aspects of their lives. The *sensei* has reached a state of mastery by passing through all the stages of a rigorous apprenticeship, a disciplinary practice through which the *sensei* then guides the students. Students learn the eight basic postures of *kyudo* and practise them for years, gradually perfecting them and integrating them with breathing techniques and the regulation of mental activity that allows full concentration. The postures, breathing techniques and mental exercises, however, are only means to an end. *Kyudo* distinguishes between *ri*, or skill, and *ji*, or inspiration. *Ri* involves discipline, repetition and specific configurations of mind and body, but *ji* is allied to genuine mastery of the principles of the art of *kyudo*.

> Understanding the principles underlying a Zen art is not based on cognitive or intellectual understanding. Rather it is based on an intuitive awareness of the underlying principles of the Universe as they apply to that particular art. [. . .] The philosophy of teaching in the Zen arts is to teach underlying principles through the repetitive practice of techniques. The techniques of the arts represent formalizations of the masters' understandings of the principles. They can be seen as approximations of the underlying principles. [. . .] Each student ultimately must see into those underlying principles by himself. This can only be done by endless repetition of the eight stages of kyudo. (Kushner 2000: 17)

Kyudo means literally 'the way of the bow', *do* being the suffix that means 'way' (the Japanese equivalent of the Chinese 'tao'). Hence, the designation of karate as *karatedo*, the way of the empty hand, or the Zen art of sword fighting as *kendo*, the way of the sword. The various ways of the martial arts, as well as the art of writing (*shodo*), the art of tea (*chado*), and so on, are 'fractional expressions of Zen in limited fields. [. . .] These actions become Ways when practice is not done merely for the immediate result but also with a view to purifying, calming and focusing the psycho-physical apparatus, to attain to some degree of Zen realization and express it' (Leggett 1978: 117). The final goal, then, is to go 'beyond technique, and indeed beyond thought' (Leggett 1978: 118) and reach a point at which the *ri* of technique gives way to the *ji* of inspiration.

The *ri* of philosophy, its ensemble of skills and techniques, is the history of philosophy. The *ji* of philosophy is the inspiration that arises in the process of creating concepts. The discipline of philosophy, 'a violent training, a culture or *paideïa* which affects the entire individual' (DR 165), gradually takes shape through the collective practices of former masters of the art, such as Plato, Spinoza, Nietzsche and Bergson, each master adding something to the *ri* of the 'way' of philosophy. The master trains apprentices in the workshop of the history of philosophy, sometimes conducting group lessons, sometimes offering individual instruction. The master discloses the concepts and problems of past philosophers, and, in the process, models the activity of philosophical thought. Apprentices must undergo this rigorous *paideïa*, but only as a means of commencing a true apprenticeship in signs, one that they will pursue on their own until, perhaps, they master the 'way' of philosophy and manage to find the *ji* of philosophical creation. How this will happen, when, or by what means is mysterious, beyond any method or programme. But, if such mastery is attained, its effects will be all-pervasive. The 'way' of philosophy is a way of living, a mode of existence, and, like the way of Zen, one that applies to all aspects of life.[3] Philosophy's way is that of the event, the encounter, the forceful interference, intercession, reverberation and resonance of signs meeting signs. The master, as producer of signs, is filled with a lightness, a gentle humour, but also with a passionate intensity. When producing signs, the master is no longer a human being, but a selfless, a-personal concentration of thought itself, an amalgam of concepts, percepts and affects. In the philosophy seminar, the material vehicle of thought is the voice, and conducting a *cours magistral* is nothing other than giving voice to philosophy. The master's enunciation of the way is the affirmative Yes, hesitant, prolonged, suspended in time, in an intermezzo, a meanwhile (*entretemps*), a between-time, a floating time that opens towards the possibility of something new. It is in this Yes, a single sign of all signs, inseparable from the asignifying matter of the master's *Sprechgesang*, that the *ji* of philosophy, its inspiration, appears. At that moment, the master apprentice discloses the essence of teaching, the way towards a perpetual encounter with signs, an ongoing apprenticeship in which masters and apprentices alike continue to learn from the world.

Notes

1. There is no transcription of Deleuze's remarks in *The ABC Alphabet* available in print. Stivale, however, has written an invaluable detailed synopsis of the seven-hour video and has made it accessible on the Internet (Stivale 2000). A version of the video with English subtitles, *Gilles Deleuze from A to Z*, appeared in 2012.
2. In the *ABC Primer*, Deleuze tells Parnet that he once taught a lycée lesson by playing a musical saw, a pedagogical technique, one must assume, that he abandoned at the university level.
3. In the *ABC Primer*, Parnet asks Deleuze if he goes to art exhibits or films in the pursuit of culture, and he says no, that he is simply seeking encounters. She then asks if he ever goes to films for entertainment rather than 'work', and he replies that it's not a matter of work, but of being alert, looking for something disturbing, amusing, stirring, anything that has the energy of something 'passing', something in the process of becoming-other. This vigilance is not restricted to the realm of the arts, he suggests, but informs all of his experience. And indeed, given the wide range of subjects Deleuze addresses in his books, it is evident that the 'way' of philosophical encounters is one that he pursued in all aspects of his life.

II. The Possible and the People to Come

2

To Choose to Choose – To Believe in This World

Though one might argue that all of Deleuze's work deals with ethics, the topic itself does not arise frequently in his writings. In *Cinema 1: The Movement-Image* and *Cinema 2: The Time-Image*, however, ethics is addressed directly when Deleuze says that 'we need an ethic or a faith, which makes fools laugh' (C2 173), an ethic of choosing to choose and a faith that allows belief in this world. In the philosophy of Pascal and Kierkegaard and the cinema of Bresson and Dreyer, Deleuze finds 'a strange way of thinking', an 'extreme moralism which is opposed to morality', a 'faith which is opposed to religion' (C1 116). This conjunction of Pascal, Kierkegaard, Bresson and Dreyer, says Deleuze, 'weaves a whole set of relations of great value between philosophy and the cinema' (C1 116). Striking is the fact that this 'strange way of thinking' is usually articulated in terms of the transcendent – specifically, the transcendent terms of Roman Catholicism in the case of Pascal and Bresson, and those of Protestantism in Kierkegaard and Dreyer – whereas Deleuze consistently maintains that his thought is above all a philosophy of immanence. One might ask, then, by what means and for what purposes Deleuze appropriates this transcendent thought for an immanent ethics, and in what ways he delineates a specifically cinematic dimension of that ethics. And, beyond these issues, one might ask of this meeting of philosophy and cinema the larger question of Deleuze's conception of the basic relationship between these two enterprises. In *What is Philosophy?* Deleuze insists on the separate vocations of philosophy and the arts, but in *Cinema 2* he suggests a more intimate relationship between philosophy and cinema, and perhaps it is in the domain of this immanent ethics that cinema serves a privileged function for philosophical thought.

Pascal and Kierkegaard

The first task in exploring this 'strange' philosophical-cinematic thought is to determine the manner in which Deleuze reads the philosophers Pascal and Kierkegaard. Deleuze's earliest engagement with Pascal and Kierkegaard comes in *Nietzsche and Philosophy*, during his analysis of Nietzsche's sense of the tragic and its relationship to chance. Deleuze notes that Pascal and Kierkegaard are often labelled 'tragic philosophers' and that both formulate an ethics of risk and the aleatory: Pascal with his wager of God's existence, Kierkegaard with his leap of faith. Pascal's wager and Kierkegaard's leap of faith prefigure Nietzsche's cosmic throw of the dice, but in Deleuze's view Nietzsche's Christian antecedents remain trapped in a tragedy of guilt and dread, whereas Nietzsche embraces a tragedy of joyous affirmation. Pascal and Kierkegaard are poets of 'the ascetic ideal' (NP 36), who oppose conventional morality and reason, but only via 'interiority, anguish, wailing, guilt, all the forms of dissatisfaction' (NP 36). What they lack is Nietzsche's 'sense of affirmation, the sense of exteriority, innocence and the game' (NP 36). The Pascalian wager especially reveals a mentality of *ressentiment*, in that Pascal's gambler tries to overcome chance and hedge all bets, to transcend the insecurity of the aleatory and escape to a providential beyond. The Nietzschean throw of the dice, by contrast, is an affirmation of each aleatory cast, whatever its specific outcome.

In subsequent references to Pascal, Deleuze for the most part simply reiterates his assessment of the Pascalian wager, but his engagement with Kierkegaard is somewhat more detailed in later works. His most extended treatment of Kierkegaard is in *Difference and Repetition*, where he parallels the concepts of repetition developed by Kierkegaard and Nietzsche. The two Kierkegaardian texts on which Deleuze concentrates are *Repetition* and *Fear and Trembling*, published the same day in 1843. Kierkegaard's chief aim in these works is to challenge the reigning Hegelianism of his day and assert the primacy of religion and the personal over philosophy and the collective.[1] In Hegel's terms, Kierkegaard's position might be characterised as that of the Unhappy Consciousness, that phase of the dialectic traced in the *Phenomenology of Mind* in which consciousness recognises itself as at once finite and infinite (or delimited and undelimited), yet without any means of overcoming this fundamental contradiction. In this basically religious consciousness, spirit (or mind) is aware of itself as a finite entity, yet also as a faculty capable of determining all natures through thought, and hence capable of comprehending the infinite. But the unhappy consciousness cannot grasp itself as being both a limited entity and an unlimited capacity of mind, and as a result it attributes that unlimited capacity to an eternal and infinite God, from which consciousness is separated, despite its sensed affinities with that God. To overcome this division, says Hegel, consciousness must make a 'movement' (*Bewegung*) of thought, whereby spirit understands itself as the medium of the infinite coming to awareness of itself in time. In this higher form of consciousness, or absolute mind, the finite spirit recognises itself as the necessary manifestation of the infinite. A religious unhappy consciousness thus gives way to a superior philosophical absolute mind; the individual spirit transcends its finitude and discovers itself as one with the infinite and undelimited. The ethical and political consequences of this movement beyond unhappy consciousness are that the individual comes to comprehend itself in its universal humanness, to recognise its own goals and purposes in the communal purposes of all humanity, and to find freedom and ultimate fulfilment through the rational coordination of action within social institutions.

Kierkegaard rejects the Hegelian elevation of philosophy over religion and its valorisation of the collective over the individual, arguing instead that the religious and the individual (in a certain guise) represent the highest form of experience and thought. The movement of thought that Kierkegaard traces is not one from Unhappy Consciousness to Absolute Mind, but a three-stage movement from what Kierkegaard labels the 'aesthetic', through the 'ethical' to the 'religious'. The 'aesthetic', by which Kierkegaard means the consciousness inherent in immediate sensual experience, is a form of consciousness that is surpassed by the 'ethical', another word for Hegelian universal philosophical reason, but what Kierkegaard's calls the 'religious' is a mode of being beyond reason, ethics and the universal, in which the ethical may be suspended and the individual enters into 'an absolute relation to the absolute' (Kierkegaard 1983a: 62).

In *Repetition*, Kierkegaard initially frames the difference between the ethical and the religious in terms of contrasting conceptions of time, the one manifesting a temporality of recollection, the other a temporality of repetition. 'Repetition and recollection', he says, 'are the same movement, except in opposite directions, for what is recollected has been, is repeated backward, whereas genuine repetition is recollected forward' (Kierkegaard 1983b: 131). Obviously, with the term 'recollection' Kierkegaard is invoking Platonic *anamnesis*, that re-memoration whereby the mind recalls those universal, eternal truths that it once knew but has since forgotten. But Kierkegaard insists as well that the Hegelian movement of thought is no alternative to Platonic *anamnesis*. Rather, it is simply another version of recollection, despite its terminology of 'movement' and 'mediation'. In Platonic *anamnesis*, the true, the eternal, the non-finite, the Whole, has always been, and thought is merely a present recalling of that totality. In the Hegelian movement of mediation, the true, eternal, non-finite Whole becomes manifest through history, but, once revealed, it remains the same unchanged Whole as in Plato, and the process of its temporal revelation ultimately affects that Whole in no meaningful way. For Kierkegaard, by contrast, the infinite is beyond full comprehension and containment, a Whole that is genuinely open to change in the future, and hence an unbounded Whole. Kierkegaard's point is roughly the same as that made later by Bergson: in Plato and Hegel the Whole is *given*, that is, the Whole is presupposed as a closed, complete and knowable entity, whereas for Kierkegaard and Bergson the Whole is open, a genuinely *becoming* Whole that is constitutively unknowable in any permanent sense. To engage such an open Whole, thought must abandon the backward movement of recollection and embrace the forward movement of repetition. Kierkegaard's concise though somewhat cryptic formulation of the recollection–repetition opposition is that 'When the Greeks said that all knowing is recollecting, they said that all existence, which is, has been; when one says that life is a repetition, one says: actuality, which has been, now comes into existence' (Kierkegaard 1983b: 149). What repeats in repetition is life (not knowing, as in recollection), and that vital repetition consists of a manifestation of an open, ungraspable Whole in a concrete instant (an 'actuality') that is followed by a subsequent instant in which the open, ungraspable Whole yet again 'now comes into existence'.

What is at stake in Kierkegaard's reflection on time is the status of the future in recollection and in repetition. In recollection, the Whole is closed and knowable. Whether it is suddenly recollected in Platonic *anamnesis*, or slowly revealed through the Hegelian movement of mediation, once that Whole is fully comprehended the future is empty. At that point, the Whole, as completed entity, has exhausted its possibilities, and the future can be only a reiteration of that selfsame set of possibilities. In repetition, by contrast, the Whole is open and ungraspable, as yet undetermined and undeterminable. The instant in which this open Whole comes into existence is always full of unknowable possibilities. The future is a genuine future, in which time matters, that is, in which the forward surge of time makes a difference. To engage the time of repetition, one must go beyond the domain of the 'ethical', which belongs to a time of recollection, and enter the domain of the 'religious'.

In *Repetition*, Kierkegaard's chief exemplar of the movement beyond the ethical to the religious is Job, and in his story one can see the connection between time, knowledge and ethics in the narrow sense of the word. Job's neighbours judge him according to the communal standards of public morality. They presume to a complete knowledge of his situation and see no possible explanation for his suffering other than guilt and no possible response other than repentance. They inhabit the domain of the 'ethical', in that they have transcended their immediate existence to embrace a universal human morality and a rational, philosophical comprehension of a closed Whole. Job, by contrast, refuses to accept his neighbours' judgement; his relationship with God is beyond universal morality, and his expectation is that, despite all rational indications, God will restore everything to him in this life, for with God all things are possible.

Perhaps Kierkegaard's most illuminating example of the religious consciousness, however, is not Job but Abraham, the central figure in *Fear and Trembling*. Abraham is called to commit an incomprehensible act, one that by the standards of universal morality must be condemned as murder. He has various rational means of avoiding the dilemma of his situation, but he declines them all. He makes a leap of faith, moving beyond the human community into an immediate and personal relationship with God. As he prepares to sacrifice Isaac, there seems no possible outcome other than Isaac's death, but Abraham trusts, despite all reason, that his son will be fully restored to him in this life. For God, all things are possible, which means that for Abraham, the future is genuinely open. Unlike the tragic hero, who subordinates one ethical norm to another (such as Agamemnon, who subordinates his duty as a father to his duty as a king in sacrificing his daughter), Abraham enters a domain in which the ethical is suspended altogether. He goes beyond universal humanity to become a specific individual in an absolute relationship with the absolute. He is what Kierkegaard calls a 'Knight of Faith', and his leap beyond rational comprehension and ethical norms brings him into a cheerful enjoyment of this world. 'He finds pleasure in everything, takes part in everything' (Kierkegaard 1983a: 39), and seems no different from the average well-fed Burgher. But for him all has been transformed, since the world now is replete with possibility.

Kierkegaard and Nietzsche

In *Difference and Repetition*, Deleuze identifies four elements common to Kierkegaard's and Nietzsche's conceptions of repetition. First, both 'make something new of repetition itself' (DR 6), in that both regard repetition as the reiteration of unpredictable possibility, a repeated coming into being of an open Whole in Kierkegaard, a repeated cosmic throw of the dice in Nietzsche. Second, both 'oppose repetition to the laws of Nature' (DR 6), in that they reject the deterministic, mechanistic model of a nature regulated by linear causality and hence subject to total predictability (at least in theory). Third, they 'oppose repetition to moral law' (DR 6), Kierkegaard by positing an ultimate suspension of the ethical, Nietzsche by advocating a thought beyond good and evil. Finally, both 'oppose repetition not only to the generalities of habit but also to the particularities of memory' (DR 7), that is, both reject a thought that looks backwards via memory (be it Platonic *anamnesis*, Hegelian mediation or a Humean association of ideas through habit) and embrace a thought that forgets what it thinks it knows and thereby becomes an active power capable of engaging an emergent future.

Deleuze does not minimise the differences between Kierkegaard and Nietzsche, and he makes it clear that his own concept of repetition is much closer to that of Nietzsche than that of Kierkegaard. Indeed, if we now consider the question of how Deleuze appropriates Kierkegaard's transcendent thought of the leap of faith for his own philosophy of immanence, we might say that it is primarily by reading Kierkegaard through Nietzsche. Kierkegaard's emphasis on the transcendent is part of his rejection of Hegel's ontology of immanent absolute spirit coming to consciousness of itself through time. The domain of the religious emerges as a transcendent disruption of the continuities, regularities and inevitabilities of communal ethics and universal reason. The religious enters existence in 'the moment', a transcendent rupture in historical time, and it defies rational comprehension as well as assimilation within human morality. What Nietzsche's concept of repetition allows Deleuze to do is to make Kierkegaard's transcendent force of disruption a part of a new, non-Hegelian ontology of difference. One might say, with a great deal of caution, that what was God in Kierkegaard becomes, through Nietzsche, difference in Deleuze. Put another way, the Kierkegaardian religious force that disrupts the Hegelian cosmos of immanent absolute spirit becomes the operative force immanent within a cosmos of self-differentiating difference.

A key element of Deleuze's ontology of difference is Nietzsche's concept of the Eternal Return, which Deleuze presents as a perpetually repeated cosmic throw of the dice. In Deleuze's ontology, however, this repetition is not purely chaotic. Rather, the series of dice throws is like a Markov chain, a formal model in which a discrete set of possibilities produces a second set of possibilities, which in turn produces a third, each set in the chain of events being affected and partially determined by the preceding set, yet with each set's potential for subsequent differentiation always being multiple and undeterminable.[2] The relationship between events is at once contingent and necessary, unpredictable yet non-arbitrary. Each set, in its multiple possibilities, exceeds any identity. It is a difference in itself, unfolding into further states of self-differing difference. The cosmos, as repeated dice throw, then, may be seen as an open Whole of interconnected Markov chains, each a contingent and necessary sequence of throws of the dice, any given result of a throw having immanent within it the potential for multiple outcomes in the next throw.

In *Difference and Repetition*, Deleuze distinguishes Kierkegaard's repetition from Nietzsche's by saying that Kierkegaard leaps whereas Nietzsche dances, by which he means that Kierkegaard's leap is a one-time cosmic wager, whereas Nietzsche's dance is a perpetually repeated series of dice throws. But what is essential to the two thinkers, says Deleuze, is that they produce movement within thought, in the sense both of going beyond the false movement of Hegelian mediation, and of inventing new means of philosophical expression. Rather than represent concepts, they 'dramatize Ideas' (DR 10; trans. modified). They create a theatre within philosophy, each complete with its 'heroes of repetition: Job–Abraham, Dionysus–Zarathustra' (DR 5), a theatre that exceeds representation through 'vibrations, rotations, whirlings, gravitations, dances or leaps which directly touch the mind' (DR 8).

Choosing to Choose

'I pay attention only to the movements,' says Kierkegaard (Kirkegaard 1983a: 38), and in *Difference and Repetition* Deleuze identifies that principle as the source of Kierkegaard's theatre of repetition. But when Deleuze comments on this 'marvelous motto' in his analysis of movement in *A Thousand Plateaus*, he says that Kierkegaard 'is acting astonishingly like a precursor of the cinema'

(ATP 281). It comes as no surprise, then, that Kierkegaard appears in both *Cinema 1* and *Cinema 2*. In each volume, Kierkegaard is invoked as a guide towards an ethics of 'choosing to choose' and a faith that induces 'belief in this world'. What Deleuze finds interesting in Pascal, but especially in Kierkegaard, is that a genuine choice 'is not between terms but between the modes of existence of the one who chooses' (C1 114). One mode of life, for example, is that of the ideologue, or the true believer, for whom the answers are already given and there is nothing to choose. Another is that of the indifferent or the uncertain, those who lack the capacity to choose or never know enough to be able to choose. A third is that of the fatalists and devotees of evil, those who make a single choice that commits them to an inevitable and unavoidable sequence of actions that afford no further choice. And finally there is the mode of existence of those who choose to choose, those who affirm a life of continuous choosing. The choice in this last mode of existence, in short, 'has no other object than itself: I choose to choose, and by that I exclude all choice made on the mode of not having the choice' (C1 114).

Those who choose to choose affirm the possible. Like Kierkegaard's Knight of Faith, they leap beyond rational and ethical certainties into an open Whole, their leap being an act of trust in possibilities beyond their present comprehension. Choosing to choose is crucial for Deleuze because contemporary men and women have lost faith with this world, that is, they no longer believe in the possibility of anything new. The world is a bad movie, an endless series of banalities and clichés, platitudes and vacuous opinions. But this does not mean simply that the world is insipid and boring; it can also be an insidious and coercive film. Deleuze says that for modern directors the world as bad film constitutes 'the intolerable', but in his study of Foucault he also treats all of Foucault's work as a response to 'the intolerable'.[3] In *Discipline and Punish*, for example, the present prison system is the intolerable. As Foucault shows, within the first forty years of its existence, the prison's drawbacks and failures are evident, and within those forty years one hears the same calls for reform and recommendations for more prisons, better prisons, stricter prisons and so on that one hears today. The penal system is a bad movie, an endless recycling of practices and discourses that seem unavoidable, inescapable, devoid of real alternatives, emptied of all genuine possibility.

The only viable response to the intolerable is to think differently, to disconnect the world's networks of certainties and pieties and formulate new problems that engender as yet unmapped relations and connections. For modern film directors, thinking differently, at its most fundamental level, is a matter of disconnecting and reconnecting images. The world as bad movie consists of myriad chains of association, which in strictly visual terms may be conceived of as images linked to other images to form natural, predictable, redundant sequences. The first task of thinking differently in images is to 'disenchain' the chains, to dissolve the links of habitual association that tie images to one another (all of which links are embedded in the common-sense spatio-temporal regularities of the sensory-motor schema). The second task is to take a given image and choose another image that 'will induce an interstice *between* the two' (C2 179). Such a choice will be contingent but not arbitrary, the choice of image being the result of a search for productive juxtapositions, such that the sequence of images becomes a self-differentiating series, but one in which the gaps between images retain their primacy. Each gap in such a series, then, is the site of a choice, a throw of the dice, a leap, an experimentation in a zone of possibilities. The gap itself is off the map of the known world; it is a pure Outside uncharted by external spatial or internal psychological coordinates. The series of images formed by such choices 're-enchains' the images, but such that they form Markov chains, contingent but necessary iterations of possibilities differentiating themselves into further possibilities. In this regard, the choice of images is an ontological choice, the process of choosing constituting a mode of existence that is inseparable from the becoming of the cosmos as an open Whole of self-differentiating differences.

Bresson

In *Cinema 2*, Deleuze discusses the Pascalian and Kierkegaardian theme of choosing to choose through the films of Eric Rohmer,

Carl Dreyer and Robert Bresson, the choice of directors obviously being guided in part by their frequent treatment as filmmakers concerned with religious themes. Certainly, in the work of Bresson, if we limit our attention to that director, the religious dimension is incontestable. Besides dealing with explicitly religious subjects (*Journal d'un curé de campagne*, *Le Procès de Jeanne d'Arc*), Bresson constructs what might be considered parables of grace, the grace that like the wind blows where it will in *Un condamné à mort s'est échappé*, or the grace that miraculously brings Michel to Jeanne at the end of *Pickpocket*. *Au hazard, Balthazar* and *Le Procès* may be regarded as studies of sainthood, *Mouchette* and *Une femme douce* as films about suffering and the problematic redemption of suicide, *Le Diable, probablement* and *L'Argent* as Jansenist essays on the bleakness of a world deprived of saving grace. Yet if religious concerns are patent in Bresson's films, they are handled in a way that allows non-religious interpretations as well. If the influence of a transcendent deity or a providential grace may be regarded as shaping events in his films, it is always by invisible means. No numinous clouds, transverse shafts of light, or surging strains of angelic choirs signal the presence of the divine. Rather, the workings of grace shape a consistently sober, often grim and insistently material world whose atmosphere, especially in the black-and-white films of the 1950s and 1960s, has some affinities with that of Italian Neorealism. Bresson's ascetic reduction of compositional elements, his focus on isolated objects, his separation of elements from their usual contexts (especially hands, feet and torsos), his spare use of camera movement and contrasting angles, all suggest a de-realising formalism consistent with a certain monastic sensibility, but the same techniques may be seen as means of enhancing the intensity of sensual experience and focusing the viewer's attention on the life of the lived body. The result is that Bresson's cinema has lent itself to multiple, contradictory interpretations, especially as regards the status of the transcendent in his work. Schrader, for example, considers Bresson to be the quintessential practitioner of the transcendental style in film, whereas Rosenbaum counters that Bresson is the ultimate materialist. Those who stress the formalist aspects of Bresson's films do so often to emphasise the invisible presence of the transcendent, whereas those who focus on the centrality of sensation and the inseparable conjunction of perception and emotion in his films tend to call attention to the insistent corporeality of any supposed hidden forces. Hence, Keith Reader can say of *Un condamné* that it is a 'spiritual realist' (Reader 2000: 49) film, open at once to a transcendental and a non-transcendental interpretation, and Ayfre can say of the transcendental in Bresson that 'we are dealing with immanent transcendence, or even, one might say, with radical invisibility', in that 'the invisible world remains invisible, or rather appears only as invisible' (Ayfre 1969: 21). Clearly, if Deleuze must read Kierkegaard through Nietzsche to transform a philosophy of transcendence into a thought of immanence, no such interpretive labour is required with Bresson, since the transformation of transcendence into immanence may be regarded as having already taken place in his films.

Deleuze touches on the element of choice in the narratives of Bresson's films, and he alludes to Bresson's persistent dramatisation of the theme of grace or chance, but Deleuze's interest in Bresson is largely formal rather than diegetic or thematic. Deleuze stresses the principle of 'fragmentation' in Bresson's practice, especially as it is brought to bear in the construction of an *espace quelconque* (an 'any-space-whatever'). In the famous Gare de Lyon sequence of *Pickpocket*, for example, the conventional spatio-temporal connections between elements are broken and the space is fragmented into components capable of being reconnected in diverse ways. 'It is a perfectly singular space', says Deleuze, 'which has merely lost its homogeneity. [. . .] It is a space of virtual conjunction, grasped as a pure locus of the possible' (C1 109). Deleuze also cites Bresson as one of the great innovators in the handling of sound. Bresson treats the sonic and the visual as separate strata, thereby introducing a gap between sight and sound that complements the gap between images that structures the visual. Bresson says that he seeks in his films a '*sort of relay*' (Bresson 1986: 37) between sight and sound, and Deleuze says that a 'coming-and-going' between the visual and the sonic 'defines the modern cinema' (C2 247; trans. modified).

In his *Cinema 2* discussion of choosing to choose, however, Deleuze concentrates on a third aspect of Bresson's cinema – that of Bresson's selection, training and manipulation of actors, or, as Bresson prefers to call them, 'models'. Bresson observes that 'nine-tenths of our movements obey habit and automatism. It is anti-nature to subordinate them to will and to thought' (Bresson 1986: 17). Traditionally trained actors are incapable of performances informed by such natural automatism, so he works largely with non-professionals. He forces his 'models' to rehearse repeatedly until their gestures and words become automatic, and he demands that his models eliminate all overt signs of expressivity or intentionality during filming. Through the suppression of thought and will in his models, Bresson aims at a kind of naturalness, yet he also seeks the unexpected and the unknown, that which is beyond either the model's or the director's intentions, but which the camera alone can capture. Models, says Bresson, are '*automatically* inspired, inventive' (Bresson 1986: 18), for it is 'a mechanism [that] gives rise to the unknown' (Bresson 1986: 41). The result of this practice is a cinema inhabited by hyper-alert sleepwalkers, curiously doubled presences that seem separated from themselves, often apparently flat and affectless, yet suddenly traversed by intense and unexpected affects.

Deleuze argues that in Bresson's models we see a manifestation of the thinker within modern cinematic thought, which Deleuze labels the 'spiritual automaton' (a term borrowed from Spinoza and Leibniz). If our contemporary dilemma is that of a loss of faith in this world, the dilemma of an 'intolerable' bad-movie world devoid of genuine possibility, the only means of overcoming this dilemma is to think differently, and, indeed, only such a different kind of thought constitutes genuine thinking. To think differently, however, is in a sense to exceed our present thought, to go beyond what we know and hold certain. Only by injecting into thought something uncharted and incomprehensible, a pure Outside, can genuine thinking begin. When this occurs, another thinker arises within thought, a thinker that is a function of the breakdown of ordinary thought, and hence, one might say, a thinker that is a perpetual product of the 'impotence of thought'. In the modern cinema, thinking differently consists of unchaining the image-chains of received opinions and beliefs and then re-enchaining images through the gaps between then. Each gap is a locus of the Outside, within which conventional thought stutters and collapses, while in that same gap another thinker within thought begins to arise, an alien, non-human (or a-human) thinker, an automaton produced by and productive of the Outside.

Bresson's screen models, then, are both manifestations of the spiritual automaton and figures of that alien thinker within thought that is generated in the modern cinema. The spiritual automaton, finally, is not something limited to embodiment in the humans on the screen, but a function distributed across a given film through its gaps, as well as a function generated within spectators when the film succeeds in meeting its ends. Such a function arises through a practice, that of unchaining conventional chains of images and re-enchaining, each new juxtaposition being a throw of the dice, a choice to trust in the possibilities of the unpredictable and unknowable. The modern cinematic practice of unchaining and re-enchaining via the gap of the Outside is a practice of choosing to choose, a mode of existence that generates the spiritual automaton. We should note as well, however, that choosing to choose is not entirely a matter of will and personal decision. Kierkegaard's leap of faith is a leap beyond reason and into the absurd, but it remains a leap of the individual thinker possessed of an identity and a will. In appropriating Kierkegaard for his immanent ethics Deleuze might be suspected of simply repeating Sartre's existential modification of Kierkegaard, but choosing to choose is not a matter of authenticity or a personal commitment to freedom. Rather, it is a matter of generating an alien thinker within thought, one that emerges only at the limits of will and reason. The spiritual automaton is such a thinker, one proper to the modern cinema, and in Bresson's handling of his models we find an instance of the practice of choosing to choose. Bresson 'radically suppress[es] the *intentions* of [his] models' (Bresson 1986: 13), and he frees their movements from any subordination 'to the will and to thought' (Bresson 1986: 17). Once they 'become automatic, protected against any thought' (Bresson 1986: 68), they become '*automatically* inspired, inventive' (Bresson 1986: 18), instances of 'a mechanism [that] gives rise to the unknown' (Bresson 1986: 41).

Spiritual Automatons and Conceptual Personae

Bresson's cinematic models may be regarded as figures of the spiritual automaton, but in one specific sense they may also serve as guides to an understanding of Deleuze's conception of cinema's relationship to philosophy. Bresson's models deliver their lines as if their words were someone else's. As they speak, linguistic signs begin to separate from visual signs; the verbal and the visual diverge into separate strata of sound and sight. This splitting of seeing from speaking, and this assimilation of language within a sonic continuum, are fundamental to modern cinema and to its potential for inducing new thought.

What does Deleuze find most appealing about cinema? Deleuze is fascinated by the visual, and especially by the possibility of seeing differently. The basic obstacle to seeing differently is conventional narrative, and, by extension, language. In his study of Francis Bacon, Deleuze identifies Bacon's primary aim as that of rendering images devoid of narrative connotations. In his essay on Beckett's television plays, Deleuze argues that Beckett attempts to move beyond words, to dry up the voices that incessantly tell their mundane stories, and to bring forth pure images, both visual and sonic, which are freed from all narrative associations. Even in his many writings on literature, Deleuze pays little attention to narrative per se, and in his book on masochism, he shows that Sacher-Masoch's fictions are mere stagings of frozen visual tableaus. And in his last book, *Essays Critical and Clinical*, Deleuze asserts that one of literature's primary functions is to create within language what he calls Visions and Auditions, visual and sonic images at the limits of language that arise within the verbal, like hallucinatory presences looming between or floating above the words.

For Deleuze, thinking differently is fundamentally a matter of seeing differently, and for him cinema is above all a visual medium. What distinguishes cinema from painting is, first, that movement and time are directly rendered within the visual cinematic image, and, second, that cinema immediately engages the problem of vision's relation to language and conventional narrative. With the collapse of the sensory-motor schema in modern film, detached, 'unchained' visual images arise, while at the same time common-sense narratives fall apart. Language is cut loose from its network of conventional associations with visual images, and it becomes part of a sonic continuum. Language enters into a back-and-forth relay with visual images, but as a component of the sonic continuum, it also tends towards its own aural limit as a-signifying affective sound. Cinema's distinction among the arts, then, is that of being the art that most fully and most directly engages the crucial philosophical problem of thinking differently by seeing differently.

The cinematic agent of this new mode of seeing is the spiritual automaton, a strange kind of agent in that it is less the cause of a new seeing than the produced locus within which such seeing arises. In this regard, it has as its analogue in philosophy what Deleuze and Guattari call the 'conceptual persona', the similarity between the spiritual automaton and the conceptual persona suggesting one final aspect of cinema's privileged relationship with philosophy. In *What is Philosophy?*, Deleuze and Guattari approach philosophy as the invention of concepts, arguing that such invention requires three elements: concepts, a plane of immanence and a conceptual persona. The conceptual persona 'is not the philosopher's representative, but, rather, the reverse: the philosopher is only the envelope of his principal conceptual persona' (WP 64). The conceptual persona at once precedes and follows the plane of immanence, in this regard both producing and being produced by thought. It is 'the becoming or the subject of a [given] philosophy' (WP 64) that arises within the philosopher as a separate, 'other' thinker. And, above all, it is a locus of movement in thought. 'In philosophical enunciations', say Deleuze and Guattari, 'we do not produce something by saying it, but produce movement by thinking it, through the intermediary of a conceptual persona' (WP 64–5; trans. modified).

In *What is Philosophy?* Deleuze and Guattari assert that the conceptual persona is a component of all genuine philosophical thought, but it is clear that their inspiration for the notion comes primarily from such 'philosophers of the future' as Kierkegaard and Nietzsche. In *Difference and Repetition* Deleuze says that Kierkegaard and Nietzsche are the first philosophers to put movement within thought, and they do so by fashioning a theatre of philosophy, with its heroes being Abraham and Job in the one theatre, and Dionysus and Zarathustra in the other. Those actors are the conceptual personae of Kierkegaard's and Nietzsche's thought, vectors that arise within thought as a-personal agents of movement. Given the similarity between the conceptual persona and the spiritual automaton, perhaps, then, we should rephrase Deleuze and say that Kierkegaard and Nietzsche create not a theatre but a cinema of philosophy, with conceptual personae that function like spiritual automatons, generating and being generated by different ways of thinking.

In *What is Philosophy?*, Deleuze and Guattari outline the fundamental elements of philosophy, and then differentiate philosophy first from the sciences and then from the arts. The domain of the arts is said to be that of sensation, the aim of the arts being the creation of affects and percepts on a plane of composition. Philosophy, by contrast, has as its goal the creation of concepts on a plane of immanence. The arts' plane of composition is identified as a plane of the possible, whereas philosophy's plane of immanence is a plane of the virtual. In *What is Philosophy?* Deleuze and Guattari's treatment of the arts focuses almost exclusively on painting, music and literature, with virtually no references to film, an absence explained perhaps by Deleuze's having already written at length on cinema, but perhaps also by the fact that cinema blurs the line between philosophy and the arts, a line Deleuze and Guattari are intent on sharpening in *What is Philosophy?* This neat demarcation of philosophy from the arts seems especially challenged by the notion of the possible in *Cinema 1* and *Cinema 2*, for the possible in those works is the dimension of creation in general, whether it be a creation in philosophical concepts or a creation in cinematic images. The possible is the domain of experimentation on the real, a zone in which possibilities are produced through disruptive critical practices, but in which as well the possibility of the new is anticipated as an outcome of each experimentation. The possible, thus, is the domain of an ethics and a faith common to thought in general.

The 'strange thought' Deleuze finds in the philosophy of Kierkegaard and the cinema of Bresson is one that affirms an ethic of choosing to choose and a faith of belief in this world. Kierkegaard fashions a cinematic philosophy, whose conceptual personae produce genuine movement within thought, leaping beyond universal reason and morality into a future of unknowable possibilities. Bresson constructs a philosophical cinema, whose models are embodied spiritual automatons, their speech and actions manifesting a split between words and images, between hearing and seeing, that split inducing fissures in the continuities of conventional narratives. Kierkegaard and Bresson's common ethic may have a transcendent religious dimension, but its practice promotes an immanent ethics. Choosing to choose is a mode of existence, a way of living in this world, and the faith that informs it is a belief in the possibilities of this world as well. The single aim of philosophy and cinema is to think differently, to unchain the sequences of inevitabilities governed by received opinion and belief, and then to reconnect the pieces in contingent yet necessary Markov chains. Thinking differently entails choosing to choose, adopting a way of living that allows a belief in the world's 'possibilities of movements and intensities so as once again to give birth to new modes of existence' (WP 74). As Deleuze and Guattari say in *What is Philosophy?*, 'it may be that believing in this world, in this life, becomes our most difficult task, or the task of a mode of existence still to be discovered on our plane of immanence today' (WP 75).

Notes

1. There are, of course, many different readings of Kierkegaard. My own is largely consonant with that of Alistair Hannay (1982); see esp. pp. 19–89. For a different, deconstructive reading of Kierkegaard and *Repetition*, see Roger Poole (1993), esp. pp. 61–82.
2. Deleuze himself makes reference to the Markov chain to describe the principle of historical succession in Foucault's philosophy. See F 17. In 'Michel Foucault's Main Texts', an essay written shortly after Foucault's death in 1984 and published in *Two Regimes of Madness*, Deleuze says of Foucault's diagrams of systems of thought, 'Between two diagrams, between two states of diagrams, there are mutations, reworkings of the relationships of forces. Not because anything can

connect to anything else. It is more like successive drawings of cards, each one operating on chance but under external conditions determined by the previous draw. It is a combination of randomness and dependency like in a Markov chain' (2R 258–9). Deleuze most likely draws his understanding of the Markov chain from one of his favorite writers, the philosopher of biology Raymond Ruyer, who discusses Markov chains in *La Genèse des formes vivantes* (Ruyer 1958: 170–89).

3. Deleuze underlines the significance of the intolerable in Foucault's thought in a 1986 interview, saying that Foucault 'In a way, he was a kind of *seer*. And what he saw was actually intolerable. [. . .] His ethics was to see or grasp something as intolerable. He did not do it in the name of morality. It was his way of thinking. If thinking did not reach the intolerable, there was no need for thinking. Thinking was always thinking at something's limit' (2R 279–80).

3

Speranza, Island of the Possible

In the June 1967 issue of *Critique*, Deleuze published a review essay of Michel Tournier's first novel, *Vendredi, ou Les Limbes du Pacifique* (*Friday: Or the Limbo of the Pacific*), and in 1969 he included a slightly modified version of the essay as an appendix to *The Logic of Sense*. Neither Tournier's novel nor Deleuze's analysis of it features prominently in Deleuze's later work, but both have played a significant role in two well-known critiques of Deleuze: Alice Jardine's 1985 feminist critique of Deleuze and Guattari's concept of 'becoming woman', and Peter Hallward's 2006 political critique of Deleuze's supposed theoretical disengagement from the conflict-laden world of the Other. Both Jardine and Hallward treat the essay as symptomatic of general tendencies in Deleuze's thought that extend well beyond the text. Reviewing their critiques thus provides an opportunity not only to evaluate the merits of their readings of Deleuze's essay but also to address the broader question of the status of the essay in Deleuze's work as a whole. Rather than seeing the essay as a symptom of deficiencies in Deleuze's thought, I view it as a precursor of things to come, an early manifestation of the philosophy of nature articulated in *A Thousand Plateaus* and of the concept of fabulation developed in *Cinema 2*, *What is Philosophy?* and *Essays Critical and Clinical*. Crucial in both regards is Deleuze's approach to the concept of the possible in his commentary on Tournier's novel.

Tournier's *Friday*

Tournier's *Friday* is a retelling of Defoe's *Robinson Crusoe*, which maintains the basic elements of the original plot: an eighteenth-century Englishman shipwrecked and stranded alone on a desert island, who spends the last few years of his island residence with a non-Western companion whom Crusoe names Friday. Within this framework, however, Tournier fashions a story markedly different from Defoe's, one that emphasises psychological, philosophical and sociohistorical themes only latently present in, or entirely absent from, the original. Tournier's novel is too rich to summarise adequately in a short space, but these are the primary details pertinent to Jardine's and Hallward's critiques.

After Robinson has been shipwrecked on the island and has assessed his situation, he names the island the Island of Desolation. For the first several months of his stay, he desperately and fruitlessly labours to build a boat for his escape. After failing, he resorts to submerging himself for hours in a swamp he calls 'the mire', where he begins to lose his mind, seeing at one point a vision of his sister Lucy, who had died as a child. To save his sanity, he institutes an administrative rationality for himself, raising crops, gathering goat herds, building a shelter, writing an island charter, constructing a water clock, recording dates, keeping a diary and so on. He maps the island and renames it Speranza, the island of hope, noting that its shape resembles that of a headless woman. He pursues a kind of hyper-capitalism, concluding ultimately that accumulation is the sole good and that consumption is evil. Yet he senses that beyond the administered island lies 'another Speranza'. He comes closer to that Speranza when he bathes his naked body in milk and slips into a womb-like cavern, discovering a foetal warmth that reminds him of the rising bread his mother had kneaded when he was a child. Eventually he comes to embrace the feminine Speranza as his wife. He begins copulating with the earth, burrowing his erect penis in the ground and inseminating the soil, his semen mysteriously producing mandrake flowers, which he regards as his daughters.

Then someone else arrives. Neighbouring Aracauna Indian tribes use the island for sacrificial rites, and one day Robinson witnesses a would-be victim escape his torturers. Robinson fires his rifle, causes the torturers to flee, and saves the escapee, whom he subsequently names Friday. Robinson initially regards Friday as a savage and considers it his duty to civilise the fifteen-year-old. Friday, however, is a recalcitrant subject, who exasperates Robinson to such an extent that he begins to adopt the habits of a tyrannical slave driver. But Robinson is also becoming weary of the strict order of his island regime, and he senses beneath the savage Aracauna 'another Friday'. So, when Friday inadvertently ignites Robinson's stored powder kegs and blows Robinson's settlement apart, it is with a secret relief that he leaves that administrative order and enters a nomadic existence with Friday. He learns from Friday, who seems an aerial spirit. The terrestrial Robinson, under the guidance of the aerial Friday, comes to discover a new Robinson, a solar spirit who inhabits the island with an animal immediacy and experiences each day as the eternal return of a new present. Not surprisingly, when a ship named the *Whitebird* eventually lands and Robinson begins talking with the crew, he has misgivings about leaving the island and returning to the civilisation he now sees as alien. He decides to stay and continue his existence with Friday. Yet, as the *Whitebird* departs, he discovers that Friday has departed as well, and in near despair he faces the prospect of dwelling alone on the island for ever. He then hears a voice and finds that a twelve-year cabin boy has jumped ship to avoid the constant beatings the boy had been subjected to. With equanimity restored by the promise of the boy's companionship, Robinson 'drew a deep breath, filled with a sense of utter contentment, and his chest swelled like a breastplate of brass' (Tournier 1969: 234).

Jardine

Jardine's 'Woman in Limbo: Deleuze and His (Br)others' is one of the earliest critiques of the concept of 'becoming-woman', appearing only five years after the publication of *A Thousand Plateaus*. Unlike many feminists who come after her, she does not centre her critique on the political efficacy of becoming-woman as part of an affirmation of an identity politics.[1] She cites Deleuze and

Guattari's caveat that embracing a politics of becoming-woman does not lessen the importance for women 'to conduct a molar politics, with a view to winning back their own organism, their own history, their own subjectivity' (ATP 276), but rather than simply challenge the viability of combining a molar politics with a minor politics of becoming-woman, she questions the status of women within 'becoming-woman' per se as well as the position of woman within the various becomings Deleuze and Guattari embrace – becoming-woman, becoming-child, becoming-animal, becoming-molecular and becoming-imperceptible. Deleuze and Guattari assert that 'all becomings begin with and pass through becoming-woman' (ATP 277), but they also argue that 'the woman as a molar entity *has to become-woman*' (ATP 275). Their logic is that the conventionally coded identities of male and female are both defined via male power, and hence that both men and women must undo those categories through a process of becoming-other. But Jardine sees this requirement that 'molar women' enter a becoming-woman as a surreptitious positioning of 'molar woman' as man, which thereby implies that all becoming-woman is only a *man's* becoming-woman. Jardine also objects to Deleuze and Guattari's hierarchy of becomings, which grants becoming-woman primacy as an initiatory phase in becoming other, but which identifies becoming-imperceptible as 'the immanent end of becoming, its cosmic formula [. . .], the end of all the molecular becomings that begin with becoming-woman' (ATP 279). This trajectory from becoming-woman to becoming-imperceptible, Jardine argues, is one that concludes, as does most male discourse on women, in the erasure of women. Jardine thus asks,

> But to the extent that women must 'become woman' *first* (in order for men, in D + G's words, to 'follow her example'), might that not mean that she must also be the *first* to disappear? Is it not possible that the process of 'becoming woman' is but a new variation of an old allegory for the process of women becoming obsolete? There would remain only her simulacrum: a female figure caught in a whirling sea of male configurations. A silent, mutable, head-less, desire-less, spatial surface necessary only for *His* metamorphosis? (Jardine 1985: 54)

Jardine supports her argument by emphasising the continuities between *Anti-Oedipus* and *A Thousand Plateaus*, by stressing the psychological aspects of desire and the Body without Organs, and by identifying the Body without Organs as a feminine body. She rightly observes that in their introduction of the concept of the Body without Organs in *Anti-Oedipus* Deleuze and Guattari make use of Schreber's psychotic experience of his organless body as feminine, but she does not explain how such a feminine Body without Organs might be related to the social Bodies without Organs of the primitive machine (the body of the earth), the despotic regime (the body of the despot) and the capitalist machine (the body of capital), none of which is described in markedly feminine terms, and all of which have an importance equal to, or (in my judgement) greater than, that of the individual human's Body without Organs. She notes that the desiring machines of *Anti-Oedipus* are replaced by assemblages in *A Thousand Plateaus*, but she says nothing about the assemblage's correlative concept of the plane of consistency, which Deleuze and Guattari identify with the Body without Organs, but which they tend to favour over the latter term, thereby avoiding the misleading implication that the Body without Organs is strictly limited in its purview to human or even animal bodies.

Deleuze and Guattari do state that 'the reconstruction of the body as a Body without Organs, the anorganism of the body, is inseparable from a becoming-woman, or the production of a molecular woman' (ATP 276), but the sense of the phrase 'molecular woman' is lost if it is not linked to the cosmic dimension of becoming and the plane of consistency. In the Becomings Plateau, bodies ultimately are defined by differential speeds and intensive affects on a plane of consistency (ATP 256). A molecular woman, therefore, is a particular configuration of speeds and affects. 'Becomings are affects' (ATP 256), and affects are powers of affecting and being affected. What is spoken of as desire in *Anti-Oedipus* is largely rearticulated in *A Thousand Plateaus* in terms of affects, a terminological shift that makes clear how broadly desire is to be construed and to what extent human becomings participate in the countless becomings that span the natural world.

Becomings may involve humans, but not necessarily. A paradigmatic example of becoming is that of the orchid and the wasp, an instance of aparallel evolution in which the orchid's colouration comes to resemble a female wasp with which the wasp engages in an 'unnatural nuptial' (ATP 241) and helps pollinate another orchid. Deleuze and Guattari return repeatedly to this example (ATP 10, 12, 25, 44, 69, 190, 238, 265, 293–4, 314), viewing it as a becoming-wasp of the orchid and becoming-orchid of the wasp that entails various powers of affecting and being affected. Other non-human becomings include the tick and mammals (ATP 51, 257, 264), the cat, baboon and C virus (ATP 238), and young roots, certain microorganisms and the leaves of trees (ATP 238). All of these becomings, at the level of speeds and affects, are instances of becoming-molecular. Becoming-molecular, however, is not the final stage of becoming. 'The imperceptible is the immanent end of becoming, its cosmic formula' (ATP 279), but becoming-imperceptible is not a matter of simply becoming invisible; rather, becoming-imperceptible is a process of becoming one with, and making, a world. To become-imperceptible 'is to world (*faire monde*), to make a world (*faire un monde*)', and the exemplar of becoming-imperceptible is 'the camouflage fish, the clandestine: this fish is crisscrossed by abstract lines that resemble nothing, that do not even follow its organic divisions; but thus disorganized, disarticulated, it worlds with the lines of a rock, sand, and plants, becoming imperceptible' (ATP 280). To become-imperceptible, then, is not to disappear, but to enter into the cosmic becoming of the world, the universal symbiosis of organic and inorganic entities in a single 'anorganic life' (ATP 503).

Jardine does not relate becoming-woman to Deleuze and Guattari's philosophy of nature, but restricts her attention to the human psychological dimension of becoming-woman as it is presented in *A Thousand Plateaus*. Yet she does address the subject of nature to a certain extent in the closing section of her essay, where she claims to expose the gender prejudices implicit in becoming-woman by examining the images of woman and the discourse on the feminine in Tournier's *Friday*. Jardine treats Tournier's novel as an allegory of the position of women in the thought of Deleuze (and Deleuze and Guattari), and she justifies this reading by identifying *Friday* as a privileged text in their work.

'Most important theorists have a repertory of exemplary fictions,' she observes, 'fictions that they call upon frequently to interact with their specific theories in creative if predictable ways' (Jardine 1985: 54). She identifies Marguerite Duras' *The Ravishment of Lol V. Stein* as one of Lacan's exemplary fictions and Blanchot's *L'Arrêt de mort* as one of Derrida's. She then asserts that 'D + G's exemplary fiction writers include Lewis Carroll, Franz Kafka, Pierre Klossowski, and Michel Tournier – to mention only a few' (Jardine 1985: 54). Of the four writers cited, Kafka certainly figures prominently in the writings of Deleuze and Guattari, but the others are seldom referenced in their works.[2] Especially dubious is the identification of Tournier as an exemplary fiction writer for Deleuze or Guattari, let alone the two together. Deleuze and Guattari cite Tournier only twice in their co-authored works: they devote two sentences of *A Thousand Plateaus* to Tournier's novel *Les Météores* (ATP 261) and mention *Friday* in a footnote on possible worlds in *What is Philosophy?* (WP 220) (the latter reference being unavailable to Jardine in 1985). Guattari never mentions Tournier in his single-authored works, and Deleuze's references to Tournier, outside of his essay on *Friday*, are minimal, and restricted to *The Logic of Sense* (LS 49, 336) and *Difference and Repetition* (DR 306, 352).

It would seem, then, that *Friday* is an exemplary fiction, not for Deleuze or Guattari, but for Jardine, who sees in it an anticipatory allegory, written thirteen years before *A Thousand Plateaus*, which reveals Deleuze and Guattari's ultimate subordination of women to male desire in the concept of 'becoming woman'. The key elements of the allegory are: Robinson's decision to name the island Speranza after viewing a map he had drawn of the island, which, in his eyes, 'resembled a female body, headless but nevertheless a woman, seated with her legs drawn up beneath her in an attitude wherein submission, fear, and simple abandonment were inextricably mingled' (Tournier 1969: 47–8); Robinson's identification of Speranza as his mother and then later as his wife; Robinson's transcendence of his relation to Speranza as his wife through his bonding with Friday; Robinson's eventual characterisation of Friday as his brother; and the appearance of the twelve-year-old cabin boy at the novel's conclusion. In this allegory, Speranza is a mere 'simulacrum' of a woman, 'a female figure caught in a whirling sea of male configurations', 'a silent mutable, head-less, desire-less, spatial surface necessary only for *His* metamorphosis' (Jardine 1985: 54). Robinson's libidinal disengagement from Speranza and subsequent supra-sexual bonding with Friday lead to 'a new world of brotherhood . . . without any women at all' (Jardine 1985: 59). And the appearance of the cabin boy, as Speranza, 'shedding her veil of mist', emerges 'virgin and intact' (Tournier 1969: 234; trans. modified), represents the ultimate male fantasy – that of creating children without the need of women.

Is this a truly *Deleuzian* allegory? Hardly. The fundamental elements of the allegory do not appear in Deleuze's essay: Deleuze does not cite the description of Speranza as a head-less woman, nor does he treat the island as feminine; he says nothing about Friday being Robinson's brother; and he does not mention the cabin boy. What Deleuze does instead is frame his analysis of the novel in terms of Defoe's original work and Tournier's reconfiguration of that text. Deleuze observes that Defoe's novel has often been seen as 'an "instrument of research" – a research which starts out from the desert island and aspires to reconstitute the origins and the rigorous order of works and conquests which happen with time' (LS 302). Defoe conducts an experiment: he places a lone individual on a desert island, and then shows how, from that originary solitude, *homo economicus* builds a world that resembles eighteenth-century Europe. Deleuze takes this reading of Defoe from Pierre Macherey, whose Marxist analysis of *Robinson Crusoe* demonstrates, in Deleuze's summary, 'how the theme of origin is tied to an economic reproduction of the world and to the elimination of the fantastic in the interest of an alleged "reality" of the world' (LS 366). Deleuze argues further that the absence of the fantastic is related to 'the elimination of all sexuality in Defoe's Robinson' (LS 303). By contrast, Tournier's counter-fiction is an 'inductive experimental novel' (LS 305; trans. modified), in which Robinson is a sexual being (*sexué*, literally 'sexed', as opposed to *asexué*, 'asexed'), whose development is determined, not by origins, but by '*ends quite different and divergent from ours*', which produce 'a fantastic world which has itself deviated' (LS 303). By reconfiguring the Robinson experiment in these terms, 'Tournier makes it impossible for him to allow Robinson to leave the island' (LS 303), since the world that has emerged is a world alien to our own.

Deleuze opens his essay with a passage from Tournier's novel describing Friday's confrontation with a large goat he has named 'Andoar', which climaxes in Friday slaying the charging goat. Friday vows to honour Andoar via a 'mysterious project: the dead goat will fly and sing – it will be a flying and musical goat' (LS 301). Friday skins the goat and turns its pelt into a kite, and he fashions an Aeolian harp from Andoar's sun-cured entrails stretched across the horns of the goat's skull. In Deleuze's reading of this episode, the terrestrial goat becomes celestial, and in this way 'the great goat frees the Elements' (LS 302). The earth and air serve 'less as particular elements than as two complete and opposed figures, each one, for its part, gathering the four elements' of earth, air, fire and water. The earth 'holds and subsumes' the elements, whereas 'the sky, with the light and the sun, sets them in a free and pure state' (LS 302). The island is the surface upon which the conflict of terrestrial and aerial elements takes place, and the story of Robinson's libidinal engagement with the island represents a movement from human desire (in Robinson's case, heterosexual desire), which anthropomorphises the elements and buries them in the earth, to a non-human desire that engages the elements in a cosmic eros. 'The end, that is, Robinson's final goal, is "dehumanization", the coming together of the libido and of the free elements, the discovery of a cosmic energy or of a great elemental Health which can surge only on the isle – and only to the extent that the isle has become aerial or solar' (LS 303).

Deleuze says that 'the isle is as much the hero of the novel as Robinson or Friday' (LS 302), but he does not identify the island as feminine, Jardine's assertions to the contrary.[3] Deleuze does mention the phase in which Robinson identifies Speranza as a mother, but in Deleuze's reading this is a sign of Robinson's psychotic regression under the pressures of his isolation, and this maternal regression is related to his hyper-capitalist obsession with producing objects without consuming them. Robinson sees his descent into the cave of mother earth as diametrically opposed to his administration of his island economy of crops and flocks, but in Deleuze's judgement,

> The impression one has, however, is that these two very different behaviors are singularly complementary. In both cases, there is frenzy – a double frenzy defining the moment of psychosis – which appears clearly in the return to the Earth and the cosmic genealogy of the schizophrenic, but no less in work, in the production of nonconsumable schizophrenic objects which proceeds by way of piling up and accumulation. (LS 314)

This psychotic phase is only an intermediary stage on the way towards a cosmic pansexuality that defies description in human terms. In Robinson's words, which Deleuze cites,

> If this solar coition is to be translated into human language, I must consider myself feminine and the bride of the sky. But that kind of anthropomorphism is meaningless. The truth is that at the height to which Friday and I have soared, difference of sex is left behind. Friday may be identified with Venus, just as I may be said, in human terms, to open my body to the fecundation of the Aster Major. (LS 304; trans. modified)

Jardine cites these same lines, commenting that here 'Speranza's primary configuration – the feminine – has been left behind' (Jardine 1985: 58), but she argues that the novel's ending, with the appearance of the cabin boy as Friday's replacement, reveals the bad faith behind this cosmic pansexuality, which is only a disguise for Tournier's and Deleuze's desire for a world without women. But, of course, the revelatory moment of male parthenogenesis does not occur in Deleuze's text.

Perhaps, then, the allegory is Tournier's, rather than Deleuze's. This hypothesis, however, is also problematic. Much of the motivating force of the bad faith allegory Jardine discovers in the novel is lost if the work is not contextualised within Deleuze and Guattari's advocacy of becoming-woman. One could argue that Tournier's text is an exercise in male becoming-woman *avant la lettre*, but there are other ways of viewing the figuration of woman and man in the novel. Tournier's project is to take the basic elements of the Robinson Crusoe story and rework them. Tournier's Robinson, like Defoe's, is an eighteenth-century Englishman, and, though he is much more introspective and philosophical than Defoe's hero, throughout much of the novel he acts and thinks like an eighteenth-century man. For example, Tournier's Robinson is initially as much an enterprising capitalist settler as Defoe's protagonist; like Defoe's Crusoe, for much of the novel Robinson seeks guidance in the Bible and interprets events within a Protestant framework of punishment and reward; and when Tournier's Robinson meets Friday, he is as openly and unapologetically racist as Defoe's hero. The topic of sexuality does not arise directly in Defoe's novel, but at the conclusion of the tale Crusoe reports that after his rescue he married and had two children, and hence one may assume that he is a heterosexual male. So, too, is Tournier's Robinson, and it comes as no surprise that his attitudes towards male–female relations are consonant with those of an eighteenth-century male. In short, Tournier's Robinson is a fictional character, and Tournier's thought always passes through the filter of his protagonist's mentality and language.[4]

Hence, when Robinson maps the island and sees in it a headless woman 'wherein submission, fear, and simple abandonment were inextricably mingled' (Tournier 1969: 47–8), he is expressing an eighteenth-century attitude towards women that is the complement of his eighteenth-century colonialist understanding of nature and the earth – as something to be dominated and rendered submissive. But Robinson is alone on the island, and the awakening of libidinal impulses initiates an increasing split in his relationship to nature. His administrative self continues to dominate nature, but his libidinal self pursues a diverging engagement with the land, a potentially subversive trajectory that Robinson articulates in terms of traditional European conceptions of male–female relations. Initially, he imagines the earth as his mother, but when he ejaculates while he is sleeping in the womb-cave, he recognises with horror the incestuous nature of his sensual contact with the earth and renounces that metaphor. Later he finds a more acceptable figure for his libidinal connection to the island, that of a wife. Yet it is crucial to observe that Robinson's passage to the island as wife is through contemplation of the unnatural nuptials of the orchid and the wasp (Tournier 1969: 114) (a detail noted by Deleuze in his essay [LS 313]). Robinson studies the sexual interaction of the flower and the insect and then explores means of consummating his own unnatural nuptials. For six months, he copulates with the mossy crevice of a tree, abandoning this outlet for his desire only when a spider bites his penis. Eventually he finds a more satisfactory sexual relation with nature when he mates with a grassy meadow, burrowing his penis in the earth and inseminating it with mandrake flowers that he identifies as his daughters. Robinson tries to conceptualise his sexual relation with plants – what he terms 'his "*vegetal way*"' (Tournier 1969: 115; trans. modified) – in human terms by considering the island his wife, but he senses that the course he is pursuing is leading to the creation of 'an increasingly dehumanized Robinson' (Tournier 1969: 112). What he comes to learn, after Friday blows up his administrative world and initiates him into the living realm of 'another Speranza', is that this anthropomorphic model of husband and wife is inadequate to represent his emergent libidinal connection to nature. He has become 'dehumanised' in that he has ceased to see himself as a human fundamentally separated from the non-human world, and the metaphors and myths of European civilisation, with which he tries to express his new, elemental connection with nature, only point obliquely towards the reality he is discovering: 'I grope in search of myself in this forest of allegory' (Tournier 1969: 214). The metaphor that figures the human–nature bond as that of husband and wife is among those that he must abandon.

Robinson's feminisation of the island, then, has to do less with relations between men and women than with relations between humans and nature, and what Jardine sees as evidence of Tournier's and Deleuze's latent sexism is actually the product of a fictional character's attempt to go beyond his culture's anthropocentric understanding of the cosmos. The erasure of woman in *Friday* also entails the erasure of man – at least as man is conceptualised in Robinson's European world view.

Nonetheless, as Jardine points out, the world of *Friday* is a world without women. But so is the world of Defoe's novel, and

Tournier's project is to start with the rudiments of Defoe's fictional world and rewrite them. As Tournier says in reflections on his first novel, Defoe's narrative has assumed a mythic status in two ways. First, Defoe's protagonist is 'a hero of solitude' (Tournier 1988: 184), a representative of the modern world's isolation of the individual as a result of the fragmentation of community, someone who suffers that isolation and yet triumphs over it. But 'Crusoe's years of solitude', says Tournier, 'are overshadowed by the novel's other great theme, for which in the end they merely lay the necessary groundwork, namely, the appearance of Friday' (Tournier 1988: 188). 'Crusoe and his man Friday', then, are the mythic givens of Tournier's experiment, and his effort is to reverse the power relationship between the two figures, as is signalled in the title of Tournier's novel. As Robinson begins to change under Friday's guidance late in the narrative, he comes to regard Friday as a brother, yet only after abandoning his paternalistic condescension. 'For years he had been both Friday's master and his father. Now in a matter of days he had become his brother; and he was not even sure of being the elder brother' (Tournier 1969: 182–3). Defoe's myth is that of a hero of solitude who is also the hero of white colonial domination of savages. The brotherhood of Tournier's Robinson and Friday represents a reconfigured power relationship that counters Defoe's myth. That they are males is a given of the myth; that they are brothers, at least in Robinson's eyes, is a sign that they treat each other as fellow human beings. And, most importantly, Robinson treats Friday as his elder brother, under whose tutelage he learns to engage the world in a different way.

So, what of the appearance of the cabin boy at the end of the novel, the linchpin of Jardine's critique? In Defoe's fiction, Crusoe readily leaves the island, virtually unchanged by his exile, ready to take up his career as a planter and merchant. By contrast, in Tournier's novel, as Deleuze observes, Robinson's development is determined by '*ends quite different and divergent from ours*', which produce 'a fantastic world which has itself deviated' (LS 303), and, as a result, he cannot leave the island. He decides to stay, but he assumes he will share his island existence with Friday. When he learns that Friday has departed, his ecstatic solar engagement with the world is shattered, and he sinks into utter desolation. What Tournier is clearly indicating is that his Robinson is not a hero of solitude, but a hero who needs other people. Tournier could have ended the novel with Robinson in despair, but he chose instead to provide Robinson with a companion. Given the constraints of the fiction's eighteenth-century world, the likelihood of a woman being aboard a merchant vessel would be remote, and hence narrative plausibility would dictate that any deserter from the ship would be male. By making the deserter a mistreated cabin boy Tournier supplies a plausible rationale for the deserter's decision to opt for island exile over life aboard ship. But Tournier's motivation for providing Robinson with a cabin boy companion, obviously, is above all thematic. At the novel's end, Robinson can now occupy Friday's role and serve as an older brother, teaching the young man to lead an alternative mode of existence.

But let us suppose that the final tableau of Robinson and the boy alone on the island is a male fantasy. Is it necessarily a fantasy of male parthenogenesis in the absence of women? Tournier was a gay man, and in his fiction he thematises various forms of sexuality – heterosexual, homosexual, androgynous and so on. In interviews, he promoted a 'genial' or 'general' sexuality rather than a restrictively genital sexuality, arguing that eroticism hurts no one, not even children (see Petit 1991: 84–5). Tournier's Robinson comes to discover such a 'general sexuality', and he prefaces his comments on his solar pansexuality by saying, 'As for my sexuality, I may note that at no time has Friday inspired me with any sodomite desire' (Tournier 1969: 211). But, if one were psychoanalytically inclined, one might read Robinson's denial as the symptom of the homoeroticism that pervades his relationship with Friday. In such case, the concluding fantasy would be one less of male parthenogenesis than of homoerotic desire, the twelve-year-old cabin boy being an *ephebe* and Robinson the boy's older lover.[5] I'm not inclined to endorse such a reading, but I find it as plausible an interpretation as Jardine's.

The allegory Jardine discerns in *Friday* is a rhetorically effective tool for exposing what she sees as a failure of imagination in Deleuze and Guattari's concept of 'becoming-woman', one that is rooted in the unexamined biases of their male perspective on questions of gender and sexuality. Deleuze's reading of the novel, however, mentions none of the elements central to her allegory. What Deleuze finds in Tournier's text is the story of the dehumanisation of Robinson's desire, a passage from an anthropocentric conception of desire that separates humans from nature to a pansexuality that integrates humans within the natural world. This reading is consonant with the thematic development of the novel, and it complements Tournier's critique of Eurocentrism, racism and colonialism, which is inseparable from the work's exploration of alternative conceptions of sexuality. Jardine's objections to Deleuze and Guattari's becoming-woman deserve serious consideration, and the allegory she draws from *Friday* bears decided polemical force. But it is a reading against the grain, an exercise in the hermeneutics of suspicion. It is not Deleuze's allegory, nor is it Tournier's.

Hallward

In Peter Hallward's *Out of This World* (2006), Tournier's novel assumes a markedly different function than in Jardine's analysis. Hallward couples his remarks about Deleuze's essay on *Friday* with an extended meditation on Deleuze's early unpublished essay 'Causes and Reasons of Desert Islands' (written sometime in the 1950s, published posthumously in 2002), emphasising the motif of a 'world without others' in the two essays. In Deleuze's 1950s essay, he treats the island as a figure of absolute origin and creativity. Under certain circumstances, the island remains 'deserted and unpeopled', no matter how many people may occupy it, for the island has become 'only the dream of humans, and humans, the pure consciousness of the island' (DI 10). In the moment of its desertion, the island gives rise to 'uncommon humans, absolutely separate, absolute creators, in short, an Idea of humanity, a prototype, a man who would almost be a god [. . .] a pure Artist, a consciousness of Earth and Ocean' (DI 11). It is from the perspective of this vision of the island as a pure creative consciousness untroubled by others that Hallward reads Deleuze's analysis of the notion of the Other presented in *Friday*. Hallward concludes that, for Deleuze, the only meaningful form of creative thought entails 'the sacrifice of that most precious sacred cow of contemporary philosophy – *the other*'; hence, Hallward argues, 'a liberating return to the immediate and the impersonal will requires elimination of the other' (Hallward 2006: 92). Hallward treats this movement beyond the Other as a symptom of Deleuze's weakness as a political philosopher. Hallward concludes that 'there is no place in Deleuze's philosophy for any notion of change, time or history that is mediated by actuality'. Deleuze is 'indifferent to the politics of this world', to 'mechanisms of exploitation and domination', 'conflicts and contradictions', and to 'relations of conflict or solidarity, i.e., relations that are genuinely *between* rather than external to individuals, classes, or principles' (Hallward 2006: 162), and primarily because his model of thought and creation is that of a world without others.

Hallward's reading of Deleuze's Tournier essay is more tangential than Jardine's, focusing on only a small portion of the essay, in which Deleuze comments on Robinson's disorienting experience of living in a world without others before Friday's arrival. For the most part, Deleuze merely rewords Robinson's highly philosophical reflections on the effects of his solitude (which are prefaced by Robinson's amusing protestation that 'I am not versed in philosophy' [Tournier 1969: 91]).[6] Robinson observes that in the absence of other people, his fundamental spatial and temporal orientation in the world begins to crumble. He reasons that the object behind his back, which he does not perceive, has permanence and solidity only because he assumes that it is the object of perception for another person. Every person expresses a possible world, he concludes, and it is the coordination of these possible worlds in a single world that gives reality its coherence. In the absence of other people, that coordination of the possible collapses. In Deleuze's formulation, 'the Other is that which possibilises' (LS 320; trans. modified), and a world without others is a world without the categories of the possible. Deleuze argues that what Robinson has discovered through his isolation is the '*a priori Other*' (LS 307), a structure that organises common-sense reality before the appearance of subject or object, assigning them positions within the realm of the possible and orienting them in a chronological time. This a priori Other functions in roughly the same way as the agencies of common sense and good sense in *Difference and Repetition*, or, even more roughly, as the sensory-motor schema of hodological space in the cinema books.

'What is the sense of the "Robinson" fiction?', Deleuze asks. His answer, 'A world without Others' (LS 318–19), is evidence for Hallward that Deleuze 'is indifferent to the politics of this world' and interactions with the Other. But Hallward ignores an essential distinction Deleuze maintains throughout his essay.[7] Whenever he speaks of the world without others, or the a priori Other, he always uses the word *autrui*, a noun that refers only to human beings, 'the other person'. He does not employ the much broader term *autre*, which may be applied to anything 'other' – the other day, the other colour, the other side of the road. This allows him to assert that 'Friday does not function at all like a rediscovered Other [*comme un autrui retrouvé*]' (LS 316), that Friday is 'not an Other, but something wholly other than the Other [*non pas un autrui, mais un tout-autre qu'autrui*]' (LS 317). Deleuze denounces only the Other as structure of limiting possibility, *l'Autrui a priori*, leaving room for an alternative world of 'otherwise Others [*des Autres qu'autrui*]' (LS 320). And such a conception is not simply hypothetical or imposed on Tournier's text. Throughout his meditation on the effects of the absence of others, Robinson uses the word *autrui*, not *autre*, to refer to the Other. Tournier also says repeatedly that Robinson sensed beneath Speranza and Friday 'another Speranza', 'another Friday', and the relationship of two individuals as 'otherwise other' is directly presented in the interactions of Robinson and Friday in the novel's final section, as is the 'otherwise other' pansexual relation Robinson has formed with the natural world of the island.

At this point, it is worth considering Tournier's own reading of his novel, since his analysis of the work stresses elements of the novel that supplement Deleuze's interpretation and that Deleuze could assume his audience would already be aware of. In his autobiographical book *The Wind Spirit*, Tournier argues that myth is central to human culture:

> Man rises above animality only by grace of mythology. Man is nothing but a mythological animal. He becomes man – he

> acquires a human being's sexuality and heart and imagination – only by virtue of the murmur of stories and kaleidoscope of images that surround him in the cradle and accompany him all the way to the grave. (Tournier 1988: 158–9)

Myth is 'a fundamental story' (Tournier 1988: 156), '*a story that everybody already knows*' (Tournier 1988: 157). An allegory, by contrast, is 'a dead myth', and 'the writer's function is to prevent myths from becoming allegories' (Tournier 1988: 160). (We might note that Deleuze, in his early essay on desert islands, says 'Literature is the attempt to interpret, in an ingenious way, the myths we no longer understand, at the moment we no longer understand them, since we no longer know how to dream them or reproduce them' [DI 12].) For Tournier, Defoe's *Robinson Crusoe* is a myth in danger of becoming an allegory. Tournier revivifies the Crusoe myth in part by rendering it in the elemental terms of earth, air and sun, in part by uncovering the psychological dynamics of isolation buried by Defoe, and in part by envisioning a world outside the conventional real. The meeting of Robinson and Friday, says Tournier, represents not 'the marriage of two civilizations', but 'the elimination of every last vestige of civilization in a man subjected to the corrosive effect of an inhuman solitude: the very roots of his life and being are laid bare, and he must then create from nothing a new world, groping in the dark, feeling his way toward discovery, clarity and ecstasy' (Tournier 1988: 190–1).

Tournier also imbues the novel with a mythical-philosophical structure, whereby, as Tournier observes, 'the three stages of Robinson's evolution are related to the three types of knowledge described by Spinoza in the *Ethics*' (Tournier 1988: 196). Robinson submerged in the swampy mire corresponds to Spinoza's first form of knowledge that operates through 'the senses and emotions'. Robinson's administered island aligns with Spinoza's second form of knowledge, that of 'science and technology', a rational knowledge 'but superficial, mediated, and for the most part utilitarian'. Finally, Robinson's solar ecstasies represent Spinoza's third form of knowledge, that of 'an intuition of the essence of the absolute' (Tournier 1988: 196). But most important in his resurrection of the Crusoe myth is Tournier's focus on Friday. In *The Spirit Wind*

Tournier reflects on his years of study at the Musée de l'Homme and the condescension with which Defoe treats Friday. That exposure to traditional cultures' wisdom and that awareness of Western racism, says Tournier, led him to vow that in his novel the cultural Other would not be dismissed or reduced to a distorted reflection of the West. Hence, part of Tournier's mission is, first, to reconfigure Defoe's mythical presentation of Crusoe as *homo economicus* and lay bare the logic of capitalism and colonialism in the first section of the novel, and then to counter Western racism and infantilising primitivism in the novel's closing section. In the novel's middle section, we might note, Tournier provides an analysis and critique of the eros of exoticism through his exploration of Robinson's libidinal engagement with Speranza. One can see, then, that in Tournier's mythic project there is a political dimension. His treatment of capitalism, colonialism, exoticism and primitivism engages historical forces that continue to play through the present world. It is for this reason that Tournier remarks,

> I wanted to dedicate my book to all of France's immigrant workers, to those silent masses of Fridays shipped to Europe from the third world – some three million Algerians, Moroccans, Tunisians, Senegalese, and Portuguese on whom our society depends and whom we never see or hear, who have no right to vote, no trade union, and no spokesperson. (Tournier 1988: 197)

It is startling to note the degree to which Tournier's characterisation of his novel conforms to the Deleuzian notion of fabulation, which Deleuze only begins to articulate in *Cinema 2*, *What is Philosophy?* and *Essays Critical and Clinical*. The engagement with historically situated assemblages of power; the detection of the diabolical forces of the future; the hallucinatory invocation of the names of history; the mythic 'legending *in flagrante delicto*'; the exploration of the floating time of the event; the invention of a new earth and a new people to come – all are present in Tournier's description of *Friday*.[8] Hallward's charge of a lack of engagement with the divisions, conflicts and inequalities of the socio-historical world certainly cannot be sustained against Tournier's fiction. A reader once asked him why he had not dedicated *Friday* to Defoe, and Tournier admits that 'the thought never even occurred to me, for it seemed obvious that every page of the book paid tribute to its English model' (Tournier 1988: 197). One might argue similarly that Deleuze need hardly stress in his essay on *Friday* that Tournier is reworking the Crusoe myth, that he is touching on central issues in the rise of capitalism and colonialism, and that he is countering European racism in his depiction of Friday (and he does show awareness of Tournier's political project at various points in the essay). Such things are so obvious that they go without saying, and it would be odd were Deleuze deliberately labouring against the basic thrust of the novel and arguing that the work's theme and his own point is that one must eliminate the Other, escape historical contingency and move somewhere 'out of this world'.

Tournier was one of Deleuze's oldest friends, a close companion during their years as students at the Lycée Louis le Grand and the Sorbonne, and in later years as well. As Stivale has shown us (Stivale 2008), friendship has always been an important component of Deleuze's thought and values, and no other individual as close to Deleuze as Tournier, save perhaps François Châtelet, has been the subject of Deleuze's writing. All creators need intercessors, says Deleuze (N 125–8), and Tournier in this essay is an especially intimate intercessor, which raises the question of the status of Deleuze's essay. In his works on Spinoza, Leibniz, Hume, Bergson and Nietzsche, it is not always clear when Deleuze is explicating the philosopher and when he is presenting his own views, and separating Deleuze from Tournier is especially difficult in this case. The essay is a generous offer of friendship, and a contribution to a collective thought about the Robinson Crusoe myth. As such, it certainly cannot be taken as an antithetical negation of the fundamental texture and spirit of the novel.

Deleuze and the Tournier Essay

'Michel Tournier and the World without Others' occupies an interesting position within Deleuze's oeuvre. In 1967, when first written, and in 1969, when appended to *The Logic of Sense*, Deleuze is still using psychoanalytic terminology to articulate his thought about desire. *Friday* is a novel of perversion, in Deleuze's analysis, a representation of the deviation of desire. Perversion 'is not defined by the force of a certain desire in the system of drives; the pervert is not someone who desires, but someone who introduces desire into an entirely different system and makes it play, within the system, the role of an internal limit, a virtual center or zero point' (LS 304). It is the concept of perversion that brings together the problematics of psycho-sexual desire, which Jardine addresses, and the phenomenological, epistemological and ethical implications of the Other, which Hallward discusses. The a priori Other is a transcendental structure that organises space according to Cartesian coordinates and a Newtonian, Laplacean causality. The emergence of subject and object within this regulated space in turn gives rise to an organised sequential time of past, present and future. But, most importantly, the a priori Other structures desire: 'In all these respects', says Deleuze, 'my desire passes through Others, and through Others it receives an object. I desire nothing that cannot be seen, thought, or possessed by a possible Other. That is the basis of my desire. It is always Others who relate my desire to an object' (LS 306). When Robinson enters a world without others, his desire loses its object – it turns away from its normative object, 'per-verts', and becomes first telluric, then vegetable and finally solar. In this turning aside, in this 'per-version', Robinson discovers a different space, a new temporality and a social relation that is 'otherwise other'.

Deleuze links the perversion of *Friday* to the perversion of Sade's fictions, in which victims and accomplices are always apprehended 'as "otherwise Others" [*Autres qu'autrui*]' (LS 320). In so doing, Deleuze suggests that the Tournier essay is a continuation of his thought in *Masochism: Coldness and Cruelty* (1967), yet Tournier's novel adds a new dimension to the notion of perversion in its conception of nature. In *Masochism*, Deleuze contrasts Sade and Masoch, finding in each a dual conception of nature, a secondary and a primary nature, according to which each writer organises desire, attempting through perversion to surmount secondary nature and gain access to primary nature. Sade's secondary nature is one of destruction and creation, a confused mixture of birth and death, whereas his primary nature is one of pure negation, an 'original delirium, a primordial chaos made solely of furious and lacerating molecules' (M 25).[9] Masoch, by contrast, posits a bipolar secondary nature, whose extremes are unconstrained sensuality and eroticised violence, which the masochist transcends through participation in a primary nature that is cool, suprasensual and purifying in its cathartic order. In *Friday*, there are also two natures, Speranza, the administered isle of colonial domination, and the other Speranza, the domain of Robinson's solar pansexuality. But the differences between the other Speranza and the primary natures of Sade and Masoch are striking. This is no nature of lacerating molecules or suprasensual coldness, but one of proliferating unnatural nuptials, within which Robinson participates in its ecstatic pansexuality. If the other Speranza is a primary nature, it is much more positive than the primary nature of Sade or Masoch, much more the subject of affirmation than negation. In this sense, the nature of the Tournier essay is a harbinger of the nature found in *A Thousand Plateaus*, Speranza being a nature of becoming-molecular and becoming-imperceptible, in which Robinson 'worlds' with the island.

The Tournier essay also marks a significant point in Deleuze's thought about the possible. Deleuze's analysis of the a priori Other represents perhaps his strongest rejection of the concept of the possible. In *Difference and Repetition*, he takes up Bergson's critique of the possible, arguing that the possible must be replaced by the virtual. Here, Deleuze explicitly associates the possible and the a priori Other with Leibniz's possible worlds and Sartre's regard of the Other (LS 366), but the unspoken object of his critique is Kant's conception of space and time as the a priori intuitions that establish the conditions of possible experience. Kant's 'possible experience' denotes the experience of good sense and common sense, and hence only the world of established, conventional modes of understanding reality. The structure of Leibnizian possible worlds expressed by Sartrean Others merely confirms the good sense and common sense of Kantian possible experience.

Deleuze also claims Kierkegaard as a defender of the possible as structured by the a priori Other, citing Kierkegaard's passage in *The Sickness unto Death*, in which a bourgeois gentleman, like a spectator overcome by the heat of a crowded theatre, crying out,

'Water! Water!', suddenly rushes to the window and exclaims, 'The possible! The possible! or I shall suffocate' (LS 318). This gentleman, says Deleuze, 'is only invoking the a priori Other' (LS 318). What is noteworthy is that this same reference receives a diametrically opposed interpretation in *Cinema 1* (C1 240) and *What is Philosophy?* (WP 178). In those works, the cry 'The possible! The possible! or I shall suffocate' signals a desperate search for possibilities beyond the conventional world, that is, something outside the structure of the a priori Other. Indeed, in *What is Philosophy?* the possible is identified as the domain specific to the arts, as opposed to the virtual domain of philosophy and the actual domain of the sciences. Such universes as the 'Rembrandt-universe or Debussy-universe' are 'neither virtual nor actual; they are possibles, the possible as aesthetic category ("the possible or I shall suffocate")' (WP 178). What allows this reversal in the deployment of Kierkegaard is the dual sense of the word 'possible'. It can denote that which is practicable, feasible, predictable, a sense picked up in Bismarck's quip that politics is the art of the possible, and this is the possible of the a priori Other. But a second meaning is that of alternatives beyond expectations, new conceptions and approaches outside conventions, a sense epitomised in the Pauline dictum, so important to Kierkegaard in *Fear and Trembling*, that with God all things are possible. Throughout Deleuze's essay on Tournier, the first sense of the possible prevails. But there is one point at which the second emerges. Deleuze observes that as Robinson's world crumbles in the absence of the Other, he is lost 'unless there be some sort of salvation for Robinson; unless he invents a new dimension or a third sense for the expression "loss of Others"; unless the absence of the Other and the dissolution of its structure do not simply disorganize the world but, on the contrary, open up a possibility of salvation' (LS 315). And, in fact, the dissolution of the a priori Other does open a possibility beyond the possible, that of another Speranza and another Friday.

The Tournier essay, then, articulates a view of nature and desire that anticipates the affective becoming-imperceptible of *A Thousand Plateaus*, and, though it concentrates on the negative sense of the possible as constraint and limitation, it also uses the word in its positive sense as the realm of the new and the as yet undisclosed. This latter sense is at work in what Deleuze comes to call fabulation, which consist of the creation of new possibilities for life, the invention of a new earth and a people to come. What is important to note is that the essay's elements that assume the most importance in Deleuze's later writings – affective nature and the invention of a new earth and new people – come from Tournier's novel. Sade and Masoch serve Deleuze as models of perversion, but it is Tournier's fiction that extends the category to include the affirmation of a nature of pansexual becoming-other – and perhaps, in so straining the limits of the category of perversion, opens a way beyond the analytic framework of psychoanalysis as a whole. And *Friday* provides a template of the fabulation Deleuze will later embrace, one that discloses uncharted possibilities for the invention of a new earth and a people to come.

Jardine and Hallward are correct that the Tournier essay has a special place in Deleuze's career, but not as a symptom of men's erasure of women or of a retreat from the political world of the Other. *Friday* is not an exemplary fiction, called upon frequently 'to interact with [. . .] specific theories in creative if predictable ways' (Jardine 1985: 54). Deleuze engages the novel only once, and the results of that engagement are far from predictable. Rather, *Friday* is an initiatory and prefigurative fiction, one that introduces important Deleuzian themes and anticipates their later development. Tournier is a friend and intercessor, and hence his novel is also an intercessory fiction, an intervention in Deleuze's thought that produces an event – an event within the possible that discloses the prospect of a new earth and a people to come.

Notes

1. See Braidotti (1993), Griggers (1997) and Grosz (1994) for succinct summaries of the attacks on 'becoming-woman' and thoughtful responses to those attacks. Also illuminating is the collection *Deleuze and Feminist Theory* (Buchanan and Colebrook 2007), especially Colebrook's introduction to the volume.
2. Carroll, of course, is at the centre of *The Logic of Sense*. Otherwise, Deleuze's references to Carroll are fleeting and of minor significance

(see DR 51, 124, 156; D 49, 65, 69, 73, 119; OLM 241; FB 17, 25; C1 202; CC 21–2, 69, 168; DI 175, 186). Guattari mentions Carroll twice, once in *Molecular Revolution in Brazil* (Guattari 2008: 456), and once in a citation from Nicolas Ruwet in the posthumously published *Lines of Flight* (Guattari 2016: 257). Deleuze and Guattari also make only brief reference to Carroll: AO 138, 188; K 93; ATP 76, 437. Deleuze includes an essay on Pierre Klossowski's fiction in *The Logic of Sense* (LS 280–301), but elsewhere he alludes to Klossowski's fiction only twice (CC 205, DI 79), citing him otherwise as a commentator on Nietzsche. Guattari never mentions Klossowski's fiction. Deleuze and Guattari make passing reference Klossowski's fiction six times: AO 77, 189, 330; ATP 131–2, 530; WP 222. For a complete list of Deleuze's literary references, see Drouet (2007).

3. Readers of Jardine's essay relying solely on her translation of Deleuze's text might think that Deleuze does feminise the island. On the second page of his essay, Deleuze writes 'L'île est la frontière ou le lieu de ce combat. C'est pourquoi il est si important de savoir de quel côté elle basculera, si elle est capable de déverser dans le ciel son feu, sa terre et ses eaux, et de devenir elle-même solaire.' Jardine paraphrases the first sentence, and then translates the second sentence as follows: 'That's why it's so important to know which side she'll turn towards, whether she's capable of pouring into the sky her fire, her earth, and her waters, and to herself become solar' (Jardine 1985: 56). 'L'île' is a feminine noun, and hence must take the pronoun 'elle', but there is no indication in Deleuze's text that he means by 'elle' anything other than 'it'. The English translation of *The Logic of Sense*, unavailable to Jardine in 1985, renders the passage in these terms: 'The isle is the frontier or field of this struggle. This is why it is so important to know which way the struggle will swing, and whether it is capable of pouring out into the sky its fire, earth, and water – or of becoming solar' (LS 302).
4. In *The Wind Spirit*, Tournier says that *Friday* is not a true anthropological novel, which remains to be written. Such a novel, he says 'would be the confrontation and fusion of two civilizations personified by two representative narrators, and it would take place as if under laboratory conditions on a desert island. Robinson is an Englishman of a certain social class of the early eighteenth century, Friday is an Araucanian, a Chilean Indian, of the same period. Both civilizations would have to be described in full detail: economy, legal, system, literature, art, religion, and so forth. The writer would then observe the encounter between the two, their struggle and fusion, and the emergence of a

new civilization combining elements of both' (Tournier 1988: 190). Although Tournier did not write such an anthropological novel, he did approach *Friday* with the same awareness of the historical and cultural specificity of his characters that he shows in this passage.

5. In the short story 'The Taciturn Lovers', Tournier briefly alludes to the sexual status of the cabin boy on board ships. In the story, an older man recalls having gone to sea as a cabin boy at the age of thirteen. 'But for a ship's boy on a deep-sea fishing boat, it was hell. As the Larousse dictionary of the time coolly wrote at the entry for "scape-goat": "the ship's boy was the crew's scapegoat". He was exploited, trampled underfoot, beaten and sodomized' (Tournier 1991: 5–6).
6. It comes as no surprise that Deleuze should follow the lines of Robinson's argument so closely. In his first publication, 'Description de la femme', which appeared in 1945 when he was twenty years old and still a Khâgne student at the Lycée Louis le Grand, Deleuze defines the Other (*Autrui*) as 'the expression of a possible world', citing as his source for this phrase his fellow lycée student Michel Tournier (LET 254). In this same essay Deleuze calls for a conception of *l'autrui* that is *sexué*, arguing further that Sartre's *Autrui* is an *Autrui-mâle*, which needs to be complemented by a philosophy of woman (LET 255). In his third publication, 'Dires et profils' (1946), Deleuze reiterates Tournier's characerisation of the Other as the expression of a possible world and introduces the concept of the '*Autrui a priori*' (LET 277). Deleuze rejected these works as juvenilia, but they make clear the long-standing nature of his ties to Tournier and the interconnections of their thought on the question of *l'autrui*.
7. See Boundas (2007) for a thorough critique of Hallward's reading of the Other in Deleuze.
8. For a detailed account of Deleuze's concept of fabulation, see Bogue (2006).
9. In the Tournier essay, Deleuze includes the footnote 'In Sade there is the ever-present theme of molecular combination' (LS 367).

4

The Art of the Possible

In *What is Philosophy?*, Deleuze and Guattari assert that the realm of the arts, unlike the virtual domain of philosophy and the actual domain of the sciences, is that of the possible. The work of art, they argue, 'does not actualize the virtual event but incorporates or embodies it: it gives it a body, a life, a universe. [. . .] These universes are neither virtual nor actual; they are possibles, the possible as aesthetic category' (WP 177). In the same work, Deleuze and Guattari second Nietzsche's view that philosophy should 'invent modes of existence or possibilities of life' (WP 72). For anyone familiar with Deleuze's writings, the tripartite division of virtual, actual and possible must give something of a start, for the controlling opposition throughout most of his thought is that of the virtual and the actual, with no mention of the possible as a third category. And the association of art with the possible and philosophy with possibilities of life hardly helps clarify matters. Hence, two questions arise: what relation does the possible have to the virtual and the actual; and what connection might there be between 'the possible as aesthetic category' and philosophy's invention of 'possibilities of life'? Deleuze and Guattari offer only limited clarification of these issues in *What is Philosophy?*, but if one examines Deleuze's scattered remarks on the possible in other philosophers and writers, the contours of a response begin to emerge.

The A Priori Other

Deleuze's most extended treatment of the possible is his essay on Michel Tournier's novel *Vendredi, ou les Limbes du Pacifique* (*Friday: Or the Limbo of the Pacific*) (1967), reprinted as 'Michel Tournier and the World without Others' in *The Logic of Sense*. In *Friday*, Tournier offers a retelling of the Robinson Crusoe story, his Robinson being a decidedly philosophical exile who develops a new mode of consciousness through isolation and his eventual meeting with Friday. For Deleuze, the novel is primarily about Robinson's discovery of the deep-seated influence of the Other (*Autrui*) on perception. In his solitude, Robinson comes to realise that his world presumes the existence of other people at a very fundamental level. What he cannot see behind his back may be visible to someone else; the hidden side of an object, the objects coming into or passing out of his field of visibility, the objects that fade at dusk and re-emerge at dawn, all have a reassuring stability, continuity and mutual orientation, and essentially because they are potentially the objects of others' perception. Deleuze argues that what Robinson discovers is not a dialectic of self and other but a structure that precedes any concrete self or other, a transcendental structure organising experience, within which individual selves and others may occupy any number of positions. This transcendental structure Deleuze names the 'a priori Other', and he describes it as 'the structure of the possible' (LS 307), in that it is the structure provided by the presupposition of a possible Other at any vantage point within one's perceptual field. In the absence of the Other, Robinson experiences a dissolution of 'the category of the possible' (LS 306). Objects assume a menacing harshness, a disorienting abruptness in their appearance and vanishing, since they are no longer interrelated through the field of Others' possible perceptions of them. Yet in this experience Robinson also uncovers the impoverished nature of the world of the a priori Other. Before his island exile, Robinson's eye brought with it the entire history of his structured experience, such that his eye projected a dead past on to the objects it perceived. This structure created not only a spatial but also a temporal disparity between subject and object, for 'if the Other is a possible world, I am a past world'; there is no 'contemporaneity of subject and object' since the 'one [the present object] is constituted only through the annihilation of the other [the past subject]' (LS 310).

Robinson is terrified by the disintegration of the world of the a priori Other, but eventually he finds in this loss 'a possibility of salvation' (LS 315), a new world of simulacra and surfaces, in which there is no division of subject and object and no fundamental disjunction of past and present. A celestial awareness emerges in which consciousness is in dispersed overflight (*survol*) above the surfaces it surveys, immanent within a play of images that includes itself and the territory it flies over. 'Consciousness ceases to be a light cast upon objects in order to become a pure phosphorescence of things in themselves' (LS 311). Time is rectified, for the absence of the a priori Other 'allows consciousness to cling to, and to coincide with, the object in an eternal present' (LS 311). The world Robinson discovers is 'a world without Others, and thus a world without the possible' (LS 320). It is a world 'in which the category of the necessary has completely replaced that of the possible' (LS 320), that necessity not marking a deterministic destiny but an affirmation of each moment as a contingent event that is embraced as inevitable.

In this formulation, it would seem, the possible is primarily a negative force, something that blocks the emergence of the world of simulacra (a world described at length in *The Logic of Sense*). 'In short, the Other, as it encompasses the possible worlds, prevents the doubles from standing erect. The Other is the grand leveler' (LS 312). Yet in this essay Deleuze indirectly suggests that the possible may also have a positive function that is related to the arts. To illustrate the connection between the Other and the possible, Deleuze considers the sight of a frightened face that one sees before knowing the source of the other individual's fear. Such a face 'is the expression of a frightening possible world, or of something frightening in the world' (LS 307). This possible world exists, 'but it does not exist (actually) outside of that which expresses it' (LS 307). The frightened face enfolds, or implicates, a possible world, which the viewer may subsequently unfold, or explicate, in an actual, concrete reality as the viewer comes to 'develop and realize the corresponding possible world' (LS 307).

There is no resemblance between the terrified face and the object of terror; the frightening world exists only as a possibility enfolded within the face. This logic of expression, of enfolding and unfolding, of implication and explication, is of course fundamental to Deleuze's *Proust and Signs*. In this 1964 study of Proust's *À la recherche de temps perdu*, Deleuze traces the course of the narrator's apprenticeship in signs, in which Marcel learns to explicate the worlds implicated in various signs, until he recognises that the greatest signs are those of art, since they are signs that enfold pure essences. Marcel confronts a possible world in the face of his beloved Albertine, but far from reinforcing a limited domain, that face leads him towards the signs of art, which are signs of a generative difference that creates its own world. At least in *Proust and Signs*, then, the Other as expression of a possible world holds the potential for liberating one from the constraints of common-sense reality (which constraints I take to be roughly the same as those of 'the a priori Other') rather than reinscribing one within them.

The Possible and the Virtual

No doubt Deleuze's negative treatment of 'the possible' in the Tournier essay stems in part from his cognisance of, and sympathy with, Bergson's critique of the concept of the possible, a critique that Deleuze rehearses in *Bergsonism* (B 96–8) and reiterates in *Difference and Repetition* (DR 211–15). Bergson points out that the possible is commonly construed as something that precedes an actual event, and that what actually transpires is a mere realisation of one of many pre-existing possibilities. Bergson counters that, in fact, the possible is only a retroactive extrapolation from an actual event. We observe what happened, and then we reflect on all that might, or might not, have happened, and based on that mental operation, we hypothesise the existence of various possibilities that preceded the actual event. In the common conception of the possible, there is an inherent contradiction. In one sense, the possible opposes the real, in that the possible has no genuine existence until it is realised in an actual event. In another sense, however, the possible is more real than the real, in that what actually transpires is seen as a mere realisation of one of many possibilities.

In this confused view of the possible, the process of realisation is governed by rules of resemblance and limitation. The actual event resembles one of the many pre-existing possible events, simply having the quality of existence added to it (and in this sense there is no genuine difference between the possible and the actual). And since every possible event is not realised, the actual event is merely a limitation or filtering of possibilities, one possibility passing into existence while others are sorted out and discarded. Deleuze argues that in Bergson one must distinguish clearly between this notion of the possible and the Bergsonian concept of the virtual. Unlike the possible, which opposes the real, the virtual is real, though not actual. Both the virtual and the actual are real, the one immanent within the other. Rather than obeying rules of resemblance and limitation, the virtual is informed by processes of difference and creation. The virtual is self-differentiating difference, and there is no resemblance between the virtual and that which is actualised. Nor is the actual a limitation of the virtual; rather, the virtual as generative difference diverges from itself, differentiates itself and produces the actual, thereby creating something new. In an analogy that is only roughly approximate, one might say that the Bergsonian virtual is like a single-cell embryo, which develops via a cascade of divisions into an organism that in no way resembles that initial single-cell entity.

What Deleuze says of the Bergsonian virtual holds true of his own conception of the virtual, and in *Difference and Repetition* Deleuze restates this opposition of the possible and the virtual in nearly the same terms as he used in *Bergsonism*. The possible, he says, 'is opposed to the real', whereas the virtual 'possesses a full reality by itself' (DR 211). If the possible is 'produced after the fact, as retroactively fabricated in the image of what resembles it', the virtual by contrast 'always takes place by difference, divergence or differenciation' (DR 212). Since the actual terms 'never resemble the singularities they incarnate [. . .] actualization or differenciation is always a genuine creation' (DR 212). Yet in *Difference and Repetition*, as in the Tournier essay, the possible also seems open to a positive treatment. In discussing once again the a priori Other, Deleuze returns to the image of the frightened face, stating that this face 'expresses a possible world: the terrifying world' (DR 260). Deleuze clarifies, however, that 'by 'possible' we do not mean

> any resemblance but that state of the implicated or enveloped in its very heterogeneity with what envelops it: the terrified face does not resemble what terrifies it, it envelops a state of the terrifying world. In every psychic system, there is a swarm of possibilities around reality, but our possibles are always Others. (DR 260)

The possible world expressed by the terrified face, then, may reinforce the restricting categories of the a priori Other, but it may as well function as a force of virtual differentiation, its unfolding, or explication, disclosing a world unlike that structured by the a priori Other.

Clearly, two basic senses of the possible are at work here, one restrictive, in which the possible denotes the foreseeable, practicable, plausible or conceivable; the other nonrestrictive, in which the possible denotes an opening towards something new, beyond orthodox notions and expectations. Something of this opposition is brought to the fore in *Difference and Repetition* when Deleuze considers a remark of Heidegger's about the possibilities inherent in a problem. Deleuze asks, 'What is this possible at the heart of a problem which stands opposed to the possibilities or propositions of consciousness, to the currently accepted opinions which make up hypotheses?' (DR 201). His answer is that the possible inherent in the problem is a virtuality in thought, something that undoes and goes beyond the restrictive possibilities of consciousness, accepted opinions and established hypotheses. This contrast of the two senses of the possible is even more dramatically displayed in *A Thousand Plateaus* at the conclusion of Deleuze and Guattari's treatment of the concept of faciality. The face in the modern Western world, they claim, is primarily a disciplinary mechanism, its smiles, grimaces, glares and twitches enforcing social codes, identities and power structures. Yet the face is also open to 'defacialization', to a usage that decodes and unfixes identities, faces mutating into '*probe-heads* (*têtes chercheuses*, guidance devices)' (ATP 190) that counter the restricting operations of the socially constructed face. Probe-heads open 'a rhizomatic realm of possibility effecting the potentialization of the possible, as opposed to [the face's] arborescent possibility, which marks a closure, an impotence' (ATP 190). We might say, then, that if rhizomatic possibility effects a potentialisation of the possible, arborescent possibility marks an opposing 'impotentialization' of the possible.

Keirkegaard and Belief in This World

A figure Deleuze frequently associates with the possible is Kierkegaard, and one can find in Deleuze's scattered remarks on Kierkegaard a shift from an arborescent to a more rhizomatic reading of Kierkegaard's sense of the possible. In the 1967 Tournier essay, Deleuze cites for the first time a phrase from Kierkegaard that he will frequently repeat in later works,[1] observing that 'when Kierkegaard's hero demands "the possible, the possible or I shall suffocate", [. . . he is] only invoking the a priori Other' (LS 318). Kierkegaard's hero, Deleuze suggests, is here calling for an arborescent possibility, a return to the possible as reassuring, orthodox structure. Such a reading is consistent with Deleuze's earlier contrast of Nietzsche and Kierkegaard in *Nietzsche and Philosophy* (1962), where Nietzsche's joyous, affirmative cast of the dice is opposed to the Kierkegaardian leap of faith, this notion informed by 'interiority, anguish, wailing, guilt, all the forms of dissatisfaction', Kierkegaard's thought fashioned 'under the sign of *ressentiment*: Abraham and Job' (NP 36). A similar, though somewhat more sympathetic treatment of Nietzsche and Kierkegaard can be found in *Difference and Repetition* (DR 5–11), in which Kierkegaard's leap of faith is likened to Nietzsche's throw of the dice, the main difference being that Kierkegaard's leap is a one-time venture into unknown possibilities, whereas Nietzsche's wager is constantly reiterated, with no expectation of a reestablishment of comforting certainties.

In *Cinema 1* (1983) and *Cinema 2* (1985), however, Deleuze presents Kierkegaard in a basically positive light. Here, Kierkegaard's cry for the possible is treated as a plea for the new, and his leap of faith is seen as an index of an affirmative mode of existence. The leap of faith may exhibit belief in a transcendent God, but what Deleuze finds most important is that the leap of faith is a commitment to a way of living in this world. The 'fascinating idea' Kierkegaard develops is that in the matter of individual choices 'the alternative is not between terms but between the modes of existence of the one who chooses' (C1 114). Some people think they have no choice and hence surrender to a passive mode of existence. Others make a choice, but then feel condemned to a subsequent course of action from which they cannot escape, thereby sinking into a mode of existence in which no further choices can occur. In the leap of faith, however, one chooses a mode of existence in which one must continually choose: 'I choose to choose, and by that I exclude all choice made on the mode of not having the choice' (C1 114). To choose to choose is to embrace an immanent ethics of belief in this world, in that such an act manifests a faith that there are always genuine choices to make and that something new is always possible in this life. Such an immanent ethics is an ethics of possibility, an affirmation of the possible – the unexpected, the unforeseen, the novel – as an ever-present dimension of this world.

In *Cinema 1* and *Cinema 2*, Deleuze introduces the notion of choosing to choose as part of his discussion of the films of Robert Bresson, Carl Dreyer and Eric Rohmer, arguing that these directors, so deeply concerned with religious themes of transcendence in their films, ultimately affirm an immanent ethics of belief in this world. And, although the practices of these directors are peculiar to themselves, Deleuze sees their aim of restoring belief in this world as the central task of all modern cinema. We live in a world of clichés, of readymade images and narratives, and our great despair is that we are caught in a bad movie from which we cannot escape. As a result, our connection with the world has been broken. 'Only belief in the world can reconnect man to what he sees and hears. [. . .] Restoring our belief in the world – this is the power of modern cinema' (C2 172). Cinema does this by countering orthodoxies, disrupting common-sense categories, relations and perceptions, while selecting and recombining images in ways that suggest new modes of thought and life. The great modern films teach us 'to believe, not in a different world, but in a link between man and the world, in love or life, to believe in this as the impossible, the unthinkable, which none the less cannot but be thought: "something possible, otherwise I will suffocate"' (C2 170). The genuinely new is what seems impossible and unthinkable, and only by seizing on the failures of conventional thought, the 'powerlessness [*impuissance*] of thought', can we move beyond the clichés of our world. We must 'make use of this powerlessness [of thought] to believe in life, and discover the identity of thought and life' (C2 170).

In *What is Philosophy?*, Deleuze and Guattari elaborate on the themes of belief in this world, possibilities of life, and modes of existence, in this case relating those themes to the aims of philosophy. Kierkegaard, they argue, may leap into the transcendent, but what is restored to him is an immanent belief in this world's possibilities, and the creation of such a belief is philosophy's goal. A possibility of life 'is evaluated through itself in the movements it lays out and the intensities it creates on a plane of immanence. [. . .] A mode of existence is good or bad, noble or vulgar, complete or empty, independently of Good and Evil or any transcendent value: there are never any criteria other than the tenor of existence, the intensification of life' (WP 74). Philosophy's concern is to create 'the one who believes in this world, and not even in the existence of the world but in its possibilities of movements and intensities, so as once again to give birth to new modes of existence, closer to animals and rocks. It may be that believing in this world, in this life, becomes our most difficult task' (WP 74–5). It would seem, then, that philosophy and the arts share the common goal of creating possibilities of life, new modes of existence. Such a suspicion may be confirmed if one connects the theme of possibilities of life to yet another motif, that of 'the invention of a people to come'. Deleuze and Guattari consistently situate all ethics within a collective politics, always treating the individual human as an immediately and irreducibly social being. The problem in contemporary social action is that a genuine, self-directed collectivity does not exist. What is needed is the invention of a new people, a 'people to come'. In *What is Philosophy?*, Deleuze and Guattari do not directly link possibilities of life to the people to come, but in Deleuze's essay 'Literature and Life', published just two years after *What is Philosophy?*, the link is made explicit.

'The ultimate aim of literature', says Deleuze, 'is to set free, in the delirium, this creation of a health or this invention of a people, that is, a possibility of life' (CC 4). Hence, when Deleuze and Guattari assert in *What is Philosophy?* that 'the creation of concepts in itself calls for a future form, for a new earth and people that do not yet exist', and that 'art and philosophy converge at this point: the constitution of an earth and a people that are lacking' (WP 108), we may conclude that this task of inventing a people is the same as that of creating possibilities of life.

The Possible and the Arts

Philosophy and the arts, then, share the common goal of creating possibilities of life, yet the question remains: what differentiates the arts from philosophy, and why are the arts 'neither virtual nor actual' but possible, 'the possible as aesthetic category ("the possible or I shall suffocate")' (WP 177)? In *What is Philosophy?* Deleuze and Guattari characterise philosophy as the creation of concepts on a plane of immanence, in contrast to the arts, which create sensations on a plane of composition. By sensations Deleuze and Guattari do not mean ordinary perceptions and feelings, but 'percepts' and 'affects', '*beings* whose validity lies in themselves and exceeds any lived [*vécu*]' (WP 164), a-personal perceptions in which the perceiver is, at it were, dissolved and dispersed within a landscape, a-subjective feelings that pass through the body and into the surrounding world. Artworks preserve sensations, and each work is '*a bloc of sensation, that is to say, a compound* [un composé] *of percepts and affects*' (WP 164). The work of art 'is a being of sensation and nothing else: it exists in itself' (WP 164). The preservation of sensation takes place on a plane of composition, where the *composés* of various affects and percepts are composed in new configurations.

Sensation is itself a form of preservation; it 'is preserved or preserves its vibrations [. . .] it itself vibrates because it contracts vibrations [. . .] it preserves itself because it preserves vibrations' (WP 211). Here Deleuze and Guattari make use of a Humean line of thought Deleuze first delineated in *Empiricism and Subjectivity* (1954) and then developed in *Difference and Repetition* (DR 70–9).

Hume notes that causal relations could never be established if sequences of discrete events were not somehow held together, such that event A was not simply followed by event B, the one erasing the other, but A was preserved and contracted into B, the two successive moments coexisting in moment B as AB. This contraction of A into B is less an action than a reception, a passive synthesis of time in which the past is preserved in the present. Deleuze argues that for Hume this passive synthesis of time takes place within the imagination, as within a receptacle in which the past is preserved in the present. This preservation is at once a passive contemplation and an incipient habit, or rather, a basic instance of our habit of forming habits, that is, of our propensity to form regular sequences of actions by preserving the past in the present and extending that past-present towards a future. In *Difference and Repetition* Deleuze treats this passive synthesis as not simply something that occurs in the human imagination, but as a process that takes place throughout nature.

> What we call wheat is a contraction of the earth and humidity, and this contraction is both a contemplation and the auto-satisfaction of that contemplation. [. . .] What organism is not made of elements and cases of repetition, of contemplated and contracted water, nitrogen, carbon, chlorides and sulphates, thereby intertwining all the habits of which it is composed? (DR 75)

Within each individual human being, multiple preservations, contractions and contemplations take place, and in each there is a corresponding 'contemplating mind', or 'soul'. 'A soul must be attributed to the heart, to the muscles, nerves and cells, but a contemplative soul whose entire function is to contract a habit' (DR 74). In this larger sense, 'we are contemplations, we are imaginations' (DR 74).

In *What is Philosophy?* Deleuze and Guattari posit a similar ubiquitous process of passive synthesis/preservation/contraction/contemplation. They concur with Plotinus that all things are 'contemplations, not only people and animals but plants, the earth, and rocks' (WP 212). Wherever there is a contraction of a past into a present, there is a corresponding 'soul' or 'microbrain'. 'Not every organism has a brain, and not all life is organic, but everywhere there are forces that constitute microbrains, or an inorganic life of things' (WP 213). Sensation is fundamentally such preservation/contraction/contemplation. 'Sensation is pure contemplation, for it is through contemplation that one contracts [. . .] Contemplating is creating, the mystery of passive creation, sensation' (WP 212). The arts' plane of composition, then, is a plane of sensation that extends throughout nature and involves an 'inorganic life of things'. The raw materials of the arts are these innumerable sensations, human and non-human, that pass through us and through which we pass into things, and the artist's task is to seize 'the composite sensation [*la sensation composée*], made up of percepts and affects', and separate it from its common-sense coordinates, 'deterritorialize the system of opinion that brought together dominant perceptions and affections within a natural, historical, and social milieu' (WP 197). Once that composite sensation is extracted from its common-sense milieu, the artist creates a material artwork within which the sensation receives a new embodiment, and in this regard the sensation 'is reterritorialized on the plane of composition' (WP 197).

Hume provides Deleuze with the theme of a passive synthesis of contraction and contemplation within the imagination, and it would seem that the motif of art's deterritorialisation and reterritorialisation is also of Humean provenance. In *Empiricism and Subjectivity* (1954), Deleuze says that for Hume taste is a rule, and that 'a rule in general is the distinction between power and the exercise of power' (ES 57). Only the imagination can effect this distinction, 'since it reflects both the passions and their object, separating them from their actuality and recuperating them in the mode of the possible' (ES 57). Hume argues that a handsome and vigorous man in prison may not be able to exercise his powers, but we can still appreciate the beauty of his appearance, and indeed we find our imagination impassioned by the beautiful characteristics that we come to recognise as a result of this separation of the man's powers from their exercise. When Hume addresses the puzzle of the genre of tragedy, in which we enjoy events that in real life we would find painful, he concurs in part with those who say that the fictional representation of suffering makes it palatable by distancing us from it and thereby diminishing the intensity of our response to it, but he adds that a new passion arises in the creation of a work of art, one that is qualitatively distinct from the passions represented. What Deleuze finds essential in Hume is that the passion, when reflected in the imagination, 'changes its quality: the sadness and bleakness of the represented passions are eliminated in the pleasure of the almost infinite play of the imagination. The work of art has therefore its own particular mode of existence, which is not the mode of a real object nor the mode of an actual passion' (ES 58). Art separates powers from their exercise, thereby creating new objects for contemplation that have their own mode of existence and that stimulate an infinite play of the imagination. Hence, one may say that aesthetics 'is the science which envisages things and beings under the category of power or possibility' (ES 57).

The parallels between Hume and Deleuze are only rough at best, yet sufficient to suggest at least one reason Deleuze identifies the arts with the possible. In deterritorialising sensation, the artist separates sensation from its actual context; the sensation is then open to deployment within multiple possible worlds, and in its decontextualisation it is revealed as a being of sensation, an entity whose mode of existence is that of the possible. But there is yet one more aspect of the possible that must be dealt with, and that is embodiment. In *What is Philosophy?*, Deleuze and Guattari say that art 'does not actualize the virtual event but incorporates or embodies it: it gives it a body, a life, a universe' (WP 177). Deleuze and Guattari provide only vague indications of what this might mean, but the logic seems to be the following. The virtual is a domain of self-differentiating differences, and that domain expresses itself in the actual domain of our common-sense world. There is a constant passage of the virtual into the actual, an actualisation of the virtual, although the virtual is never exhausted or depleted by that passage, instead continuing to exist as an immanent presence within the actual. The point at which the virtual passes into the actual is the domain of sensation, the point at which the virtual is sensed within the actual. Philosophy begins with a disturbance of the senses, a break in common-sense experience that reveals the immanent virtual. It then extracts the virtual from the actual and engages the virtual by establishing its own virtual domain of concepts on a plane of immanence. The arts, by contrast, extract the same virtual that is immanent within the actual, but rather than engaging it directly, the arts invent a material embodiment of that virtual, the artwork having a kind of hybrid being at the intersection of the virtual and the actual, a being of sensation. What allows this mode of existence to emerge is the deterritorialisation of sensation from its common-sense coordinates and its reterritorialisation in a new material, that of an embodied possible world.

This association of the possible and embodiment also appears in Deleuze's *The Fold: Leibniz and the Baroque* (1989), and its treatment there helps shed light on the motif as it is used in *What is Philosophy?* In Deleuze's discussions of possible worlds in *Proust and Signs*, the Tournier essay and *Difference and Repetition*, of course, Leibniz was always present, and in *Difference and Repetition* Deleuze recognises Leibniz as one of the great thinkers of difference, albeit one whose ambiguous use of the concept of the possible betrays a vacillating attitude towards difference (DR 212–13). In *The Fold*, however, Deleuze offers no critique of the Leibnizian possible and instead shows how it functions in relation to the virtual. Deleuze argues that for Leibniz monads are virtuals that are actualised in the world, whereas bodies are possibles that are realised in the world. God chooses one world from an infinity of possible worlds, within all of which monads may become actual. Only with God's choice does a possible world become real. Hence, 'the actual does not constitute the real; it must itself be realized' (TF 104). Since monads and bodies are qualitatively different entities, their emergence in the world is governed by parallel but separate processes of actualisation of the virtual (monads) and realisation of the possible (bodies). One problem this system raises for Leibniz is to explain the connection between monads and bodies as well as the necessity of the monads' embodiment. If, after all, monads are self-contained, self-complete entities, what need do they have of bodies and in what way do the monads 'belong' to their corresponding bodies? Deleuze sees Leibniz grappling with this question in his late speculation about the *vinculum substantiale* (literally, the 'substantial chain'), the mysterious link that ties monads to bodies. The *vinculum* is neither monad nor body, but a pure relation created by God. It induces a 'back-and-forth from the soul [monad] to the body, and from bodies to souls' (TF 120; trans. modified). In this back-and-forth movement bodies realise the possible, but what makes them real is the animation provided by their corresponding monads. Bodies become real as that which is actual in the monad is realised in those bodies. There is finally no genuine explanation for this elusive passage from monads to bodies; it is simply the mystery of incarnation and creation in general, a divine process beyond human comprehension. But the process itself suggests that, if monads do not need bodies, God wants them to have bodies, and their embodiment is evidence of a harmonious interfolding of monads and bodies in which the actualisation of the virtual animates bodies and the realisation of the possible embodies and gives reality to monads.

Leibniz is not Deleuze, of course, but in both the problem of embodiment is associated with the concept of the possible. In Leibniz, the interfolding of monads and bodies is central to the mystery of creation; in Deleuze, 'Contemplating is creating, the mystery of passive creation, sensation' (WP 212). For Leibniz, the *vinculum* is a mediating concept that accounts for the back-and-forth communication between monads and bodies, between the parallel actualisation of the virtual and realisation of the possible. For Deleuze, the possible itself plays an intermediary role, denoting the dimension of sensation, in which the virtual is sensed in the process of its actual embodiment. The arts explore this dimension, seizing the virtual within sensation, separating it from its common-sense coordinates, and then re-embodying it within a material artwork that renders sensate the non-rational becoming of the virtual immanent within the actual.

The Art of the Possible

If politics is said to be the art of the possible, for Deleuze the possible is the politics of the arts. The category of the possible is produced by the structure of the a priori Other, but its restricting, limiting force may be counteracted by non-restrictive possibilities. The terrified face is the sign of a possible world, one that may be unfolded in ways that reinstate an arborescent possibility, or in ways that activate a rhizomatic possibility, a potentialisation of the possible. To engage a non-restrictive possibility is to invent possibilities of life, modes of existence in which one chooses to choose as a means of believing in this world. Philosophy and the arts share the common goal of inventing possibilities of life, but the arts operate within the domain of sensation, which is that of the continuous passage of the virtual into the actual. Sensation is the domain of the possible in that it is the site at which contemplation/contraction/preservation/creation takes place within the imagination (an imagination made up of passively contracting souls or microbrains), and the site of sensation's deterritorialisation and its subsequent reterritorialisation within material artworks that enfold possible worlds beyond the world we inhabit. That invention of possible worlds proceeds through embodiment, by way of an experimentation on the sensations that traverse bodies such that the virtual, which is immanent within those sensations, is given a new material form. Within each material artwork, a being of sensation emerges, a palpable virtual inviting us towards new possibilities, new modes of existence.

Notes

1. In *Cinema 1*, Deleuze refers to Kierkegaard's *Traité du désespoir* (*The Sickness unto Death*) and 'the story of the bourgeois who takes his breakfast and reads his newspaper with his family and suddenly rushes to the window shouting, "I must have the possible, or else I will suffocate [*Du possible, sinon j'étouffe*]' (C1 233). I have not found any passage in *The Sickness unto Death* or other works by Kierkegaard that corresponds precisely to this characterisation. At one point in the *Traité du désespoir*, however, Kierkegaard does speak of the despair of those who cease to believe in possibility. When someone faints, we cry 'Water! Water!' 'Mais pour quelqu'un qui désespère, on s'écrie: du possible, du possible! [. . .] Un possible: et notre désespéré reprend le soufflé, il revit, car sans possible, pour ainsi dire on ne respire pas' (Kierkegaard 1949: 98–9). Howard V. Hong and Edna H. Hong's English translation of the passage is the following: 'but when someone

wants to despair, then the word is: Get possibility, get possibility [. . .] A possibility – then the person in despair breathes again, he revives again, for without possibility a person seems unable to breathe' (Kierkegaard 1980: 38–9).

5

Deleuze and Guattari and the Future of Politics: Science Fiction, Protocols and the People to Come

My purpose is, first, to reflect on the concept of fabulation as the invention of a people to come, and then to consider the manifestation of the concept in science fiction, or, as it is sometimes called, speculative fiction – a term I prefer to the former. Rather than speak abstractly about the genre as a whole, I will concentrate on a limited corpus: the fiction of Octavia Butler, the first and still, I believe, the foremost African-American female exponent of speculative fiction. My inquiry will be guided by four questions, the first of which will serve as the general context in which questions two, three and four are situated. The first question is: when is the future? The second: why is utopia a bad concept and in what way is fabulation its superior counterpart? Question number three: if the object of fabulation is the creation of a people to come, how do we get from here and now to there and then, from the present to the future? And question four: what is a people to come? Octavia Butler's fiction will be especially helpful in thinking about a people to come as a literary element, that is, as a component of the possible, the plane of composition, the realm in which the event takes finite, material form in order to create the infinite in its own special way.

Four Questions

From the point of view of common sense, the question 'When is the future?' must seem absurd – the future is the future, and it is what will happen, in contradistinction to what has already happened and what is happening now. But as we all know too well, common sense is no guide to the thought of Deleuze. If we look at *Difference and Repetition*, we may distinguish three futures, one for each of the three passive syntheses of time. In the first synthesis, that of the present, the future is something like the forward edge of a moving present. A common but mistaken concept of time is that of a line of infinite points, each point representing a present 'now'. Such a conception leads to Zeno's paradoxes, to which Bergson responds by positing time as composed of indivisible movements. The present in this regard contains many points along a line, and in that sense we can say that the present is a contraction of past, present and future within a single movement. Husserl makes essentially the same point when speaking of the retention of the past and pretension of the future in a moving present. The present contracts chunks of time, as it were, and in theory the present contraction could be infinite – and, indeed, the Stoics said that the present of the gods included all time. But other creatures have limited capacities for contraction, and hence they reach a point of fatigue. The rhythm of any entity's contractions of the present marks the pattern of that entity's powers and fatigue. Cells, organs and organisms all have different capacities for contracting the present, such that bacteria, the heart, insects and whales inhabit different presents. But, for all of them, there is a future of the present, the leading edge or avant-garde of each temporal contraction on its way towards the limit of fatigue.

In the second synthesis of the past, the past coexists with the present as a virtual double and continues to exist in itself as a retention of all virtual presents within an ever-expanding field of the past. Since the present always passes, it must pass into something which will continue to be doubled by the virtual past, which in turn will perpetually retain itself. In this regard, the past pre-exists the present as its necessary condition, and thus, there is a future of the past. (My explanation here is truncated and inadequate, admittedly, but sufficient for the present purposes.)

The third passive synthesis is that of the future. The third synthesis is a pure form of time which 'unfounds' time and splits the subject, or 'I'. But, as James Williams has so eloquently shown, the third synthesis is not simply time out of joint, '*hors de ses gondes*', but also a cut, an assembly (*un ensemble*), an ordering and a seriation. The third synthesis as a novel action requires a cut, a caesura in time, which produces a before and an after. The cut must assemble the before and after within itself, but also tear them apart. Once torn apart, an ordering of before, cut and after emerge. The cut produces an asymmetrical division in which the before and after are incommensurable. As asymmetrical elements, the before and after are thus distinguished not simply as an order, but as a series (see Williams 2010: 79–112).

We may say, then, that there is a future of the present as contraction, a future of the past as retention and precondition, and a future of the future as cut, assembly, ordering and seriation. But why raise these issues? When Deleuze speaks of a people to come, he often cites Paul Klee's remark that 'the people are missing', *c'est le peuple qui manque*. The implication seems clear: in the present there is no people, and the people to come, *le peuple à venir*, is only possible in some future that has not yet arrived. In *What is Philosophy?*, Deleuze and Guattari say that philosophy creates a plane of immanence and that 'deterritorialization of such a plane does not preclude reterritorialization but posits it as the creation of a future new earth [*une nouvelle terre à venir*]' (WP 88). Philosophy works '*to summon forth a new earth, a new people*' (WP 99). Philosophy's problem is that '*We lack resistance to the present*. [. . .] Art and philosophy converge at this point: the constitution of an earth and a people that are lacking as the correlate of creation' (WP 108). And yet, Deleuze and Guattari also say that philosophical thought is a matter of

> acting counter to the past, and therefore on the present, for the benefit, let us hope, of a future – but the future is not a historical future, not even a utopian history, it is the infinite Now, the *nun* that Plato already distinguished from every present: the Intensive or Untimely, not an instant but a becoming. (WP 112)

For Foucault, they observe,

> what matters is the difference between the present and the actual. The actual is not what we are but, rather, what we

> become, what we are in the process of becoming – that is to say, the Other, our becoming-other. [. . .] It is not that the actual is the utopian prefiguration of a future that is still part of our history. Rather, it is the now of our becoming. (WP 112)

It would seem, therefore, that the new earth and new people are also present, that the future is now – but, of course, that now is an infinite Now, the Nietzschean Untimely, the time of our 'becoming', the time of Aion. 'When is the future?', then, is a serious question when considering *un peuple à venir*. Is such a people 'to come', or is it 'at hand', that is, in the process of becoming in an Untimely Now? I will speak further about this issue when addressing my fourth question, 'What is a people to come?'

Now to my second question: 'Why is utopia a bad concept and in what way is fabulation its superior counterpart?' Deleuze makes explicit the relationship between utopia and fabulation in a 1990 interview with Toni Negri. There he says, 'Utopia isn't the right concept: it's more a question of "fabulation" in which a people and art both share. We ought to take up Bergson's notion of fabulation and give it a political meaning' (N 174). Why is utopia not 'the right concept', or, as Deleuze and Guattari put it in *What is Philosophy?*, 'not a good concept' (WP 110)? In the fourth chapter of *What is Philosophy?*, when the subject of a new earth and a new people is addressed, for a while Deleuze and Guattari use the word 'utopia' without apology. They remark that

> *utopia is what links* philosophy with its own epoch, with European capitalism, but also already with the Greek city. In each case it is with utopia that philosophy becomes political and takes the criticism of its own time to its highest point. Utopia does not split off from infinite movement: etymologically it stands for absolute deterritorialization but always at the critical point at which it is connected with the present relative milieu, and especially with the forces stifled by this milieu. (WP 99–100)

Yet reservations soon emerge, as they state, 'The word utopia therefore designates *that conjunction of philosophy, or the concept, with the present milieu* – political philosophy (however, in view of the mutilated meaning public opinion has given to it, perhaps *utopia* is not the best word)' (WP 100). The initial problem, then, is one of public opinion and degraded usage. But beneath such superficial misconstrual lurks a deeper potential for misunderstanding: 'Utopia is not a good concept because even when opposed to History it is still subject to it and lodged within it as an ideal or motivation' (WP 110). As an ideal, utopia functions as a kind of Platonic Idea, something above this world, static and perfect. If utopia is a motivation, then it is something external to action, something aimed for as a goal. We might add that utopias frequently are spatial rather than temporal – places, rather than times.[1] The architecture of utopias is often complete and contained, and processes take place within their spatial confines as components of a self-regulated system. In all these regards, utopias are the antithesis of becoming, process and movement towards a future that is genuinely new and thus inherently unpredictable, defiant of any mapping. Motivation cannot be external to the process of becoming, and becoming cannot be goal-directed.

Fabulation is a superior concept because its essence is to activate the 'powers of the false', to falsify orthodox truths in the process of generating emergent truths. To fabulate, in Pierre Perrault's words, is to 'legend *in flagrante delicto*' (cited in C2 150; trans. modified), and in doing so, to summon forth a 'people to come'. As Deleuze says in *Negotiations*,

> What we have to do is catch someone else 'legending', 'caught in the act of legending'. Then a minority discourse, with one or many speakers, takes shape. We here come upon what Bergson calls 'fabulation' [. . .] To catch someone in the act of legending [*Prendre les gens en flagrant délit de légender*] is to catch the movement of constitution of a people. A people isn't something already there. A people, in a way, is what's missing, as Paul Klee used to say. (N 125–6)

Fabulation does not presume an ideal, nor does it have an external goal as its motivation. It is its own end, an irreducibly temporal process of becoming-other that is open-ended, and if it is a process of summoning forth a future people, it is one that cannot move beyond itself without involving the participation of a collectivity in its action. Fabulation commences with resistance, since 'to create is to resist' (WP 110), but if it is resistance to the present in the hope of a better future, that future cannot be predicted, nor can its superiority to the present be assured.

Yet one might ask, do we simply start blindly becoming, with no coordinates, no point of inception? This brings me to my third question: if the object of fabulation is the creation of a people to come, how do we get from here and now to there and then, from the present to the future? Let us remember first that, if the becoming of fabulation involves resistance, such resistance is always contingent and specific. One resists the intolerable where one finds it, when one can no longer tolerate it – hence the point of inception is no problem. But what about the coordinates of becoming? Here, I would like to suggest that protocols of experimentation can provide a certain scaffolding for resistance. Deleuze and Guattari state that 'To think is to experiment', although they add that 'experimentation is always that which is in the process of coming about – the new, remarkable, and interesting that replace the appearance of truth and are more demanding than it is' (WP 111). Yet experimentation is not a haphazard activity. In *Kafka: Toward a Minor Literature*, Deleuze and Guattari find in Kafka's letters to Felice

> a prodigious operation by which [Kafka] translates this horror [of impending matrimony] into a *topography of obstacles* (where to go? how to arrive? Prague, Vienna, Berlin?). The Surveyor. And also the other operation by which he enumerates a numbered *list of conditions* that the subject of the statement thinks can dissipate horror when, in fact, it is this very horror in the subject of the enunciation that inspires them (a Life Plan, or a Life Program, à la Kleist). (K 31–2)

The reference to Kleist is intriguing, if in need of further clarification. In several letters to his half-sister, Ulrike, Kleist does indeed speak of the need for a *Lebensplan*, a life plan, but he seems to mean something quite mundane. He tells his sister that he cannot achieve anything if he does not have a plan for his life. He then complains in subsequent letters that he cannot create a satisfactory plan, that one plan soon gives way to another, and, once adopted, each plan proves inoperable. But Deleuze and Guattari give this innocuous concept of a life plan a more interesting sense. They see the life plan as a programme for experimentation, which suggests that Kafka's 'topography of obstacles' and 'list of conditions' are also elements of an experimental protocol. In *Dialogues*, Deleuze contrasts French literature with minor literature, in which there is no longer

> the infinite account of interpretations which are always slightly disgusting, but finite processes of experimentation [*des procès finis d'experimentation*], protocols of experience [*protocoles d'expérience*]. Kleist and Kafka spent their time making programs for life [*programmes de vie*]. Programmes are not manifestos – still less are they phantasms, *but means of providing reference points for an experiment which exceeds our capacities to foresee*. (D 47–8)[2]

What, then, are the coordinates of resistance? They are the 'reference points for an experiment that exceeds our capacities to foresee', and it is by way of such reference points, such protocols, that we may move from the present towards the future. It is worth noting that in *Anti-Oedipus*, something of this experimental spirit is invoked indirectly in Deleuze and Guattari's remarks about utopias. The elaborate plans, structures and proposed institutions of utopian thinkers are not maps of achieved perfection. Rather, they say, 'the great socialist utopias of the nineteenth century function [. . .] not as ideal models but as group fantasies – that is, as agents of the real productivity of desire, making it possible to disinvest the current social field, to "deinstitutionalize" it, to further the revolutionary institution of desire itself' (AO 30–1). As they remark at another point in their text, 'if we must still speak of utopia in this sense, à la Fourier, it is most assuredly not as an ideal model, but as revolutionary action and passion' (AO 63).[3]

And now my fourth question: 'What is a people to come?' In the concluding paragraph of *What is Philosophy?*, Deleuze and Guattari offer an image of philosophy, science and the arts as brains submerged in chaos. And in this submersion, they say, 'it seems that there is extracted from chaos the shadow of the "people to come" in the form that art, but also philosophy and science, summon forth: mass-people, world-people, brain-people, chaos-people' (WP218). In *Essays Critical and Clinical*, Deleuze says that the people to come is

> a minor people, eternally minor, taken up in a becoming-revolutionary. Perhaps it exists only in the atoms of the writer, a bastard people, inferior, dominated, always in becoming, always incomplete. *Bastard* no longer designates a familial state, but the process of drift of the races. I am a beast, I am a Negro of an inferior race for all eternity. (CC 4)

The ultimate aim of literature, says Deleuze, 'is to set free [. . .] the creation of a health, [the] invention of a people, that is, a possibility of life' (CC 4). We might note that the 'people to come' is in many ways a version of the 'subject-group' of *Anti-Oedipus*, 'a group whose libidinal investments are themselves revolutionary' (AO 348).

The people to come, then, seems to be simply resistance that initiates group becoming towards an unknowable future. In this regard, any actually fully formed 'people' would seem to be a utopian collectivity, and the process of resistance a movement towards an impossible goal. Perhaps no one has more vociferously and thoroughly made the case for such a reading of the concept of the people to come than Philippe Mengue, and his critique is worth examining in detail, since it reveals many of the ways in which Deleuze's thought is often misconstrued.

Mengue's Critique

Mengue finds a decidedly anti-democratic strain in Deleuze, which he attributes to a latent leftist radicalism and an aristocratic scorn for the masses. Micropolitics, he asserts, 'risks sinking into a pragmatic vitalism of subversion, which encloses micropolitics in an avant-gardism that is nothing more than the last burst of an exhausted modernism' (Mengue 2003: 203). In this view, micropolitics proves to be a rejection of the realm of true politics, which is one of *doxa*, negotiation and compromise. The 'radical dissidence' of Deleuzian micropolitics, claims Mengue, 'leads to the impasse of the retreat of the political, and, finally, to the abstract and indeterminate retreat into the vain and utopian waiting for a Revolution and a "people to come"' (204). What Deleuze seeks is a 'metapolitics' above the messiness of genuine politics, a collectivity that is a '*totality* which is in principle' incapable of 'any possible realisation', a human community that is 'radically new (whatever the form one attributes to it), in which humans would be "other" (desire for an "other" human) because they would lead an "other life", in an "other society" (one of total and faultless peace, justice, liberty and equality)' (192; emphasis in original). This is what Deleuze seeks when he calls for a 'new earth' and a 'new people'.

Deleuzian micropolitics, nomadism, the untimely Event, resistance to the intolerable, the people to come – all, in Mengue's reading, are symptoms of an unconscious idealism and a scorn for the unavoidable imperfections of genuine politics. What Deleuze refuses to recognise is 'the undeniable fact that the juridico-political order is *forever situated in the impossibility of fully satisfying human desire as such*' (Mengue 2003: 193; emphasis in original). Given the inherent constraints of the political, Mengue judges democracy to be the best system for conducting politics. The political is by nature a domain of opinion, and the best one can hope for in any political system is 'a little *solidarity* and *consensus* concerning what needs to be done, here-now' (52; emphasis in original). Deleuze's contempt for *doxa* and discussion constitutes contempt for democracy, since in the democratic public space, opinions are put forward, discussed, critiqued, reformulated, amalgamated in compromised formulations, and once temporarily formed, left open to an endless process of future discussion. This *is* the thought of the *polis*, in which 'opinions become *views* to discuss, their authors become *friends* or citizens" (53; emphasis in original). Such friendship is not formed to seek 'knowledge or truth, but for something that is also beautiful, and which requires wisdom – friendship that links and creates harmony in disharmony itself, "discordant harmony" [*l'accord discordant*], not among the faculties of the mind, but among humans and their opinions' (54). A true understanding of politics and democracy shows that 'political *doxa* can be "right". Granted, not "true" or even "remarkable" (even if it might prove to be so eventually), but acceptable, allowable – at a given moment for a given assembly or community' (56).

Ironically, democracy is the most fully Deleuzian of politics, claims Mengue. 'Democratic politics alone is without foundation, because it is the only possible logic in the fact of the plurality and rivalry of opinions and political actions' (Mengue 2003: 47). Deleuze's antipathy towards democracy betrays a hidden longing for the foundation of a stable, ideal political order. Mengue concurs with Deleuze that thought is a confrontation with chaos, but chaos, for Mengue, is a gap, lack, the void. 'Philosophical thought, in its ultimate dimension, never ceases to think about chaos, to think about its *gap* [*béance*]' (198; emphasis in original). What characterises democracy is that it explicitly takes into account what Mengue calls '*the hole* [*trou*] *of the political*' (199; emphasis in original). What is fundamental in democracy is

> the clear and explicit consciousness – and which is said, and never ceases to be said in all tones, from lamentation to exaltation – of its absence of foundation. Democracy is the only political form in which power is 'sworn to remain in search of its foundation'. It goes forth from an absence, a lacuna in *knowledge*. (Mengue 2003: 199; emphasis in original)

Deleuze retreats from this absence and instead posits a counter-absence, the missing people (*le peuple qui manque* – literally the people who 'lack', who 'are lacking'). The people to come, then, is for Mengue nothing more than an attempt to fill this lack and thereby put an end to genuine politics, which must permanently deal with its own constitutive lack.

Mengue is correct that Deleuze speaks disparagingly of democracy, especially late in his life. He also consistently declares war on all forms of *doxa*, and he frequently admits that he despairs when others ask him to 'discuss' philosophical issues. But it is not at all certain that Deleuze's critique of democracy signals a total rejection of the concept itself. Rather, his critique is directed against democracy as it is practised in the West. The polemical and perhaps exaggerated tone of his remarks – most often proffered in interviews, a venue that seeks a wider audience than that of professional philosophers alone – is meant to counter the complacency and self-satisfaction implicit in standard political discourse in contemporary democracies. Likewise, his critique of *doxa* is a critique of the commonplace, that which goes without saying, the thoughtless, mindless slogans of received wisdom. What Mengue labels 'opinion' is much broader than that, and there is no indication that Deleuze rejects the exchange and mutual examination of serious views about politics and the political. He despairs of 'discussion' because discussion all too often is a matter of egotistical combat, an effort to defeat the opponent in a battle of fixed commitments and positions. In that sense, discussion is the opposite of exchange and cooperative interaction, a mere contestation of competing ideologies, fixed forms of *doxa*. Throughout his work, Deleuze shows a willingness to examine others' ideas, and he welcomes exchange that might lead to the emergence of something new. Deleuze embraces interaction with others in the form of 'interference' and 'intercession',[4] which could easily be seen as types of discussion (in Mengue's broad sense of the term). Such interference and intercession aim at 'resonance' among forces and the emergence of new truths via the 'powers of the false' (N125–6). Deleuze nowhere suggests that processes of interference, intercession, resonance and exchange cannot take place in the domain of the political. And despite the apparent utopian aura of the term 'people to come', such a people, I believe, is ultimately not one that has reached the perfection of an ideal society – whether that of total liberty, equality, benevolence, harmony or justice.

There is certainly something of an anarchic strain to Deleuze's concepts of nomadism, the war machine and becoming. But he insistently reminds us that deterritorialisation and reterritorialisation always occur ceaselessly and simultaneously. Further, he recognises the dangers of unbridled deterritorialisation. Absolute deterritorialisation is the leading edge of innovation and creativity, but it must be engaged with caution, not with mindless and total abandon. Mengue's characterisation of chaos as lack, gap or absence is not Deleuze's. For Deleuze, chaos is plenitude, but a fullness that perpetually issues forth in temporary and provisional forms of organisation. Chaos's absolute deterritorialisation is inseparable from processes of reterritorialisation, and such reterritorialisations themselves oscillate between movements towards relative deterritorialisation and returns to homeostatic forms. As Simondon argues, the ubiquitous process of nature is that of individuation, an actualisation of metastability in locally stable entities, those entities themselves simultaneously sustaining elements of metastability that make them vital, living and changing entities. Chaos and its differentiation are immanent and inextricable, and the becoming of the world is always a liminal phenomenon, at the interface of absolute chaos and the restricted chaos of half-stable, half-metastable processes of individuation. Thought, for Deleuze, is like the cosmos, at 'the edge of chaos', as Jeffrey Bell aptly puts it (Bell 2006). When Deleuze and Guattari say that thought must confront chaos, it is not in order to vanquish chaos, but to delineate a plane of consistency that makes chaos productive and usable, a force of creativity. The invention of a people to come entails an engagement with a chaotic plane of consistency, and when viewed exclusively in terms of its movement towards the new, it seems anarchic. But, just as thought aims at creating concepts, so the invention of a people to come is directed towards something that is not absolutely chaotic and anarchic, towards some form of collectivity that is simultaneously metastable and temporarily stable, always engaged in processes of negotiation, dissolution and reformation.

It must also be granted that Deleuze and Guattari's call for the creation of a 'new earth' and a 'new people' has a millennial aura about it, but such newness need not be ideal, simply better than what we have at present. Ian Buchanan makes a useful distinction between utopia as a process and utopia as 'a place, a mythical island in an unknown sea' (Buchanan 2000: 164),[5] a distinction that Eugene Holland has framed as an opposition between 'utopia as a fixed "product"', and 'what may be called "utopianism as a process"' (Holland 2006: 217), both arguing that Deleuze and Guattari advocate the latter rather than the former. By maintaining the designation 'utopian' in characterising this process, Buchanan and Holland establish a degree of continuity between Marxist and leftist traditions of thought, a continuity that is suggested in *What is Philosophy?* when Deleuze and Guattari say that philosophy's effort '*to summon forth a new earth, a new people*' is 'closer to what Adorno calls "negative dialectics" and to what the Frankfurt School called 'utopian'" (WP 99), and when Deleuze and Guattari affirm Ernst Bloch's distinction between 'authoritarian utopias, or utopias of transcendence, and immanent, revolutionary, libertarian utopias' (WP 100). (Buchanan and Holland's notion of utopianism as process, in fact, seems roughly equivalent to Bloch's 'immanent, revolutionary, libertarian' utopianism.) What Buchanan and Holland emphasise is the initial phase of the emergence of new possibilities for life through resistance to the present and 'the *diagnosis* of becomings in every passing present' (WP 113), a phase that is undoubtedly central to Deleuze and Guattari's thought, but one that can easily be misconstrued as simply anarchistic and a nostalgic remnant of Deleuze and Guattari's immature May 1968 radicalism (which is Mengue's reading of this phase).

In a trenchant and extended critique of Mengue, Paul Patton proposes an argument in line with my own, remarking that Deleuze and Guattari's 'political philosophy is not so utopian that it is completely disconnected from the normative and conceptual horizons of the present' (Patton 2010: 162), for which reason Patton, in another essay, adopts Rawls's distinction between an 'extravagant utopianism' and a 'realistic utopianism', arguing that Rawls's advocacy of a realistic utopianism is one shared by Deleuze and Guattari (Patton 2010: 186).[6] Patton systematically demonstrates that Deleuze's negative assessments of democracy are not expressions of a fundamental antipathy to the broad concept of democracy as 'a form of society characterized by the absence of class or caste privilege and by the implementation of the egalitarian principle of the equal worth of individuals such that no person's life, beliefs, or values are inherently worth more than those of anyone else', nor necessarily to a narrow sense of democracy as 'a form of government in which the governed exercise control over governmental bodies and their policies, typically through regular and fair elections' (Patton 2010: 164). Patton demonstrates that it is on the basis of such a broad conception of democracy that Deleuze formulates his critique of contemporary democracies, which claim to be democratic in both senses of the word, but which in fact are neither. Patton concedes that 'the Deleuzian theory of micropolitics is only a partial account of the process of political decision making', but such incompleteness does not indicate antipathy, 'and there is no reason to suppose that Deleuzian theory proposes an alternative rather than a supplement to democratic political theory' (Patton 2010: 167). In a parallel fashion, Patton rebuts Mengue's claim that Deleuze's critical remarks about 'human rights' express a blanket hostility to the normative principles of fairness and justice purportedly endorsed in the concept, but instead that Deleuze is critiquing the function of the term 'human rights' in contemporary discourse as well as the ways in which this concept purportedly are implemented.

What is crucial in Patton's analysis is that Deleuze's critiques are not to be taken as endorsements of lawlessness and anarchy. Deleuze focuses on the failures of contemporary governmental and judicial institutions and on philosophy's task of critiquing those institutions and initiating a process of 'thinking otherwise'. Deleuze does not address broad questions of the means whereby justice and equality might be actualised, and it is for this reason that Patton proposes that we extend Deleuze's analysis and consider the general institutional conditions under which the fundamental principles of justice and equality might be articulated. Put bluntly, Deleuzian political philosophy should be seen as an endorsement of democracy and a justice which may be actualised through a proper use of law.[7] Patton's effort to extend and complete Deleuzian political analysis, in my judgement, is an attempt to answer the oft-posed question: what do we do if the revolution succeeds? What do we do if a becoming results in something approaching an actual 'people', a viable collectivity? A key to approaching these questions is to recall that Deleuze characterises the invention of a people to come not simply as a becoming-minor of resistance, but also as the invention of alternative modes of existence, new possibilities of life (CC 4).

Clearly, if we want to theorise further about a different collectivity, we must rethink the notion of such a people as merely an accursed race defined by resistance. Were this characterisation of the people to come the sole means of describing this collectivity, the concept might well be construed as one that is defined from without. An accursed race as constituted by the sanctioned, dominant race, and the centrality of resistance invites a conception of the people to come as solely a people *against* something. All of this smacks of Hegelian negation and even of Nietzschean *ressentiment* and the negative Will to Power. We must also reject any idealistic conception of the people to come, in which universal harmony prevails and the rule of consensus puts an end to any genuine politics. In *Anti-Oedipus*, when Deleuze and Guattari discuss 'subject groups', they cite with approval Jean-Pierre Faye's assertion that in genuinely revolutionary groups, 'What counts, what is effective in our opinion, is not such and such a group, but rather the dispersion or the Diaspora produced by their splinterings [*éclats*]', a position they see as asserting 'the necessarily polyvocal character of subject-groups and their writing' (AO 349). 'Subject-groups' possess heterogeneous desires, since collectivities are multiplicities, not aggregates that form an amorphous mass (like the fascist mobs that so fascinated and frightened Canetti in *Crowds and Power*).[8] If indeed collectivities are heterogeneous multiplicities, then they must incorporate genuine differences, that is, differences that make a difference, and hence differences that signal conflict and the need of resolution or some form of mutual accommodation of differing interests and desires. The people to come, in short, will be a people perpetually generating differences, potential asymmetries of power, and sites of resistance for those who find themselves faced with the intolerable. The means whereby differences are negotiated, we hope, will be better than those currently in effect. No matter what social order emerges in a process of becoming, there will be a politics of the future, and that politics will not be defined from the outside, but from within the people to come *as that people continues its becoming.*

Butler's Science Fiction

This is where I find Octavia Butler's fiction helpful. Science fiction is above all other genres primarily a literature of the future. Dystopian fiction is always set in a near future, and speculative fictions of various sorts, utopian or not, generally are set in a future time. This holds true for Butler's works as well. She endorses the common view that science fiction 'uses science, extrapolates from science as we know it to science as it might be [,] to technology as it might be' (Butler 2010: 84). But her speculations take a specific form that is especially germane to our concerns. She recalls in one interview that

> When I was in my teens, a group of us used to talk about our hopes and dreams, and someone would always ask, 'If you could do anything you wanted to do, no holds barred, what would you do?' I'd answer that I wanted to live forever and breed people – which didn't go over all that well with my friends. (Butler 2010: 18)

In fact, all of Butler's fiction is directed towards the invention of a people to come. When asked in another interview if she tries to create new types of communities in her writings, she replies, 'I'd say more that I don't try to create communities; I always automatically create community' (Butler 2010: 111). And those communities often literally involve new people – hybrids, genetic alterations, parasite-induced mutations and so on.

The five-novel Patternmaster series spans several centuries, from the late eighteenth century to some distant, undesignated future.[9] The first novel tells of Doro, a 4,000-year-old Nubian mutant who has gained the power of immortality, but only at the cost of inhabiting a succession of human bodies and discarding their empty, dead shells when he enters a new body. He has undertaken a eugenics project to breed other mutant beings with exceptional powers, and in the course of his wanderings he has encountered Anyanwu, a central-African woman who has lived for 400 years, healing others and maintaining a rejuvenated form without possessing other bodies. She comes under the sway of Doro and becomes part of his breeding programme. In the second novel, which takes place in the twentieth century, successful mutant humans are finally created, and they develop 'the pattern', a psychic force field that greatly enhances the powers of all its participant members. Doro tries to maintain control of the pattern, but in a struggle with Doro's daughter he is defeated and killed. In successive generations, the patternmasters sponsor journeys to other planets, and following one such expedition a returning astronaut brings an alien virus that genetically alters its human hosts and induces mutant offspring whose appearance combines human, feline and porcine characteristics in an otherwise monstrous form. These mutant becomings-animal are labelled 'Clayarks', and their characteristics seem those of pack animals with intuitive intelligence and territorial aggressivity. In the concluding novel (actually the first one written) set in the distant future, the established order consists of a feudal aristocracy of patternmasters, the servant class of humans who are totally dominated by the mind control of the patternmasters, and the feral Clayarks who roam the wilds outside patternist settlements. This, then, is the ultimate configuration of the series' 'people to come'.

Butler's two Parable novels, *Parable of the Sower* (1998) and *Parable of the Talents* (1998), are at once her most dystopian and most utopian fictions. Set in the near future of a collapsed American society, the novels envision a world of ecological degradation, technological breakdown and widespread poverty and drug addiction. Gated communities have become walled fortresses surrounded by masses of homeless derelicts, most of whom are desperate, many violent, and some addicted to substances like 'pyro', a designer drug that went out of control and created humans who gain intense sexual pleasure from setting fires and especially from incinerating other humans. The teenaged heroine, Lauren, must flee when her walled enclave is overrun, and throughout the first novel she walks the interstate highway I-5 (now used only by pedestrians) from Los Angeles to northern California. Along the way, she gathers other survivors and brings them together through her self-generated personal religion, Earthseed, in which she teaches two basic lessons: first, that 'God is change', and that being shaped by and shaping God are the sole means of becoming-other in a productive fashion in this new world; and, second, that our species' destiny is to inhabit other planets. Eventually, she and her incipient community, which she consistently calls 'her people', settle in a secluded part of northern California, and there they form the community of Acorn, something like a communal collective. In the second novel, fundamentalist Christian paramilitary forces raid Acorn, kill most of its inhabitants, and enslave the surviving women via 'slave collars' that induce powerful, debilitating electrical impulses at the first sign of resistance to their captors. Lauren stages a successful revolt, and the inhabitants of Acorn flee and disperse. She learns that spreading the movement of Acorn cannot proceed via the proliferation of isolated communal settlements, but must focus on the ideas of her religion, since the spread of ideas is much less difficult to control than the physical spread of concrete bodies, and since the specifics of Acorn's socioeconomic organisation are subordinate to the ultimate goals of the religion. Eventually she succeeds in forming a broad network of community groups of various kinds, many of them integrated into urban environments and partially enmeshed in capitalist market institutions. The movement gains economic power, helps fuel widespread economic recovery and the restoration of a modicum of sociopolitical cohesion on the continent of North America, and achieves a certain institutional prominence and autonomy. At this stage, the 'people to come' are no longer practitioners of a counter-capitalist communal sociopolitical culture, but exponents of the religion of Earthseed, and with economic success they are able to begin the pursuit of their ultimate goal: to leave earth and colonise other planets. Lauren's initial inspiration in formulating this component of the Earthseed project was the belief that humans can form a viable community only by uniting in a collective cause that leads to struggle against an alien and challenging environment. Hence, the community of the people to come issues in a creative line of flight, but that line of flight is to other worlds, since humans cannot coexist peacefully on this world alone – a conclusion which, for those of us condemned to remain on earth, signals a decidedly non-utopian future.

Butler's masterpiece, the *Xenogenesis Trilogy*,[10] provides the fullest and most intriguing account of various becomings, the invention of a new people, and the establishment of alternative modes of existence and possibilities of life. After a global nuclear holocaust, a small number of humans have survived in suspended animation, thanks to the intervention of an alien species called the Oankali, who have saved the humans and gradually detoxified the earth for recolonisation. The Oankali, who call themselves genetic 'traders', search for interesting life forms and, when they find them, engage in the collective procreation of hybrid organisms. The Oankali have three sexes: male, female and ooloi, the ooloi being a definite 'it', not some male–female combination. The Oankali have saved the humans in order to mate with male and female humans in pentads of a human male and female couple, an Oankali male and female couple, and one Oankali ooloi. Each ooloi, by combining the genetic materials of the human and Oankali couples, and then manipulating those materials through use of its vast, cosmic stock of genetic materials gathered by generations of ooloi on countless planets and preserved in the ooloi's special organ called its Yashi, fashions human-born and Oankali-born 'constructs' who then go on to produce further iterations of a new, hybrid people. The first novel recounts the initial resuscitation of humans and the formation of pentads for settlement on earth. The second and third novels trace the development of Oankali family units and construct children on earth.

Many readers have seen the Oankali as utopian beings. They value life and embrace difference. They naturally heal, their relationships are nurturing, they cannot cause pain without feeling that pain themselves, their connections to the environment are all-embracing and ecologically sound, and they govern the collectivity through consensus. Yet others have argued that the Oankali are insidious beings, one critic labelling them symbols of neoliberal capitalist globalisation. They embrace difference, but in Oankali constructs the organelle that inhabits every cell of the Oankali (the word 'Oankali' is also the name of that organelle) is present in every construct cell as well. The Oankali only *seem* to surrender their identity. Whatever hybrids they fashion continue to have a fundamental Oankali identity. They are like global capital, capable of embracing everything and assimilating it within the capitalist machine. Disturbing as well is the human–ooloi relationship. The ooloi injects its 'ooloi substance' when in contact with humans, and that substance, while deeply pleasurable and healing, also is intensely addictive, and it makes the human male and female incapable of physically touching one another. The entirety of Oankali culture is based on neurochemical bonding, and their consensus only occurs because of those bonds. Unlike the familial bonds of humans, the Oankali bonds preclude conflict among males. No male, female or ooloi need fear that a partner will be taken, since the ooloi has chemically marked the couple as its own. Hence, the political order of the Oankali, humans and constructs is one of consensus and non-violence, but made possible only through addiction and the deep control of ooloi intermediaries.

In all of Butler's novels she invents a people to come. In each case, new modes of existence and possibilities of life are delineated. But in all of them politics continues. The new possibilities are not necessarily better, just different. The sociopolitical structures include versions of primitive collectivism, family-centred social networks, feudal class relations, master–slave institutions, and international ecumenical movements. If we add to the mix the world of Butler's last novel, *Fledging* (2005), we would have examples of tribal cultures, matrilineal and patrilineal settlements, and mixtures of polyandry and polygamy with various forms of homo- and heterosexual alliances. Each novel is a form of experimentation, an investigation of the possible outcomes of becoming-other and thereby creating a people to come. As experimentation, each novel introduces a protocol, a '*means of providing reference points for an experiment which exceeds our capacities to foresee*'. This I regard as an important positive function of science fiction, one way in which art renders concrete the realm of the possible. In this way, fiction promotes the thought of a people to come as something that actually might take any number of definite forms, and perhaps may assist us in *our* attempts to imagine, invent and enact alternative modes of existence, new possibilities of life.

Notes

1. In *Spaces of Hope*, David Harvey makes a useful distinction between 'the utopianism of social process' and 'utopias as spatial form'. If there is a utopian strain in Deleuze (and, with sufficient qualification, one could say that indeed there is), it would be such a 'utopianism of social process'. See esp. Harvey 2010: 164–81.

2. In the second essay of *Essays Critical and Clinical*, 'Louis Wolfson; or the Procedure [*procédé*]', Deleuze assigns a negative connotation to the word 'protocol', opposing it to the term 'procedure'. Deleuze's essay is devoted to two books by the schizophrenic Louis Wolfson, *Le Schizo et les langues* and *Ma mère musicienne est morte*. Deleuze is fascinated by the mental gymnastics Wolfson performs in transforming words via various foreign languages in order to defend himself from malignant influences in his environment. Deleuze argues, however, that Wolfson, unlike Raymond Roussel and Antonin Artaud, is not an artist in his linguistic experimentation. 'Wolfson's book, however, is not a literary work, and does not claim to be a poem. What turns Roussel's procedure into a work of art is the fact that the interval between the original sentence and its conversion is filled with marvelously proliferating stories, which make the starting point recede until it is entirely hidden. [. . .] But there is nothing similar in Wolfson: between the word to be converted and words of the conversion, and in the conversions themselves, there is nothing but a void, an interval that is lived as pathogenic or pathological. [. . .] The transformations never reach the grandiose level of an event, but remain mired in their accidental circumstances and empirical actualizations. The procedure thus remains a protocol. The linguistic procedure operates in a void, and never links up with a vital process capable of producing a vision' (CC 10–11). It is worth noting that in the original version of 'Louis Wolfson; or the Procedure', which Deleuze published as a preface to Wolfson's *Le Schizo et les langues* (1970) and titled 'Schizologie', no such distinction between 'protocol' and 'procedure' exists. In the opening paragraph of the original preface, Deleuze says that 'One of the great originalities of this book is that it sets forth a protocol of experimentation or activity' (this sentence is retained in the 1993 version of the essay). But Deleuze clearly is simply offering a synonym for 'procedure' when he speaks of Wolfson as a practitioner of 'a protocol of experimentation or activity'. Only in 1993 does Deleuze make use of that opening sentence later in the essay to contrast protocols and procedures (and the sentence contrasting the two is the only sentence in the 1993 essay that addresses that distinction). Clearly, 'protocol' was a positive term for Deleuze in 1970, and it remained so in the 1977 text of *Dialogues*, where 'protocol' is treated as a synonym of 'process' (*procès*, a cognate of *procédé*). (We might note that the words *procès*, *processus* and *procédé* appear frequently in Deleuze's works, and often in related if not interchangeable ways.)

3. At two points in *Anti-Oedipus*, Deleuze and Guattari come close to embracing the term 'utopian' themselves. In the first, they cite with approval an extended passage from Pierre Klossowski, praising him as the philosopher who has most fully described the schizoid dimension of desire, 'but still within the category of an active utopia' (AO 367–8). At another point, they pose the rhetorical question, 'In what sense does the schizoid investment constitute [. . .] a real investment of the sociohistorical field, and not a simple utopia?' (AO 367). In my judgement, however, these passages still indicate an underlying resistance to adopting the term 'utopian' to describe their own position.
4. In *Negotiations*, where Deleuze elaborates on the concept of 'intercessors' (translated as 'mediators' by Joughin), Deleuze introduces the concept by saying, 'The important thing has never been to accompany the movement of one's neighbor, but to make one's own movement. If no one begins, no one budges. Interferences are also not exchange: everything takes place through gift or capture' (N 125; trans. modified). For some reason, Joughin renders 'Les interférences' as 'interplay', which obscures an important element in Deleuze's concept of intercession. Intercession and mediation can easily be thought of as relatively peaceful, cooperative activities, whereas interference suggests, if not violent opposition and conflict, at least a meeting of different forces that is less than irenic. The addition of 'interference' to 'intercession' counters the tendency to read intercession as a utopian process. Likewise, Joughin's decision to translate 'capture' as 'taking' tends to reduce an agonistic process to a gentler form of interaction. Finally, Joughin's choice of 'giving and taking' as equivalents of 'gift and capture' obscures Deleuze's implicit reference to traditional cultures (termed 'primitive' in *Anti-Oedipus*), in which entities pass from one individual according to the logic of the gift, as delineated by Marcel Mauss, or through capture in war, as well as Deleuze's allusion to the Nietzschean master's affirmative will to power in *The Genealogy of Morals*, a will that proceeds via the donation of value.
5. One of the more insightful aspects of Buchanan's *Deleuzism* is the correlation he draws between the utopian strain in Deleuze and Guattari and the concept of utopia developed by Fredric Jameson (see Buchanan 2000: 164–9). Buchanan also provides incisive commentary on the utopian dimension of *Anti-Oedipus* in *Deleuze and Guattari's Anti-Oedipus: A Reader's Guide* (2008); see esp. pp. 124–32.
6. Both Holland and Patton cite Deleuze and Guattari's statement in

What is Philosophy? that 'The word utopia therefore designates *that conjunction of philosophy, or the concept, with the present milieu*' (WP 100), but neither includes the parenthetic remark that completes the sentence: 'however, in view of the mutilated meaning public opinion has given to it, perhaps utopia is not the best use of the word', and neither makes use of Deleuze's remark in *Negotiations* suggesting that utopia be replaced by the concept of 'fabulation'. I do not see this as an oversight or a mistake, however. Deleuze and Guattari make frequent reference to fabulation in Chapter 7 of *What is Philosophy?*, which concerns the arts, whereas the comments on utopia occur in Chapter 4, 'Geophilosophy', which is focused on philosophy. In *What is Philosophy?*, Deleuze and Guattari emphasise the qualitative differences between philosophy and the arts, which suggests, I believe, that, even though 'utopia is not the best word' in philosophy or the arts, the concept of fabulation should replace that of utopia only in the arts, and that some other, never specified term might be used instead of utopia in philosophy. Since Deleuze and Guattari never provide such a term, it seems reasonable to propose such terms as 'utopia as process' or 'realistic utopia' as a means of delineating the bad use of 'utopia' from those more in keeping with Deleuze and Guattari's non-idealistic, processual conception of utopian change.

7. Laurent de Sutter makes a related argument in his *Deleuze: La pratique du droit* (2009). De Sutter differentiates between a critical and a clinical conception of law in Deleuze, the former generating Deleuze's frequent critiques of law, the latter, only vaguely sketched late in Deleuze's career, suggesting the possibility of a positive conception of law. De Sutter argues that Hume's conception of institutions as vehicles for the establishment and expansion of social relations, which Deleuze discusses in his early *Expression and Subjectivity: An Essay on Hume's Theory of Human Nature*, is implicit in Deleuze's endorsement of jurisprudence, which de Sutter glosses as a positive mode of expanding the sphere of law in ways that promote genuine equality and fairness. See esp. Sutter (2009: 63–106).
8. Hardt and Negri distinguish among a 'people', which 'has traditionally been a unitary conception', the 'masses', which, while being 'composed of all types and sorts', is nevertheless one within which 'all differences are submerged and drowned', and the 'multitude', which 'is composed of innumerable internal differences' (Hardt and Negri 2004: xiv). My reading of Deleuze's 'people to come' is in accord with Hardt and Negri's 'multitude'.
9. The volume *Seed to Harvest* contains four of the five Patternmaster

novels: *Patternmaster* (1976), *Mind of My Mind* (1977), *Wild Seed* (1980) and *Clay's Ark* (1984). The fifth, *Survivor* (1978), is the one work Butler has expressed displeasure with, for which reason she chose to omit it from *Seed to Harvest*. (In my view, Butler evaluation of the novel is unnecessarily harsh, and in fact the novel is equally as interesting and engaging as the other works in the series.)

10. The three novels of the trilogy, *Dawn* (1987), *Adulthood Rites* (1988) and *Imago* (1989), have been reprinted in a single volume, titled *Lilith's Brood* (1989).

6

Protocols of Experience and the Experimental Novel

'Protocols of experience' is a minor term in Deleuze's vocabulary, but one whose explication helps reveal the fundamental elements of his conception of literature. For Deleuze, linguistics is a subdivision of pragmatics, and language is a mode of action inseparable from discursive and non-discursive formations of power, themselves inextricable from their material components. Language operates within assemblages of words, ideas, representations, institutions, objects, artefacts and organisms that ultimately admit of no absolute distinction from one another. Literature is simply a specific mode of language action. Hence, Deleuze insists that no differentiation should be made between a writer's life and works (K 41; ATP 4), and that writing is a means of intervening in the real. Literature is both critical and clinical, its critical function being that of diagnosing the diseases of society, its clinical function that of initiating new possibilities for life. Literature intervenes in the world by resisting the intolerable – 'death, slavery, infamy, shame' (N 174) – by undoing repressive codes and destabilising asymmetrical power relations. Its interventions seek no predetermined cure, however. Their aim instead is to open the future to new modes of existence, the precise nature of which cannot be determined ahead of time. Literature is a form of experimentation, which seeks through its interventions in the real to invoke a 'people to come', but which has no guarantee of success. It is this notion of literature as experimentation that informs Deleuze's use of the term 'protocols of experience'.

Experimentation and Protocols of Experience

The phrase 'protocols of experience' occurs only four times in Deleuze's writings: first in *Kafka: Toward a Minor Literature* (1975), next in *Dialogues* (1977), and then twice in *A Thousand Plateaus* (1980). In *A Thousand Plateaus*, the French 'protocoles d'expérience' is translated as 'protocols of experience' at one point (ATP 283), but 'un protocole d'expérience' is rendered elsewhere as 'the protocol of an experiment' (ATP 162). The differing translations of 'expérience' are legitimate, since *expérience* can mean both experience and experiment, and the double meaning of the word is significant. The word 'protocol' has various meanings – a set of rules dictating behaviour in formal situations; a document detailing the terms of a treaty or formal agreement between two countries; a list of the specific measures of a medical course of treatment; and a plan for a scientific experiment. The conjunction of 'protocole' and 'expérience' thus suggests that Deleuze is using 'protocol' primarily in the sense of 'a plan for a scientific experiment'.

Experimentation itself is an important theme in Deleuze's later works, first making its appearance in the exposition of his 'transcendental empiricism' in *Difference and Repetition* (1968). There Deleuze argues that Kant's focus on the conditions of possible experience necessarily leads to a bifurcation of the aesthetic into the realm of sensible experience on one hand, and the realm of the arts on the other, such that 'the theory of the sensible [. . .] captures only the real's conformity with possible experience', whereas 'the theory of the beautiful [. . .] brings together the reality of the real insofar as it is reflected elsewhere' (DR 68; trans. modified). By contrast, in Deleuze's transcendental empiricism, which seeks the conditions of *real* experience, 'the two senses of the aesthetic become one, to the point where the being of the sensible reveals itself in the work of art, while at the same time the work of art appears as experimentation' (DR 68). Art, then, is experimentation; what it experiments on is the sensible, or real experience; and what it reveals is the being of the sensible.

In *Anti-Oedipus*, Deleuze and Guattari touch again on art as experimentation during their discussion of desiring-production as open-ended process (*processus*). In modernity, they say, art reaches a breakthrough – that of 'art as a *process* [*processus*] without goal, but that attains completion as such' (AO 370). When artists abandon 'meanings and aims' [*sens et buts*],

> art accedes to its authentic modernity, which simply consists in liberating what was present from its beginnings, but was hidden underneath aims and objects, even if aesthetic, and underneath recodings and axiomatics: the pure process [*processus*] that fulfills itself, and that never ceases to reach fulfillment as it proceeds [*en tant qu'il procède*] – art as 'experimentation'. (AO 370–1)

To the final word 'experimentation', they add a footnote citing John Cage's remark that 'the word *experimental* is apt, providing it is understood not as descriptive of an act to be later judged in terms of success and failure, but simply as of an act the outcome of which is unknown' (cited in AO 371). Deleuze and Guattari also give as instances of modern experimentation 'l'expérience Artaud, l'expérience Burroughs' (AO French 445), translated as 'the Artaud experiment, the Burroughs experiment' (AO 370).

Experimentation receives considerable stress in *Kafka: Toward a Minor Literature*, and here 'protocols of experience' (translated as 'tests of experience' [K 7]) appears for the first time. After rejecting psychoanalytic, hermeneutical and structural interpretations of Kafka, Deleuze and Guattari state: 'We believe only in a Kafka *politics* that is neither imaginary nor symbolic. We believe only in one or more Kafka *machines* that are neither structure nor phantasm. We believe only in a Kafka *experimentation* that is without interpretation and signification and rests only on protocols of experience' (K 7; trans. modified). A writer, they say, 'is not a writer-man; he is a political man, a machine-man, an experimental man' (K 7; trans. modified). When Deleuze and Guattari discuss *The Trial* in terms of machinic assemblages, they say that the characteristics of Kafka's novelistic machinic assemblage 'impose not an interpretation or a social representation of Kafka but an experimentation, a socio-political protocol' (in the English translation, 'a socio-political investigation') (K 49).

I will use Deleuze and Guattari's *Kafka* as the framework for the rest of my discussion, but before considering further what they mean in *Kafka* by 'experimentation', 'protocols of experience' and 'a socio-political protocol', I would like to remark briefly on Deleuze's preface to Louis Wolfson's *The Schizo and Languages* (*Le Schizo et les langues*), which first appeared in 1970, and then was published in a much revised version as 'Louis Wolfson; or The Procedure' in Deleuze's last book, *Essays Critical and Clinical* (1993). Wolfson's book provides a third-person account of himself as '"the student of schizophrenic language", "the mentally ill student", "the student of demented idioms"' (CC 7) who fends off his mother and his maternal tongue (American English) by developing elaborate mental operations to undo and deform English and create new sentences in an amalgam of sonic and/or semantic equivalents of the English sentence drawn from French, German, Russian or Hebrew. For example, the sentence 'Don't trip over the wire!' becomes '*tu'nicht* (German) *trébucher* (French) *über* (German) *èth hé* (Hebrew) *Zwirn* (German)' (SZ 6). In his 1970 preface, Deleuze praises Wolfson for inventing such operations, which Deleuze calls 'procedures' (*procédés*), saying that 'one of the great originalities of this book is to be a protocol of activities or occupations'; in the 1993 version of the text, Deleuze praises Wolfson for setting forth 'a protocol of experimentation or activity' [*un protocole d'expérimentation ou d'activité*] (CC 7/18). Deleuze finds Wolfson's practices similar to those of the novelist Raymond Roussel, who developed narratives through slight modifications of germinal sentences (such as 'les lettres du blanc sur les bandes du vieux billard' [the white letters on the cushions of the old billiard table] and 'les lettres du blanc sur les bandes du vieux pillard' [the white man's letters about the gangs of the old plunderer]), or by creating from a single sentence homonymous fragments that he subsequently incorporated into a narrative (for example, 'j'ai du bon tabac' [I have good tobacco] yields 'jade tube onde aubade' [jade tube wave morning-song]) (CC 20). Wolfson's book, however, unlike a novel by Roussel, is 'not a literary work, or a work of art, nor does it claim to be so' (Wolfson 8). Roussel's procedures lead to texts unrelated to the circumstances of their creation, whereas Wolfson's procedures remain tied to the specific situation in which he finds himself, and hence they lack aesthetic autonomy. In 1993 Deleuze articulates this difference between Wolfson and Roussel by saying 'the transformations never reach the grandiose level of an event, but remain mired in their accidental circumstances. The procedure thus remains a protocol' (CC 11). In the 1970 text, however, Deleuze does not oppose procedure and protocol, but instead equates protocol and procedure, distinguishing Wolfson from Roussel via their respective uses of procedures.

Protocols and Kafka

One sense of a literary protocol, then, is that of a procedure or set of procedures whereby one experiments on linguistic elements – letters, sounds, meanings – deforming them, and then reassembling them in new ways. In *Kafka: Toward a Minor Literature*, Deleuze and Guattari assert that such linguistic experimentation is present in Kafka's use of German, which they label a 'minor' usage facilitated by German's status as a deracinated 'paper language' in Prague and by Kafka's exposure to Czech, Hebrew and Yiddish speech and idioms. Yet Deleuze and Guattari give no specific examples of such linguistic deterritorialisation, focusing instead on other forms of experimentation in Kafka. Deleuze and Guattari divide Kafka's writings into three groups: the letters, the short stories and the novels. In all three forms, Kafka's problem is to avoid closure and keep his literary machine running.

In the letters, notably those to his fiancée Felice, the danger is that his exchanges will lead to marriage, and hence to an end of the correspondence – and, Kafka fears, to an end of his activity as a writer altogether. Hence, his strategy is to ward off conjugality and perpetuate an endless correspondence through the imposition of obstacles to any physical meeting with Felice.

> The horror of Kafka toward all forms of conjugality. A prodigious operation by which he translates this horror into a *topography of obstacles* (where to go? How to arrive? Prague, Vienna, Berlin?). The Surveyor. And also the other operation by which he enumerates a numbered *list of conditions* that the subject of

> the statement thinks can dissipate horror when, in fact, it is this very horror in the subject of enunciation that inspires them (Program or Life Plan, à la Kleist). (K 31–2; trans. modified)

The relationship between these 'operations' (*operations*) and experimental protocols is made clear in Deleuze's 1977 *Dialogues*, where he speaks of Kafka and Kleist passing their time 'drawing up programs for life' (D 48; trans. modified). If Kafka is forever composing programmes of obstacles and numbered conditions, Kleist in his early correspondence with his half-sister speaks repeatedly of his need for a *Lebensplan*, a life plan. Deleuze argues that neither Kafka nor Kleist is attempting to map the future in a fixed way. Rather, each is using a programme or life plan to live an experimental life, to engage in a 'life-experimentation' (D 47). A life programme as mode of experimentation is 'always modified in the process of coming into being, betrayed in the process of being hollowed out, like river banks that branch off or canals that are arranged in order that a flux may flow' (D 48; trans. modified). Life programmes or plans are 'finite processes [*procès*] of experimentation, protocols of experience', which serve as '*means of providing reference points for an experimentation which exceeds our capacities to foresee*' (D 48; trans. modified, emphasis in original).

In Kafka's letters, then, we find something like the procedures of Wolfson and Roussel, specific techniques, or *opérations*, exercised in language. These operations, however, are also components of programmes, plans, sets of obstacles, numbered lists of conditions, which function as reference points for experimentation. In this sense, such protocols outline a set of future operations, but only as the basis of an improvisatory process of constant adjustment of the plan as experimentation continues. And most important, these protocols of experience do not have linguistic deformation as their goal. They are meant instead to have the real-world effect of keeping Felice at a distance.

Deleuze and Guattari deal with Kafka's short stories primarily as stories of animal metamorphosis, or what they call 'becoming-animal'. When they say that the writer is an 'experimental-man', they add parenthetically that he is one 'who thereby ceases to be a man in order to become an ape or a beetle, or a dog, or mouse, a becoming-animal, a becoming-inhuman' (K 7). Such becoming-animal, they assert, is not metaphorical, symbolic or allegorical but real. Not that people magically become beetles or dogs; rather, a process of becoming-other passes between the categories of the human and the animal, such that a new, a-human mode of being opens up through the metamorphic interrelation of the two via a 'line of flight', a vector of deterritorialisation. The stories, Deleuze and Guattari say, 'attaining to the real, writing themselves within the real itself, [. . .] are nonetheless caught up in the tension between two opposing poles or realities. Becoming-animal effectively shows a way out, traces a line of flight' (K 36; trans. modified). Becoming-animal is also 'a map of intensities. It is an ensemble of states, each distinct from the other, grafted onto the man insofar as he is searching for a way out. It is a creative line of flight that means nothing other than itself' (K 36; trans. modified).

Becoming-animal is but one of several forms of becoming-other – becoming-woman, becoming-child, becoming-molecular, becoming-imperceptible, and so on. Central to becoming-other is experimentation, which Deleuze associates with Spinoza's observation that we do not know what a body can do. In *Spinoza: Practical Philosophy* (revised and augmented edition 1981), Deleuze says that on the great plane of immanence of Nature, each thing, whether natural or artificial, living or non-living, is defined by its affects – that is, its powers of affecting and being affected – and by its differential speeds. Spinoza's *Ethics*, according to Deleuze, is an 'ethology', a study that defines 'bodies, animals, or humans by the affects they are capable of [. . .] The approach is no less valid for us, for human beings, than for animals, because no one knows ahead of time the affects one is capable of; it is a long affair of experimentation' (SPP 125). In *A Thousand Plateaus*, Deleuze and Guattari address experimentation on the body, first in Plateau Six, 'How Do You Make a Body without Organs', then in Plateau Ten, 'Becoming-Intense, Becoming-Animal, Becoming-Imperceptible . . .'. The Body without Organs is roughly the same as the plane of consistency, a deterritorialised dimension of nothing but affective intensities and differential speeds. The Body without Organs is a limit that is never fully reached, but approaching that limit can only take place via experimentation. The Body without Organs, Deleuze and Guattari say, 'is not a concept but a practice [*une pratique*], a set of practices [*un ensemble de pratiques*]' (ATP 150). The hypochondriac, the schizophrenic, the drug addict, and the masochist experiment on their bodies, trying to make a Body without Organs, with varying degrees of success or failure. Each is engaged in a set of practices, a 'programme' like that of the masochist who enumerates the operations the dominatrix is asked to perform on his body: tie me to a table; whip me one hundred times; sew up this orifice; burn that organ, and so on. Carlos Castaneda, who writes of his experiences with the Mexican sorcerer Don Juan, is also making a body without organs when he follows the various stages in his training in sorcery. Castaneda's books, Deleuze and Guattari say, are less an ethnographical study than 'a protocol of experience' (ATP 162; trans. modified). All these efforts to make a Body without Organs proceed via processes of becoming-other, and in Plateau Ten Deleuze and Guattari provide further details of becoming-other, all of which involve experimentation on the body and tend towards the Body without Organs or the plane of consistency. In this plateau, they speak of Henri Michaux's experimentation with drugs as 'minute protocols of experience' (ATP 283), but it is clear in this plateau that all becomings, including Kafka's becoming-animal, are experiments connected to sets of practices, to protocols of experience.

Kafka's letters, then, employ the protocols of programmes, life plans, sets of obstacles, lists of conditions; and his short stories engage protocols of becoming-other, especially becoming-animal. To these protocols the novels add practices much more clearly political than those in the letters and stories. Paradigmatic among the novels in this regard is *The Trial* – *Le Procès* in French. Kafka's fundamental goal, according to Deleuze and Guattari, is to perpetuate active desire – desiring-production in the terminology of *Anti-Oedipus* – and avoid any closure in such desiring. Desire, they say, is 'not form, but a procedure, a process [*le désir n'est pas forme, mais processus, procès*]' (K 8), and in *The Trial*, Kafka explores the law as desire, converting the *procès* as court proceeding into a *procès* as open-ended process of experimentation. (We will recall that in *Anti-Oedipus* Deleuze and Guattari characterised modern art as 'the pure process [*processus*] that fulfills itself, and that never ceases to reach fulfillment as it proceeds [*en tant qu'il procède*] – art as "experimentation"'.) The fundamental operation or procedure of *The Trial* is 'to extract from social representations assemblages of enunciation and machinic assemblages and to dismantle these assemblages' (K 46). 'Writing has this double function', say Deleuze and Guattari: 'transcribe into assemblages, dismantle assemblages' (K 47; trans. modified). Such transcription and demolition 'is a procedure [*procédé*] much more intense than any critique'. *The Trial* 'is not an interpretation or a social representation', but 'an experimentation, a socio-political protocol' (K 48–9; trans. modified). The application of this procedure takes place through Josef K., who is less a character than a function, the 'K-function' (D 73). At each stage of the narrative, as representations are converted into assemblages, K produces an experimental dismantling, which then leads to another stage, and then another, the sequence following no predetermined plan, episode after episode exploring the law as repressive institution and converting it into an immanent line of desiring production. Through this sociopolitical protocol, Kafka neither interprets nor represents reality, but instead experiments directly on the real, and in so doing uncovers not simply the material power structures and processes in effect in Kafka's present, but also the 'diabolical powers of the future' immanent within the Austro-Hungarian Empire – those of Nazi Germany, Stalinist Russia and American capitalism. These diabolical powers of the future are metastable potentialities that are being actualised in the present, yet that have the possibility of other actualisations, both negative and positive. For this reason, Kafka's disclosures of immanent forces of the future are always double-edged, revealing both 'diabolical powers to come' and 'revolutionary forces to be constructed' (K 18).

Zola and the Experimental Novel

For Deleuze, writing is experimentation, an intervention in the real meant to produce something new. In this regard, literature involves not only formal aesthetic experimentation but also something like scientific experimentation. This association of literature with science cannot help but bring to mind Zola's essay 'The Experimental Novel' (1880), which calls for the development of the novel as an experimental science.[1] The differences between Deleuze's and Zola's conceptions of literary experimentation are significant, but helpful in clarifying Deleuze's thought.

Zola organises his essay around Claude Bernard's *Introduction to the Study of Experimental Medicine*, arguing that just as medicine is becoming less an intuitive art and more an experimental science, so literature should abandon its rhapsodic and metaphysical intuitions and embrace the scientific method. Bernard notes that medical experimentation is more complicated than experimentation in physics and chemistry, since it involves milieus both external and internal to humans, yet nonetheless it is a feasible and necessary enterprise. Zola admits that literature's domain is even more complex than that of medicine, in that it includes social milieus as well those of the physical and the physiological environment. But such complexity, Zola argues, should not deter writers from developing literature as an experimental science that, like medicine, will extend the range of human knowledge. Says Zola, 'We have experimental chemistry and medicine; we shall have an experimental physiology, and later on an experimental novel' (Zola 1964: 16). And the novel's field of experimentation will be not the physiological body but 'the passionate and intellectual acts of man' (Zola 1964: 16).

Experimental novelists, Zola explains, choose a set of characters and their environment, develop a hypothesis of how the characters might react under certain circumstances, induce a modification of the social situation, and then observe the results of that modification. As Zola says, 'The idea of experiment carries with it the idea of modification', and 'we must modify nature, without departing from nature, when we employ the experimental method in our novels' (Zola 1964: 11). Once a given experiment is completed, the novelist deduces the natural laws that governed the characters' behaviour. Zola argues, however, that the discovery of such deterministic laws does not lead to fatalism, since humans can use knowledge of these laws to act and thereby further modify their situation. Experimental novelists are 'experimental moralists', and

> In our role as experimental moralists we show the mechanism of the useful and the useless, we disengage the determinism of the human and social phenomena so that, in their turn, the legislators can one day dominate and control these phenomena. In a word, we are working with the whole country toward that great object, the conquest of nature and the increase of man's power a hundredfold. (Zola 1964: 31)

Among the many problems with Zola's concept of the experimental novel, two are particularly striking: first, Zola ignores the fact that the writer's imaginary laboratory is qualitatively different from the scientist's material laboratory, and in no way subject to the constraints of factual and counterfactual verifiability fundamental to legitimate experimentation; and second, Zola leaves unexplained how scientific determinism accommodates the free will necessary for humans to conquer nature and create an ideal world. Deleuze addresses both these problems. Since language is a mode of action, there is no separation between art and life, fiction and the world. Like Zola, Deleuze conceives of experimentation as modification, as an intervention in which writers, in Zola's words, 'modify nature, without departing from nature' (Zola 1964: 11), but the aim of such intervention is not the discovery of scientific laws. Indeed, nature as Deleuze conceives it is not deterministic but probabilistic. It is a 'chaosmos' of non-linear systems far from equilibrium, dissipative structures, strange attractors, metastable states and emergent phenomena, and literary experiments are meant to test potentials and instigate unpredictable modifications of the chaosmos. For this reason, Deleuze has no difficulty in reconciling literature as experimental method and as activist politics, since his is not a deterministic world and the results of any experimental intervention can never be known in advance. Zola likens the experimental novelist to the experimental doctor, the one diagnosing social wounds and disease, the other corporeal ailments, and both finding cures through their scientific investigations. Deleuze, too, links medicine and literature, affirming Nietzsche's designation of writers as 'civilization's doctors' (N 143). Unlike Zola's experimental novelist, however, the Deleuzian experimental writer seeks no specific cure, but merely a way 'to free life from what imprisons it' (N 143) and open possibilities for new, uncharted modes of existence.

Protocols of Experience as General Method

Whereas Zola's aim is to make literature a science, Deleuze seeks only to appropriate certain scientific practices for discretely literary ends. Indeed, in *What is Philosophy?*, Deleuze and Guattari make a sharp differentiation among philosophy, science and the arts, arguing that each has its own provenance and purpose. Yet all three, they claim, have a common goal – that of summoning forth a people to come. And it is in this regard that the concept of protocols of experience is most suggestive. I have identified various literary protocols of experience, ranging from Wolfson and Roussel's linguistic procedures; to Kleist's life plans and Kafka's programmes of obstacles and enumerated conditions; to masochistic programmes, Castaneda's training regimens and Michaux's controlled exploration of drugs; to various becomings – becoming-woman, becoming-child, becoming-animal, becoming-imperceptible; and to the sociopolitical operations whereby Kafka transcribes representations into assemblages, dismantles them, and discloses the immanent forces of potential futures. In all these case, protocols serve as '*means of providing reference points for an experimentation which exceeds our capacities to foresee*' (D 48; trans. modified). What I would argue is that this conception of protocols as 'means of providing reference points for experimentation' is indicative of a basic political practice informing Deleuze's conception of philosophy, science and the arts. To utilise protocols of experience entails the following: (1) to assess the present configuration of powers that imprison life and identify those points most susceptible to modification; (2) to develop specific protocols – plans, programmes, procedures, practices and so on – to guide a future experimental intervention; (3) to implement those protocols in an experimental intervention in a given situation; (4) to evaluate the results of the experiment and determine the extent to which it has or has not furthered the goal of inventing a people to come; and (5) to reassess the new, post-experimentation configuration of powers that imprison life and commence another round of experimentation guided by protocols of experience appropriate to the new situation.

Philosophers, scientists and artists develop protocols of experience in divergent fashions, but they do so to face a common problem. Their shared goal is to invoke a people to come, yet they cannot produce such a people on their own, nor can they know in advance what such a collectivity would be. Their project is utopian but only in a certain sense. In *What is Philosophy?*, Deleuze and Guattari say 'Utopia is not a good concept' (WP 110), their reasoning being that utopias are usually complete blueprints of an ideal world, which inevitably project into the future the limitations of the present. Hence, they argue that if one must use the concept 'utopia', one must 'distinguish between authoritarian utopias, or utopias of transcendence, and immanent, revolutionary, libertarian utopias' (WP 100). The former are utopias as completed, future *products*, the latter are utopias as *processes*. Philosophy, science and the arts have resistance in common – 'resistance to death, to the intolerable, to shame, and to the present' (WP 110) – and in all three domains, 'to create is to resist' (WP 110). In all three, 'to think is to experiment, but experimentation is always that which is in the process of coming about – the new, remarkable and interesting' (WP 111). How, then, should one proceed in resistance to the present, in a utopian process of experimentation, if there is no fixed goal to orient one's actions? Not haphazardly, but through protocols of experience, '*reference points for an experimentation which exceeds our capacities to foresee*' (D 48; trans. modified). The protocols of experience detailed here are those used by writers to invoke a people to come. They are specific to the art of literature, but the fundamental process of experimentation that underlies them may be applied to philosophy and science as well. In philosophy, science and the arts, protocols of experience serve as guidelines for movement from an intolerable present to an unknowable future.

Note

1. Deleuze in fact alludes to Zola's text when he calls Michel Tournier's novel *Friday, or the Limbo of the Pacific* 'an inductive experimental novel' (LS 305; trans. modified).

III. Music and Philosophy

7

The New Harmony

In a 1988 interview, Deleuze remarks that philosophy needs 'not only a philosophical understanding, through concepts, but a non-philosophical understanding, rooted in percepts and affects. You need both. Philosophy has an essential and positive relation with nonphilosophy: it speaks directly to non-philosophers' (N 139–40). Deleuze views the arts as the domain that is 'rooted in percepts and affects', and hence as one that affords a particularly vital non-philosophical comprehension of philosophy. Philosophy's primary goal is the invention of concepts, he says, but the concept includes 'two other dimensions, percepts and affects'. For this reason, 'the affect, the percept and the concept are three inseparable powers [*puissances*], running from art into philosophy and from philosophy into art' (N 137; trans. modified). In *What is Philosophy?* (1991), Deleuze and Guattari speak at length of philosophy's relationship to the arts, but perhaps the best examples of this relationship, as Deleuze understands it, are to be found in *The Fold: Leibniz and the Baroque* (1988). *What is Philosophy?* is filled with references to various philosophers and artists, but it provides no detailed analyses of any single philosopher's relationship to the arts. *The Fold*, by contrast, offers an extended reading of Leibniz's thought as a philosophical counterpart of the Baroque sensibility expressed in the arts of the late seventeenth and early eighteenth century. An especially intriguing and instructive instance of the philosophy–arts parallels established in *The Fold* is that which Deleuze draws between Leibniz's concept of harmony and the harmonic practices of Baroque composers. In Deleuze's presentation of Leibniz's 'new harmony', one can see clearly how Deleuze envisions philosophy's relationship to the arts. And, perhaps as importantly, one can see from this example what Deleuze regards as the role the history of philosophy and its encounter with the arts should play in contemporary philosophical and aesthetic endeavours.

Baroque Music

In *The Fold*, draws on several of the arts to characterise the Baroque and establish Leibniz as a philosopher responding to the aesthetic concerns of his age. Chief among those arts are architecture and painting. Deleuze likens Leibniz's differentiation of monads and bodies, for example, to a two-storey Baroque building, the upper storey representing the domain of monads, the lower that of bodies. The upper storey is an essentially interior space, a monastic cell or *camera oscura*, like the monads, 'without doors or windows'. The lower storey, by contrast, is an exterior façade, horizontally organised in the rhythms of its components (doors, windows, columns, pediments) but with no meaningful relationship between those components and the interior space (just as bodies constitute a causally interconnected domain without being linked in any simple or direct way to the domain of monads). Deleuze finds that opposition of lower corporeality and upper monadic spirituality in Baroque painting, and he argues that the motif that organises both levels and allows for their intercommunication is that of the fold. In Baroque still lifes, the folds of draperies and tablecloths communicate with the whorls of wood grains and marble veins, the curves of goblets, plates, medallions and armour, the flowing contours of fruit, wild game and flowers. In El Greco, twisting bodies pulsate within undulating landscapes, earthly figures intertwining and often ascending into unearthly realms of vortical spirituality. The Baroque fold is one that 'goes out to infinity' (TF 121), just as Leibniz's bodies and monads form infinite series, bodies folded within bodies, monads within monads, each monad enfolding the infinite cosmos, each body unfolding a specific constituent of the infinite whole, the folds of bodies and folds of monads communicating through the additional mysterious folds of the *vinculum substantiale*.

Clearly, Deleuze's conception of the Baroque is predominantly visual, with architecture, painting and, to a lesser extent, sculpture providing him with models of the period's aesthetic. Yet Deleuze does note that Leibniz makes regular use of the musical metaphor of harmony, and, unlike most commentators, Deleuze regards this as more than a casual figure of speech.[1] It would be a mistake to seek in Leibniz's thought 'a direct transposition of musical chords [*accords*, the French word *accord* capable of denoting both a musical chord and the general notions of agreement, harmony, linkage or entente] in the way they are developed in the Baroque', Deleuze observes. And yet 'it would also be erroneous to conclude with Leibniz's indifference in respect to the musical model: the question, rather, involves analogy. And we know that Leibniz was always trying to bring it to a new rigor' (TF 131). That new rigour depends on a deep sensitivity to the new harmonic practices of Baroque composers.

Deleuze's primary guide to Baroque music is Manfred Bukofzer, whose *Music in the Baroque Era* (1947) is one of the pioneering modern works in the field. Bukofzer differentiates Renaissance from Baroque music first by observing the emergence of a plurality of styles in the Baroque. Unlike other transitions in music history, in which one period's style is replaced by another, at the beginning of the Baroque 'the old style was not cast aside, but deliberately preserved as a second language, known as the *stile antico* of church music' (Bukofzer 1947: 3). Theorists of the late sixteenth and early seventeenth century frequently opposed the *stile antico* to the *stile moderno*, framing the opposition as well in terms of a *stylus gravis* versus a *stylus luxurians*, or a *prima prattica* versus a *seconda prattica*. Later in the seventeenth century, another classificatory scheme became common, one dividing the field into church, chamber and theatre music (*musica ecclesiastica*, *cubicularis*, *theatralis*), the *stile antico* roughly (but not entirely) coinciding with that of *musica ecclesiastica*. This rather confusing discourse of two practices and/ or three styles, argues Bukofzer, was a sign that the Renaissance unity of style had been lost and that with the Baroque development of a plurality of styles had come a heightened consciousness of style per se.

For many seventeenth-century theorists, the *prima prattica* and *seconda prattica* could be differentiated primarily by their handling of music and word, the first practice giving precedence to music, the second to text. Advocates of the second practice often claimed that they alone represented the emotions in their settings of texts, but, as Bukofzer points out, neither Renaissance nor Baroque composers attempted a direct, psychological representation of emotions, instead relying on a conventional ensemble of coded figures to render fixed emotional effects. What set the two practices apart was a Renaissance predilection for 'the affections of restraint and noble simplicity' and a Baroque love of 'the extreme affections, ranging from violent pain to exuberant joy' (Bukofzer 1947: 5). Renaissance settings also often muted emotional effects by allowing multiple voices to sing different words simultaneously, a tendency early *seconda prattica* composers deliberately countered through the development of the recitative – the rhythmically free, declamatory solo component of opera – which from its inception was intended to render extremes of pathos and affective violence by following the inflections of natural speech. Indeed, Bukofzer argues, that impulse to render powerful emotions was the primary motivation for the Baroque's creation of opera, not (as is often claimed) a vague desire to 'imitate the Ancients', something Renaissance and Baroque musicians both professed. Although Baroque representations of emotions tended to adhere to conventional musical codes, the recitative's adoption of oratory as a guide to the handling of speech opened music to extra-musical elements (much to the dismay of *prima prattica* composers). Hence, concludes Bukofzer,

> renaissance and early baroque concepts of music stand, at this point, clearly opposed. The renaissance artist saw in music a self-contained autonomous art, subject only to its own laws. The baroque artist saw in music a heteronomous art, subordinated to words and serving only as musical means to a dramatic end that transcended music. (Bukofzer 1947: 8)

In strictly musical terms, Renaissance and Baroque compositions may be differentiated in several interrelated ways. In the Renaissance, dissonance occurred only on the weak beat or as a suspension of the strong beat. Harmony was conceived of as a concordant sounding of individual voices on strong beats, the voices maintaining an equal and relatively autonomous role. In the Baroque, harmony was thought of as a sequence of vertical chords, and, as a result, dissonance on the strong beat became possible as long as the chord was clearly delineated. The Renaissance's equality among the voices gave way to a dominance of the outer voices, the bass line supplying the foundation for the chord, the melody providing an expressive ornamentation of the harmonic structure. The prominence of the bass line and melody was especially evident in the convention of the thorough-bass, or *basso continuo*, a convention virtually coextensive with the Baroque era. According to this common practice, the *continuo* keyboardist accompanying a violin soloist, for example, was simply given a bass line with a sequence of numerical figures accompanying each note, the numbers merely indicating the chord to be played but not the specific notes of the chord. In such a composition, while the bass line and melody were written out by the composer, the subordinate inner voices of the chord were improvised by the keyboardist.

Of course, Renaissance compositions also had bass lines, but the Baroque bass voice, while still a line with a horizontal continuity, was constructed to emphasise a system of tonal chordal relations. Unlike Renaissance harmonies, which were primarily modal, Baroque harmonies were tonal, that is, organised around the attraction of a tonal centre. In Renaissance intervallic harmony, individual voices were coordinated so that concords sounded on strong beats, but with no pressing concern about the sequence of chords from one strong beat to the next. In Baroque tonal harmony, by contrast, the progression of chords was regulated by a system of relations between chords, the tonic (the C triad in the key of C major) providing maximum stability, the dominant (G major triad in C), the subdominant (F major triad in C) and various other chords having degrees of instability that required resolution according to fixed sequential movements from one chord to the next. This tonal foundation of chord sequences made possible a much greater freedom in the treatment of the melody, both harmonically and rhythmically. Not only was the Renaissance dictum that all dissonance be resolved by downward movement no longer observed in the melody, but dissonance occurred on strong beats and melodies made use of a wider range of intervals, most notably chromatic steps and intervals corresponding to augmented and diminished progressions. That increased chromaticism in melodic construction had as its corollary a greater harmonic chromaticism, Baroque composers significantly expanding the Renaissance palette of triads and sixth chords by introducing unprepared seventh chords, augmented triads and diminished chords. The heightened freedom of the melodic line was manifest especially in the Baroque system of ornamentation, whereby melodies were embellished with various grace notes (mordents, trills, turns, appoggiaturas and so on), those additional melodic notes either indicated by signs above the melody or simply improvised by the performer without any explicit instructions from the composer.

Rhythmic innovations also informed Baroque practices. Renaissance compositions typically were organised by the *tactus*, an even flow of beats maintained throughout a given section of music. A strict system of mathematical proportions governed the rhythms of individual voices, and all voices were coordinated by the unifying *tactus*, yet the autonomy and equality of the voices tended to weaken the sense of a dominant, emphatic measure controlling all voices. Duration rather than dynamic stress was the primary technique for creating melodic syncopation or accent. Baroque composers, by contrast, exploited the rhythmic extremes of a freely pulsed, expressive lyricism and a heavily stressed, insistently repetitive dynamism. The first extreme was on display in the opera recitative, which followed the fluid cadences of spoken speech, at times entirely without any regular pulse. The other extreme was manifest especially in the dance forms (allemande, courante, sarabande, gigue, gavotte, minuet) that so intrigued Baroque composers. Like their Renaissance predecessors, Baroque composers exploited a full range of contrapuntal techniques, but they handled the individual voices in such a way that the overall metrical organisation of the composition was seldom obscured.

The Baroque saw as well the introduction of idiomatic writing, whereby composers exploited the features peculiar to a given voice or instrument, or a group of voices and instruments. Renaissance music typically was conceived in terms of a single part-writing practice common to vocal and instrumental music. Choral compositions generally could be performed a cappella or with instrumental doubling of the lines, or they could be performed by instruments alone. Conversely, instrumental compositions often bore the inscription 'to be played or sung'. With the invention of opera, Baroque composers explored the lyrical possibilities specific to solo voices. In their church music, they exploited a-cappella sonorities that would be compromised by instrumental accompaniment. They developed differentiated vocalic and instrumental practices in operas, oratorios and cantatas. And they gradually formulated distinct styles for various families of instruments, especially strings and keyboards. Such idiomatic writing made possible as well an exchange of idioms, a violin line adopting a vocalic idiom, a lute ornament appearing in a harpsichord composition. These exchanges and interpenetrations could also take place at the level of entire compositions, the idiom of an organ prelude shaping a choral work, the recitative idiom dominating an instrumental piece. Finally, idiomatic writing informed the widespread practices of the Baroque 'concertant style', in which groups of instruments were opposed to one another as contrasting compositional blocks (that contrast of groups frequently taking the form of an opposition of homophonic chord blocks that stressed vertical harmonic relations).

We may say in general, then, that Baroque music displayed an increased heterogeneity and heteronomy in comparison with Renaissance music. Baroque composers developed three separate styles and two distinct practices. They made use of the rhythmic extremes of unpulsed recitatives and heavily stressed dance forms. They expanded the Renaissance harmonic vocabulary to include various altered chords. Melodic composition gained a new freedom, chromatic variation and ornamental elaboration providing options for linear construction unavailable to Renaissance composers. The development of idiomatic writing complemented the Baroque's increased sensitivity to stylistic differences, the Renaissance's single part-writing technique giving way to divergent techniques suitable for individual voices, instruments and ensembles. The Baroque's fascination with emotional extremes in early opera was gradually communicated throughout a number of other forms, and opera's openness to textual, extra-musical influences gave evidence of an increased sensitivity to extra-musical affectivity in general. What made all this possible was a new harmonic system, one based on tonality and a chordal conception of harmony, with a privileging of the outer voices of a foundational bass and an expressive, ornamental melody. This harmonic system was the force designed to bring unity to the multiple styles and idioms, the extremes of rhythm, intervallic movement and harmonic palette, and the centrifugal influence of extra-musical concerns.

Leibniz and Pre-established Harmony

In this opposition of Renaissance and Baroque conceptions of musical harmony Deleuze sees a parallel to the opposition of Malebranche's occasionalism and Leibniz's pre-established harmony.[2] In Malebranche, the occasion of God's constant intervention ensures a harmonious relationship between bodies and souls. The occasion, says Deleuze, 'plays the role of a sort of counterpoint that still belongs to a melodic or polyphonic conception of music' (TF 128). In other words, Malebranche thinks of bodies and souls as equal and autonomous melodic voices brought into regular harmonic relations through a single unifying force, as in Renaissance musical practice. Leibniz's pre-established harmony, by contrast, is a harmony of accords, one that is analogous to Baroque musical harmony in its emphasis on vertical relations and the production of unity within a pervasive heterogeneity.

Like many before him, Leibniz finds inspiration in the Pythagorean conjunction of music and mathematics when articulating his notions of harmony. In Deleuze's analysis, the controlling metaphor in Leibniz's conception of pre-established harmony is that of the relationship among inverse, or reciprocal, numbers (for example, 5/1 is the inverse, or reciprocal, of 1/5). Pre-established harmony 'is a numerical unity, insofar as it envelops a multiplicity' (TF 128). The one of God envelops the multiplicity of monads. Each monad is an unfolding of the one, and each monad expresses the entirety of the one from a specific point of view. God is the infinite one, and God envelops an infinity of monads; each of the infinite monads, though only an infinitely small entity, expresses the infinite one from its individual point of view. Hence, if God = ∞ / 1, the individual monad is the inverse of God, or 1 / ∞. According to Leibniz's principle of indiscernibles, however, no two monads are exactly alike, and thus we must insist as well that each monad has a specific value, say 1/3 or 1/7, even though the number of monads is infinite, each monad is infinitely small, and each expresses the entirety of the infinite one. Leibniz reconciles this dual nature of the monad by asserting that 'each monad expresses the world (1 / ∞), but clearly expresses only a particular zone of the world (1 / n , n having in each case a specific value)' (TF 130; trans. modified). Each monad is like the singular point at which a curve meets a tangent straight line. The straight line and the curve are made up of an infinity of points, the line and curve converging at the singular point, the distance between the line and curve decreasing by infinite gradations as the two near the singular point. The singular point may be said to integrate the differentials of this particular relation between tangent and curve, and it is in this sense that each monad's zone of clarity may be characterised by the convergent series of differentials it is capable of integrating. From this analogy, Deleuze concludes that

> in its own portion of the world or in its clear zone, each monad *thus presents accords*, inasmuch as an 'accord' can be called the relation of a state with its differentials, that is, with the differential relations among infinitely small elements that are integrated into this state. (TF 130)

Pre-established harmony, then, is a harmony of accords. The accords produced in the individual monad are of three basic types, which Deleuze sees as analogous to the basic chords (again, in French *accords* = musical chords) of the tonal harmonic system – major chords, minor chords and dissonant chords. Each monad is a point of view on the world, and as such it has perceptions and affections specific to its point of view. Each monad perceives and senses the entire world in a confused way, but only a small portion of the world in a clear fashion. That clear perception is like the sound of waves at the shore (a favourite example of Leibniz's). That sound is an integration of unconscious, differential micro-perceptions of the infinite sounds of individual waves, individual drops of water, individual molecules and so on. The monad's zone of clarity is its clear perception of the sound of the sea, but its perception extends confusedly to include an infinity of vague and decreasingly distinguishable micro-perceptions. Likewise, a monad's specific affection is like a moment of hunger, a conscious feeling that integrates a differential series of moments passing by infinite gradation from unconscious appetitive inclination, to vague gastric unrest, to full-fledged hunger. Major accords are those integrations that allow the monad to expand its zone of clarity, to continue its pleasures in proliferating accords. Minor accords are those integrations that are unstable and temporary, 'simple pleasures that are inverted into their contrary, unless they are attracted by a perfect [i.e., major] accord' (TF 131). And dissonant accords are those integrations that interrelate negative and positive series, such that dissonance is, according to standard Baroque musical practice, either prepared or resolved. When a dog enjoying a juicy bone seems to be abruptly sent into pain by a blow from a stick, it actually has already been sustaining a watchful alertness to possible danger, has had a vague sense of some approaching movement, an unconscious awareness of the scent of a human, and so on, and in this regard it has been preparing itself for the dissonant blow, thereby integrating the series of its eating pleasure into the series of corporal pain. Conversely, the martyr at the stake resolves the dissonance of rising flames by integrating her torments into the prospect of an imminent eternal glory.

The accords of monads are constantly forming and unforming, tending 'toward a resolution or a modulation' (TF 132). Although each monad's accords express the entire world, and hence extend through all other monads, its accords arise from within, for each monad is without doors or windows, a self-enjoying, self-contained locus of unfolding. And though that unfolding occurs as a temporal process of constant transformation, through major and minor integrations of differential series, through preparations for and resolutions of dissonance, the accords of each monad trace a trajectory of instants that exist in a co-present, virtual simultaneity.

In each moment of a monad's unfolding, the entire history of the world is implicit, as is the future course of the world. The course of each monad's unfolding has been inscribed in it from its creation; that course is like a musical score that the soloist monad performs without promptings from its sonic surroundings. The monad's unfolding, then, though manifested in a horizontal temporality, exists vertically as a virtual score, the total history of the monad's changing accords already written in its soloist part. In the simplest terms, one may say that the monad's accords are like arpeggios, melodies made up of the notes of a chord, temporal unfoldings of simultaneous, virtual forms. In that each monad integrates multiple series, however, we must imagine its solo score as one made up not solely of monodic arpeggios but also of multi-voiced chordal progressions (perhaps the score of a truly grand piano).

Spontaneity and Concertation

Each monad acts spontaneously, without prompting from without, and hence its accords constitute a harmony of spontaneity. Yet, in addition to spontaneity, there is a harmonious arrangement of all monads among one another, a harmony Deleuze calls 'concertation' (a harmony, he suggests, that may be seen as the analogue of Baroque music's 'concertant style'). Although each monad plays its individual part without regard to other monads, all the monads belong to a single world and perform the music of that world together as a harmoniously coordinated orchestra. Concertation is 'an accord of spontaneities themselves, an accord among accords' (TF 132). The cosmos is God's great orchestral score, each monad a separate part in the score, the whole composition a manifestation of an unfolding pre-established harmony. Deleuze insists, however, that Leibniz's God does not so much create the individual monads as he creates the world within which the monads unfold, that world incapable of existing outside the monads that express it. The harmonies of spontaneity and concertation are mutually implicated, then, in that God's orchestral composition is a total world, selected from all possible worlds, a world already replete with its monads, which are the necessary expressions of that world.

The harmony specific to concertation is one of clarity and

obscurity, of pre-established mutual adjustments of relations among monads. Each monad is characterised by its zone of clarity, no two monads possessing precisely the same range and degree of clarity. As a given monad expands its zone of clarity, necessarily somewhere else another monad's zone contracts. All monads express the same world, but, in a given event, that which expresses it with greater clarity is a cause, and that which expresses it with less clarity is an effect. The causality among monads is not like mechanical causality, since each monad is an autonomous entity and hence unaffected by any other monad. Rather, it is an ideal causality, the causality of mutually coordinated harmonious relations that constitute the unified world created by God. Ideal causality always proceeds from clarity to obscurity, or from the more-clear to the less-clear. Concertation, then, may be defined as 'the sum of ideal relations of causality'. Ideal causality

> is concertation itself, and therefore is perfectly reconciled with spontaneity: ideal causality goes from the more-clear to the less-clear, but that which is more-clear in a substance is produced by that substance by virtue of its own spontaneity, and that which is less-clear in the other is likewise produced by virtue of its own spontaneity. (TF 134; trans. modified)

The *Vinculum Substantiale*

In addition to spontaneity and concertation, Deleuze proposes the existence of a third element of Leibnizian harmony, one that parallels the *basso continuo* of Baroque music: the *vinculum substantiale*, or substantial link (*vinculum*, literally 'fetter', 'chain').[3] Late in his life, Leibniz addressed the question of transubstantiation in a series of letters to Father Des Bosses, and in the process took up the question of the identity of bodies as they change through time. We humans have bodies that are more than aggregates of particles (such as buckets of sand). Our bodies are organisms, collectively organised entities, and yet they also include various organs, themselves more than aggregates. And while the components of our bodies function together as unified entities, they are routinely replaced (skin is shed and regrown, blood is lost but then replenished). The body, as Leibniz frequently expresses it, is like Theseus' ship, patched and repaired piece by piece such that the ship that docks is entirely different from the ship that set out at the voyage's beginning, and yet it is the same ship. Every monad has a body, and that body's formal unity comes from its related monad. The human body's organs are also bodies, and hence bodies with their own corresponding monads (a heart monad, a liver monad, a blood cell monad, a bile cell monad). The monad of an individual human body is a dominant monad, the monads of its components are dominated monads, and that which puts the dominant and dominated monads in relation to one another is the dominant monad's *vinculum substantiale*. Itself not a monad, the *vinculum* is a pure relation, created by God, one that produces a cooperative cohesiveness among monads, while also allowing for periodic reassemblages of monads, as some dominated monads break away from the *vinculum* and other, new monads fall under its sway. What the *vinculum* adds to Leibnizian harmony is an element of flux and variation. The *vinculum* is like the Baroque *basso continuo*, the anchoring harmonic foundation that supplies a solid tonality, yet that also makes possible a new freedom in the melodic line. The *continuo*'s subordination of inner voices secures the piece's chordal harmonic structure, thereby ensuring that the wide-ranging chromatic, intervallic, rhythmic and ornamental variations of the melody do not compromise the work's tonal logic. In a similar fashion, the *vinculum* of a given body establishes its dominant tonality, while allowing its assemblages of dominated monads to form, partially dissolve, and reform again in a flux of changing combinations.

Yet the *vinculum* effects more than links among monads. Though it is itself neither monad nor material body, and though it only links monads to monads, in its linking of a dominant monad to its dominated monads it induces a 'back-and-forth from the soul [of the dominant monad] to the body [that belongs to the dominant monad], and from bodies [that belong to the dominated monads] to souls [of the dominated monads]' (TF 120; trans. modified). Monads actualise the virtual, whereas bodies realise the possible, and the domain of actualised monads remains separate from that of realised bodies. Leibniz generally explains the alignment of monads and bodies as the result of God's pre-established harmony, but in his speculations about the *vinculum* Deleuze sees an additional principle at work, one that connects monads and bodies in a new way. The back-and-forth induced by the *vinculum* suggests that it serves an intermediary role, one that presides over the incarnation of monads. Bodies realise the possible, but that which makes them real is their animation by their attendant monads. Bodies become real as that which is actual in the monad (a given perception or affection) is realised in those bodies. 'One does not realize the body, one realizes in the body that which is actually perceived in the soul. The reality of the body is the realization of phenomena in the body. That which realizes is the fold between the two stories [i.e., the two domains of monads and bodies], the *vinculum* itself' (TF 120; trans. modified). This mysterious passage from monads to bodies, this realisation of the actual within bodies, is the principle of incarnation and creation in general, a divine principle beyond human comprehension. By interfolding monads and bodies, the *vinculum* animates matter, creating a harmony that is characteristically Baroque in its simultaneous spirituality and insistent sensuality. Because of the *vinculum*, in Leibniz

> there is not only harmony within harmony [that is, spontaneous harmony within the harmony of concertation], but harmony between the harmony and the melody. In this sense harmony goes from the soul to the body, from the intelligible to the sensible, and extends into the sensible. [. . .] It is in the melody that the harmony realizes itself. (TF 135; trans. modified)

The New Harmony

Deleuze sees many parallels between the new harmony of Baroque music and the Leibnizian harmony of spontaneity, concertation and the *vinculum substantiale*, but that analogy, though brought by Leibniz 'to a new rigor' (TF 131), by no means provides the programme for a mechanical or rigid construction of philosophical concepts. The Baroque harmonic system has an internal coherence as well as a specifically musical relationship of continuity with, development of and departure from Renaissance contrapuntal practices. Likewise, Leibniz's harmony is part of a philosophical system, with its own inner coherence and a strictly philosophical relationship to the systems of his contemporaries and predecessors. The Baroque's musical harmony of chords, tonality and *basso continuo*, its heterogeneity of styles and extremes of rhythm, its idiomatic handling of instruments and concertant-style contrast of ensembles, its free-flowing chromatic and intervallic ornamentation of melodic lines, its heteronomous, oratorical approach to the setting of texts, and its pervasive expressive sensuality – all may have their counterparts in Leibniz's thought, but the relationship among the elements differs from the musical to the philosophical system, and there is no way one could predict what role the *basso continuo* might play once one had established the role of accords/chords in the Leibnizian system. Nor could one predict what form Leibniz's thought would take based on an identification of occasionalism with Renaissance harmony, for Leibniz's response to occasionalism, though principled and systematic, is an inventive and unforeseeable transformation of the questions and terms informing occasionalism, just as Baroque tonality represents a creative and unpredictable metamorphosis of Renaissance polyphonic counterpoint.

Yet there remains a common concern in Leibniz and Baroque music, an effort to conceive of the One and the Many in a new way, to develop a model that stresses heterogeneity and differences among components, that provides for cohesiveness while admitting flux and variation, and that allows for both centripetal and centrifugal forces, thereby ensuring the internal structural integrity of the One while making possible its expansive engagement with new elements. Leibniz's philosophical response to the non-philosophy of Baroque music remains philosophical, yet his concept of harmony reverberates with the new harmony of the music of his age, especially with that music's percepts and affects, its expressiveness, its delight in extremes, its play with contrast and variation, and its incessant effort to engage the spiritual within the sensual. Leibniz and the composers of his era pursue their separate ends, but they all inhabit the world and attempt to engage that world through thought, Leibniz via a thought in concepts, the composers via a thought in sonic percepts and affects. And

Leibniz's thought in concepts and the composers' thought in sonic percepts and affects meet in a permeable membrane that forms the outside of each thought, one that affords passages from concepts to percepts and affects and back again.

The New New Harmony

Deleuze regards Leibniz's system as a last, valiant effort to sustain theological order in a rapidly disintegrating world, and in Voltaire's critique of 'the best of all possible worlds' he sees evidence of the system's demise.[4] Yet Deleuze finds much in Leibniz that is of more than historical interest. *The Fold* is not a mere exercise in the history of philosophy, for while Leibniz's system may have collapsed, its component concepts have a potential for exploitation that goes beyond his times, an 'untimely' potential that Deleuze is intent on exploring. In a parallel fashion, Deleuze discovers in the contemporary arts certain tendencies that echo Baroque artistic practices, such that he can speak of a 'new Baroque and a neo-Leibnizianism' (TF 136) in modern aesthetic practice. Those contemporary tendencies in the arts and his own philosophical explorations have in common the practice and concept of the fold within a new harmony, a harmony that is Leibnizian, but with a difference. Leibniz's world of infinite folds-within-folds, of monadic minds/spirits interfolded with matter and topological folds of reversible insides and outsides, remains a potent model, but the harmony of that world can no longer be conceived of as a unity, since our interfolded universe is not circumscribed and complete. Leibnizian monads are subject to two interrelated conditions, 'one of closure and the other of selection' (TF 137). Each monad is without doors or windows, entirely closed in upon itself, spontaneously expressing the entire world. Its spontaneous harmonic interrelationships with other monads arise from God's selection of the best world from among the infinite number of possible worlds. In our neo-Leibnizian cosmos, by contrast, the principle of selection no longer holds. Multiple possible worlds coexist, worlds that are incompossible and yet co-present. Each monad expresses a world, but not necessarily the same world, nor does a given monad express the same world from moment to moment. Hence, with the demise of the principle of selection, the principle of closure also falls away, as the monad opens on to the various divergent, incompossible worlds with which it is attuned.

> To the degree that the world is now made up of divergent series (the chaosmos), or that the throw of the dice has replaced the game of Plenitude, the monad is now unable to contain the entire world as if in a closed circle that can be modified by projection. Instead, the monad now opens itself on a trajectory or an expanding spiral that moves further and further from a center. (TF 137; trans. modified)

In *The Fold*, Deleuze offers an extended example of the ways in which a given philosopher may respond to the arts. Leibniz's pre-established harmony is analogous to the new harmony of Baroque music in many respects, but the musical analogues take on different functions in their philosophical milieu, and their transfer from the aesthetic to the conceptual sphere obeys no simple transformation rule or procedure. For Deleuze, philosophy has an internal integrity and rigour, and its thought in concepts is incommensurable with other modes of thought. Yet it also opens itself to the non-philosophical, finding counterparts to artists' thought in percepts and affects within its own conceptual field. The new harmony of the Baroque is Leibnizian, in part because Baroque composers and Leibniz operate within a similar world, attempting to think the One and the Many in new ways. Yet their musical and philosophical innovations possess an untimely potential as well, their practices and concepts capable of assuming unexpected configurations and functions in other contexts. For this reason, the history of philosophy is a vital component of contemporary philosophy, just as the history of the arts supplies invaluable inspiration for modern artistic practice. And if philosophy bears an essential relationship to the non-philosophy of the arts, that relationship is not restricted to one with the contemporary arts. The new harmony of the Baroque is as much a contributing element of Deleuze's thought as is the new new harmony of Cage, Berlioz, Stockhausen and Berio. In philosophy and in the arts, a continuing co-presence of untimely elements from both domains prevails, each with its own mode of thought, but each open to the movements of the other. Hence, at the conclusion of *The Fold*, Deleuze can say of both philosophy and the arts,

> we are all still Leibnizian, although accords no longer express our world or our text. We are discovering new ways of folding, akin to new envelopments, but we remain Leibnizian, because what always matters is folding, unfolding, refolding. (TF 137)

Notes

1. Christiane Frémont (1981), for example, says of Leibniz's use of the word 'harmony' and other musical terms that he 'makes use of these musical notions without worrying too much about their technical sense or the difficulties that they imply' (32).
2. At another point in *The Fold*, Deleuze proposes a tripartite parallel between philosophical approaches to the soul–body problem and musical conceptions of harmony. 'Leibniz likes to compare diverse concepts of the soul–body to modes of correspondence between two clocks: either influx [the soul directs the body through a direct influence], or occasion [occasionalism], or harmony (which Leibniz judged to be superior). These are the three "ages" of music: monodic, or unison [medieval music], polyphonic or counterpoint [Renaissance music], harmonic, in chords – that is, baroque' (TF 136; trans. modified). This periodisation is unfortunately obscured in the English translation of *The Fold*.
3. Deleuze bases his reading of the *vinculum substantiale* on the analyses of Frémont (1981: 31–42) and Yvon Belaval (1952: 240–53).
4. Deleuze does not offer this historical reading of Leibniz in *The Fold*, but in an interview about *The Fold* Deleuze comments: 'The relation between Leibniz and Voltaire marks a fundamental transition in the history of thought. With Voltaire, we're in the Enlightenment, that is, precisely a regime of light, of matter and of life, of Reason, completely different from the Baroque regime, even if Leibniz prepared the way for this new age: theological reason had crumbled and become purely and simply human. But the Baroque already marks a crisis in theological reason: it was a final attempt to reconstruct a world in the process of disintegrating' (N 161; trans. modified).

8

Deleuze, Mann and Modernism: Musical Becoming in *Doctor Faustus*

Thomas Mann's *Doctor Faustus* (1947) may well be the greatest novel ever written about music. Although some have questioned the depth of Mann's understanding of music, pointing to his lack of formal training in music and his status as a mere enthusiast of the art rather than a practising musician, his attention to strictly musical elements of the work's imagined compositions, his grasp of the fundamentals of the art and their relation to literature, and his sense of music's position in the history of the West in general and Germany in particular are undeniably sophisticated and, in my judgement, quite profound. In preparation for the writing of *Doctor Faustus*, Mann undertook an ambitious course of study in music theory, and during the compositional process he made use of the considerable talents of Theodor Adorno, an accomplished musician and formidable philosopher, to fashion the musical sections of the work. Detractors of Mann's achievement have suggested that Adorno's importance is so great that he should be given equal credit for the novel, but for anyone who has attempted to fathom the complexities of Adorno's difficult essays on music, Mann's lucid presentation of the musical elements of *Doctor Faustus*, whatever their source, must be viewed as a victory in itself. That he is then able to integrate such musical materials within a moving and complex narrative is surely one of the great triumphs of the literary imagination.

Undoubtedly, the most significant of *Doctor Faustus*'s imaginary musical works are *Apocalipsis cum figuris* and *The Lamentation of Doctor Faustus*, the last major compositions of Adrian Leverkühn, the novel's protagonist. The two works are presented as masterpieces of atonal music that voice the torment of modernism's struggle to reconcile an ascetic, intellectual rigour and a fascination with the mystical demonic. Notable in *Apocalipsis cum figuris* are experimental elements that Mann sees as representative of a dangerous tendency within modernism towards decadence, barbarism and animality. Some of those elements are honed, perfected and brought to an even greater level of intensity in *The Lamentation*, the result being a 'breakthrough' (Mann 1997: 509) that allows Leverkühn to transcend the perilous practices of the *Apocalipsis* and discover a way beyond the impasses of modernism. When approached through the aesthetics of Deleuze and Guattari, however, these same elements in the *Apocalipsis*, so decried by Mann, emerge as positive components of a general musical 'becoming-other', whereas the breakthrough practices of *The Lamentation* assume the guise of a negative betrayal of the potential created in the earlier work. Although Mann makes no simple equation of atonal music and Nazism, he does suggest that loose parallels exist between the cold detachment and demonic expressivity of musical modernism and the cynical, calculating rationality and cruel barbarity of Nazi politics and ideology. Some have criticised Deleuze and Guattari's philosophy, especially as articulated in *Anti-Oedipus*, as promoting a politics of libidinal fascism. Such critiques, however, are based on the same assumptions that underlie Mann's critique of musical modernism, assumptions that are antithetical to the concept of becoming as a mode of aesthetic and political invention. When viewed from the perspective of Deleuze–Guattarian becoming, Leverkühn's *Apocalypsis cum figuris*, finally, may be regarded as a model for musical innovation and creative activity in general, unlike *The Lamentation*, which represents a limited practice, and possibly a musical dead end.

Music and Literature

Doctor Faustus purports to be the biography of the fictional German composer Adrian Leverkühn, as told by Serenus Zeitblom, his lifelong friend. The novel follows two narrative lines. The first details the life of Leverkühn, from his birth in 1885, through his early education, his gradual decision to abandon the study of theology for music, his contraction of syphilis at a house of prostitution in 1906, his ascent as a composer, culminating in the production of his masterpieces *Apocalipsis cum figuris* in 1919 and *The Lamentation of Doctor Faustus* in 1930, to his collapse into madness that same year and his death in 1940. (The parallels between Leverkühn's and Nietzsche's lives are deliberate.) Zeitblom writes the biography from May 1943 to April 1945, interspersing his narrative of the composer's career with comments on the declining fortunes of Germany during World War II and his own anguished responses to the evils perpetrated by his country.

Zeitblom is a classical philologist and staunch defender of culture, learning, the arts and the values of what he calls the era of 'bourgeois humanism' (Mann 1997: 372), stretching from the end of the Middle Ages to the outbreak of World War I. In his enthusiasm for 'ancient languages and their classical poets and writers' (Mann 1997: 49), Zeitblom savours

> that inner and almost mysterious bond between [. . .] classical philology and a lively and loving eye for man's beauty and the dignity of his reason – a bond made manifest in the very name we give the study of ancient languages, the 'humanities', whereby the psychological connection between linguistic and human passion is crowned by the idea of pedagogy. (Mann 1997: 11)

He claims that one may teach the exact sciences, of course, but never as a true pedagogue, and the same may be said of music:

> And it seems to me that that other, perhaps even more internal and yet strangely inarticulate language, the language of tones (if one may call music that) cannot be included, either, in the pedagogic, humanistic sphere, though I am well aware that music played an ancillary role in Greek education and in the public life of the *polis* generally. It seems to me, however, that despite the logical, moral rigor music may appear to display, it belongs to a world of spirits, for whose absolute reliability in

> matters of human reason and dignity I would not exactly want to put my hand in the fire. (Mann 1997: 11)

Language, literature and the humanities, then, are fundamentally different from music and the sciences, if only as the pursuits responsible for cultural pedagogy. Music may be a language, but it is a 'strangely inarticulate language' and one that lacks 'reliability in matters of human reason'.

Zeitblom, like Leverkühn, sees music as an art allied in complex ways with mathematics, theology and the experimental sciences. Zeitblom notes that mathematics, 'as applied logic, which nevertheless stays within pure and lofty abstraction, holds a curious intermediate position between the humanistic and the realistic sciences' (Mann 1997: 50). In its abstraction, music belongs to the theological realm, as Leverkühn suggests in his remark to Zeitblom that music is ordered relationship and that 'Studying ordered relationships is ultimately the best there is. Order is everything. Romans thirteen: "For what is of God is ordered"' (Mann 1997: 50). Music has an 'inherent lack of sensuality', according to Leverkühn's mentor, Kretzschmar, and hence 'a secret bias toward asceticism' (Mann 1997: 67). Music '*per se*, music as pure abstraction', Kretzschmar asserts, may have as its 'deepest desire not to be heard at all, not even seen, not even felt, but, if that were possible, to be perceived and viewed in some intellectually pure fashion, in some realm beyond the senses, beyond the heart even' (Mann 1997: 68).

Music, then, as Leverkühn remarks, '"has always seemed a magical union of theology and the fine sport of mathematics"' (Mann 1997: 140). Its alliance with theology, however, makes Zeitblom uneasy. He views religion as 'the feeling and taste for the infinite' (Mann 1997: 97), and as such a subject of study better left to 'our sense of piety, to the fine arts, to free contemplation, indeed to exact research as well' (Mann 1997: 98) than to formal theological argumentation. Yet Zeitblom knows that religion has always been, and will continue to be, a subject of logical disquisition, and 'in all ages theology has willy-nilly let itself be influenced by the scientific currents of its era' (Mann 1997: 98). In the Renaissance and the Enlightenment, this gave rise to 'liberal theology', which

Zeitblom regards as an oxymoronic fusion of the rational and that which defies rational comprehension. Such a theology is 'cultured, but shallow' (Mann 1997: 99), in that it ignores the mysterious and darker sides of human experience. He notes that nineteenth-century theology has seen 'the infiltration of theological thought by irrational currents within philosophy, in whose domain the nontheoretical, the vital, the will or instinct – in short, once again, the demonic – had long since become a major theoretical issue' (Mann 1997: 99). But if such thought is less shallow than liberal theology, it is also something the 'civilized human mind' cannot help but sense as 'uncanny'. 'For by its very nature, theology, once it is linked with the spirit of Life Philosophy, with irrationalism, runs the risk of becoming demonology' (Mann 1997: 99).

Zeitblom also finds this alliance of theological thought with the irrational in the natural sciences. When Leverkühn and Zeitblom were children, Leverkühn's father liked to entertain them with scientific demonstrations, which, says Zeitblom, 'always moved along one particular path, that is the mystical or intuitive semi-mystical, down which, it seems to me, human thought is almost inevitably led when in pursuit of the natural world' (Mann 1997: 20). Zeitblom finds the natural world 'eerie' (Mann 1997: 20) and ultimately demonic, for which reason Zeitblom later develops a 'lack of interest, bordering on distaste, for the pranks and mysteries of natural phenomena, for "nature" in general', and a 'devotion to the sphere of humane letters' (Mann 1997: 285). The natural sciences inevitably lead thought into mysticism, but they also do so through an engagement with the world of the senses, and in this regard they resemble music. Although music has an 'inherent lack of sensuality' (Mann 1997: 67), it nonetheless cannot exist independently of the senses and material reality. According to Leverkühn, the purpose of rigid order in musical composition is to induce a 'chilling effect' in a work, since 'music has so much warmth of its own – like a cow stall, bovine warmth, one might say' (Mann 1997: 76). Music 'always does prior penance for its sensual realization', and its 'rigor, or what you might call the moralism of its form, must serve as the excuse for the bewitchments of its actual sound' (Mann 1997: 76). Music, thus, is open to the allure of the mystical, but also to the bewitching, animal warmth of sensuality. If, as Zeitblom asserts, the domain of the demonic is that of 'the nontheoretical, the vital, the will or instinct' (Mann 1997: 99), then clearly music, like the natural sciences, has affinities with the demonic. And if, as Leverkühn claims, music is 'energetic will, energetic will *per se* – not as an idea, but in its reality', and 'this is almost a definition of God' (Mann 1997: 87), then theology, too, partakes of that same demonic domain, one that is at once elemental and mystical.

If music and literature meet at any point, it is in the voice. Language, after all, has a sonic dimension, and hence an inherent musicality. In its oral enunciation, language is embodied, rendered sensual, and imbued with emotional and affective nuance. For Leverkühn, music's sensuality is most evident in 'the resonating breath of the human voice, which probably has the most bovine warmth of any sounding board imaginable' (Mann 1997: 76). The human voice may be abstract, he claims, 'the abstracted human being, if you like. But it is an abstraction in about the same way as the naked body is abstract – it's practically genitalia' (Mann 1997: 76). In this sense music is a concrete abstraction, an essence of sensuality and sexuality manifest in matter, just as, in Leverkühn's words, music may be regarded as 'energetic will *per se* – not as an idea, but in its reality' (Mann 1997: 87). In Leverkühn's view, music and speech 'belonged together, were ultimately one – language was music, music a language' (Mann 1997: 174). Zeitblom does not contradict Leverkühn when he makes this observation, but he clearly sees the music–language relationship as more problematic than does Leverkühn. Perhaps music is a language, but to Zeitblom it is a 'strangely inarticulate language, the language of tones' (Mann 1997: 11), and thus outside the domain of the humanities. Zeitblom distrusts music, yet loves it, a position that he recognises as paradoxical: 'That I am nevertheless devoted to it with all my heart is one of those contradictions which, whether a cause for joy or regret, are inseparable from human nature' (Mann 1997: 11). Perhaps that essential contradiction stems from the human voice, at once the vehicle of linguistic enunciation and musical expressivity.

Apocalipsis cum figuris

Zeitblom deeply admires Leverkühn's music, yet finds in his works disturbing tendencies that Zeitblom regards as symptomatic of a general malaise within modernism. The problem facing the modern composer is that the possibilities of tonal music have been exhausted traditional forms seem clichéd, expressive devices empty and insincere. The bond between art and world has been shattered, and as a result the complete work of art as analogue of a social totality is no longer viable. To move beyond this impasse, Leverkühn develops an atonal approach to composition whose outlines are roughly similar to those of Schoenberg's twelve-tone method. Leverkühn aspires not only to invent the vocabulary of a renewed polyphony but also to enable the formation of a genuine community of artist and audience. Zeitblom, however, discerns a cold rationality in the composer's calculated manipulation of twelve-tone rows, one that ultimately denies freedom and agency. And in Leverkühn's revival of Renaissance and medieval forms and techniques, as well as his experimental violations of musical conventions, Zeitblom sees not the creation of a new community but the activation of the barbaric forces of the demonic.

The composition that Zeitblom presents as the best example of Leverkühn's tendency towards 'bloody barbarism and bloodless intellectuality' (Mann 1997: 393) is his 1919 oratorio, *Apocalipsis cum figuris* (Apocalypse with pictures). Loosely based on Dürer's 1498 series of fifteen woodcuts of the same name, the *Apocalipsis cum figuris* incorporates texts from various sources, including the Revelation of St John of Patmos, the fourth-century *Vision of St Paul*, the writings of the Venerable Bede, Mechtild of Magdeburg and Hildegard of Bingen, and Dante's *Inferno*, the end result being 'a new apocalypse of [Leverkühn's] own, a résumé in some sense of all previous proclamations of the end', a 'descent into hell, into which visionary power has worked the images of the beyond from both earlier, shamanistic levels and those of antiquity and Christendom, on up to Dante' (Mann 1997: 377). According to Zeitblom, the work is written in 'a compositional style subject to the strictest laws of intellectual and technical complexity' (Mann 1997: 378). The oratorio is clearly atonal, although its technique apparently is that of a 'free atonality', rather than a strictly Schoenberg-like row methodology, since it subsumes both tonal and atonal materials within its general design, the entire work governed by the paradox 'that its dissonance is the expression of everything that is lofty, serious, devout, and spiritual, while the harmonic and tonal elements are restricted to the world of hell or, in this context, to a world of banality and platitudes' (Mann 1997: 394). Leverkühn offers 'parodies of diverse musical styles', including 'burlesqued French impressionism, bourgeois drawing-room music, Tchaikovsky, music hall songs, the syncopations and rhythmic somersaults of jazz', yet 'always sustained by the main orchestra, speaking its serious, dark, difficult language and asserting with radical rigor the work's intellectual status' (Mann 1997: 395).

These are what Zeitblom regards as the oratorio's broad characteristics, which it shares with other works of Leverkühn. Its more specific features, however, are found only in this composition, and it is here that any reader familiar with the works of Deleuze and Guattari must be struck, for they bear a remarkable resemblance to the elements of musical 'becoming-other' that Deleuze and Guattari discuss in *A Thousand Plateaus* and other texts.[1] (The resemblances may well be more than fortuitous, given the fact that Deleuze and Guattari briefly cite *Doctor Faustus* – without specific textual attribution – at one point in their discussion [ATP 97].) First, Leverkühn's *Apocalipsis* makes frequent use of the glissando, a musical device in which Zeitblom has 'always tended to hear something anticultural, indeed anti-human, even demonic' (Mann 1997: 393). In Zeitblom's analysis, music begins when humans 'wrest from chaos a system of tones' and 'assign individual notes to song – which originally among primitive humans must have been a howl that glided over several pitches' (Mann 1997: 393). Hence, the glissando for him is 'a barbaric rudiment of premusical days' (Mann 1997: 393). Deleuze and Guattari also observe the disturbing effects of the glissando's dissolution of individual pitch differentiations, but they see in this device a positive means of activating a virtual line of continuous variation immanent within musical material. The glissando's sliding sounds create zones of indiscernibility, passages of becoming, and, if extended, the device discloses 'the plane of a generalized "glissando" implying the constitution of a statistical space in which each variable has, not an average value, but a probability of frequency that places it in continuous variation with the other variables' (ATP 96). Deleuze and Guattari cite pieces by Berio and Schnebel as creative uses of a generalised glissando, arguing as well that *Sprechgesang*, *parlando* and other uses of the voice to create indiscernible passages across a continuum from speech to singing are extensions of the principle of the glissando. Not surprisingly, in Leverkühn's *Apocalipsis* we find

> ensembles that begin as speaking choruses and only by stages, by way of the oddest transitions, arrive at the richest vocal music; choruses, that is, that move through all the shades of graduated whispering, antiphonal speech, and quasi-chant on up to the most polyphonic song – accompanied by sounds that begin as simple noise, as magical, fanatical African drums and booming gongs, only to attain the highest music. (Mann 1997: 392–3)

And, at the conclusion of the first part of the oratorio, we hear another continuum of sonic becoming, a 'pandemonium of laughter', in which 'the giggle of a single voice' gradually gives way 'to a dreadful mayhem of yowls, yelps, screeches, bleats, bellows, howls, and whinnies, to the mocking, triumphant laughter of hell' (Mann 1997: 397).

The apocalyptic oratorio also elides gender distinctions in its treatment of the voice, as well as distinctions between the human voice and non-human instruments. The narrator of the oratorio, a role 'traditionally given to a tenor, is also written here for a male voice, but one almost in the range of a castrato, whose cold, reporterlike, matter-of-fact crowings stand in horrible contrast to the contents of his catastrophic message' (Mann 1997: 396). (Zeitblom notes that in the oratorio's premier performance, 'the role was sung in masterly fashion by a eunuchoid tenor named Erbe' [Mann 1997: 396].) The merging of voice and instrument is found in the role of the whore of Babylon, which is assigned 'to the most graceful coloratura soprano, and her virtuoso runs are at times so completely like a flute that they melt into the orchestra' (Mann 1997: 394). Conversely, the instruments often mime human voices: 'variously muted trumpets imitate the most grotesque vox humana – as does the saxophone as well' (Mann 1997: 394–5). (Admittedly, the vox humana is an organ stop, but that stop, as its name implies, is designed to imitate the human voice, and it is not certain whether Zeitblom is referring to the organ stop or simply displaying witty erudition in likening the trumpets and saxophone to human voices.) This elision of gender and material distinctions Zeitblom regards with alarm, but Deleuze and Guattari see the practice as a creative 'machining of the voice' (ATP 303). In their discussion of Dominique Fernandez's eccentric book on the disappearance of the castrato in opera and the subsequent partitioning of voices by gender, Deleuze and Guattari treat the castrato as an instance of the becoming-woman and becoming-child of the voice. In the castrato, it is not a question of 'imitating a woman or a child', but of deterritorialising the voice, such that it becomes 'unengendered' (ATP 304). And although Deleuze and Guattari agree with Fernandez that in Verdi and Wagner one can find a treatment of the voice that accentuates the differences between male and female voices, they argue that a compensatory tendency is activated in their works, whereby voice and instruments become increasingly indiscernible. Such practices represent a 'new threshold of deterritorialization of the voice', 'no longer that of a properly vocal becoming-woman or becoming-child, but that of a becoming-molecular in which the voice itself is instrumentalized' (ATP 308). This becoming-molecular they see as the guiding principle of modern music, especially evident in Varèse and Messiaen, whose works manifest in sound the molecular's 'capacity to make the *elementary* communicate with the *cosmic*' (ATP 308). One aspect of this molecular capacity which they discern in modern music is its exploitation of electronic media – something, we should note, that Leverkühn also employs, loudspeakers being used in his oratorio 'to produce directional and acoustic gradations that had never been achieved before' (Mann 1997: 396).

Zeitblom finds the oratorio's 'bloodless intellectuality' disquieting, but what disturbs him most is its 'bloody barbarism' (Mann

1997: 393). Zeitblom holds the traditional view that nature is opposed to culture, and that the rational order of culture is fashioned through the domination of irrational human nature, which he associates with 'the nontheoretical, the vital, the will, or instinct – in short, once again, the demonic' (Mann 1997: 99). The irrational cannot be eradicated, but it must be controlled hence Zeitblom's definition of culture as 'the reverent, orderly, I may even say, propitiatory inclusion of the nocturnal and monstrous in the cult of the gods' (Mann 1997: 12). Music's origin is paradigmatic of the formation of culture. '[T]he earliest achievement of the art of music', says Zeitblom, 'was to separate sound from nature, to wrest from chaos a system of tones, and to assign individual notes to song – which originally among primitive humans must have been a howl that glided over several pitches' (Mann 1997: 393). For this reason, the glissando is ultimately 'anticultural, indeed anti-human, even demonic' (Mann 1997: 393), as are the other devices of musical becoming that Leverkühn employs.

The Lamentation of Doctor Faustus

But the *Apocalipsis* is not Leverkühn's final work, nor is it his greatest achievement, according to Zeitblom. Between the composition of the *Apocalipsis* in 1919 and the completion of his last work, *The Lamentation of Doctor Faustus*, in 1930, Leverkühn finds a means of realising his long-held ambition – that of creating music in an absolutely 'strict style' involving 'the total integration of all musical dimensions' (Mann 1997: 205), such that 'free notes would no longer exist' (Mann 1997: 205). Leverkühn's means of realising his ambition is that of a Schoenberg-like twelve-tone row method of composition. During those same years of 1919 through 1930, while developing his twelve-tone technique, Leverkühn also suffers his greatest personal loss: the death of Nepomuk, nicknamed 'Echo', an innocent child who suffers excruciating and prolonged pain before succumbing to cerebrospinal meningitis. Echo is one of the few individuals Leverkühn has genuinely loved, and the demise of the child instils in Leverkühn utter despair and a dark vision of the cosmos. It is in *The Lamentation* that Leverkühn gives full expression to his grief at Echo's death within the language of his new-found dodecaphonic 'strict style'.

In the *Apocalipsis*, Leverkühn had concluded part one with a chorus of 'hellish laughter', and then opened part two with 'the totally strange and wonderful children's chorus [. . .] whose sound is so sweet, might I say, so inaccessibly alien and superterrestrial that it fills the heart with hopeless longing' (Mann 1997: 397). The utter contrast between the two sections, however, is only superficial, for as Zeitblom realises, 'in its musical substance', the children's chorus 'is, for him who has ears to hear and eyes to see, a reprise of the Devil's laughter' (Mann 1997: 397). The technique that in the *Apocalipsis* generates 'the inner sameness of its children's angelic chorus and hell's laughter' (Mann 1997: 511) Zeitblom later finds extended to the entirety of *The Lamentation of Doctor Faustus*. What is realised in the *Apocalipsis*, he says, 'is a formal utopia of terrifying ingenuity, which now becomes universal in the *Faust* cantata, taking possession of the entire work and allowing it, if I may put it that way, to be totally consumed by its thematic element' (Mann 1997: 511). Early in the novel, Kretzschmar had established an opposition between 'harmonic subjectivity' and 'objective polyphony' (Mann 1997: 57) that Zeitblom and Leverkühn had both come to embrace, and in *The Lamentation* Zeitblom sees a reconciliation of the seemingly antithetical elements of subjective expressivity and objective contrapuntal order. In Zeitblom's presentation of Western music history, the rise of harmonic music in the late seventeenth and eighteenth centuries, in which the melody and bass line take precedence over the other voices, eventually reaching the point that inner voices function primarily as simple chord accompaniments, represents an increased emphasis on the expressive and the individualistic in music. That harmonic system is a departure from the genuine polyphony of Renaissance compositions, in which all voices have equal importance. The movement from Renaissance polyphony to eighteenth- and nineteenth-century harmonic expressivity is paralleled by an increasing separation of music from ritual and religious functions, this growing secularisation being identified by Zeitblom as a movement from a 'cultic' to a 'cultural' epoch (Mann 1997: 65), from traditional communalism to bourgeois individualism. Paradoxically, it would seem, Leverkühn's *Lamentation*, says Zeitblom, 'this, his strictest work, a work of utmost calculation, is simultaneously purely expressive' (Mann 1997: 512).

Zeitblom's explanation of this paradox is that in this 'formal arrangement of ultimate rigor that knows nothing that is unthematic', in which 'free notes no longer exist', the music 'can now unfold outside all restraints – that is to say, abandon itself to expression' (Mann 1997: 512). *The Lamentation* is the product of 'the dialectic process by which strictest constraint is reversed into the free language of emotion, by which freedom is born out of constraint' (Mann 1997: 510). What is liberated by such constraint is expressivity. The essence of expressivity, Zeitblom claims, is to be found in the lament, and *The Lamentation* is one 'gigantic *lamento*' (Mann 1997: 511). The lament 'is expression *per se*, one might boldly say that all expression is in fact lament' (Mann 1997: 510). '[T]he expression of lament', Zeitblom adds, is 'expression in its first and primal manifestation' (Mann 1997: 512). Zeitblom's implicit argument, though never directly articulated, is that the personal, emotional dimension of music arises through the human consciousness of death and the experience of mourning. The lament is 'the expressive cry of the soul' (Mann 1997: 509–10), and as a primal element in music it marks the emergence of organised musical sound from the chaos of spontaneous noise emitted by human animals, a noise 'which originally among primitive humans must have been a howl that glided over several pitches' (Mann 1997: 393). The universal nature of the lament's expressivity allows its articulation in all voices of a composition, and hence expression can exist in a work of the strictest polyphony, such as *The Lamentation*. Although expressivity is always individual, 'there are no solos in *Faustus*' (Mann 1997: 512), the individual expression of lament being subsumed within the universal polyphony of *The Lamentation*'s strict order. The result is an essence of lament, 'and as such, negatively related to the finale of the Ninth Symphony [of Beethoven] with its variations on jubilation' (Mann 1997: 511), a renunciation of the Ode to Joy, a 'proudly despairing "No!" spoken against false and flabby bourgeois piety' (Mann 1997: 515). Yet in this despair Zeitblom discovers one final paradox: from this essence of lament, this 'irredeemable despair', emerges 'hope beyond hopelessness, the transcendence of despair', 'a light in the night' (Mann 1997: 512).

For Zeitblom, *The Lamentation* is a 'breakthrough' that transcends the 'bloody barbarism and bloodless intellectuality' (Mann 1997: 393) of the *Apocalipsis*. The barbarism of the *Apocalipsis* resides in such elements as its prehuman howls, its confusions of laughter, weeping, speech, and song, its mixtures of high art and popular entertainment, and its periodic interjections of primitive, non-Western musical idioms. That barbarism is reinforced by the work's cold intellectuality, which manifests itself in Leverkühn's pastiche of styles and the parodic detachment with which he mocks traditional tonal devices. Early in his career, Leverkühn exclaims, 'Why must almost everything appear to me as its own parody? Why must it seem to me as if almost all, no, all the means and contrivances of art nowadays are good only for parody?' (Mann 1997: 143). In his various compositions from that early moment through the *Apocalipsis*, a thorough-going parodic sensibility informs his style. In *The Lamentation*, however, the extreme discipline of the twelve-tone method purges the work of all parody, all popular idioms and all non-Western elements. The barbarism of the prehuman gives way to the primal human expressivity of lament, an emotional freedom paradoxically made possible through the formal constraints of the twelve-tone row. And in the polyphonic manifestation of individual lament within each of the voices, a new collectivity is discovered.

From the perspective of Deleuze and Guattari, *The Lamentation* seems a much less transcendent achievement than Zeitblom claims. There is nothing wrong with exploring the possibilities of the twelve-tone row, but it represents only one way of renewing Western music, and Zeitblom's implicit praise of strict serial composition is that it rejects several lines of development that Deleuze and Guattari would no doubt find promising. The danger of the serial technique is that it can lead to a hermetic elitism, and that its rigours can limit invention to the exploitation of fixed, finite permutations within a closed system. There is little to suggest that the constraints of the serial method represent a genuine breakthrough rather than a temporary escape from traditional tonality that may soon lead to academic stagnation. Even more suspect than the exclusive triumph of *The Lamentation*'s formal method, however, is the explanation Zeitblom offers for the work's success. Zeitblom frames the work as a reconciliation of expressive subjectivity and polyphonic objectivity, achieved through 'the dialectic process by which strictest constraint is reversed into the free language of emotion' (Mann 1997: 510). What kind of dialectic this process may be, whether Hegelian or otherwise, is not specified, but it implies a transcendence of contradictions, limited in number and generated within a closed historical tradition. Deleuze and Guattari's philosophy is decidedly anti-Hegelian, stressing difference as a generative, mutative force antecedent to the formation of any full-fledged contradictions. The object in Deleuze and Guattari's thought is not to overcome given contradictions, but to exploit multiple differences that are immanent within a situation, though unrecognised in dominant conceptualisations of that situation. From this perspective, the *Apocalipsis*, with its heterogeneous disruptions of musical conventions, represents a much more promising source of future invention than *The Lamentation*. The rigours of *The Lamentation*'s method are designed to overcome the contradictions of an unavoidable historical impasse, whereas in fact its dilemma is a function of the narrow range of possibilities this conception of Western art music's history and development makes available. *The Lamentation*'s expressivity, in turn, exploits a negative, life-denying mentality, one in which primal emotion is found in a universal 'being unto death', the source of all expressivity. *The Lamentation* counters the Ode to Joy, and though Deleuze and Guattari would join Zeitblom in rejecting the 'false and flabby bourgeois piety' (Mann 1997: 515) often associated with Beethoven's Ninth, they would not reject all joy and celebrate instead human mortality and loss. Paramount in Deleuze and Guattari's thought is the embrace of a Spinozistic joy and a Nietzschean affirmation of life, an affirmation of affirmation that runs counter to the Hegelian negation of negation and the nihilistic being unto death. Rather than loss and the absence of death, Deleuze seeks modes of invention that stress the active forces of life.

Music and Nazism

Although Mann nowhere makes explicit the precise parallels he is drawing between aesthetics and politics in his novel, he clearly suggests that Leverkühn's *Apocalipsis* is informed by principles similar to those that shaped fascism, even if those principles have markedly different results, especially from an ethical standpoint, in the separate spheres of politics and music. (Less certain are the political parallels to be drawn to *The Lamentation*, which for Mann may represent a solution to the dilemma posed in the *Apocalipsis* that is without a counterpart in the realm of politics.[2]) The 'bloody barbarism' of the *Apocalipsis* has as its political counterpart the Nazi racial and national ideology of blood, soil and will, a form of 'naturalistic atavism' (Mann 1997: 393) that overwhelms humanist culture with a cultic celebration of demonic energy and desire. The 'bloodless intellectuality' of the *Apocalipsis* perhaps corresponds to the disciplinary order of the repressive Nazi state and the cynical, cold efficiency of its death machine. More important, however, are the mystical tendencies behind this intellectuality, tendencies that reinforce the irrational forces of barbarism. Music's mysterious elements, in Zeitblom's analysis, ally it to theology and natural science. Zeitblom describes religion as 'the feeling and taste for the infinite' (Mann 1997: 97), and music, in its religious guise, is, in Leverkühn's words, 'energetic will *per* se – not as an idea, but in its reality', and 'this is almost a definition of God' (Mann 1997: 87). In its alliance with natural science, music furthers a mystical affirmation of the demonic infinite within the material world. What brings bloody barbarism and bloodless intellectuality together, then, is a celebration of will and the demonic, at once ethereally detached and sensually engaged, and this coincidence of mysticism and barbarism informs both the *Apocalipsis* and Nazism.

If one were to accept the terms of Mann's analysis, one might well conclude that the musical becoming advocated by Deleuze and Guattari is as misguided as that of Adrian Leverkühn in the *Apocalipsis*. And, indeed, some have argued that Deleuze and Guattari are simply promoting a rehash of Schopenhauer, Nietzsche and Marinetti that is as dangerously fascistic now as it was in the first half of the twentieth century.[3] Such an identification of Deleuze and Guattari's musical becoming as proto-Nazism, however, is indefensible. The Nazi ideology of blood and soil seeks a fixed identity, one grounded in an essential biological, racial 'Germanness', which itself has permanent bonds to a traditional, primeval territory. Far from affirming dynamic processes of metamorphosis, as do Deleuze and Guattari, Nazi apologists oppose all forces of 'becoming-other', especially the forces of racial impurity and territorial usurpation. The Nazi celebration of the will, too, has no parallel in Deleuze and Guattari's thought. The Nazis' appropriation of Nietzsche's will to power, in Deleuze's analysis, is a perversion of Nietzsche's thought. In Deleuze's reading, the affirmative will to power is an affirmation of metamorphosis, a will to expand one's powers of affecting *and being affected by* other entities. The Nazi 'triumph of the will', by contrast, is a negative will to power *over others*, and, as a result, a will to resist outside influences. It is essentially a reactive will that opposes any becoming-other – indeed, a will that aims at the complete domination of the other and its mutative force. Deleuze and Guattari do indeed stress music's inextricable connections with our biological existence within a material environment, but never in the service of racial, national or territorial identities. And, although they second Nietzsche's call for an art and a way of life that affirm metamorphosis, they never embrace an irrational mysticism of power and domination.

But one might also use Deleuze and Guattari to critique Mann's analysis and to show that Leverkühn's apocalyptic oratorio, rather than representing the dead and dangerous end of modernism, suggests creative paths for the future development of music. For Deleuze and Guattari, music is not structured by any clear-cut divide between nature and culture, or the rational and the irrational. Deleuze and Guattari characterise music as the 'creative, active operation that consists in deterritorializing the refrain' (ATP 300). The refrain is Deleuze and Guattari's term for any rhythmic pattern that organises an environmental system. According to this definition, a bird in its habitat may be characterised in terms of a multitude of refrains, including those of: the bird's developmental trajectory from gestation through maturation to its death; the regular movements of the bird as it forages, mates and interacts with conspecifics; the developmental trajectories and movements of surrounding conspecifics, as well as those of other species with which the bird interacts (predators, prey, symbionts); ambient climatic patterns, rhythms of plant growth, cycles of microbial florescence; and so on. Within this network of refrains, the bird's song constitutes an additional refrain, one that is emergent within its lifeworld, and thus, though distinguishable from the other refrains, ultimately inseparable from its world. Likewise, human music emerges from the refrains of a human lifeworld, gaining relative autonomy as it 'deterritorialises' the refrains that constitute a given environment. What Deleuze and Guattari mean by the musical deterritorialising of refrains is that music engages the surrounding patterns of a lifeworld, extracts them from their context, and thereby detaches them or 'decodes' them, and then gives them a new function within the self-referential system of a given musical language. As an illustration of this process of 'deterritorialising' a natural refrain, Deleuze and Guattari offer the instance of Olivier Messiaen, who employs birdsongs in may of his compositions.[4] Messiaen claims to reproduce birdsongs in his music with absolute fidelity; however, he adds that the tempi of the birdsongs must be slowed to a human speed, their micro-intervals must be stretched to fit a chromatic scale, and their timbres must be rendered in complex chords and combinations of instruments. The end result, he confesses, is a rendering of birdsong that few ornithologists would be able to recognise, and it is this resultant product that Messiaen then combines with other rhythmic, melodic and harmonic elements within his compositions to form a coherent work of art. In Deleuze and Guattari's terms, Messiaen has 'deterritorialised' the birdsong, subjected it to a mutative 'becoming-other', and 'reterritorialised' it within a musical composition. Although Messiaen's handling of the refrains of birdsong may seem idiosyncratic, Deleuze and Guattari insist that it is paradigmatic of the art of music as a whole.

For Deleuze and Guattari, refrains come into existence as regularised, relatively fixed patterns emergent within zones of variation, continuums of flux and modulation. These zones of variation, flux and modulation remain immanent within each refrain.

The refrain 'territorialises' the metamorphic variations, restricting and regulating them, but the potential for destabilising the refrain, or 'deterritorialising' it, continues to play through the refrain. When the potential of this deterritorialising force is activated, a process of 'becoming-other' is inaugurated, a process that may lead to the formation of new, unforeseeable and unpredictable refrains. In musical terms, what this means is that immanent within the chromatic scale of Western art music is a continuum of sonic material in continuous variation, and that the exploitation of the glissando is an activation of that continuum and the instigation of a 'becoming-other' of the intervallic system. Likewise, a zone of variation includes male and female voices in a single continuum that the composer may exploit in a 'becoming-other' of gendered voices; another zone of indiscernibility allows a 'becoming-other' among voices and instruments; a third continuum traverses wails, cries, laughter, speech and song, which may give rise to yet another 'becoming-other' of these expressive components; and so on.

Also, immanent within all zones and continuums of variation and the refrains that organise them is a primal affectivity, which is present in all natural entities and determinable through their relative powers of affecting and being affected by other entities. This primal affectivity is manifest in diverse forms of perception, emotion, behaviour, cognition and so on, each particular manifestation of that affectivity being characteristic of a given organism. In this view, therefore, no radical distinction may be maintained between the various degrees of inner experience that in a given creature may range from sensate responses to the most abstract cogitation. In Deleuze and Guattari's view, then, any analysis that predicates a qualitative opposition between emotion and reason, such as Zeitblom posits in his characterisations of music, is misguided. Just as the human lifeworld emerges within and is inseparable from the lifeworlds of other natural organisms, and the productions of human culture are themselves inseparable from the larger lifeworld of human beings, so too the most elevated of intellectual activities, such as composing and performing music, can never be separated from the affective forces that play through humans and their surrounding environment.

Hence, processes of deterritorialisation and reterritorialisation

– those of stratification and destratification, fixing and unfixing, coding and decoding – are constantly at work in our world. The immanent lines of deterritorialisation within material, social and mental structures provide modes of invention that are not exclusively rational or irrational, and they are operative to varying degrees in all such structures. Human culture is not separate from but emergent within nature; it is a specific dynamic configuration of de- and reterritorialising forces embedded in a cosmic lifeworld. Musical deterritorialisation modifies refrains, transforms them, but does not radically separate them from the natural world, since the materials of the musical composition are organised, or reterritorialised, within the work, which itself participates in the play of forces within the world. The lines of musical deterritorialisation are paths of becoming, and Deleuze and Guattari recognise the dangers of activating virtual processes of becoming. Those dangers, however, cannot be escaped by avoiding all becoming – in fact, such an effort would be impossible. The dangers are related to speed and contagion. Deterritorialisation can proceed too rapidly, everywhere and all at once, the result being a suicidal rush into a black hole. This is the apocalyptic becoming of addiction, terrorism, the suicidal state and so on. Deterritorialisation can also become cancerous, as specific sites of repressive organization multiply and choke out competing structures and processes. Such becoming gives rise to what they call the fascist Body without Organs.[5] Thus, the horrors of the Nazi state, according to Deleuze and Guattari, are a matter of destructive speeds and cancerous contagion, the Nazi death machine being an all-consuming black hole and the myths of blood, soil and will being manifestations of an ever-spreading ideological metastasis.

Leverkühn's oratorio is open to the dangerous forces of apocalyptic, suicidal becoming and cancerous, fascistic becoming, and perhaps Zeitblom is right to fear those forces. But such forces need not lead to destruction or barbaric repression. If treated with caution, they may foster new forms, processes and relations. The oratorio's uses of the voice, its becoming-woman, becoming-child and becoming-molecular, offer possibilities for the transformation of vocal music. Its animalistic elements disclose the existence of paths like that taken by Messiaen, who incorporates motifs from birdsongs and sonic landscapes into his compositions. The so-called 'primitive' components of the oratorio, its 'magical, fanatical African drums and booming gongs' (Mann 1997: 393), far from undermining culture, open Western art music to the musics of diverse non-Western cultures, with their complex rhythms, micro-tone scales, subtle timbres and alternate practices. And Leverkühn's parodies of popular musical form – especially jazz – might well lead not to mockery but to the renewal of Western art music via an appropriation of alternative ways of music making. Perhaps Leverkühn's oratorio is excessive, in that it exploits all these modes of becoming at the same time, but if explored with caution, if activated selectively and slowly, these becomings could disclose lines of powerful musical invention.

It is perhaps too easy to find fault with Mann from the vantage of the twenty-first century. When Mann began writing *Doctor Faustus* in 1943, Germany and much of the world were engaged in a conflict whose outcome was far from certain, and by the time he finished the novel in 1946, the consequences of that struggle were still largely undetermined. Understandably, and correctly, he viewed his historical situation as a moment of crisis, in which something had gone terribly wrong in Western culture, and specifically in German culture. His sense that Western art music had entered a similar period of crisis in the years leading up to World War II was also accurate, at least from the perspective of many serious composers, and his effort to draw parallels between the political and aesthetic developments of modernity represented a valiant attempt to correlate the spheres of politics and the arts, without reducing one to the other, and to diagnose the problems, attempted solutions and ultimate failures that have arisen in the modern era. The proliferation of alternative musical practices and vocabularies in post-World War II art music has no doubt made Mann's high-modernist stance – either a regressive repetition of tonal platitudes or an aggressively experimental atonality – seem arbitrarily limited. But we would be hopelessly deluded were we to think that we have learned the lessons of Nazism and Auschwitz and moved definitively beyond those crises. In Mann's view, the era of bourgeois humanism came to an end in 1914, and that humanistic culture found no adequate replacement in the ensuing decades. Mann recognised that a return to such a humanistic culture was impossible, but his analysis of the possibilities for developing alternative cultural formations, I believe, was limited by his fundamental conceptions of human nature and human culture, conceptions that also shaped his approach to music and aesthetics as a whole. In Deleuze and Guattari's thought I find more promising means of reconceiving the situation of humans, their histories and their cultures within the world. That thought furnishes a new perspective on the compositions of Leverkühn, one that confirms the perspicuity of Mann's perception of modernism's tendencies while indicating the limitations of Mann's understanding of those tendencies. Deleuze and Guattari also help us reframe Mann's narrative of the political events of his day, such that the parallels Mann draws between aesthetics and politics may be seen as much less certain than Mann believed. By no means, however, do I see Deleuze and Guattari's thought as a definitive guide to an understanding and transcendence of the fascist mentality and the abyss of the Holocaust. But their thought does, I believe, suggest fruitful ways of construing Mann's political narrative that open possibilities he did not envision – and perhaps could not envision, given his historical situation.

Notes

1. I discuss Deleuze's writings on music at greater length in Chapters 1 through 3 of *Deleuze on Music, Painting, and the Arts* (Bogue 2003).
2. For an illuminating, suggestive and admittedly speculative reading of the musical-political parallels of *Doctor Faustus*, see Evelyn Cobley's *Temptations of Faust* (Cobley 2002). For a more restrained treatment of the subject, see Patrick Carnegy's *Faust as Musician* (Carnegy 1973). Useful commentary on this topic is also provided by Susan von Rohr Scaff in *History, Myth, and Music: Thomas Mann's Timely Fiction* (Scarff 1998).
3. A particularly stark instance of this critique may be found in Manfred Frank's *What is Neostructuralism* (Frank 1989: 315–58). Frank characterises *Anti-Oedipus* as a 'kind of political and intellectual flipping-out, a spiritual Calibanism', which he regards as inflected with deleterious associations and tendencies. 'We only have to remind ourselves of the already fascistically colored neovitalisms that, as a result of the redis-

covery of Gobineau, Nietzsche, and Chamberlain, are creeping back, this time not so much in Germany, the homeland of blind respect for blind productivity, as in France. And they are all the more dangerous due to their anarchist touch that displeases the average bourgeois. But to displease the bourgeois is, as I have said, in itself not enough: after all, even Nazism was a "completely unbourgeois adventure"' (Frank 1989: 342). For an especially odious effort to associate Deleuze and Guattari with Nazis and fascism via their philosophy of nature, see Luc Ferry's *The New Ecological Order* (Ferry 1995: 112–14).

4. See Chapters 1 and 3 of my *Deleuze on Music, Painting, and the Arts* (Bogue 2003) for a more detailed exposition of Messiaen's compositional methods.
5. For Deleuze and Guattari's most detailed treatment of the issues of speed, contagion, black holes and the fascist Body without Organs, see ATP 161–6.

9

Scoring the Rhizome: Bussotti's Musical Diagram

During the last decade I have taught a semester-long seminar on *A Thousand Plateaus* five times, and last autumn I thought I was well prepared for the fifth iteration. But at the end of my lecture on the book's first section, a student who had been an aspiring opera soprano in a previous life asked, 'What do you have to say about the musical score on the opening page?' and all I really had to say was 'I've never given it much thought'. I managed to improvise a few vague observations until the class period came to a welcome end, but after class I began studying the score and its provenance, discovering very soon that the work is not only fascinating in its own right, but also of great significance for *A Thousand Plateaus*. Like so many references in *A Thousand Plateaus*, the Bussotti score operates both internally and externally, reverberating within the book while opening the text to proliferating connections with the outside world, those rhizomatic connections extending so seamlessly that it is impossible to determine which elements are intentionally referenced by Deleuze and Guattari, and which are fortuitously evoked through the citation.

The Images of *A Thousand Plateaus*

Each of *A Thousand Plateaus*' fifteen textual sections is preceded by a visual image, and that of Bussotti's score is the most important of them all. Aside from Bussotti's score, few of the visual images add a great deal to the text. Some are mere visual examples of specific elements in the plateau that follows (the Ark of the Covenant preceding 'On Regimes of Signs', the wooden chariot drawing at the beginning of the Nomadology plateau, the photographs of an Etruscan amphora and plate prefacing the Becoming plateau, the crazy quilt before 'The Smooth and the Striated'). Others have a humorous or sardonic edge: the lobster of 'The Geology of Morals' ('God is a Lobster, or a double pincer, a double bind' [ATP 40]); the Buster Brown comic of 'Three Novellas'; the partridge trap of 'Apparatus of Capture'; the Postulates of Linguistics plateau's image of the ominous Doctor Mabuse issuing *mots d'ordre*; the Conclusion's 'Computer Einstein' portrait, representing the machine–human interface of the electronic, the inorganic, the corporeal and the mythical.

A few require more careful elucidation. Deleuze and Guattari's poetic caption for the photograph preceding 'One or Several Wolves', 'Field of Tracks, or Wolf Line', only attains full clarity after one consults the list of Illustrations and learns that the photograph is titled 'Wolf Tracks on Snow'. Here, the text–image relation is more complex than in many other plateaus, in that the literal wolf's trace is a figurative image of the Freudian erasure of wolves as packs and the wolf as animal (rather than substitute father). The image captioned 'Dogon Egg and Distribution of Intensities', which precedes the Body without Organs plateau, has a textual counterpart in the reference to 'the BwO as the full egg' and 'The tantric egg' (ATP 153), but its full significance is only made evident in *Anti-Oedipus*, where Deleuze and Guattari expound at length on the Dogon's world-egg as Body without Organs and its relation to the status of incest within the Dogons' complex mythology (AO 154–8). A similar expanded resonance emerges if one uncovers the reference that inspired Deleuze and Guattari to preface the Faciality plateau with Duccio's *The Calling of Saint Peter and Saint Andrew*. Deleuze and Guattari's contrast of the frontal face and the profile is mapped on to the distinction between the despotic and passional regimes, but only upon consultation of Jean Paris's *L'Espace et le regard*, a central source in the plateau, can one appreciate the rich network of artistic associations that Duccio's painting is capable of activating.

If there are images that might rival Bussotti's score in importance, they would be Léger's *Men in the Cities* (preceding the

Segmentarity plateau) and Klee's *Twittering Machine* (placed before the Refrain plateau). Without Léger's title (provided solely in the list of Illustrations), the relationship between the image and the plateau is only intuitively evident, but, once identified, the painting lends the plateau added resonances, linking it to discussions of the city in the Nomadology and Apparatus of Capture plateaus, while retaining its implicit echoes of the Faciality plateau through its 'probe-head' images of abstract frontal and profile faces. Klee's *Twittering Machine* obviously evokes birds and refrains, but the reference to Klee itself brings to mind Klee's writings on music and painting and his own practice as a painter, dancing to music as he painted. In the cases of both Léger and Klee, modern painting's polysemic densities lend the images a considerable power as components of *A Thousand Plateaus*, and this power is only reinforced by their association with such key concepts as micropolitics, segmentarity and the refrain.

The Bussotti Image

Nonetheless, Bussotti's score still remains *A Thousand Plateaus*' most important image, and for a number of reasons. If nothing else, it has pride of place – it is the first image you see when you start reading the book. The 'Authors' Note' ('avant-propos' in the French) advises the reader that 'To a certain extent, these plateaus may be read independently of one another, except the conclusion, which should be read at the end', and in the English translation, the reader could possibly choose to turn first to a plateau other than the Rhizome plateau and thereby avoid viewing Bussotti's score, since the Authors' Note is on a right-hand page facing a blank left page. But in the original French edition the 'avant-propos' is on the left page directly opposite Bussotti's score on the right. Hence, even if you should choose to read other plateaus before the rhizome plateau, you've already seen this image. Of course, you have also seen the opening text of the Rhizome chapter, but, significantly, seeing the text provides very little information about the section in question. No doubt you can't help instantly deciphering the plateau's large-font title, but the rest of the text is merely generic typography, meaningful only when you actually start reading the smaller font text. By contrast, the image of Bussotti's score is absorbed as a single entity, and, as we shall see, this fact is central to Bussotti's interrogation of the relationship between the visual and the aural, as well as the verbal.

Further, the Rhizome plateau itself has a special significance among the fifteen sections. It is titled 'introduction', and if the conclusion should be read last, it would seem that the introduction should be read first, even if Deleuze and Guattari do not say as much. The rhizome text was published as a separate book in 1976, the only plateau to appear by itself. ('One or Several Wolves' and 'How Do You Make Yourself a Body without Organs?' also were published before 1980, but as articles in the journal *Minuit*.) In the 1976 book, as in *A Thousand Plateaus*, the text is labelled 'introduction' (though the word followed 'rhizome' rather than preceding it), which indicates that even in its early formulation, the section possessed an introductory function, though in its 1976 form, the question must arise, 'introduction to what?' An introductory exposition of a concept that deserves further exploration? Or an introductory harbinger of things to come, a tantalising preview of the rhizomatic complex that will be published as *A Thousand Plateaus*? Both seem plausible, and both stress the text's position as something preceding something else.

More important, the concept of the rhizome, among all those of *A Thousand Plateaus*, best characterises the book itself, and indeed Deleuze and Guattari directly address the questions of the Book and their own status as authors in the rhizome plateau. And, finally, 'Introduction: Rhizome' is something like an operatic overture to the book, densely packed with motifs whose full significance will become apparent only after reading the entire text. If read first, and read carefully, the Rhizome plateau should be confusing, difficult, even opaque at times, and in that sense it is a baptism by fire, a fitting introduction to the authors' uncompromising strategy of always working in the middle and of forcing readers to leap unprepared into the middle with them.

Bussotti's score has a similar inaugural, introductory function. It was not included in the 1976 book *Rhizome: introduction*, which, despite what one might initially think, indicates not the score's lesser but its greater importance. Both the plateau and the score can stand alone, and hence the image has a certain autonomy. It is a fitting image to introduce the first plateau, but it should also be seen as the entire book's master image. If the Rhizome plateau is the work's overture, Bussotti's composition is its score. It tells us how to perform *A Thousand Plateaus*, how we should play the book.

Bussotti's 'Aserialism'

Bussotti is a multi-talented artist whose productions include music, drawings, paintings, costumes, theatrical productions, films, poems and prose works. Born in 1931, he came to international prominence in 1959 with the composition under consideration here, *Five Piano Pieces for David Tudor*, a piece inspired by his experiences the previous year when he first attended the Internationale Ferienkurse für Neue Musik (International Summer Courses for New Music) in Darmstadt, Germany. Initiated in 1946 by Wolfgang Steinecke, the Darmstadt Ferienkurse in its early years focused on works of quasi-tonal modernism, but by 1952 three young composers had emerged as leaders of an increasingly influential avant-garde: Luigi Nono, Karlheinz Stockhausen and Pierre Boulez. They were proponents of atonal serialism, a rigorous and severe formalism that severed musical elements, in Attinello's words, 'from any continuous and meaningful context and reformulated [them] as nondirected, temporally arbitrary (i.e. reversible) patterns' (Attinello 2007: 29). However rich the variations in serial practice, 'the *style* (as distinguished from the technique) of serialism, as it is usually understood, [was] one of nearly mathematical purity' (Attinello 2007: 29).

The year Bussotti first attended the Ferienkurse, 1958, was also the year John Cage made his inaugural appearance at Darmstadt. On 3 September, Cage collaborated with David Tudor in two-piano performances of works by Earle Brown, Morton Feldman, Christian Wolff and Cage himself; later, Cage delivered three lectures, during which Tudor played various works by Cage and others. Cage's presentations were highly controversial and their subsequent influence on avant-garde music was profound. For some composers, Cage's experimentations with sonic textures and chance were inspirational; for others, they were anathema. Among those most opposed to the aleatory aspect of Cage's approach was Boulez, who later caustically derided the post-Cage adoption of chance as a compositional practice:

> Notable in several composers of our generation at the present time is a constant preoccupation, not to say obsession, with chance. [. . .] The most elementary form of the transmutation of chance is located in the addition of a philosophy dyed with Orientalism and masking a fundamental weakness in the technique of composition; this would be a recourse against the asphyxia of invention, recourse to a more subtle poison that destroys every embryo of artisanship; I should willingly qualify that experience – if it is one – in which the individual, not feeling responsible for his work, simply throws himself into a puerile magic out of unavowed weakness, out of confusion, for temporary assuagements – I should willingly qualify that experience as chance by inadvertence. (Boulez 1968: 35)

Bussotti, by contrast, was among those who responded positively to Cage's experimentations with chance, adopting aleatory effects in many of his compositions in the decade following 1958, as is evident in the *Five Piano Pieces for David Tudor* of 1959.

It is important to note, however, that Bussotti's embrace of chance was idiosyncratic and, in one major regard, antithetical to Cage's sensibility. Boulez saw in Cage's aleatory methods a retreat from the responsibilities of a rigorous serialism, but both composers treated sounds in a detached and intellectual fashion, whereas Bussotti approached music as a personal, emotional and erotic medium. In the prefatory note to *Due voci*, composed between May and December 1958, Bussotti declared himself an advocate of 'aserialism', which he defined as the 'dialectical rebellion of the humanistic attitude in the man who writes music, against the stiff aridity of systems' (cited in Ulman 1996: 188). As Ulman observes, what Bussotti sought in *Due voci*, and in many of his subsequent compositions, was to infuse 'the gestural and sonic world of the serial avant-garde with the intimacy and subjectivity which serialism had sought through impersonal rationality to avoid' (Ulman 1996: 188). The aim of Bussotti's aleatory methods was not, as Cage advocated, 'to let sounds be themselves' (Cage 1961: 10), but to invite performers to participate with the composer in an affective interpersonal event. In this regard, Tudor's influence was essential. A champion of American new music and the leading avant-garde pianist of his generation, Tudor was not simply a technical virtuoso but also a gifted improviser whose manipulations of all components of the piano greatly expanded the instrument's range of sonic possibilities. He tapped, thumped and beat the wooden frame, operated the pedals as percussive accessories, reached inside the piano and plucked, scratched, rapped and strummed the strings, sliding fingers up and down, coaxing overtones and eerie whispers from the instrument. Of necessity, given the elaborate gestures and broad movements required to execute the score, Tudor's stage performances, besides generating exotic sounds, also functioned as theatrical events, during which, as Richard Toop writes of another Bussotti piano composition for three players, the piano becomes 'a prone body, alternately caressed, cajoled and assaulted by its suitors' (cited in Griffiths 1981: 127).[1] It is no doubt in large part this theatrical and affective dimension of improvisatory practice that drew Bussotti to experimentations with chance.

Bussotti's theatrical and libidinal proclivities, it should be noted, were manifest not only in his music but also in his person. Many have remarked on the tumultuous effect of Cage's presentations at Darmstadt in 1958, the theoretical repercussions of which were compounded by the personal animosities Cage's appearance unleashed – Boulez and Stockhausen had long vied for dominance at Darmstadt, often acrimoniously, and it was Stockhausen who had invited Cage to Darmstadt and who defended Cage's music from the vociferous attacks launched by many of the participants in the 1958 Ferienkurse. But Smith and Attinello argue persuasively that Bussotti may well have been an even more disturbing presence than Cage at Darmstadt in 1958, chiefly because of his flamboyant and forthright gay sexuality. Boulez and Cage, like many gay men in the 1950s, were quiet about their sexual orientation, and in the closed, hothouse atmosphere of Darmstadt, Bussotti's frank behaviour seems to have provoked considerable unease.

> Bussotti made certain underlying connections between music, avant-gardism and homosexuality all too evident; while inspiring some of the younger gay figures to be less secretive about their behaviour, and even apparently introducing some participants to sexual experiences heretofore only imagined by them, he also definitely alarmed and annoyed the senior figures, particularly Boulez. (Ormond-Smith and Attinello 2007: 110)

Bussotti's homoerotic approach to music was already implicit in his 1958 *Due voci*, with its text from La Fontaine celebrating voluptuousness, and it was explicit in the texts of *Pièces de chair II*, composed between 1959 and 1960. In the fifth of the *Five Piano Pieces for David Tudor*, Bussotti provides above the two-stave piano score a third line labelled 'voce', apparently meant to be sung, with a text reading, 'I don't say no to the boys with clear eyes / but I LOVE / more than all those the ones with / black eyes that shine' (cited in Smith and Attinello 2007: 112). Bussotti's eroticism reached full efflorescence in his 1964 composition *La Passion selon Sade*, a musical and theatrical work whose score combines musical notations, complex charts, diagrams, drawings of characters and other graphic elements. As Ulman comments,

> In *La Passion* the latent eroticism of Bussotti's graphic style and opulent instrumental writing becomes explicit: the flautist must strip partially, the singer and conductor lie together on a divan, the percussionist functions as torturer, and the two pianos characteristically alternate between violent deluges and delicate explorations of unusual sonorities [. . .] Cage's theater of the absurd had been transformed, with the added inspiration of Artaud's 'theatre of cruelty', into Bussotti's 'theatre of Eros', which would grow ever more expansive: by the end of the sixties, Bussotti had even embarked on his first grand opera, *Lorenzaccio* (1968–72). (Ulman 1996: 189)

Bussotti and Graphism

The chance Cage advocated, then, was for Bussotti a mere vehicle for creating improvisatory music-theatre. Yet, if Bussotti responded favourably to Cage's experiments with chance, he was even more deeply affected by Cage's explorations of the graphic dimension of musical scores. A number of Cage's scores from the 1950s departed radically from standard notational practices. Many consisted solely of graphic, non-musical elements, as in *Variations 1* (for any instrument), *Aria* (for solo voice) and *Fontana Mix* (electronic score), all produced in 1958. *Variations I* consists of a prefatory page of instructions and six plastic transparencies, the first of which bears twenty-seven dots of various sizes, the following five of which have five randomly drawn lines each. The performer(s) is (are) to superimpose the lines on the dots in any way, using the dots as notes and the lines as trajectories of five sonic elements. *Aria* is a twenty-page setting of words and word fragments in Armenian, Russian, Italian, French and English. The vocal lines, Cage explains, 'are drawn in black, with or without parallel dotted lines, or in one or more of 8 colors. These differences represent 10 styles of singing. Any 10 styles may be used and any correspondence between color and style maybe established' (Cage 1960: preface [no pagination]). Near each squiggle are snippets of text that the soloist is to render in song. *Fontana Mix* includes ten pages with six curved lines each, ten transparencies with randomly placed points, and a transparency with a rectangular, ruler-like grid of small squares, 100 squares long, 20 squares wide. The performer generates the score by placing a transparency of points on a sheet of lines, and then superimposing the grid at any chosen angle. Once assembled, the given complex of points, lines and grid are translated into electronic sounds according to Cage's general instructions for utilising the graphic elements to generate the tone, colour and pitch of sonic events.

The influence of Cage's treatment of the score as visual artefact is immediately evident in the *Five Piano Pieces for David Tudor*, especially in Piece Four, and throughout much of his career Bussotti continued to make dual use of the score as musical notation and graphic medium – to such an extent that he is typically classified in music histories as an exponent of 'graphism' (a movement all too often dismissed as a frivolous musical dead-end).

Three of the *Five Piano Pieces for David Tudor* premiered at Darmstadt in 1959, with Tudor at the keyboard, and from its initial execution Bussotti's aleatory methods came under fire. Following the performance of one of the pieces, an audience member asked Tudor to play the piece again – obviously, in an effort to question the validity of the entire improvisatory enterprise. Stockhausen refused to allow a repeat performance.[2] That same year, the complete score appeared in print. Since then, the piece has remained one of the best known of Bussotti's compositions, and the image of Piece Four perhaps the most often reproduced of all Bussotti's scores.

Thus, the opening visual image of *A Thousand Plateaus*, when contextually situated, brings together a number of themes. Generated amid the 1958 Darmstadt turmoil surrounding Cage's lectures, Tudor's performances and Bussotti's gay flamboyance, the *Five Piano Pieces for David Tudor* represents a challenge to the ascetic serialism of Boulez, an 'aserial' amalgamation of aleatory composition, theatrical performance, unconventional graphic notation and affectively charged textures. To label the score as inherently 'homoerotic' would be far-fetched, but, as I hope to show, it does possess a decided sensuality that unsettles the score's more conventional, geometric elements. This interplay of chance, corporeal performativity, graphic experimentation and affective intensity provides a fitting preface to the entirety of *A Thousand Plateaus*.

Five Piano Pieces for David Tudor

To understand Piece Four of *Five Piano Pieces for David Tudor*, we must first consider the composition's prefatory page, which bears a brief text by Bussotti in Italian and German translation. In English (my translation), the text reads as follows:

> The expression 'David Tudor' used in the title is not a dedication but, so to speak, a kind of indication of the instrument.
>
> The written musical characters realise a scale that goes from traditional written notes to signs as yet musically unknown: *disegno* [drawing, design].
>
> In one case (piano piece 4), an autonomous *disegno* by the author, from ten years earlier, is pianistically adapted. Often the

> sonic acts that such a *disegno* may generate remain in the hands of the pianist.
>
> The five pieces, taken from a vaster cycle and hence dissociated from that cycle, reunite here in a minor cycle virtually placed within the global cycle. Thus, a finished part (piano piece 2) in its global context becomes unfinished, a complete part (piano piece 5) incomplete.

Bussotti's first prefatory sentence tells us that the musical instrument is the machinic assemblage 'Tudor-piano' (and since Tudor died in 1996, the composition is now unplayable – at least if one takes Bussotti's comment literally). Just as Deleuze and Guattari insist that the book is a machine plugged into other machines (ATP 6) and that there is no separation between the lives and times of authors and their works (K 41), so Bussotti writes for a Tudor-piano machine, and invites us to view the composition as a machinic assemblage of 'Bussotti-score-Tudor-piano' and to plug that machine into other machines. Bussotti then states that the score's components run the gamut from conventional musical notation to unknown graphic signs. A quick glance at the score's five pieces confirms Bussotti's assertion, although it would seem that in each piece conventional notation is scarcely present, and is almost immediately sent speeding along a deterritorialising line of flight into a galaxy of cryptic signs and designs.

Bussotti's score stages a confrontation of the aural and the visual, of music and the plastic arts, a fact Bussotti explicitly states in the preface's third sentence, informing us that Piece Four started as an autonomous 1949 *disegno* that was 'adapted pianistically' ten years later. As Roland Barthes says in a profound one-page essay on Bussotti, the composer's basic principle is that 'writing is not a simple instrument'. A Bussotti score

> constructs a homological space [. . .] one part wizard's book of multiple signs, refined, coded with infinite minutiae, and one part vast analogical composition, in which the lines, the locations, the flights, the stripes are charged with suggesting, if not imitating, *what is actually happening* on the concert stage [. . .] A Sylvano Bussotti manuscript is *already* a total work [. . .]

> visibly, it is an ordered jumble of drives, desires, obsessions, which expresses itself graphically, spatially, *in ink*, one might say, independently of what the music communicates. (Barthes 1995: III, 387–8)

As overture to *A Thousand Plateaus*, Piano Piece Four juxtaposes two of the book's central aesthetic concerns: painting (the faciality plateau) and music (the refrain plateau), each art with its own problem – painting, that of the face-landscape, and music, that of the refrain. But just as music proves to have '*rhythmic faces or characters* and [. . .] *melodic landscapes*' (ATP 318), so painting has its refrains, and in Bussotti's score, sonic and visual landscapes and refrains enter a zone of indiscernibility that opens on to a plane of consistency composed of speeds and intensities within an unformed matter.

Piano Piece Four

And now to the score of Piano Piece Four (Fig. 9.1). The composition title is preceded by the Roman numeral XIV, indicating that this is part fourteen of the virtual 'global cycle' from which it has been extracted. (That global cycle, consisting of fourteen

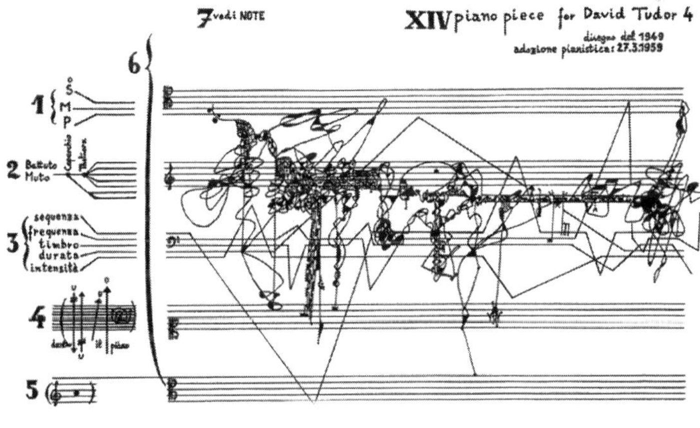

Figure 9.1 Score of Bussotti's Piece Four, *Five Piano Pieces for David Tudor* © 1959 Ricordi, Milano

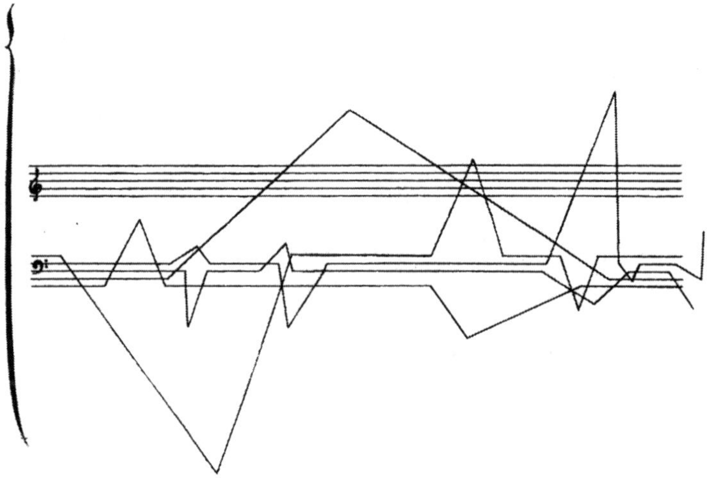

Figure 9.2 Treble and bass clef of Piece Four

sections, was published in 1960 as *Pièces de chair II*.) The other four piano pieces for David Tudor are labelled in accordance with their positions within *Pièces de chair II*, as 'V b)', 'VIII', 'd)', and 'I a)'. The basic unit of a traditional piano score consists of a two-stave system, the top stave most often registering notes for the right hand and marked with a treble clef, the bottom, bass clef stave bearing notes for the left hand. Lines two and three of the score have the traditional treble and bass clefs, but the five lines of the bass stave zigzag wildly across the other four staves (Fig. 9.2). Lines one, four and five have C-clefs, the line bisecting the capital-B-like shape representing middle C. The C-clef on line one is conventionally referred to as a 'tenor clef', line four a 'soprano clef', and line five an 'alto clef'. C-clefs have specialised uses for certain instruments, and are virtually unheard of in piano music, as are piano scores with five staves (designed for five-handed pianists, perhaps?). And, as we will see, only line five's C-clef actually designates a specific musical note.

In my reading of the score, the left-hand margin units numbered one through five indicate the performance components that will be activated when the full composition, labelled six, is actually played.[3] Unit One is the most obscure of the score's components.

No explanation of the significance of the P, M and S is provided in the score, but, according to Bussotti (personal communication), 'The three letters in question signify: P = pizzicato M = muted (stop the sonority) and S = *sordina* [muffled] with all the means of directly transforming the sounds; introduction of paper between the strings, application of different pieces of material between the same.'[4] Hence, when graphic marks touch the top stave, the performer is to reach into the piano, pluck the strings (*pizzicato*), dampen the strings with the hands (muted), and sound the strings prepared with paper and other materials, either by striking the corresponding keys of the keyboard or by sounding the strings directly (plucking, striking). (The use of the 'prepared piano' was one frequently employed by David Tudor in compositions he performed, and hence an appropriate component of a score dedicated to him.)

Unit Two designates the two fundamental operations of all piano playing: striking strings and muting them. But Bussotti extends these operations beyond the keyboard to the lid of the piano, scored with an additional two lines. If you follow stave two left to right, in fact, you find that midway through the piece two extra lines appear, replete with enigmatic markings. Hence, all the standard keyboard functions of piano playing are represented by one treble clef stave, rather than the two-stave, treble–bass clef system, and the lid is assigned a role comparable to that of the keyboard.

Unit Three is the most complex and most important of the five units. Its components are the basic elements of any sound. Each of the five zigzag lines charts movements in an analogue scale of less and more, of increases and decreases in some continuum. The intensity line charts volume, louder and softer. The duration line registers the tempo, faster and slower (the peak of the duration triangle marking the composition's fastest tempo). Timbre in music designates the quality of a sound, that which differentiates a flute from an oboe, for example. The timbre line's continuum, I propose, is that of dark and light, or, if you have a synaesthetic mind, like Olivier Messiaen's, the line might be seen as traversing the sonic analogue of the visual chromatic spectrum from the edge of the infrared to the limits of the ultraviolet, or from cool to warm colours, or from light to heavy saturation. (Such visual analogues of sonic qualities are legitimate here since Bussotti's score is both an aural and a visual artefact.) The frequency line designates variations in pitch, lower and higher sounds, from 20 Hertz to 20 kiloHertz. I have concluded that 'Sequenza', the most puzzling of the terms, refers to the sequentiality of sonic elements, that is, the differentiation of separate sonic events via the temporal gaps between sounds. The continuum charted by the sequence line ranges from a maximum distance between sounds, to the minimum of simultaneity. Thus, the base of the sequence line marks a moment of simultaneity, in which the player makes all sounds at once – and that nadir coincides with the greatest concentration of design marks on the score.

If you extract the five lines (Fig. 9.3), what you have is the diagram of the composition, in Bonta and Protevi's words, 'the outline of the traits of expression of an abstract machine, the "nonformal functions" linked to the "phyla" of "unformed matters" or "traits of expression"' (Bonta and Protevi 2004: 79). The five components of Unit Three name the unformed matter and non-formal functions of sound in general, and the lines outline the specific disposition of that matter/function within this composition.

Unit Four, 'inside the piano', directs the performer to reach into the piano, strum the undampered strings up, down and in an outward spiral motion. Unit Five is Bussotti's little joke. The score's drawing touches the fifth stave only at one small point atop the stave. That point, if read as a musical note on the alto clef, is

Sequence
Frequency
Timbre
Duration
Intensity

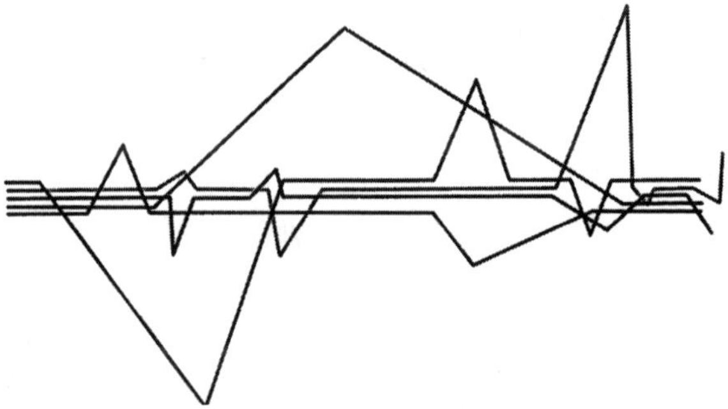

Figure 9.3 Unit Three of Piece Four

A above middle C. Five's parenthesis notates the same pitch with the more common treble clef, as if to remind the performer how to read the unusual alto clef, lest he or she forget how to do so.

The Score and the *Disegno*

Unit Seven, atop the score, says 'see note', in other words, see the prefatory sentence indicating that the score was originally a 1947 *disegno* that was 'pianistically adapted' on 27 March 1959. With some laborious graphics editing, you can expose the original drawing, which, to my eye, is a thoroughly rhizomatic design (Fig. 9.4). The clear horizontal axis of the drawing delineates the plane of some undetermined rhizomatic growth suspended in space, such that the elements below the horizontal axis are as rootless as the elements that rise above the axis. The drawing's forms are non-representational, but decidedly organic rather than geometrical. Amid the drawing, one finds shapes resembling a tendril and fruit, a spider-like creature suspended from a thread, a column of shapes resembling plant cells or rock crystals. Tubers, polyps, leaves, stamens, pistils, shoots and stems may be discerned in the thicket of forms (Fig. 9.5).

The composition has a vertical axis, and if one wishes to formulate an analysis correlative to that which Deleuze conducts in

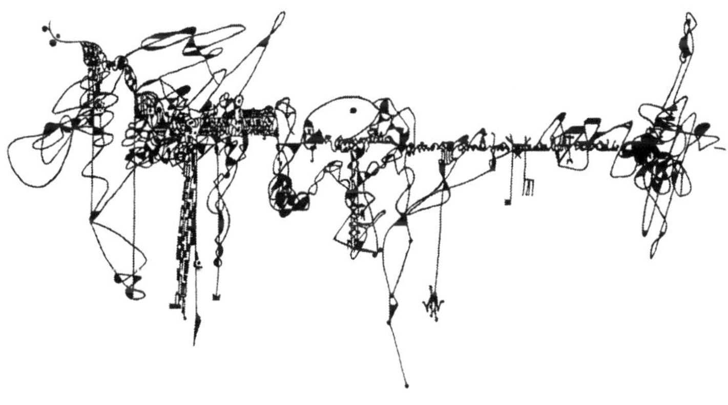

Figure 9.4 Bussotti's 1947 *disegno*

Figure 9.5 Tubers, polyps, leaves, stamens, pistils, shoots and stems

Francis Bacon, one might situate the drawing's generative locus of chaos, which Bacon calls the 'graph' ('diagram' in the French translation), in the zero point of the X–Y axes (Fig. 9.6). From that site, one can imagine the form emerging. But any one of the lines of flight so designated could be an initiating line of

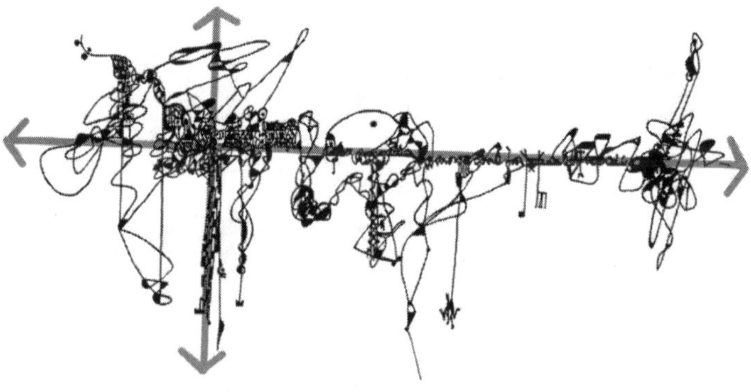

Figure 9.6 Horizontal and vertical axes of Bussotti's *disegno*

involution, from which the acentered rhizomatic design emerges. My hypothesis, however, is that the point on the bottom stave, the A above middle C, is the generative source of the composition (Fig. 9.7). It is Paul Klee's 'grey point', a 'nowhere-existent something' or 'somewhere-existent nothing' (cited in Bogue 2004: 80), a fundamental point of chaos that leaps out of itself, tracing a line that may eventually delineate all forms and volumes. Deleuze and Guattari invoke Klee's originary point of chaos at the inception of the Refrain plateau, providing a visual analogue of music's generation of refrains from a sonic point of chaos. In Bussotti's A above middle C, then, the sonic and visual meet. That point may be read as a musical symbol and as a drawing component. There the realms of sound and sight converge in a point of undecidability, which generates the soundscape and landscape inscribed on the ink-covered paper of the score. If music and art are envisioned as planes of consistency, the musical score exists on one plane, the drawing on the other (Fig. 9.8). The A above middle C, the point common to the two planes, fixes the line of intersection of the two planes. If the planes are then rotated towards one another, they merge in a single plane, a plane of consistency common to the drawing and the sound score, and that plane is embodied in the score itself, a sheet of paper diagraming an abstract machine.

But Piano Piece Four is also the score of A *Thousand Plateaus*. It

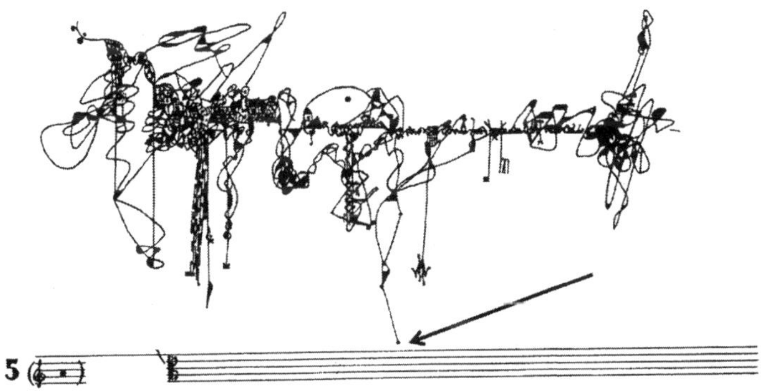

Figure 9.7 A above middle C (Klee's 'grey point')

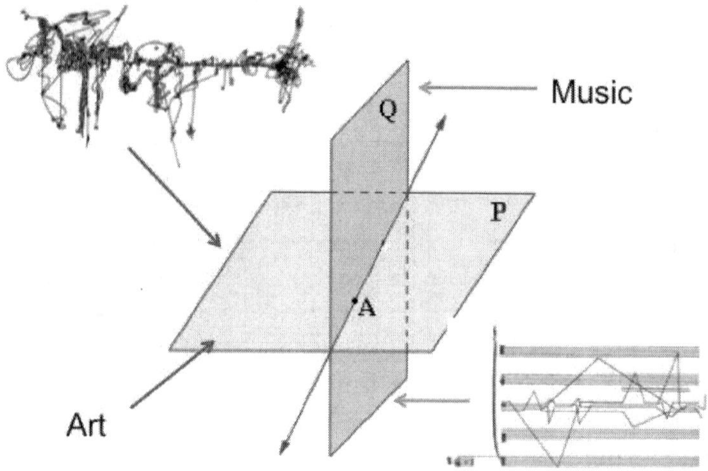

Figure 9.8 Planes of art and music

serves as an overture to the book, replete with strata of sedimentation, abstract lines of flight, becomings-animal, plant and mineral, supple and rigid lines of segmentarity (Fig. 9.9), white wall–black hole machines of faciality (Fig. 9.10), regimes of signs (Fig. 9.11), smooth and striated spaces. Bussotti's score tells us how to perform the book – to follow and enact its variations in intensity; to explore the varying duration of tempos of reading; to savour the timbres of tones, voices and vocabularies; to discover the work's varying frequencies and resonances; and to sample its component textual passages in sequences separated by varying distances, or to perform components in simultaneities assembled in the virtual memory space of coexisting sheets of the past. In engaging these five elements, we activate the diagram of *A Thousand Plateaus*' abstract machine, a realm of pure speeds (duration, frequency, sequence) and affects (intensities, timbral qualities).

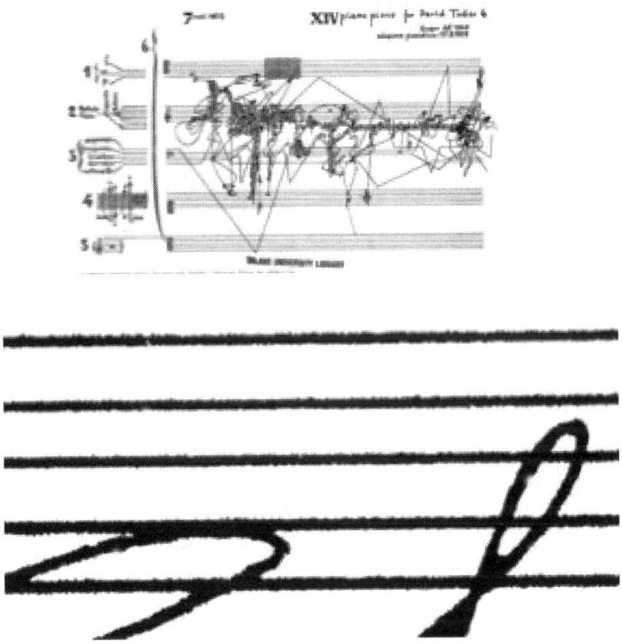

Figure 9.9 Supple and rigid lines of segmentarity

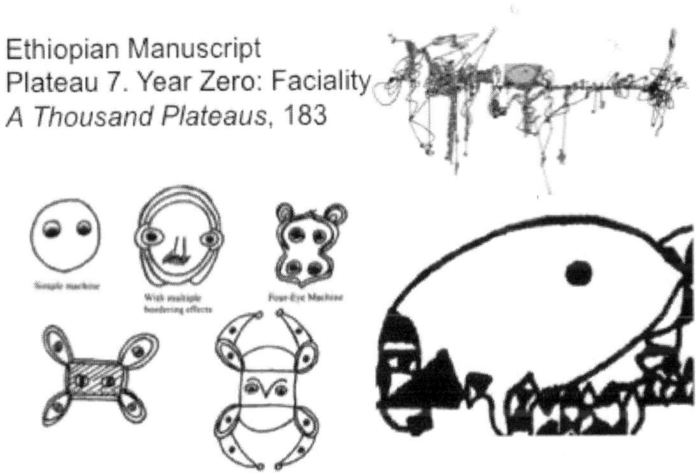

Figure 9.10 Machines of faciality in A *Thousand Plateaus* and Piece Four

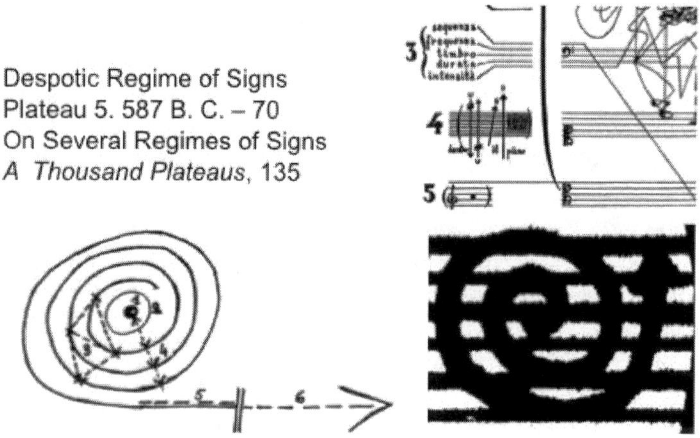

Figure 9.11 Regimes of signs in *A Thousand Plateaus* and spiral arrow in Piece Four

Notes

1. Besides playing a key role in the development of the New York School's early piano music, Tudor was also an influential force in the dissemination of American new music in Europe. As Beal shows, 'Over a brief but fertile period of unprecedented international exchange, Tudor operated as an ambassador of [American new music], and his diplomatic presence at key new music venues in West Germany – especially at the *Internationale Ferienkurse für Neue Musik* (International Holiday Courses for New Music) in Darmstadt between 1956 and 1961 – established American experimentation's controversial yet ultimately stimulating presence in conversations about new music' (Beal 2007: 78).
2. Similar objections to the improvisatory nature of the composition arose during performances of *Five Piano Pieces for David Tudor* in other venues. Cope records that 'Bussotti's *Five Pieces* was performed in Los Angeles three times in one concert, by three different performers. More conservative members of the audience, obviously appalled by the lack of recognizable similarities among the performances in structure, length, instrumentation, or motive, reacted antagonistically to both performers and work. [. . .] In reference to these performances Halsey Stevens has pointed out that: ". . . if Mr. Bussotti had wandered into the hall and didn't know what was going on, he would not have had

the remotest idea that those three performances, or any one of them, might have been his own piece. They were so totally different in every respect that the only thing he could lay claim to was having designed the score, not to have composed the piece. Aleatory music, it seems to me, as it is frequently pursued, is an amusing parlor game . . ."' (Cope 1989: 165).

3. Other readings of the score, of course, are possible. Erik Ulman, in personal correspondence, argues that the numbered elements (save number seven) are to be performed in sequence. No doubt his alternative is but one of several other possibilities, all of which may be justified by Bussotti's prefatory remark that the execution of the score rests 'in the hands of the pianist'.
4. Bussotti's email message of 18 October 2012, written in French, reads as follows: 'Les trois lettres en question signifient: P = pizzicato M = muted (estomper la sonorité) et S = sordina avec tous le moyens de transformer directement les sons; introductions de papier entre les cordes, applications de morceaux différents entre les mêmes.'

IV. Literature and Philosophy

10

Deleuze, Guattari and the Kafka–Kleist Connection: Towards a Literature of War

In *Kafka: Toward a Minor Literature*, Deleuze and Guattari remark that the only author Kafka

> will take as his master is Kleist, and Kleist also detested masters; but Kleist is a different matter even in the deep influence that he had on Kafka. We have to speak differently about this influence. Kleist's question isn't 'What is a minor literature and, further, a political and collective literature?' but rather, 'What is a literature of war?' This is not completely alien to Kafka, but it is not exactly his question. (K 55)

Deleuze and Guattari do not elaborate on this notion of a Kleistian literature of war in *Kafka*, nor do they further specify the concept explicitly in any subsequent publications. And yet, if one traces Deleuze's and Deleuze and Guattari's references to Kleist in works from *Kafka* on, one finds not only the outlines of such a concept but also the traces of a significant genealogy of rhizomatic thought that spreads from Kafka through Kleist and beyond into topics and concerns far afield from those commonly associated with literature.

It would be nice if there were a companion volume to Deleuze and Guattari's *Kafka* which would provide a detailed reading of Kleist's literature of war, and in fact, after a certain fashion, such a volume exists: Mathieu Carrière's *Für eine Literatur des Krieges, Kleist* (1981), translated into French in 1985 as *Pour une littérature de guerre, Kleist*. Carrière is an actor, writer and director who has appeared in well over 100 films and television shows. He made his film debut at the age of thirteen as Tonio in *Tonio Kröger*, and two years later starred in Volker Schlöndorff's widely acclaimed *Young Törless*. Besides working steadily in film throughout his life, as a young man he developed a strong interest in philosophy and studied with Deleuze for several years during the 1970s. In a 3 May 2010 interview concerning his role in the Ruhr Theatre Festival's upcoming production of Kleist's fragment *Robert Guiskard*, Carrière alluded to his connection with Deleuze while explaining his long-standing interest in Kleist:

> I've been infected by Kleist for forty years, but I have never acted in any of his texts. When I was twenty years old [1970], in Paris I had the most important encounter of my life, with the philosopher Gilles Deleuze, and with him I worked on, among other things, the project 'Nomadic Literature and the War Machine'. From that work came my book *For a Literature of War, Kleist*. Since then I have been in love with Kleist and with his *Penthesilea*. (*Der Westen* 2010; my translation)

Signs of this important relationship between Carrière and Deleuze appear in *A Thousand Plateaus* when, after two extended passages about Kleist, Deleuze and Guattari cite as their source 'an unpublished study of Kleist by Mathieu Carrière' (ATP 542, 553), which, most certainly, is a version of Carrière's 1981 publication. If one follows Deleuze and Guattari's suggestion and consults Carrière's book, one discovers that the passages in *A Thousand Plateaus* are highly condensed synopses of Carrière's analyses, albeit with slight modifications and shifts in emphasis. And one finds in Carrière's text an argument framed in Deleuze–Guattarian terminology and articulated in a voice that is subtly inflected with a Deleuze–Guattarian tone.

My object is to explore the Kafka–Kleist connection that Deleuze and Guattari first draw in *Kafka*, and to do so by bringing to more complete articulation Deleuze and Guattari's concept of a Kleistian literature of war, using as the primary resources in this endeavour Deleuze's and Deleuze and Guattari's scattered remarks about Kleist, as well as Carrière's detailed treatment of Kleist and his literature of war. I hope to show that Kleist provided Deleuze and Guattari an important means of developing the concept of minor literature presented in *Kafka* and extending the notion of the literary in their subsequent works, especially *Dialogues*, *A Thousand Plateaus*, *What is Philosophy?* and *Essays Critical and Clinical*, by tracing the interpenetrating connections between writing and the world beyond (and yet already within) the text.

Kleist and the War Machine

Although in *Kafka* Deleuze and Guattari distinguish Kafka and Kleist by differentiating minor literature from a literature of war, the distinction between the two writers is presented elsewhere in somewhat different terms. In *Dialogues*, Deleuze and Parnet say that

> what is important in Kafka is precisely the way in which, throughout the regimes of signs, [. . .] he puts them in flight or movement on a plane of consistency [. . .] here we have Kafka putting literature into an immediate relationship with a minority machine [. . .] See how Kleist put literature into an immediate relationship with a war machine. (D 123; trans. modified)

And in *A Thousand Plateaus* Deleuze and Guattari speak of 'Kleist and a mad war machine, Kafka and a most extraordinary bureaucratic machine' (ATP 4). What these passages suggest, I believe, is that the pertinent difference between Kafka and Kleist should be viewed, not in terms of an opposition of minor literature and a literature of war, but in terms of literature's immediate relationship with a war machine in Kleist and literature's immediate relationship with a bureaucratic machine in Kafka.[1] I will return later to Kafka's bureaucratic machine and focus now on Kleist and the war machine.

If indeed Kleist puts literature into an immediate relationship with a war machine, the obvious question must be, what is a war machine? In *A Thousand Plateaus* Deleuze and Guattari speak at length about the war machine, especially in the Nomadology plateau, connecting the terms to a dizzying network of themes and concepts. In *Le Vocabulaire de Gilles Deleuze*, Sasso and Villani capture some of the essential elements of this network of associations in their brief entry on the war machine:

> What characterises the war machine is the exteriority of its relation to the State [. . .] Consubstantially linked to nomadism, to its displacement (even when stationary), to its absolute speed, [. . .] to its unstriated and unmarked space, [. . .] the war machine also has a relation to the invention of the 'numbering' number [. . .] and to the activity of a 'thought of the outside'. (Sasso and Villani 2003: 354; my translation)

To this we might add that in *A Thousand Plateaus* Deleuze and Guattari remark that a war machine is 'an assemblage that makes thought itself nomadic' (ATP 24). Yet, despite articulating these multiple connections between the war machine and other concepts, nowhere in *A Thousand Plateaus* do Deleuze and Guattari provide a straightforward definition of the war machine. It is only in a 1980 interview following the publication of *A Thousand Plateaus* that Deleuze explicitly defines the term:

> We define the 'war machine' as a linear assemblage that is constructed on lines of flight. Thus understood, the aim of war machines isn't war at all but a very special kind of space, *smooth space*, which they establish, occupy, and extend. *Nomadism* is precisely this combination of war machine and smooth space. We try to show how and in what circumstances war machines aim at war (when state apparatuses take over a war machine that's initially no part of them). War machines tend much more to be revolutionary, or artistic, rather than military. (N 33; trans. modified)

It would seem, then, that the essence of Kleist's art is that it puts literature into an immediate relationship with 'a linear assemblage that is constructed on lines of flight'. Yet, if war 'is not the aim of the war machine', what do we make of the fact that war is often the central subject in Kleist's work, and war itself seems to be inseparable from his 'mad war machine' (ATP 4)? Kleist's 'mad war machine', in fact, does have war as its aim, which compels us to ask, what is war? On this point Carrière is particularly helpful. Carrière defines Kleistian war via the notion of 'infection', saying that infection

> is the invasion of a multiplicity of bodies by another multiplicity; the invasion's project is the disorganisation, the deterritorialisation of the affected body [. . .] Infection is the encounter of at least two enemy populations on the same territory, on the same battlefield. It is a form of affective encounter [. . .] War is the climate of infection which, alone, makes love possible. (Carrière 1981: 9; 1985: 9–10)[2]

A preliminary definition of a literature of war, then, might be 'a literature that immediately engages a war machine (an assemblage on lines of flight) and war (the climate of infection, the encounter of at least two opposed forces, or affective intensities)'.

One means of fleshing out this skeleton of a definition is to examine the major passages in which Deleuze and Deleuze and Guattari mention Kleist. Doing so not only provides a detailed account of a literature of war but also reveals the elements within that literature that are common to Kafka's minor literature (for, as we recall, Kleist's literature of war 'is not entirely alien to Kafka' [K 55]).[3]

Five Commonalities

First, the commonalities, of which there are at least five.

(1) In A *Thousand Plateaus*, Deleuze and Guattari argue that

> the ideal for a book would be to lay everything out on a plane of exteriority [. . .], on a single page, the same sheet: lived events, historical determinations, concepts, individuals, groups, social formations. Kleist invented a writing of this type, a broken chain of affects and variable speeds, with accelerations and transformations, always in a relation to the outside. Open rings. His texts, therefore, are opposed in every way to the classical or romantic book constituted by the interiority of a substance

> or a subject. The war-machine book against the State apparatus-book. (ATP 9)

Although the specifics of this Kleistian writing are peculiar to his works, the description of a writing in which 'lived events, historical determinations, concepts, individuals, groups, social formations' are laid out 'on a plane of exteriority' applies equally well to Kafka's texts. Deleuze and Guattari insist repeatedly in *Kafka* that the diaries, letters, short stories and novels form a single writing-machine, expressive of no hidden inner meaning or subjective interiority, but instead directly connected to and imbedded in the outside world, always immediately social and political in nature. If, as Deleuze and Guattari insist, Kafka takes Kleist as his master, then one clear element of that apprenticeship is in Kafka's developing his own writing-world laid out on a single plane of exteriority.

(2) Kleist and Kafka also draw up programmes for living, or life plans, rather than drafting manifestos for a fully envisioned future literature (as do most French writers). 'Kleist and Kafka spent their time making programmes for life. Programmes are not manifestos – still less are they phantasms, *but means of providing reference points for an experiment which exceeds our capacities to foresee*' (D 48). In an early letter (May 1799) to his half-sister, Ulrike, Kleist speaks at length of an individual's need to adopt 'a master plan for life', a 'life plan [Lebensplan]'; in a 16 August 1800 letter to his fiancée, he says that his 'plan has suffered a change'; five days later he writes to Ulrike that 'I am keeping a journal, in which I daily improve and perfect my plan'; yet he laments to Ulrike on 5 February 1801 that 'I resolved not to leave my room until I had decided on a definite life plan; but eight days passed and in the end I had to leave my room after all, and as undecided as ever' (Kleist 1982: 27, 40, 43, 91). As Deleuze points out, Kleist's life plans orient his action, but they are 'always modified in the process of coming into being, betrayed in the process of being hollowed out' (D 48). Their counterparts in Kafka are the strategies Kafka adopts to keep his fiancée, Felice, at a distance, 'a *topography of obstacles* (where to go? how to arrive? Prague, Vienna, Berlin?) [. . .] a numbered *list of conditions* [. . .] (a Life

Plan or a Life Program, à la Kleist)' (K 31–2). For both Kleist and Kafka, the life plan/programme, then, is not the map of a fixed life journey but a device for orienting experimental trajectories with no foreseeable destination, 'processes of experimentation, protocols of experience', which are 'modified in the process of coming into being' (D 48).

(3) In their writings, Kleist and Kafka both engage an abstract line on a plane of consistency, that abstract line being characterised variously as a line of flight, as a line of the steepest gradient, and as a line traced by the displacements of a centre of gravity. Demonstrating the equivalence of these descriptions of the abstract line and their connection to Kleist, Kafka and the plane of consistency will require some careful exegesis.

In the description of the abstract line as displacement of a centre of gravity, reference is being made to Kleist's essay 'On the Puppet Theatre', in which a master dancer explains to the narrator the principle behind the graceful dancing of the marionettes. The narrator assumes that the puppeteer would need multiple strings to manipulate the puppet, but the master dancer explains that only one string is necessary, since the puppet's movements are controlled through the manipulation of the puppet's 'center of gravity'. The line traced by the movement of the centre of gravity is to all appearances quite simple, but when carefully considered, the master dancer observes, this same line 'is something very mysterious. For it is nothing less than the *path of the dancer's soul*; and he doubted whether it could be found except by the puppeteer transposing himself into the center of gravity of the marionette; or, in other words, by *dancing*' (Kleist 1982: 212).

In a 1974 lecture, Deleuze uses Kleist's marionette essay to distinguish three kinds of lines: a rigid molar line, a supple molecular line and a line of flight. (These three lines, of course, form the thematic core of Plateaus Eight and Nine of *A Thousand Plateaus*.) The rigid molar line 'corresponds to the moments of the story represented by the play of the puppets' (2R 12). The supple molecular line consists of 'movements of an entirely different kind: tangible, representative curves, an arm that rounds itself out, a head that tilts'. This line is made up of 'very supple segments – one gesture, then another gesture' (2R 11–12). And the line of flight is the one traced by the puppeteer's manipulation of the puppet's centre of gravity.

> The puppeteer does not operate according to movements that already represent the figures to be achieved. He makes his puppet move according to a vertical line, wherein the puppet's center of gravity, or rather, center of lightness, is displaced. It is a perfectly *abstract* line, not in the least *figurative*, and no more symbolic than figurative. The line is mutant because it is made up of as many *singularities* as stopping points, and yet these do not break up the line. There is never any binary relationship or bi-univocal relation between this vertical, abstract line – which is for this reason all the more real – and the concrete movements of the puppets. (2R 11; trans. modified)

The crucial elements in this description of the third line, we should note, are that the puppet's actual movements bear no resemblance to the line; that the line is abstract yet real; and that it is characterised through its singularities, that is, the points at which the puppeteer's up-and-down manipulations of the puppet change direction. (A simple instance of singularities, or singular points, is that found in a square, which possesses four singular points at each of its corners, the corner point being singular in that it is the only point that belongs simultaneously to the two lines that converge at that corner.)

In *Dialogues*, Deleuze explicitly links Kleist and the centre of gravity to the plane of consistency. Following Spinoza's conception of the 'plane of consistency, plane of immanence',

> the trinity Hölderlin – Kleist – Nietzsche already conceived writing, art and even a new politics [. . .] as successions of catatonic states and periods of extreme haste, of suspensions and shootings, coexistences of variable speeds, blocs of becoming, leaps across voids, displacements of a centre of gravity on an abstract line, conjunctions of lines on a plane of immanence. (D 95; trans. modified)

In another passage, while describing the molar line, molecular line and the line of flight, Deleuze says that the third line 'is simple, abstract, and yet is the most complex of all, the most tortuous: it is the line of gravity or velocity [*célérité*], the line of flight and of the greatest gradient [*de plus grande pente*]' (D 125). In a third passage, Deleuze states that in reading Kafka and Kleist, one 'should follow the line of steepest gradient in a work, at the same time as reaching its plane of consistency', and, by doing so, one will see 'Kafka putting literature into an immediate relationship with a minority-machine' and Kleist putting literature 'into an immediate relationship with a war machine' (D 123; trans. modified). And, finally, Deleuze asserts that in literature

> the essential point, in the end, is the way in which all these regimes of signs move along a line of gradient, variable with each author, tracing out a plane of consistency or composition which characterizes a given work or group of works: [. . .] Virginia Woolf's Wave, Lovecraft's Hypersphere, Proust's Spider's Web, Kleist's Programme, Kafka's K-function. (D 122; trans. modified)

(We might note that in Deleuze's equation of Kleist's programme, or life plan, and Kafka's K-function, the continuity between the writer's life and the writer's fiction is made explicit, which suggests as well that the 'plane of exteriority', which includes the lives and writings of Kleist and Kafka, is also a 'plane of consistency' or 'plane of immanence'.)

(4) Kleist and Kafka's conception of writing is antithetical to that of Goethe. According to Deleuze and Guattari, Goethe is the quintessential bourgeois writer, a man of the State and the literary equivalent of Hegel in philosophy. Kleist and Kafka, by contrast, are part of an anti-Goethe, anti-State tradition in German letters that also includes Lenz, Hölderlin, Büchner and Nietzsche (see D 42, 95; K 18; ATP 24, 268–9, 356, 378, 482; CC 110). Deleuze and Guattari nowhere elaborate on their association of Goethe (and occasionally Schiller) with Hegel, nor on their classification of Lenz, Hölderlin, Büchner, Nietzsche and Kafka as Goethe's literary enemies. Their characterisation of the Kleist–Goethe opposition, however, while sketchy, is slightly more detailed than that offered in fleeting remarks about the other

members of the anti-Goethe tradition, and the details of their characterisation of the Kleist versus Goethe/Hegel opposition are drawn primarily from Carrière.

Citing an 1811 letter in which Kleist speaks briefly of his musical conception of literature and contrasts it with Goethe's painterly mentality (see Kleist 1982: 196), Carrière argues that the differences between music and painting aptly capture the differences in Kleist's and Goethe's aesthetics. According to Carrière, painting for Goethe renders visible the forms of organic nature 'in its eternal and reasonable continuity'; 'on the canvas, there are no holes, no leaps. Color is visible or it isn't'. By contrast, the art of music is full of discontinuities, gaps and sudden movements, and for someone like Goethe, 'music, with its silence, its holes and leaps, is nothing but the noise of undesirable and obscure forces' (Carrière 1981: 27–8; 1985: 26–7). Kleist's musical writing, replete with discontinuities, fragments, sudden shifts in speed and affect, is thus repugnant to Goethe (and it is indeed the case that Goethe generally disliked Kleist's work – see Kleist 1982: 175–80).

Carrière also draws a parallel between Goethe and Hegel during his discussion of the Goethe/painting versus Kleist/music opposition. Ultimately,

> Goethe sees and explains the world as a two-legged construction, which rests on the pillars of 'reflection on the absolute' and 'sacred mystery'. And just as the new bourgeois economy required a fluid continuity between the two poles, so the powerful Hegelian dialectic, developing between a totalitarian mirror and a hidden signifier, makes its appearance. The movement of existence is accumulation, the administrator of the mystery is the *Weltgeist*, and the State is reflected in the eye of God. (Carrière 1981: 26; 1985: 25)

From this analysis Carrière concludes that 'Statesmen and State-poets are painters. Anarchists play music' (Carrière 1981: 26; 1985: 25).[4]

(5) Kleist and Kafka both write in affects. In *What is Philosophy?*, Deleuze and Guattari assert that art's goal is to capture '*a bloc of sensations, that is to say, a compound of percepts and affects*' (WP 164).

Percepts are not perceptions, nor are affects affections. Percepts are like landscapes in which no distinction between perceiver and perceived may be made, in which 'the landscape *sees*', in which, in Cézanne's words, man is '"absent from but entirely within the landscape"' (cited in WP 169). Affects in turn are processes of becoming-other that pass through individuals – becoming-woman, becoming-child, becoming-animal, becoming-molecular. Hence, '*Affects are precisely these nonhuman becomings of man*, just as percepts – including the town – are *nonhuman landscapes of nature*' (WP 169). In a 1988 interview, Deleuze directly ties Kleist and Kafka to affects: 'The great English and American novelists often write in percepts, and Kleist and Kafka in affects' (N 137). What Deleuze seems to mean by this remark is that English and American novelists use landscapes as a generative element from which the plots, characters and settings of their works emanate – in *What is Philosophy?*, Deleuze and Guattari speak of 'the moor as percept' in Thomas Hardy, 'oceanic percepts in Melville' and 'urban percepts in Virginia Woolf' (WP 168–9) – and that in Kleist and Kafka the same generative function is fulfilled by becomings, especially becoming-animal (as in Kleist's *Penthesilea* and in Kafka's 'The Metamorphosis', 'A Report to an Academy', 'Investigations of a Dog', 'The Burrow' and so on).

After surveying these common elements, we might pause to consider once again Deleuze's definition of the war machine as 'a linear assemblage that is constructed on lines of flight'. It should be evident from this catalogue of commonalities that, according to Deleuze's definition of the war machine, Kleist and Kafka both engage a war machine in their lives and fiction. Obviously, the notion of a literature of war has not yet been given sufficient specificity to allow a differentiation of Kleist's writing from Kafka's.

Penthesilea

Perhaps the most direct means of capturing the essence of Kleist's literature of war is to consider the work of Kleist that is at the centre of Deleuze and Guattari's discussion, and the composition Carrière analyses in greatest detail: *Penthesilea* (1807). This verse tragedy on a classical topic recounts the fatal love between

Achilles and Penthesilea, Queen of the Amazons. The drama opens with the stunned Greeks trying to assimilate the news of the unexpected appearance of Amazon warriors on the battlefield of Troy. The Greeks, pitted for years against the Trojans, had assumed that when the Amazons attacked the Trojans they had obviously come as allies of the Greeks, but the Amazons had then turned and attacked the Greeks as well. For Deleuze and Guattari, the Amazons are the perfect embodiment of the war machine. In the midst of the struggle between the Greeks and the Trojans, two manifestations of the State apparatus, a pure force erupts, a machine of war exterior to the State apparatus, and in this sense, 'a pure form of exteriority' (ATP 354). 'Descendants of the Scythians, the Amazons spring forth like lightning, "between" the two States, the Greek and the Trojan. They sweep away everything in their path' (ATP 355).

Penthesilea leads the charge, fighting with abandon and fury, yet in the midst of battle, she stops and freezes. As Odysseus reports to his comrades: 'For one moment, with a pensive gaze / She stares into our ranks, void of expression'. She remains immobile until she sees Achilles, at which point 'A deepening flush spreads down unto her neck, / Blood sets her face aglow as if the world / Surrounding her were leaping into flames. / Then, with a sudden jolt, she swings herself / [. . .] Down from her horse' (Kleist 1998: 7). Transfixed by an affect that passes through her, her face aglow as if in the midst of leaping flames, Penthesilea freezes for several seconds and then moves 'with a sudden jolt'. For Deleuze and Guattari, this scene represents the essential Kleistian stutter of affect, a series of moments of catatonic stasis and lightning movement. (It is the case that many of Kleist's protagonists fall into trances, swoon, sleepwalk, stand frozen and so on.) Kleist writes in affects and speeds, claim Deleuze and Guattari, 'a broken chain of affects and variable speeds, with accelerations and transformations, always in a relation with the outside'; 'everything with [Kleist], in his writing and his life, becomes speed and slowness. A succession of catatonic freezes and extreme velocities, fainting spells and shooting arrows' (ATP 9; 268). These limits of movement, stasis and infinite speed mark the limits of a continuum of non-subjective affects, and together they establish a specific time and rhythm.

> This element of exteriority – which dominates everything, which Kleist invents in literature, which he is the first to invent – will give time a new rhythm: an endless succession of catatonic episodes or fainting spells, and flashes or rushes. Catatonia is: 'This affect is too strong for me', and a flash is: 'The power of this affects sweeps me away', so that the Self (*Moi*) is now nothing more than a character whose actions and emotions are desubjectified, perhaps even to the point of death. (ATP 356)

Penthesilea's puzzling reaction to the sight of Achilles, we learn later, is the outward sign of her betrayal of a fundamental law of the Amazons, and for Deleuze and Guattari betrayal is a central component of the warrior and the war machine. Deleuze and Guattari assert that the Amazons are 'a State-less woman-people whose justice, religion, and loves are organized uniquely in a war mode' (ATP 355), but this assertion requires some qualification. As Carrière points out, the Amazons are not so much state-less as possessed of a weak state, whose 'social structures are still young and unstable' (Carrière 1981: 86; 1985: 82), nor are their institutions 'organized uniquely in a war mode'. As Penthesilea explains to Achilles, the Amazons are descendants of a tribe of Scythians, 'obedient to the gods / Warlike and free' (Kleist 1998: 92), who had been conquered by Vexoris, King of the Ethiopians. The Ethiopians had killed all the males of the tribe and forced themselves on the surviving women. The women, however, under the leadership of Tanaïs, plotted a rebellion, and one night, as the Ethiopian men came to their beds, all the women stabbed the men to death, Tanaïs delivering the fatal blow to Vexoris. A council then declared the formation of a nation of women, with Tanaïs as their queen, and when someone objected that women could not protect themselves without men, Tanaïs seized the ritual bow of Scythian state authority and tore away her right breast, thereby ridding herself of any encumbrance to the bow and demonstrating the warlike character necessary to survival. Thereafter, all Amazons adapted themselves for war by removing their right breasts (hence the name Amazon, Greek: *a-mazon*, without-breast). The Amazons also established three institutions to ensure the reproductive continuity of the community: the Feast of Maids in Bloom, the Feast of Roses and the Feast of Ripeness. During the Feast of Maids in Bloom, fecund virgins are assembled, consecrated for battle, and then sent forth to wage war on men. 'Then, like a fire-blazing storm, we burst / Into the forest of men', and bring the surviving warriors, 'the ripest of the ones that fall', back 'to the meadows of our native land' (Kleist 1998: 97). Upon their return, the maidens commence the Feast of Roses, during which they have sex with the conquered men 'Until the seed has blossomed in our wombs', at which point the final rite, the Feast of Ripeness, is celebrated and the men are sent home. As Penthesilea tells Achilles, the Feast of Ripeness, 'alas, is not the gladdest, / Son of the Nereid – there is much weeping, / And many a heart is seized with dismal sorrow' (Kleist 1998: 98).

The Feast of Maids in Bloom and the Feast of Roses are institutions meant to rein in the potentially uncontrollable forces of war and Eros, and as such they are inherently unstable. The Feast of Ripeness is the ritual that attempts to bring the release of the affects of war and love to a definitive conclusion and thereby reconstitute social stability. One of the laws meant to reinforce these inherently weak institutions is the rule that no warrior may choose the man she fights and eventually brings back as her sexual partner, a law that enforces group identity among the warriors, depersonalises the ensuing sexual activity, and reduces the women's pain upon the men's eventual departure. Penthesilea knows that 'It is not fitting for a daughter of Mars / To seek out her opponent' (Kleist 1998: 100), yet she has deliberately violated this fundamental law. Just before her departure for battle, Penthesilea's mother, Queen Otrerë, had made Penthesilea promise that she would bring back Achilles as her prize, and hence she had chosen Achilles as her enemy. Her choice of Achilles as opponent might easily be viewed as the outcome of a venerable tragic dilemma, that of facing an impossible choice between conflicting duties to state and family (as in Sophocles' *Antigone*), but for Deleuze and Guattari the choice of an opponent is a central feature of the warrior as component of the war machine.

Deleuze and Guattari oppose conventional social groups within the state (such as families, tribes, classes and so on) to bands, packs or gangs, the first defined by stable, hierarchical relations, the second by unstable, shifting associations, such that 'a pack, a band, a population, a peopling [constitute] a multiplicity' (ATP 239), irreducible to subunits without changing qualitatively in nature. Fundamental to the pack is affect, for affect 'is the effectuation of a power of the pack that throws the self into upheaval and makes it reel' (ATP 240). Yet, despite being a multiplicity, a pack always has a demonic, anomalous element, which marks the borderline of the pack. The anomalous is the most highly deterritorialised element of the pack, and as such the element that leads the pack towards a metamorphic becoming-other. Although Deleuze and Guattari speak of the anomalous as 'an exceptional individual', they soon qualify this statement, adding 'the anomalous is neither an individual nor a species; it has only affects, it has neither familiar or subjectified feelings, nor specific or significant characteristics' (ATP 223–4). Penthesilea is one such anomalous element, and her act of choosing is the index of her anomalous status. Deleuze and Guattari liken her to Ahab, who violates the code of the whale-hunter pack and chooses Moby-Dick as his enemy:

> Ahab chooses Moby-Dick, in a choosing that exceeds him and comes from elsewhere, and in so doing breaks with the law of the whalers according to which one should first pursue the pack. Penthesilea shatters the law of the pack, the pack of women, the pack of she-dogs, by choosing Achilles as her favorite enemy. (ATP 244)

Deleuze and Guattari also state that 'the anomalous choice' is the means by which 'each enters into his or her becoming-animal, the becoming-dog of Penthesilea, the becoming-whale of Captain Ahab' (ATP 244), and this 'becoming other' is yet another important aspect of the warrior's relation to the war machine. In Kleist's drama, Penthesilea's becoming-dog is one with Achilles' becoming-woman, a mutual becoming that leads to disaster. As Kleist relates the story, after choosing her opponent, Penthesilea faces Achilles on the battlefield. In their duel, Achilles strikes a blow that renders her unconscious. He takes her to his camp, where Prothoë, Penthesilea's confidante, begs Achilles to spare Penthesilea's life. Achilles tells Prothoë, however, that he had already planned to spare Penthesilea, for he has fallen in love with her and intends to make her his queen in his kingdom of Phthia. When Penthesilea begins to awaken, Prothoë tells her that she had triumphed over Achilles, and Achilles indirectly confirms the falsehood, telling Penthesilea that 'In every nobler sense' he is 'A captive bound and fettered by your eyes' (Kleist 1998: 80). Yet soon the truth is revealed, and Achilles informs her that

> I'll not follow you to Themiscyra,
> But rather you, to blooming Phthia, me:
> For once my people's war is finished, that's where
> I'll take you, caroling for joy, and seat you,
> Blessed that I am, upon my father's throne. (Kleist 1998: 103)

Penthesilea is horrified at the prospect of receiving 'a man / Not honorably conquered by the sword' (Kleist 1998: 78). Before Achilles can take her away, however, the Amazons rally and manage to free Penthesilea from Achilles' forces. Penthesilea departs in fury, Achilles in despair. Eventually, Achilles recognises the depth of his passion and decides to leave his troops, face Penthesilea in individual combat, and deliberately lose the fight and become her prisoner. Achilles assumes that Penthesilea's love for him is so great that she will not kill him when they meet, but Penthesilea knows nothing of his intentions, and she has descended into a fury that has rendered her mad. She summons her war-dogs, and when Achilles appears before her on the battlefield, she joins the dogs in attacking him, biting, eating and killing him as if she were one of the pack. When she returns to her senses and realises what she has done, she stabs herself to death.

Penthesila, then, refuses assimilation within Achilles' State apparatus as a subservient queen. Achilles, for his part, eventually abandons the Greeks and thereby betrays his own State. He becomes the anomalous element of his war pack, entering a becoming-woman, in that he is willing to place himself in the woman's traditional position of subordination. Penthesilea has betrayed the Amazons in having chosen Achilles, but her betrayal leads to a becoming-dog. She is the anomalous element within the Amazons, but her becoming has made her a member of another pack, one that devours the object of her choice – perhaps the ultimate betrayal.

In the Nomadology plateau, Deleuze and Guattari assert that 'the regime of the war-machine is [. . .] that of *affects*', and that 'affects are projectiles just like weapons'. Hence, 'Weapons are affects and affects weapons', and the prime example of this relationship comes from Kleist, who 'presents us with a becoming-weapon of the technical element simultaneous to a becoming-passional element (the Penthesilea equation)' (ATP 400). In the play's first reports of Penthesilea we see the conversion of affect into weapon. Diomedes relates a battle scene in which the Trojan Deiphobus had struck Achilles with his sword while Penthesilea was at Deiphobus' side. She froze 'two minutes long', and then brought 'her sword plunging, like a bolt from heaven, / Down with a blaze of light into his neck' (Kleist 1998: 10). The affect induces two minutes of catatonia, and that affect then is transformed into an instantaneous flash of the sword. Throughout the play the characters use the traditional image of love's arrows, but when Penthesilea begins her final assault on Achilles, she pierces his throat with an actual arrow before jumping on him with her dogs. And in the final scene we find affect itself becoming a weapon, without the intermediary of a physical object. Penthesilea has surrendered her arrows and dagger to Prothoë, but then she fashions an immaterial dagger from her inner feelings:

> For now I shall descend into my breast,
> And dig a shaft, and quarry out the cold
> Ore of a feeling that annihilates.
> This ore I purify in fire of grief
> To hardest steel. (Kleist 1998: 148)

From this steel, she claims to fashion a dagger, and with this affect-weapon, she stabs herself to death: 'And to this dagger now I yield my breast: / So! So! So! So! Again! – Now it is done' (Kleist 1998: 148).

The Warrior and the Secret

The warrior, then, is (1) the conduit of *speeds and affects*, (2) an agent of *betrayal*, (3) an *anomalous element*, (4) whose *choice of object* marks (5) a *becoming-other*, and (6) whose *affects are weapons* and *weapons affects*. To these dimensions of the warrior and the war machine, only one more must be added: the secret. Deleuze and Guattari find 'the most uncanny modernity' in Kleist because 'the elements of his work are secrecy, speed and affect' (ATP 356). The secret 'has its origin in the war machine; it is the war machine and its becomings-woman, becomings-child, becomings-animal that bring the secret' (ATP 287), and in Kleist 'the secret is no longer a content held within a form of interiority; rather, it becomes a form, identified with the form of exteriority that is always external to itself' (ATP 356). The secret as form of exteriority is a secret with no hidden content, a point of inscrutability that has no truth to reveal other than itself. As Carrière shows at length, secrets abound in Kleist's works, and inevitably they set off a chain of affective events. In *Penthesilea*, Achilles' becoming-woman, his decision to yield to Penthesilea, is a secret to her, and her becoming-dog is a secret he cannot comprehend, but in both cases the genuine secret is the becoming-other itself, which is the exteriority of the secret with no hidden meaning at all. Perhaps the best example of the secret, however, is found in the conclusion of *Michael Kohlhaas*. The horse-trader Kohlhaas, who has waged a personal war in search of justice and has been captured and condemned to death, has in his possession an amulet inscribed with a gypsy's prediction of the fate of the Elector of Saxony's house, which prediction, some months earlier, she had written down in the Elector's presence but then given to Kohlhaas. Neither the Elector nor Kohlhaas has read the inscription, but the gypsy has told Kohlhaas that its contents, if revealed to the Elector, will later save his life. When the Elector eventually tries to acquire the amulet, Kohlhaas refuses to give it up, and just before being executed, Kohlhaas stares at the Elector, who is in disguise among the crowd, opens the amulet, reads the inscription and then swallows it just before being beheaded. The secret is Kohlhaas's weapon (when Kohlhaas consumes the inscription, the Elector is seized by a fit and falls unconscious to the ground), and though it provides the answer to the Elector's question about the fate of his house, it is not even clear that Kohlhas knows the question, and hence that the answer Kohlhaas reads in his final minutes means anything to him. The secret is irreducible, impenetrable, a pure *form* of the secret, with no content.

Kleist's literature of war, then, is a literature of the warrior, who is a vehicle of affective speeds and inscrutable secrets, 'a traitor to the world of dominant significations, and to the established order' (D 41), a wielder of affect-weapons, and an anomalous element whose choice of enemy demarcates a line of flight and a becoming-other. Affect pervades all aspects of this literature, and hence we may continue to say that Kleist, like Kafka, writes in affects, but that Kleist's treatment of affects is specific to the climate of war.

Gemüt and Grace

One additional means of differentiating Kleist's affective writing from Kafka's, less pragmatic and more theoretical, remains in the Kleistian concept of *Gemüt*, which is articulated in Kleist's essays 'On the Puppet Theatre' and 'On the Gradual Fabrication of Thoughts While Speaking'. Carrière provides a detailed analysis of *Gemüt*, and it is to this analysis that Deleuze and Guattari allude in their passing remarks on the concept. An elusive, untranslatable term, *Gemüt* may mean, among other things, 'mind', 'nature, disposition', 'soul', 'feeling' or 'warm-heartedness'. (Carrière's French translator chooses to translate *Gemüt* as 'le cœur', 'the heart'.) It was a favourite term among German Romantics and, for some writers of the period, the centre of a veritable 'cult of *Gemüt*'. In *A Thousand Plateaus* Deleuze and Guattari allude twice to Kleistian *Gemüt*. In the first passage, Deleuze and Guattari remark that Kleist 'is fascinated by bears; they are impossible to fool because their cruel little eyes see through appearances to the true "soul of movement", the *Gemüt* or nonsubjective affect: the becoming-bear of Kleist' (ATP 268). In the second, Deleuze and Guattari cite Kleist's brief essay 'On the Gradual Fabrication of Thoughts While Speaking' and argue that Kleist there articulates 'the thought of the *Gemüt*, which proceeds like a general in a war machine should, or like a body charged with electricity, with pure intensity [. . .] the *Gemüt* that refuses to be controlled, that forms a war machine' (ATP 378). To explicate these dense, somewhat cryptic passages, we must turn now to Carrière's more detailed analyses of Kleistian *Gemüt*.

For the German Romantics, says Carrière,

> *Gemüt* is neither emotivity nor soul. There are perhaps as many authors as definitions of the term. For all such authors, *Gemüt* is defined as a place suspended in a climate of the unconscious: as psychic locus, it has a Janus head, with one face examining the inner sanctum, and with the other obeying the orders of consciousness. (Carrière 1981: 24; 1985: 23)

Carrière finds in E. T. A. Hoffmann a tendency to separate *Gemüt* from the subject, and he argues that Kleist completes this movement by entirely desubjectivising *Gemüt*.

> For Kleist, *Gemüt* is nothing more than the relay of affects. By affect, in this context, what is meant is a concentration of non-subjective force whose expression is realised in a place which at no instant may be divided into an exterior or an interior. *Gemüt* is henceforth deprived of personal sensations and experiences, however divided and differentiated they may be; it becomes a charged battery, transforming murderous forces, killing anyone who commits an error in manipulation. *Gemüt* is a silent storm, from which, from time to time, lightning shoots forth. (Carrière 1981: 24; 1985: 23)

If war is a 'climate of infection', the meeting place of opposing affective intensities, then *Gemüt* is itself a war zone, a zone of indiscernibility between the psychic interior and the world outside, through which affects pass and clash, within which intensities are stored and occasionally released in explosive flashes.

Carrière, like Deleuze and Guattari, relates *Gemüt* to Kleist's fascination with bears, but in a somewhat more complex fashion than do Deleuze and Guattari. When Deleuze and Guattari say that bears 'are impossible to fool because their cruel little eyes see through appearances to the true "soul of movement", the *Gemüt* or nonsubjective affect' (ATP 268), they are alluding to the concluding section of Kleist's 'On the Puppet Theatre'. There, the master dancer recounts for the narrator a strange experience he had facing a tame bear as a fencing opponent. Try as he might, he could not strike the bear, who easily deflected all his attacks.

> It was not merely that the bear, like the world's leading fencer, parried every one of my thrusts, but to my feints he reacted not at all (a feat that no fencer anywhere could match). Eye to eye, as though he could read my very soul, he stood with his paw poised for the strike, and if my thrusts were not in earnest he simply did not move. (Kleist 1982: 216)

In this example, we find an additional attribute of *Gemüt*, beyond that of a storm centre of affective intensities: it possesses a non-subjective intuition of the soul's movements in others and maintains a centre of gravity within. Kleist closes 'On the Puppet Theatre' with the master dancer's observation that 'in the organic world, as reflection grows darker and weaker, grace [*die Grazie*] emerges more radiant and supreme'. Yet humans might still attain grace in their dancing, for 'just as two intersecting lines, converging on one side of a point, reappear on the other after their passage through infinity, [. . .] so will grace, having likewise traversed the infinite, return to us once more, and so appear most purely in that bodily form that has either no consciousness at all or an infinite one, which is to say, either in the puppet or a god' (Kleist 1982: 216). Grace, then, finds its perfection in either the automaton or a god, and the bear is an embodiment of animal 'grace', which is closer to the absolute grace of the automaton than any human grace, save that which might be attained at an infinite point when human reflection becomes that of a god. But, as Carrière notes, if the bear is an embodiment of animal grace, it also is tame, imprisoned and often awkward in its movements within its constricted world. Carrière views the Kleistian bear as a figure of a paradoxical combination of clumsiness and grace, of the adroit and the maladroit, a combination that characterised Kleist himself in his social life, and that appears in the frequent swoons, trances, stupors and dream-states his protagonists fall into before exploding into graceful action.

This combination of awkwardness and grace is also manifest in the thought of *Gemüt*, which forms the subject matter of Kleist's 'On the Gradual Fabrication of Thoughts While Speaking'. Kleist opens the essay by recounting a common experience he has while attempting to understand a difficult law case or solve a mathematical problem. He sits at his desk, stares at a light, with his sister behind him intent on her own work. He has a vague sense of the answer he is seeking, and with a 'dark notion [*dunkle Vorstellung*]' of the answer, he begins to explain it to his sister. On such occasions, 'my mind [*das Gemüt*] [. . .] shapes that muddled idea into a form of new-minted clarity, even while my talking progresses'. During this process, 'I mumble inarticulately, drawl out my conjunctions, use unnecessary appositions, and avail myself of all other dilatory tricks to gain the time required for fabricating my idea in the workshop of Reason [*Vernunft*].' The process is accelerated when his sister makes a gesture as if to interrupt him, for his 'intellect [*Gemüt*], already sorely exercised, becomes all the more agitated at this external threat to tear it away from the speech which is guiding it, and, like a great general when circumstances marshal against him, I am suddenly a degree more capable of my objective' (Kleist 1982: 218–19). What this demonstrates, Kleist argues, is that 'the lines of thought and expression move abreast, and both mental processes [*Gemütsakte*, literally '*Gemüt*-acts'] are congruent to each other. Speech [*Sprache*] is not a fetter, then, like a drag chain on the wheel of the mind [*des Geistes*], but a second wheel running parallel to it on the same axle' (Kleist 1982: 221). Moreover, there is something non-personal about this thought of *Gemüt*. When students are asked an unexpected question, such as 'What is the State?' or 'What is property?', often they stammer, even if they do know the answer, since they do not have a clichéd, pre-formed definition at hand. Only 'a foolish examiner would conclude that they did not know [the answer]. For it is not *we* who "know"; it is rather a certain condition, in which we happen to be, that "knows"' (Kleist 1982: 222).

For Deleuze and Guattari, this stammering thought of *Gemüt*, in which speech and thought run parallel on the same axle, is consonant with Kafka's minor writing, in which expression precedes content, the process of creative invention taking place through a sonic and conceptual deterritorialisation of language. Deleuze and Guattari also relate the thought of *Gemüt* to Artaud's 'incapacity' (*impouvoir*) of thought, finding similarities in Kleist's 'On the Gradual Fabrication of Thought While Speaking' and in Artaud's correspondence with Jacques Rivière. For Artaud, 'thought operates on the basis of a *central breakdown*', living 'solely by its own incapacity to take on form'. Similarly, Kleist's 'thought of the *Gemüt*, which proceeds like a general in a war machine', entails a loss of control of language, a process of 'being a foreigner in one's own tongue'. In this thought we see

> the form of exteriority, the relation between brother and sister, the becoming-woman of the thinker, the becoming-thought of the woman: the *Gemüt* that refuses to be controlled, that forms a war machine [. . .] an event-thought, a haecceity, instead of a subject-thought. (ATP 378; see also WP 55, where the Kleist–Artaud comparison is drawn in similar terms.)

Gemüt and Action

Deleuze and Guattari loosely tie the thought of *Gemüt* to war, in that *Gemüt*, by refusing to be controlled, 'forms a war machine', but Carrière's extended treatment of the concept helps specify the ways in which the thought of *Gemüt* is related to the grace, affect and violence of Kleistian *Gemüt* and to the dilemmas posed by a literature of war. Carrière points out that in 'On the Gradual Fabrication of Thought While Speaking', all the examples of the thought of *Gemüt* involve individuals who are pressured by external forces. In one example, Mirabeau rises to revolutionary eloquence during the National Assembly when the King's Master of Ceremonies enters the Assembly and delivers the King's order to disband. Under the external pressure of the King's command and the National Assembly's conflicting expectations, Mirabeau, initially unsure of what he will say, begins speaking, and then, 'leaping to the pinnacle of audacity', delivers his famous words of defiance. In a second example, drawn from La Fontaine's fable 'Les animaux malades de la peste', the fox saves his life while pleading his case before the lion-king's assembly. To put an end to the plague, the gods have demanded a sacrifice of the worst sinner among the animals, and the fox, uncertain of the means of escaping his nomination as the proper sacrificial offering, begins speaking, and in the process gradually finds the inspiration of accusing the donkey of being the worst animal sinner, thereby saving his life. The example we mentioned earlier, of students fumbling their answers when asked, 'What is the State?' or 'What is property?', is a third instance of thought under pressure – in this case, thought that may not be given sufficient time to develop if the examiners are hasty and demand ready responses. And even the apparently benign example Kleist offers at the opening of the essay, that of his formulation of a thought while speaking to his sister, involves the intervention of the sister, whose apparent movement to interrupt him is an 'external threat' that causes him to respond 'like a great general when circumstances marshal against him' (Kleist 1982: 219).

The thought of *Gemüt*, the process whereby thought passes from initial confused babbling to inspired articulation, is one of *Gemütsakte*, thought-acts, and they are *affective* thought-acts, in which an autonomous, non-personal *Gemüt* functions as the locus of conflicting forces, those both internal and external to the thinking individual. For this reason, Carrière asserts that 'the discourse of *Gemüt* [*Gemüts-Rede*] is a form of war: *Gemüt* "speaks" under the pressure of events. Its warrior discourse is a source of joy; it provokes revolutionary gestures.' Ultimately, says Carrière, '*Gemüt* is like the plane of consistency of every assemblage; it is the goal of its own desire' (Carrière 1981: 63; 1985: 60).

Thought, then, is not distinct from action or from affect, but is itself affective thought-action. And its combination of awkwardness and grace is simply one instance of the awkwardness and grace of the dancer and the warrior. If we return to the essay 'On the Puppet Theatre', the grace of the puppet's dance is explained through the example of the fencing bear. The bear is both clumsy and graceful, and its grace is revealed in the limited combat of the fencing match. Deleuze and Guattari cite the bear's graceful mastery of the 'center of gravity' as an instance of 'the *Gemüt* or nonsubjective affect: the becoming-bear of Kleist' (ATP 268), but this 'becoming-bear' also contains a hint of menace and violence, a latent content that becomes overt in Kleist's drama *Die Hermannsschlacht* (*The Battle of Hermann*, 1808). The play focuses on the Battle of Teutoburg Forest (9 CE), in which Hermann (Latin: Arminius) unites with other German tribes to decimate the forces of the occupying Romans under the command of Varus. Before organising the tribal rebellion, Hermann has maintained friendly relations with the Romans, and specifically with Ventidius, one of Varus' representatives. Hermann's wife, Thusnelda, has been courted by Ventidius, and when Hermann plans his revolt, Thusnelda decides to wreak her own vengeance on the Romans. She invites Ventidius to meet her for an evening tryst in a garden, and when Ventidius arrives, she locks him in the garden with a ravenous female bear. As the bear eats Ventidius and he cries for help, Thusnelda taunts him, asking him 'Is she resisting your advances? [. . .] Tell her, Ventidius, that you love her' (Kleist 2008: 111).

Hence, in Kleist's becoming-bear there is a continuum of affect from graceful dance to violent destruction, the fencing bear being a chained, tamed becoming, the becoming-bear of Thusnelda an unleashed, wild becoming. Thusnelda's becoming-bear is like Penthesilea's becoming-dog, a becoming in which Eros and war meet in the female's consumption of the would-be male lover. The centre of this female becoming-animal is *Gemüt*, the zone of indiscernibility between inside and outside in which combating forces meet and from which they explode.

If we return to Penthesilea and her consumption of Achilles, we may complete the circuit that links thought, speech, affect and violence in a single plane of consistency called *Gemüt*. We have seen that affects are weapons and weapons affects, and specifically that Penthesilea can reach into her breast and form an incorporeal yet deadly dagger from the iron-ore affect in her heart. But, as Carrière shows, words, too, function as affect-weapons. When Penthesilea enters her becoming-dog, she does so via an incantatory recitation of the names of the dogs in her pack, each name the invocation of an affective power of destruction. When she finally comes to her senses after eating Achilles, she asks, in a strange, dazed voice, whether she kissed him to death and concludes, 'So it was a mistake. A kiss, a bite, / The two should rhyme' (and, as the translator notes, in the German text 'the words *Küsse* and *Bisse* [kisses and bites] actually rhyme'). She says to Achilles, 'Most pitiful of mortals, you forgive me! / By Artemis, my tongue pronounced one word / For sheer unbridled haste to say another'. She explains what she means about her confusion of words by observing that many young women tell their lovers, 'I love you, oh so much / That if I could, I'd eat you up right here', whereas in her case, as she tells the dead Achilles, 'Look: When *my* arms were wrapped around your neck, / I did what I had spoken, word for word; / I was not quite so mad as it might seem' (Kleist 1998: 146). The mouth that should kiss and murmur words of love makes a mistake; kisses become bites, a figure of speech becomes a corporeal act. 'She devours her love, lapsus linguae', a slip of the tongue, which, perhaps, is 'the fulfilment of love. Body and Speech are interchangeable' (Carrière 1981: 77; 1985: 74).

In Kleist's literature of war, 'to speak with *Gemüt* means to make war, to speak in order to destroy' (Carrière 1981: 65; 1985: 62). The thought of *Gemüt* is one with the acts of *Gemüt*. *Gemüt* is the battleground of opposing affects, the site of inseparable awkwardness and grace, the awkwardness being the catatonic, still storm of accumulating affect, grace being the instantaneous flash of exploding affect. Even in the apparently harmless thought of *Gemüt*, in which *Gemüt*-acts bring Speech and Mind together, danger lurks. 'Catastrophe inhabits each thing; it is the intimate point of every centre of gravity; it is the capacity of every thing to transform itself into another, the tendency toward disintegration' (Carrière 1981: 75; 1985: 71). The moments of stasis are moments in which affects are transformed, in which becomings arise. The transformation of affects may bear on thoughts, words, weapons or bodies, leading as easily to acts of love as acts of violence. The problem Kleist addresses in his literature of war is in this regard the problem of the war machine's uncontrollable, unpredictable and dangerous power of transformation, and all his writing is engaged with this problem.

Kleist's War Machine and Kafka's Bureaucratic Machine

We may now formulate a detailed definition of a Kleistian literature of war: a literature that immediately engages a war machine (an assemblage on a line of flight, or abstract line traced by the displacements of a centre of gravity) and war (the climate of infection in which opposing forces–affects–intensities collide, accumulate and explode) on a plane of consistency (speeds and affects) that is also a plane of exteriority (the author's writings, life, historical events and so on), whose protagonists are warriors (vehicles of affective speeds and inscrutable secrets; traitors to dominant significations and the established order; wielders of affect-weapons; anomalous elements whose choice of enemy demarcates a line of flight and a becoming-other) and whose fundamental component is *Gemüt* (the zone of indiscernibility between inside and outside, in which affects engender becomings that transform thoughts, words, objects and bodies, and induce in them unpredictable, uncontrollable and dangerous metamorphic relations).

We have identified five commonalities in Kafka and Kleist: writing and life on a single plane of exteriority; life plans as protocols of experimentation; writing on a plane of consistency traced by a line of flight; writing antithetical to the aesthetics of Goethe and politics of Hegel; and writing in affects. According to Deleuze's broad definition of the war machine, Kafka and Kleist both engage a war machine in their writing. If we review Deleuze and Guattari's definition of minor literature in Chapter 3 of *Kafka* – a literature that (1) deterritorialises language, (2) operates directly at the social and political level, and (3) engages a collective assemblage of enunciation – we can see that Kleist, like Kafka, would qualify as a minor writer. Kleist's thought of *Gemüt* involves the stammering of linguistic deterritorialisation in which expression precedes content, and, at least according to one of Kleist's English translators, his prose bears the strangeness of a deterritorialising style: Kleist's 'paragraphs often stretch for pages without a break', and the sentences 'are complex syntactical puzzles, claustrophobic labyrinths of pronominally linked subordinate clauses joined by semicolons that confound any prospect of foreseeable closure'

(Afterword to Kleist 2010: 282). All Kleist's major works deal with social and political events, primarily wars, rebellions, social upheavals and mass hysteria. And Kleist's collective assemblage of enunciation points towards the problematic future of a people to come confronted with a crushing State apparatus.

What finally differentiates Kleist from Kafka is their approach to the State apparatus, in Kleist's case via the war machine, in Kafka's via the bureaucratic machine. There is one work of Kleist's that does engage a bureaucratic machine – *Michael Kohlhaas* – and it is perhaps not surprising that this was Kafka's favourite work of Kleist's. In that narrative, Michael Kohlhaas seeks justice, and when denied justice by various courts, he declares war against the State, eventually leading a band of over a hundred marauders in an increasingly indiscriminate campaign of destruction. But if Kohlhaas's story is primarily about a war machine in opposition to the State, over half of Kleist's tale relates the contorted workings of the legal machinery of sixteenth-century Germany and Austria. These sections of Kleist's narrative read like a slightly more realistic, sixteenth-century version of Kafka's *The Trial*. But *Michael Kohlhaas* is the exception; the rest of Kleist's oeuvre examines only the war machine and its relation to the State.

One might say that, whereas Kleist focuses on the deterritorialisation of the State from the outside, Kafka explores the deterritorialisation of the State from within. According to Deleuze and Guattari, *The Trial* is an extended analysis of the Law as machine, in which everything is related to the law – not simply judges, bailiffs, lawyers, courts and police officers, but also businessmen, bankers, artists, priests, maids, neighbours, young girls and so on. In this regard, the Law is an overwhelming, all-encompassing, monolithic entity. Yet what Kafka shows is that desire permeates the entire structure, that at every juncture the machine is in the process of disassembling itself, of mutating in strange and unpredictable twists and turns. K. is the line of flight that passes through the machine, opening paths of deterritorialisation in each episode of the plot. He is less a character than a function – 'the K. function' (D 122) – a generative centre of gravity tracing an abstract line of the steepest gradient. *The Castle* is the logical complement to *The Trial*, in that *The Trial* analyses the

Law component of the bureaucratic machine, whereas *The Castle* focuses on the bureaucratic machine as a whole, with the Law machine treated as merely a component of the State apparatus. Here, too, K. remains a function, and his deterritorialising path again reveals the immanent desire that plays through the State apparatus, exposing the mutative elements within the monolithic, all-pervasive institution of the Castle.

For Kafka, the central problem is to diagnose the '*diabolical powers that are knocking at the door*', especially 'Fascism, Stalinism, Americanism', and to make his literary machine 'the relay for a revolutionary machine-to-come' (K 41, 18). Kleist's problem is to conceive of a war machine as alternative to the State apparatus that does not simply become a machine of external destruction or collapse upon itself in suicidal annihilation. In Deleuze and Guattari's estimation, Kleist's view of the problem is not at all optimistic: 'Throughout his work, Kleist celebrates the war machine, setting it against the State apparatus in a struggle that is lost from the start' (ATP 355). In *Die Hermannsschlacht*, Hermann wages war against the Roman State, but his triumph leads to a new German state with Hermann himself declared king. Hermann, like Kafka's K., is less character than function, but his war machine-function is purely destructive. For example, he enlists a group of Germans to disguise themselves as Romans, and one of the disguised warriors rapes a young German woman, whose father slays her to protect her honour. Hermann hides the fact that the rapist was a German in disguise, bids the father dismember his daughter's corpse, and send its fifteen parts to the fifteen German tribes in order to unite them in hatred against the Romans – and this complex of deceit, betrayal, violence, murder and dismemberment is the foundation of the new German State. In *The Prince of Homburg*, the Prince launches a war machine at the Battle of Fehrbellin, attacking before receiving the requisite orders of the commander in chief, but he eventually surrenders himself to the State and willingly faces execution in service to the Law. Michael Kohlhaas's war machine opposes the State, but Kohlhaas ultimately disbands his forces, submits to the Law, and goes peacefully to his execution. And in *Penthesilea* the war machines disengaged from the strong Greek State and the weak Amazon state eventuate in a suicidal becoming-woman and becoming-animal that destroy Achilles and Penthesilea. Kleist's fiction as a whole poses the question:

> Is it the destiny of the war machine, when the State triumphs, to be caught in this alternative: either to be nothing more than the disciplined military organ of the State apparatus, *or to turn against itself*, to become a double suicide machine for a solitary man and a solitary woman? [. . .] Is the war machine already overtaken, condemned, appropriated? (ATP 356)

The most positive thing one can say is that perhaps

> at the moment the war machine ceases to exist, conquered by the State, [. . .] it displays to the utmost its irreducibility, that it scatters into thinking, loving, dying, or creating machines that have at their disposal vital or revolutionary powers capable of challenging the conquering State. (ATP 356)

The Place of Kleist in Deleuze and Guattari's Thought

The Kafka–Kleist connection provides an important means for Deleuze and Guattari to extend the concept of minor literature and to explore the ways in which literary concerns are inextricable from diverse social, political and historical issues outside its immediate purview. The first published reference to Kleist is in a 1974 lecture of Deleuze's, and Kleist is briefly cited only four times in *Kafka* (1975), most importantly in the differentiation of minor literature and a literature of war. In *Dialogues* (1977) and *A Thousand Plateaus* (1980), however, discussions of Kleist abound, albeit in sections that never extend beyond two pages. In *What is Philosophy?* (1991) and *Essays Critical and Clinical* (1993), Kleist is mentioned a few times, but generally to reiterate the points fully articulated in *Dialogues* and *A Thousand Plateaus*. Kafka likewise is cited regularly in texts following *Kafka*, although little is added to the 1975 analysis of Kafka's fiction in subsequent references. Clearly, in *Kafka* Deleuze and Guattari worked through the possibilities offered by Kafka for productive thought about literature, and thereafter Kleist provided them with new possibilities for approaching literature, which they had fully explored by *A Thousand Plateaus*. The concepts Deleuze and Guattari found in Kleist – the war machine, nomadic thought, the warrior, speeds and affects, the secret, the anomalous element, the choice of enemy, affects as weapons – are all embedded in separate discussions of those concepts in *A Thousand Plateaus*, and in each instance the fundamental discussion is not literary, but social, political, anthropological and historical. Kleist, perhaps more than any other writer, instantiates for Deleuze and Guattari the pervasive interconnections literature may form with the world at large. Whether Kleist played a key role in generating Deleuze and Guattari's thought about the war machine, nomadism, the warrior and so on; whether their thought about these concepts co-evolved with their analysis of Kleist's works; or whether their thought about these concepts preceded and guided their treatment of Kleist, is impossible to determine. What is indisputable, however, is that Kleist was a crucial component of a creative line of thought from 1974 to 1980, and that the Kafka–Kleist connection was one that facilitated a broadening of the concept of minor literature and an articulation of the extended implications of what it means to be a writer.

Notes

1. I believe that Kafka's immediate engagement of a bureaucratic machine is what is essential in his literature, and that its characterisation as a 'minority machine' (D 123) is not helpful in understanding the Kafka–Kleist connection, and, indeed, potentially misleading. In *Kafka*, Deleuze and Guattari tangentially link Kafka to ethnic and cultural minorities by citing Kafka's *Diary* entry concerning 'kleine Literaturen' (literally, 'small literatures'; translated as 'minor literatures'), such as Czech literature, and by discussing Kafka's short lecture on the Yiddish theatre, but for the most part they treat Kafka as a minor writer in the broad sense that he engages in a minor usage of language – that is, he deterritorialises language. In identifying Kafka's literary machine with a 'minority machine', Deleuze states that Kafka engaged 'a new collective assemblage of enunciation for German (an assemblage of minorities in the Austrian Empire had already been Masoch's idea, in a different way)'. Deleuze actually says

very little about minorities in his 1967 treatment of Sacher-Masoch, and the stress on minorities in *Dialogues* seems to be the first sign of a growing awareness of that dimension of Sacher-Masoch's work, an awareness that receives full expression only in the three-page essay, 'Re-presentation of Masoch', published in *Essays Critical and Clinical* (1993). There, Deleuze asserts unequivocally that 'Masoch's work [. . .] is inseparable from a literature of minorities' (CC 55), though he provides no evidence to substantiate this claim. My assumption is that in the course of writing *A Thousand Plateaus*, Deleuze and Guattari became increasingly aware of the importance of minority populations in literature in general, and that they therefore emphasised this aspect of Kafka and Masoch in their later writings, thereby adding a dimension to their previous analyses of these writers that had not been there initially. Hence, I will deal only with Kafka's bureaucratic machine, upon which Deleuze and Guattari place central emphasis in *Kafka*. I should add that, in appropriations of the concept of 'minor literature' by recent critics, all too often the term is used as a synonym for 'minority literatures', and through that term Deleuze and Guattari are recruited for the defence of identity politics, which, of course, is antithetical to Deleuze and Guattari's conception of minor writing.

2. All translations from Carrière are my own. I provide references to both the German original and the French translation.
3. I have chosen to ignore two interesting references to Kleist in Deleuze and Guattari: Kleist as a practitioner of a mannerism similar to Kafka's (K 79–80, 98 n. 6) and the comparison of Melville's protagonists to Kleist's Penthesilea and Kätchen von Heilbronn (CC 79–80, 192–3 n. 14). Fascinating as these references may be, the first raises issues that, in my judgement, are tangential to Deleuze and Guattari's understanding of both Kafka and Kleist, and the second broaches questions that are not central to an analysis of the Kafka–Kleist connection.
4. For anyone familiar with German literary history, this blanket opposition of Lenz, Hölderlin, Kleist, Büchner, Nietzsche and Kafka to Goethe and Hegel must seem simplistic. First, one must ask, which Goethe are we talking about? Deleuze, Guattari and Carrière seem to be speaking, not of the actual, protean writer, but of the popular image of Goethe as cultural icon that arose in the later nineteenth century and twentieth century, an image that is essentially a caricature of the late, classical Goethe as symbol of German greatness. The allegiance of Goethe with Hegel is equally problematic, both in its assumptions about Goethe and its caricatured presentation of Hegel. The relationship between any one of the supposed 'anti-Goethes'

and Goethe is complex, and in some cases complicated by personal interactions between the individual and Goethe (Lenz, Hölderlin and Kleist). Establishing the common elements in Lenz, Hölderlin, Kleist, Büchner, Nietzsche and Kafka would also require careful and discerning analysis. Finally, labelling Kafka as 'anti-Goethe' ignores the fact that all his life Kafka deeply admired Goethe. Deleuze and Guattari concede this fact (K 29), but offer only the explanation that Kafka's admiration may stem from Kafka's self-identification with Mephistopheles in *Faust*. But such a hypothesis only points to the problem of speaking of Goethe as a monolithic figure, since Goethe's major works include, among others, *Götz von Berlichingen*, *Werther*, *Faust Parts I* and *II* and *Elective Affinities*, none of which may be readily assimilated with the classicism of, say, *Torquato Tasso* or *Iphigenia in Tauris*. As for the opposition of painting and music drawn by Carrière, it serves as a useful metaphor for understanding Carrière's approach to Kleist, but it will not bear up under even rudimentary scrutiny as a general statement about the relationship between the two arts.

11

On the Superiority of Chinese-American Literature

'On the Superiority of Anglo-American Literature' is the title of Section Two of Deleuze and Parnet's *Dialogues*. In that section Deleuze speaks of English and American literature as a single phenomenon, but it is possible to distinguish between the two and determine the elements that Deleuze deems characteristic of American literature alone. Besides considering the Deleuzian image of American literature as a whole, I wish to reflect on the geographic components of his conception, especially his valorisation of the West, both as locus and as direction, and within that national and geographical context, to remark very briefly on Chinese-American literature, something Deleuze does not himself address.

English and American Literature

Deleuze and Parnet's 1977 *Dialogues* is a free-form improvisation on themes from Deleuze's earlier work and numerous motifs soon to appear in *A Thousand Plateaus*. The ostensible topic of Section Two is English and American literature's superiority to French literature, but in the course of Deleuze's divagations numerous heterogeneous concerns are loosely tied to the subject at hand. The remarks on literature per se elaborate on a paragraph on Anglo-American literature in *Anti-Oedipus* and also bring together the concepts related to minor literature, enunciated at length in *Kafka*, and the concepts of lines, becomings, nomadism and treason of *A Thousand Plateaus*.

According to Deleuze, the problem with French writers is that they don't know how to flee. They confuse escape from the world, whether mystical or artistic, with tracing a line of flight. They are mired in the imaginary, the realm of phantasms, whereas the line of flight emerges in the real. French writers, Deleuze says, 'are too human, too historical, too concerned with the past and future' (D 37), and hence unable to engage becomings. They are, he says, 'too fond of roots, trees, the survey, the points of aborescence, the properties' (D 37), and thus constitutively unrhizomatic. When they recommence any project, they seek a first principle, a point of origin, a tabula rasa, rather than starting in the middle. Theirs is a literature of treachery rather than treason, of transgression rather than conjunction. Because French writers see in flight an escape into the imaginary or a separate realm of art, they view literature as something personal (an internal reality) or formally complete and autotelic (art for art's sake, the work as finished entity). For these reasons, says Deleuze, 'French literature abounds in manifestos, in ideologies, in theories of writing, at the same time as in personal conflicts, in perfecting of perfectings, in neurotic toadying, in narcissistic tribunals [. . .] French literature is often the most shameless eulogy of neurosis' (D 49). Deleuze cites with approval D. H. Lawrence's assessment of French literature as 'incurably intellectual, ideological and idealist, essentially critical, critical of life rather than creative of life', to which Deleuze adds that 'a terrible mania for judging and being judged' (D 49–50) runs through all of French literature.

English and American writers, by contrast, know how to flee. They do not seek escape into the imaginary but engagement with the real. Their flight sets the world in flight, unmoors the fixed elements of the real. Deleuze says that in 'Thomas Hardy, Melville, Stevenson, Virginia Woolf, Thomas Wolf, Lawrence, Fitzgerald, Miller, Kerouac [. . .] everything is departure, becoming, passage, leap, daemon, relationship with the outside. They create a new Earth; but perhaps the movement of the earth is deterritorialization itself' (D 36–7). Their concern is not with the past or future, but the time of becoming, not a revolutionary future but a 'becoming-revolutionary' (D 37) in the untimely time between times, the time of haecceities and infinitives. These writers are constantly restarting, halting and starting again, but always in the middle, never at a beginning, origin or first principle. Their becomings are rhizomatic, like grass rather than trees. 'Trees are the opposite of grass. Not only does grass grow in the middle of things, but it grows itself through the middle [. . .] Grass has its line of flight, and does not take root' (D 39). Anglo-American literary flight is not neurotic, but 'a sort of delirium', a pact with demons rather than a covenant with Jehovah. Treachery and trickery – those French modes of calculating one's advantage, weighing past actions and future probabilities, gaining power from within social structures – are replaced by betrayal and treason, whereby one 'no longer has any past or future' and seeks to 'betray the fixed powers which try to hold us back, the established powers of the earth [. . .] the world of dominant significations [. . .] the established order' (D 40–1). Rather than formulate manifestos or pursue personal quarrels, English and American writers, like Kleist and Kafka, draw up 'programs of life', which Deleuze describes as 'finite processes of experimentation, protocols of experience'. Such programmes, processes and protocols are not manifestos or phantasms, says Deleuze, '*but means of providing reference points for an experimentation which exceeds our capacities to foresee*' (D 48). For the English and Americans, writing reaches no terminus, but consists of a ceaseless, open-ended process without final destination. And for them, writing is not a self-enclosed, autotelic activity. 'In reality', says Deleuze,

> *writing does not have its end in itself, precisely because life is not something personal.* Or rather, the aim of writing is to carry life to the state of a non-personal power [. . .] To write has no other function: to be a flux which combines with other fluxes – all the minoritarian-becomings of the world. (D 50)

And what is the endpoint of those minoritarian-becomings, 'the aim, the finality of writing'? asks Deleuze. 'Still way beyond a becoming-woman, a becoming-black, a becoming-animal, etc., beyond a minoritarian-becoming, there is the final enterprise of becoming-imperceptible' (D 45).

Deleuze sees in English and American literature an affinity

with English empiricism, a philosophical position that for Deleuze receives its most penetrating formulation in Hume. Hume's central insight is that relations are external to their terms. Since the same terms may have different relations in different circumstances, all terms are only contextually comprehensible, and hence variable in their function and significance. For this reason, 'Empiricists are not theoreticians', says Deleuze, 'they are experimenters: they never interpret, they have no principles' (D 55). To think empirically is to experiment with specific contextual arrangements of terms and relations, to form assemblages, conjunctions of heterogeneous elements that enter into a co-functioning. This experimentation with assemblages is what brings together English philosophers and English-American writers, for 'empiricism is like the English novel', says Deleuze. 'It is a case of philosophizing as a novelist, of being a novelist in philosophy' (D 54).

Empiricists and English–American writers also partake of the same logic of 'AND'. To experiment is to assemble, and hence to connect elements with an open-ended conjunction. 'AND' is the connective of every assemblage and the creator of genuine multiplicity. To think empirically, to think with 'AND', is to make thought stutter, and in this regard empiricism is one with minor literature's deterritorialisation of language, which seeks a 'stuttering of language in itself', a 'minoritarian use of language' (D 58).

Deleuze and American Literature

In the course of his career, Deleuze makes reference to thirty-eight American writers, most merely in passing. H. P. Lovecraft and Henry Miller are quoted several times in the two volumes of *Capitalism and Schizophrenia*, while James's 'In the Cage' and Fitzgerald's 'The Crack-Up' are given close, if compact, readings in Plateau Eight of *A Thousand Plateaus*. Deleuze includes a penetrating, brief essay on Whitman in *Essays Critical and Clinical.* But for Deleuze it is Melville who is the most important – indeed, one might say, the quintessential – American writer. Melville's pre-eminence is perhaps not immediately apparent in *Dialogues*, but it is worth observing that Deleuze begins his meditation on Anglo-American literature by making reference to D. H. Lawrence's salute to Melville's genius. Section Two's opening words are, 'To leave, to escape, is to trace a line. The highest aim of literature, according to Lawrence, is "To get away. To get away, out! . . . To cross a horizon into another life . . . So [Melville] finds himself in the middle of the Pacific. Truly over a horizon"' (D 36; trans. modified). Melville's primary function in *Dialogues* is to provide an example of becoming-animal, specifically in the figure of Ahab in his becoming-whale. (We might note that Ahab's becoming-whale is referenced seven times in the Becomings plateau of *A Thousand Plateaus*, four times as an illustration of percepts and affects in *What is Philosophy?*, and once in *Negotiations* in relation to Foucault's thought as a process of 'crossing the line' to the 'Outside' [N 111].) It is Ahab's becoming-whale that draws him into a line leading beyond the horizon, towards an open Outside. It is also through Ahab's becoming-whale that Deleuze brings together the themes of betrayal, choice and the demonic in *Dialogues*, in that Ahab's crime is that

> of having chosen Moby-Dick, the white whale, instead of obeying the law of the group of fishermen, according to which all whales are fit to hunt. In that lies Ahab's demonic element, his treason, his relationship with Leviathan – this choice of object which engages him in a becoming-whale himself. (D 42)

Melville's full significance for Deleuze, however, is only revealed in 'Bartleby; or, The Formula', one of Deleuze's finest pieces of literary criticism. Here, Deleuze reiterates *Dialogues*' points about Ahab's becoming-whale and Melville's enduring effort to trace a line beyond the horizon to an Outside, but he also connects Melville to the themes of minor literature – the deterritorialisation of language, the immediate engagement of the social and political, the activation of collective assemblages of enunciation – while delineating in Melville an American political ideal based on pragmatism, democracy and sympathy. In *Dialogues*, minor literature's deterritorialisation of language is treated in terms of making language stutter, but Deleuze offers no concrete literary instances of this practice. Instead, he concentrates on the English language itself as both a repressive force of global homogenisation and a medium open to multiple internal deformations. These characteristics he finds especially true of American English. 'The American language', he says, 'bases its despotic official pretensions, its majoritarian claim to hegemony, only on its extraordinary capacity for being twisted and shattered and for secretly putting itself in the service of minorities who work it from inside, involuntarily, unofficially, nibbling away at that hegemony as it extends itself: the reverse of power' (D 58). In the essay 'Bartleby', unlike *Dialogues*, Deleuze offers a specific instance of stuttering in literature – Bartleby's 'I prefer not to' – and submits it to an exhaustive analysis. Bartleby's 'formula' is an essence of stammering, a simple, short phrase whose iteration induces a cascade of deterritorialisations. Bartleby himself belongs to no ethnic minority, but his deployment of his formula is paradigmatic of minor literature's deterritorialising usage of language.

In 'Bartleby', then, Melville shows himself to be an exemplary practitioner of minor literature's deterritorialisation of language, but Melville's treatment of Bartleby, Deleuze shows, is connected to broader themes that echo throughout Melville's works. In Chapter 44 of *The Confidence-Man*, Melville reflects on characters in fiction, differentiating 'new, singular, striking, odd, eccentric, and all sorts of entertaining and instructive characters' from what he calls 'originals'. The original character, says Melville,

> is like a revolving Drummond light, raying away from itself all round it – everything is lit by it, everything starts up to it (mark how it is with Hamlet), so that, in certain minds, there follows upon the adequate conception of such a character, an effect, in its way, akin to that which in Genesis attends upon the beginning of things. (Melville 1964: 261)

No work of fiction may contain more than one Original, according to Melville (though Deleuze finds two in *Billy Budd*). Deleuze identifies two types of Originals in Melville: monomaniacs (Ahab in *Moby-Dick*, Claggart in *Billy Budd*, Babo in 'Benito Cereno') and hypochondriacs (Cereno and Billy Budd, but 'above all Bartleby' [CC 80]). These two types, '*monomaniacs* and *hypochondriacs*, demons and angels, torturers and victims, the Swift and the Slow, the Thundering and the Petrified' (CC 78–9), belong to a 'terrible supersensible Primary Nature, original and oceanic, which, knowing no Law, pursues its own irrational aim through them' (CC 79). By contrast, non-Originals, that is, ordinary humans, belong to sensible, rational Secondary Nature of Law. The 'biggest problem haunting Melville's oeuvre', says Deleuze, 'no doubt [. . .] lies in reconciling the two originals, *but thereby also in reconciling the original with secondary humanity*, the inhuman with the human' (CC 84).

Melville envisions that reconciliation in the annihilation of all father figures and the creation of a society of blood brothers and blood sisters. 'The American is one who is freed from the English paternal function', says Deleuze, and in founding a new world society the American vocation 'was not to reconstitute an "old State secret", a nation, a family, a heritage, or a father', but 'to constitute a universe, a society of brothers, a federation of men and goods, a community of anarchist individuals' (CC 85). Deleuze links the formation of such a universe to American pragmatism, which he regards as less a 'summary philosophical theory fabricated by Americans' than 'an attempt to transform the world, to think a new world or new man insofar as *they create themselves*' (CC 86). (In this regard, Deleuze views Melville as a pragmatist *avant la lettre*.) Pragmatism affirms the world as '*in process, an archipelago*' (CC 86), and the social order it advocates is one of 'islands and straits, immobile points and sinuous lines' (CC 86). Deleuze likens this order to a wall of stacked stones with no mortar, 'a wall of uncemented stones, where every element has a value in itself but also in relation to others' (CC 86). This order is 'an infinite patchwork with multiple joinings', 'a Harlequin's coat' (CC 86). And what holds it together is trust, hope and belief – not belief in a world to come, but belief in this world and its possibilities.

In pursuing a politics of the archipelago and belief in this world, American pragmatism faces a dual problem: that of overcoming all the particular differences among individuals that breed mistrust, but without succumbing to a fusion of souls in a grand Whole of philanthropy and charity. The solution is to counter particularities with singularities, and to replace charity with sympathy.

Singularities are becomings, apersonal intensities that retain specificity without taking on a conventional identity. In their becomings, men and women discover what Melville calls a 'democratic dignity', a radical equality of human beings without regard to their particularities, yet one that recognises each person's singularities. Such becomings, as social phenomena, give rise to collective intensities, which Deleuze identifies with 'sympathy' as opposed to 'charity'. Here Deleuze is following Lawrence in his reading of Whitman and Melville as advocates of what Lawrence describes as '"all the subtle sympathizings of the incalculable soul, from the bitterest hate to passionate love"' (cited in CC 87). Both singularities and sympathy are produced only when the individual 'takes to the open road (or the open sea) with its body, when it leads a life without seeking salvation, when it embarks upon its incarnate voyage, without any particular aim, and then encounters other voyagers, whom it recognizes by their sound' (CC 87). The open road is an American morality of sympathy, one 'with no other aim' than the journey, 'open to all contacts, never trying to save other souls, [. . .] with freedom as its sole accomplishment, always ready to free itself so as to complete itself' (CC 87).

The Specificity of American Literature

In treating Melville as the paradigmatic American writer, Deleuze is able to differentiate American from English literature in his Bartleby essay, though the distinction he draws is somewhat problematic. Melville's Original characters are inexplicable, like life itself, and hence beyond rationality. 'The founding act of the American novel,' says Deleuze, 'like that of the Russian novel, was to take the novel far from the order of reasons' (CC 81). Surprisingly, however, Deleuze contrasts the American and Russian novel in this regard with 'the English novel, and even more so the French novel' (CC 81). Deleuze also attributes the patchwork ideal of American democracy, central to the American literary project, to Americans, who, says Deleuze, 'invented patchwork, just as the Swiss are said to have invented the cuckoo clock' (CC 87), even though in *Dialogues* he describes English empiricism as 'a Harlequin's jacket or patchwork' (D 55). Yet these contradictions aside, which I regard as rhetorical strategies rather than definitive reassessments of English literature, other elements of Deleuze's analysis remain that may help us determine the specificity of American literature as Deleuze sees it. Deleuze is right to stress in Melville and American pragmatism the centrality of action, process, belief and community. American pragmatism builds on British empiricism, but, as Gérard Deledalle notes in a book cited by Deleuze, the experimentation of pragmatism, unlike British empiricism, is focused on 'the spirit of the laboratory', as Pierce expressed it, on science as method and on the collective enterprise of doing science. The stress on method entails a focus on actions and verifiable consequences, as well as on beliefs – as constituents of habits, as unavoidable in the formulation of hypotheses, and as confirmed or modified through experimentation.[1] Scientific inquiry, being an open-ended activity, envisions knowledge as process, and pragmatists situate this process within a world itself in the process of evolution. And science's collective dimension leads pragmatists to a general theory of action and inquiry as social activities, and eventually to Royce's ideal 'Community of Interpretation' and Dewey's democratic ideal.[2] Deleuze's focus on Melville and Whitman's sympathy, although not a theme in pragmatism, also helps differentiate English from American sensibilities. As Deleuze shows in his first book on Hume, sympathy figures prominently in Hume's social theory, as that which allows individuals to go beyond themselves to form larger communities. But Hume grounds his social theory in private property, whereas Melville's sympathy is part of a 'democratic dignity' that knows no distinctions of property. Sympathy regards the human as such, *homo tantum*, and in this regard, Deleuze argues, Melville's democratic ideal is the counterpart of the Russian communist ideal, Melville's ideal being envisioned as a universal community of immigrants, the Russian ideal as a universal community of workers. In sum, then, both English and American literature pursue lines of flight, deterritorialise language and form patchwork assemblages, but American literature stresses action and process more fully, and it alone articulates ideals of democratic sympathy, belief in this world, a universal community of immigrants and a camaraderie of the open road.

In principle, the open road of American sympathy has no privileged direction, but in its literary historical manifestation it has most often been the road to the West, as Deleuze notes in *Dialogues* and *A Thousand Plateaus*. In *Dialogues*, he remarks that 'American literature operates according to geographical lines: the flight towards the West, the discovery that the true East is in the West, the sense of the frontiers as something to cross, to push back, to go beyond' (D 37). In *A Thousand Plateaus*, he and Guattari state that 'directions in America are different: the search for arborescence and the return to the Old World occur in the East. But there is the rhizomatic West, with its Indians without ancestry, its ever-receding limit, its shifting and displaced frontiers' (TP 19). In both texts, Deleuze cites Leslie Fiedler's *Return of the Vanishing American* as the source of his comments, in *Dialogues* referring the reader to 'the whole analysis of Leslie Fiedler' (D 154), and in *A Thousand Plateaus* providing a succinct yet detailed summary of Fiedler's book in an extended footnote (TP 520).[3] Fiedler's argument is that in pre-Columbian Europe the West already had a mythological significance that would persist in the New World imagination. The map of pre-Columbian Europe consisted of the North (Europe), the South (Africa) and the East (Asia, which, incidentally included China from as early as the second century BCE). The West was not on the map as such, but simply an unknown territory beyond the map's edge, the mythic site of either an earthly paradise (Atlantis, the Blessed Isles) or a forbidden land of death (best represented by Dante's account of Ulysses' transgressive voyage west beyond the Straits of Gibraltar into shipwreck and sin). Fiedler argues that American literature, from its inception, is informed by an imaginary geography that views the West as an Edenic and transgressive territory, a land without women in which American males of European descent divest themselves of their past and form homoerotic bonds with Native Americans, Africans and other non-Europeans. Deleuze ignores the psychoanalytic content of Fiedler's analysis, but agrees that in American literature the journey west is the direction of deterritorialisation. From James Fenimore Cooper, through Melville to Jack Kerouac, the westward journey or voyage is the trajectory beyond the horizon to the Outside. And with Ginsberg,

Sanders and others the movement West ends in a discovery of the wisdom of the East.

In *A Thousand Plateaus*, Deleuze and Guattari oppose the arborescent West of Europe to the rhizomatic East of China, citing Henry Miller's declaration that '"China is the weed in the human cabbage patch"' (cited in ATP 18).[4] (For Miller, as for Deleuze and Guattari, the association of China with weeds is high praise, since the weed is an exemplary rhizome, something that '"*grows between*, among other things"' [ATP 55].) Midway between arborescent Europe and rhizomatic China Deleuze and Guattari situate America. They counter Haudricourt's claim that India is 'the intermediary between the Occident and the Orient', and assert instead that 'America is the pivot point and mechanism of reversal' (TP 19). In America, the movement east towards Europe is the line of reterritorialisation, whereas the movement west towards China is the line of deterritorialisation.

East and West, of course, are both locations and directions. Locations – *the* West, *the* East, West Coast, East Coast and so on – are largely defined by their pertinent landmasses, whether continents, islands or administrative territories (national, state, metropolitan, whatever). Directions, by contrast, are relations, and, as we know, relations are separate from their terms. On a globe, every point is both east and west of every other point, depending on the direction in which one travels. Geographically, if not culturally, India is as much between Europe and China as is America. The westward trajectory of much American literature is a function of the European colonisation of the New World, begun on the east coast and continued in the incremental opening of western territories to those pursuing America's Manifest Destiny. (Go west, young man!) Deleuze's focus on American literature's western vector reflects his attention primarily to white authors of European descent. Of the thirty-eight American writers Deleuze names, only three do not fit this profile: the African-Americans Chester Himes and Leroi Jones (Amira Baraka), both cited only once in passing, and, if one labels him a writer, the Hispanic-American Carlos Castaneda (a native of Peru). Deleuze, of course, is sensitive to questions of ethnicity and minorities in literary study – witness his analyses of Kafka, Sacher-Masoch and the concept of minor literature in general. In *Dialogues*, Deleuze does say that 'American is worked upon by a Black English, and also a Yellow English, a Red English, a broken English, each of which is like a language shot with a spray-gun of colors' (D 58), but he never deals with the writers of black, yellow, red or broken English. One wonders what Deleuze's portrait of American literature would have been like had he read the multiethnic literatures of the United States written by immigrants arriving from all directions. And what his geography of American literature would have resembled had he treated authors whose movement to America has been eastward – as is the case with Chinese-American writers.

Rather than offer vague generalities about Deleuze, American literature and Chinese-American authors as a whole, I would like to consider two such writers from a Deleuzian perspective: Maxine Hong Kingston, currently perhaps the most famous Chinese-American writer, and a much younger, less well-known author, Tao Lin.

Maxine Hong Kingston: Becoming Chinese-American, Becoming Woman

Born in 1940, Kingston explicitly characterises herself as a Chinese-American woman writer. Her first two publications, *The Woman Warrior: Memoirs of a Girlhood among Ghosts* (1976) and *China Men* (1980), are hybrid works of what might be called 'memoir fiction' or 'collective autobiography'. The ostensible topic of *Woman Warrior* is Kingston's childhood in Stockton, California, and her relationship with her various female Chinese relatives – mother, grandmother, assorted aunts and distant relations. Yet over half the narrative is devoted to the lives of her ancestors in China and the Chinese myths and tales she absorbed from the 'talk-story' of her kin. Her fiction engages a becoming-woman as she rejects traditional Chinese sexism, refashions folk myths from a feminist perspective, and betrays family secrets about disgraced female ancestors by telling the stories her mother says must not be told. She deterritorialises English through language that is both colloquial and poetic, engaging a wide range of indigenous American and Chinese immigrant rhythms and phrases.

Kingston's rendering of Chinese speech in English 'others' the language, such that Cantonese scholars fluent in English, when reading the Mandarin translation of her novel, told Kingston that they could hear the Cantonese rhythms of her Chinese speakers, and hence they retranslated the book into Cantonese (Skenazy and Martin 1998: 45).

If *Woman Warrior* is the story of her female relatives, *China Men* is the story of her male ancestors. More conventional in style than *Woman Warrior*, *China Men* has four principal narrative sections: one devoted to Kingston's great-grandfather's stint as a wage slave in a Hawaiian pineapple plantation; a second to her grandfather's labour on the Continental Railroad in the American West; a third to her father's emigration to California; and a fourth to her brother's army sojourn in Vietnam. In the first three narratives, the journey east is highlighted, even more so than it had been in *Woman Warrior*, the goal of that journey being the 'Gold Mountain' (*jīn shāng*) as they called America, a paradisiacal land not unlike the fabled West of European immigrants. Between these biographical chapters, Kingston intersperses smaller stories about Chinese men in America, Chinese myths and stories (including one she heard as a child about Lo Bun Sun – actually her parents' version of *Robinson Crusoe*). Throughout the work, Kingston stresses the injustices experienced by her ancestors, and in a central chapter she simply lists the racist federal laws that have been directed against the Chinese from 1868 to 1978. In this regard, the collective autobiography of *China Men* is decidedly the collective enunciation of a minor people's immediately sociopolitical experience.

In her first two novels, then, Kingston's becoming-woman is a movement westward away from Chinese sexist culture and towards Western concepts of gender equality. For her ancestors, by contrast, the movement east to America is a line of deterritorialisation, a means of escaping class and economic stratification. And in her deterritorialisation of language, she is 'othering' English via Chinese, creating a zone somewhere between East and West.

In her third prose work, *Tripmaster Monkey: His Fake Book* (1989), Kingston largely abandons autobiographical motifs and stories set in China, focusing instead on the meanderings of Wittman Ah Sing, a poet/playwright and fifth-generation American of Chinese descent living in San Francisco. Kingston has said that in her first two works she felt the burden of 'translating a whole world, all of China and its myths and history', whereas in *Tripmaster* she experienced a 'great relief' as she explored 'the American language, the language that I hear and speak' (Skenazy and Martin 1998: 141–5), incorporating the riches of canonical American literary language, which she knows intimately, as well as the vibrant slang of the early 1960s, in which the novel is set. Primary among her Euro-American inspirations is William Carlos Williams's *In the American Grain*, but she also alludes to Whitman, Melville (Bartleby in particular), Dickinson, Faulkner, Fitzgerald and Kerouac, among many others. Yet she also makes use of Chinese texts, most notably *Journey to the West* (*Shīyóujì*), the sixteenth-century novel about the monk Xuánzàng's pilgrimage to India, in the company of the monkey Sūn Wùkōng, among others. Kingston makes reference in her title both to Monkey and Xuánzàng, who is also called the 'Tang Tripitaka Master' in the Chinese narrative. Kingston's hero is a Tripitaka trickster monkey, but also a 'tripmaster' in the parlance of the 1960s, that is, someone who guides LSD users in their hallucinogenic 'trips'. Wittman's Bay Area wanderings, from his firing as a toy salesman, to a psychedelic party, to an encounter with a Caucasian girl that leads in a day to a casual marriage, then to visits with his retired vaudeville mother and his peripatetic father, eventuate in the performance of a play he has written, in which all his acquaintances, of diverse racial and ethnic backgrounds, enact an inclusive American collectivity (much like the global America Melville describes in a passage in *Redburn*, which Deleuze cites in his 'Bartleby' essay). Yet Kingston's utopian ideal is also tempered by the polemical edge of Wittman's monologue in the play, a twenty-page recitation of the racist indignities endured by every Chinese-American. Wittman travels a good deal, but ultimately his journey is neither westward nor eastward; rather, it is a *voyage sur place*, as Deleuze calls it, a journey in intensities, a 'trip', though one induced less by drugs than by the poetic imagination. Wittman's intensive becoming-other is echoed in Kingston's language, which is replete with allusions to sources high and low, suddenly shifting in diction and cadence, improvisational in its jazz-like riffs, as in this passage describing Wittman as he dances:

> In sync. In sync at last. A ballet dancer and an m.s. spastic – no different – O democratic light. Innards at one with the rest of the world. And why not when we're doing the twist, and Chubby Checker does the twist, 'Let's twist again, like we did last summer,' and the light is a strobe, and a strobili is a twisty pine cone. All right. All right. And – . And – . And – . And then – . Bang bang. Bang bang. But – . But – . But – . Banga. Banga. Lost. Found. Lost. Found. Gotcha. Gotcher teeth. Gotcher face. Boom. Boom. Bomb. The Bomb. Bomb flash. Bomb flash. In what pose will the last big flash catch me? What if. This were. Bomb practice? We're training to dig flashes. And my fellow man and woman aglow. Like fast frequent pulsations of radioactivity. (Kingston 1989: 110)

Kingston, then, clearly fits the profile of Deleuze's American writer, though the journey of her becoming is both West and East, and finally neither, instead being a journey *sur place*, on site. Her becoming-woman and her becoming-Chinese-American entail a deterritorialisation of English, first through Chinese rhythms, then through the rhythms of American polyvalent speech and writing. And her politics follows the line of Melville in seeking a people to come, a collectivity performed and enacted in the artwork of Wittman's aesthetic creation, though one pursued through acerbic critique and resistance to the present and its demonic forces.

Tao Lin: Becoming-Imperceptible

Tao Lin, like Kingston, is a Chinese-American, but as writers the two differ in virtually every way. Born to Taiwanese parents in 1983, Lin grew up in a Florida gated community, graduated from New York University, and now resides in New York City. He has written one collection of short stories, two poetry volumes and four novels, *Eeeee Eee Eeee* (2007), *Shoplifting from American Apparel* (2009), *Richard Yates* (2010) and *Taipei* (2015). Whereas Kingston identifies herself as a Chinese-American woman writer,

Lin says that being of Chinese descent has not particularly affected his life or his work. He told one interviewer that in a first draft of *Eeeee Eee Eeee*, the protagonist's parents came from Taiwan, but later he made the protagonist's parents German and replaced references to Taiwan with Germany and those to Shanghai with Berlin. He added that 'I want ideally in my fiction to edit race and name in the same way I might move or delete a comma', since in terms of what he calls 'existential issues', 'there is no difference between a Haitian or a Canadian or whatever', and his interest as a writer is in such 'existential issues' (Vizzini 2007). Most of Lin's characters are in their late teens and twenties, live in New York City, New Jersey or suburban Florida, work dead-end jobs (when they work), hang out, talk, phone, text, email and Gmail chat, go to each other's apartments, visit restaurants, bars, stores, malls and parks. In *Shoplifting from American Apparel* Lin incorporates some autobiographical material into the text – chiefly regarding his overnight incarceration for shoplifting – but otherwise the characters and settings are generic and minimally detailed. In terms of plot, things happen, but often in random if unremarkable sequence. Novels start and end, but with no clear markers of inception or closure, the story always remaining in the middle. In *Eeeee Eee Eeee* Lin indulges in the fantastic, his human characters encountering and speaking with a bear, a dolphin, a hamster, a moose and an alien, but these unlikely interactions lead to no unusual consequences. In his subsequent novels, there are no such flights of fancy, each narrative becoming increasingly spare and mundane.

Lin's interest, he says, is in 'existential issues', such as hunger, sleep, sex, boredom, death and so on, but his approach to these issues has a pervasive strangeness, each fiction creating atmospheres, moods, haecceities, which involve existential issues but extract from them an elusive ambience, difficult to pin down – one that I personally find uncomfortable, often vaguely unpleasant and troubling, yet quietly powerful. That strangeness, I believe, comes from the style. If Kingston resembles Joyce in her exuberant verbal play, Lin is like Beckett in his ascetic reduction of language to its minimal elements. Sentences are short, syntax uncomplicated, diction limited and decidedly unliterary, adjectives rudimentary (good, bad, happy, sad, stupid), descriptions spare. Verbal repetition is pervasive, as are non-sequiturs, which generally form low-key, conversational sequences that reappear as leitmotifs in the narrative. At times Lin's minimalism is used to comic effect, as in this passage from *Eeeee Eee Eeee*, when Shawn, Lelu and Andrew meet 'the president' (presumably, the President of the United States) in a sushi bar and decide that 'it would be good to network with the president'.

> They invited the president to eat sushi. At the sushi bar the president said that it was stupid to be the president.
>
> 'Power is stupid,' the president said.
>
> The president said he was an alien. He was from a different planet. He came here and was bored. 'I felt I needed a goal,' he said. 'Now I'm the president. I have no human preconceptions, because I'm from a different galaxy. Listen to me, since I'm the ruler. You chose me. People need to process what I say. [. . .] Politics is a pretend game where it is very important to block out the information that it is a pretend game. I'm the president, I think. There is no good or bad. You arrive. Here you are. No one tells you what to do. So you make assumptions. (Lin 2007: 193–5)

Generally, however, the effects of Lin's stylistic asceticism are more mundane, as in this Gmail chat between the main characters of *Richard Yates*, Haley Joel Osment, a twenty-two-year-old writer living in New York City, and Dakota Fanning, his sixteen-year-old girlfriend living with her mother in New Jersey:

> Haley Joel Osment said he wanted to funnel boiling water into his brain.
>
> 'That would be good,' said Dakota Fanning. 'I just thought of Bono and felt suicidal.'
>
> Haley Joel Osment said he was afraid of missing the train.
>
> 'If you miss the train again I'm going to shit myself,' said Dakota Fanning.
>
> 'I'm going to miss it. I feel like I can't not miss it,' said Haley Joel Osment.

> 'I got electrocuted today,' said Dakota Fanning.
> 'Sizzling hot,' said Haley Joel Osment.
> 'I'm going to be very sleepy tomorrow.'
> 'No,' said Haley Joel Osment.
> 'I'm always very sleepy the day after electrocution. I won't be able to do anything but lay'
> 'Now what,' said Haley Joel Osment. 'Drink coffee.' (Lin 2010: 41–2)

Lin's minimalism, I would argue, is aimed at becoming-imperceptible, which, we will recall, Deleuze identifies in *Dialogues* as 'the goal, the finality of writing' (D 45). Lin's language seems anodyne and innocuous, and his characters appear to be like everybody else, nearly anonymous in their lack of distinguishing features, yet a pervasive strangeness signals the unsettling becoming-other of Lin's fictional world. As befits his minimalism, Lin's political bent is decidedly molecular. His characters float over the world, each a kind of Bartleby 'preferring not to'. They show no career ambition or commitment to work, taking minimum-wage jobs, quitting abruptly or eventually getting fired for absenteeism. They routinely shoplift with no remorse. (Lin has said that he supported himself for extended periods of time by shoplifting goods and selling them on eBay.) Granted, their resistance to capital and consumerism is minimal and without collective organisation, but it is nonetheless omnipresent. Yet Lin's characters are not immune to the diseases of micro-power, which he explores with especial subtlety in *Richard Yates*. There, by the smallest of increments, Haley Joel Osment becomes a controlling, abusive figure, eventually demanding reports from Dakota Fanning of all her activities and of every lie she has ever told, no matter how miniscule. And Dakota Fanning slowly emerges as a bulimic and a compulsive self-harm cutter, the two of them forming an enabling, low-key *folie à deux*.

Kingston and Lin, then, are both Deleuzian American writers, despite their many differences. Whether they are both Chinese-American writers, however, is another question. Kingston fits the standard profile of the Chinese-American minority writer, whereas Lin seems merely a writer of Chinese descent whose fiction is unmarked by his ethnicity. The continuum I have implicitly drawn, from Kingston's becoming-woman and becoming-Chinese-American to Lin's becoming-imperceptible, could be seen simply as evidence of Chinese-American assimilation within American culture and of American-dominated globalisation as a whole. In that case, the differences between Kingston and Lin would be merely functions of time and context: Kingston was reared in the small-town America of the late 1940s and 1950s by parents who maintained in their American home the folk traditions of the pre-industrial, agrarian Gŭangdōng of their childhood, whereas Lin was reared in eighties and nineties suburbia by parents who themselves grew up in the increasingly Westernised world of postwar Taiwan.

In posing this question of Chinese-American identity, I have clearly ventured into the territory of identity politics that has made Deleuze and Guattari's concept of 'becoming' controversial from its inception. At issue is the relationship between the minor and minorities, categories that do not always coincide, as Deleuze and Guattari repeatedly stress. Kingston's affirmation of herself as a Chinese-American woman writer is an index of the diverse becomings her fiction has engaged, but also a possible sign of reterritorialisation, were one to view her works as eventuating in the reconstitution of fixed definitions of 'Chinese-American' or 'woman'. Lin's lack of interest in his ethnicity, by contrast, need not signal passive cultural assimilation. Just as a white male, like Melville, can become-other and make a minor usage of English, so can a Chinese male, like Lin, and without necessarily doing so *as* a Chinese-American. But in Lin's becoming-imperceptible yet another question arises – whether his 'othering' of the ordinary has been productive of something new or has simply devolved into a simulation of the mundane that is functionally indistinguishable from it. (Here, obviously, I am reviving old arguments about 'contestatory postmodernism' versus 'celebratory postmodernism'.)

Deleuze's conception of American literature – or at least the kind of American literature he finds superior to French literature – makes room for various minorities to pursue lines of flight, deterritorialise English, invent paths of resistance, envision a people to come, and so on, but it also allows members of majorities to do the same, and it does not declare that minorities *must* be minor as representatives of their minority status. Most important, both majorities and minorities can only attain these ends by becoming-minor themselves, whatever their class, gender, ethnicity, sexual orientation and so on. For this reason, Deleuze's inattention to ethnic writers in his characterisation of American literature is not fatal to his project, and indeed it invites us to perform a discerning and careful examination of multiethnic American literatures from a Deleuzian perspective. The lines of flight within American literature, whether westward from Europe or eastward from China, ultimately must be situated on a map of intensities, one whose nomadic coordinates are those of a new people and a new earth. Kingston, Lin and many other Chinese-American writers, as cartographers of intensities, complicate, but do not contradict, the Deleuzian image of American literature. Rather, they extend our sense of that literature's powers – of what an American literature can do, and what it might do in the future.

Notes

1. Here, too, the differentiation between English empiricism and American pragmatism is in doubt. As early as *Empiricism and Subjectivity*, Deleuze stresses the importance of belief for Hume. In his 1989 Preface to the English Edition, Deleuze lists as one of Hume's great achievements that he 'established the concept of *belief* and put it in the place of knowledge. He laicised belief, turning knowledge into a legitimate belief. He asked about the conditions which legitimate belief, and the basis of this investigation sketched out a theory of *probabilities*. The consequences are important: if the act of thinking is belief, thought has fewer reasons to defend itself against error than against *illusion*' (ES ix). If a distinction is to be drawn between Hume and American pragmatists in this regard, perhaps it is that belief among pragmatists ranges from Peircean belief as grounded in scientific method (a concept close to that of Hume) to James's belief in God and Royce's belief in an Infinite Spirit (views that Hume would have rejected) (see Deledalle 1983: 69–73, 160). For illuminating explorations of Deleuze's relation to pragmatism, see the collective volume *Deleuze and Pragmatism* (Bowden, Bignall and Patton 2015).
2. Perhaps an extension of Deleuze and Guattari's typology of

geophilosophical tendencies could help separate English empiricism from American pragmatism. In *What is Philosophy?*, Deleuze and Guattari contrast English thought with French and German philosophy by saying that 'the English are precisely those nomads who treat the plane of immanence as a moveable and moving ground, a field of radical experience, an archipelagian world where they are happy to pitch their tents from island to island and over the sea' (WP 105). We might contrast this characterisation with the geophilosophical tendencies implicit in Deledalle's analysis of the American values that underlie pragmatism: a belief in America as the promised land of liberty equality and fraternity; in the myth of the pioneer and the frontier; in individualism and democracy; in success; and in 'manifest destiny' (Deledalle 1983: 15). Of course, this is mere speculation, since Deleuze nowhere suggests that he shares Deledalle's view of pragmatism in this particular regard.

3. Deleuze and Guattari's note reads as follows: 'This book contains a fine analysis of geography and its role in American mythology and literature, and of the reversal of directions. In the East, there was the search for a specially American code and for a recoding with Europe (Henry James, Eliot, Pound, etc.); in the South, there was the overcoding of the slave system, with its ruin and the ruin of the plantations during the Civil War (Faulkner, Caldwell); from the North came capitalist decoding (Dos Passos, Dreiser); the West, however, played the role of a line of flight combining travel, hallucination, madness, the Indians, perceptive and mental experimentation, the shiftings of frontiers, the rhizome (Ken Kesey and his 'fog machine,' the beat generation, etc.). Every great American creates a cartography, even in his or her style; in contrast to what is done in Europe, each makes a map that is directly connected to the real social movements crossing America' (ATP 529).
4. Miller's China, as he himself says, is an 'imaginary China', one that bears little relation to the actual place. In his correspondence with Michael Fraenkel, published under the title *Hamlet*, Miller counters Fraenkel's contention that Hamlet is heroic, asserting instead that Hamlet is cowardly and infected with a modern, Western disease of hyperconsciousness. The diseased Western mentality divides humans into animal and vegetable halves, the first being conscious, the second oneiric. As a result, 'The dream side of life, which the plant glorifies, gets pigeon-holed through our singular vision of things as morbid phenomena. The human side of life is the waking side.' Miller speculates that 'if it were possible to imagine an intermediate state in which

one neither is nor does, then China might be regarded as the fairest example. China never becomes anything but China. By virtue of this intermediate logic China is becoming China more and more every day. China is the weed in the human cabbage patch. After every weeding China reappears as China. It has no further aspiration. [. . .] Eventually the weed always gets the upper hand. Eventually things fall back into a state of China. [. . .] If man is ever going to become himself, MAN, and not something different, he will have to stand outside the realm of Idea and, growing more and more satisfied with himself, vegetate. [. . .] My plan, then, in so far as the negation of all effort and purpose may be said to be a plan, is to stop evolving, to remain what I am and to become more and more only what I am. [. . .] I want to become nothing more than the China I already am' (Miller and Fraenkel 1946: I, 54–5).

12

Theatrum Philosophicum Asiaticum

My purpose is to stage an East–West juxtaposition of the concepts and practices of theatre and thought. On the Western side of the stage is Deleuze in a twofold role: as advocate of thought as theatre and as author of thought about theatre. On the Eastern side are ensembles of players representing three different theatrical practices and theoretical traditions: those of Beijing opera from China, Kathakali dance drama from the Kerala region of India and Nō drama from Japan. The juxtaposition is perhaps analogous to the irrational cut of modern cinema, in that Deleuze never speaks of these Asian forms of theatre, and the Asian practitioners undoubtedly have no awareness of Deleuze, but my hope is that this juxtaposition's creation of an unmotivated gap between entities will produce something not simply unexpected but worth contemplating.

Deleuze's Theatre of Thought and Thought about Theatre

Foucault, in 'Theatrum Philosophicum', his well-known essay review of *The Logic of Sense* and *Difference and Repetition*, brings a minor Deleuzian theme to centre stage – that of philosophy as theatre. A new kind of thought is present in Deleuze's texts, says Foucault, 'springing forth, dancing before us, in our midst; genital thought, intensive thought, affirmative thought, acategorical thought [. . .] This is philosophy not as thought, but as theater: a theater of mime with multiple, fugitive, and instantaneous scenes in which blind gestures signal to one another' (Foucault 1977: 196). Aside from Deleuze's recurrent references to simulacra and a one-paragraph analysis of the actor in *The Logic of Sense* (LS 150), Foucault's sole inspiration for this rhapsodic characterisation of Deleuze is *Difference and Repetition*'s six-page description of the 'theater of repetition' of Kierkegaard, Nietzsche and Péguy (DR 5–11). Deleuze says that 'theater is real movement, and it extracts real movement from all the arts it employs' (DR 10). Since Kierkegaard, Nietzsche and Péguy 'want to put metaphysics in motion, in action' (DR 8), Deleuze finds congenial the adoption of theatre as a model for their thought, a thought that aims at

> producing within the work a movement capable of affecting the mind outside of all representation [. . .] making movement itself a work, without interposition [. . .] substituting direct signs for mediate representations [. . .] inventing vibrations, rotations, whirlings, gravitations, dances or leaps which directly touch the mind. [. . .] They no longer reflect on the theater in the Hegelian manner. Neither do they set up a philosophical theatre. They invent an incredible equivalent of theatre within philosophy. (DR 8)

In their theatre of repetition, Deleuze concludes,

> we experience pure forces, dynamic lines in space which act without intermediary upon the spirit, and link it directly with nature and history, with a language which speaks before words, with gestures which develop before organised bodies, with masks before faces, with spectres and phantoms before characters – the whole apparatus of repetition as a 'terrible power'. (DR 10)

Clearly, Foucault is correct in finding the elements of Deleuze's own thought in this theatre of repetition, and we might argue that aspects of the theatrical model, most notably that of *movement* in thought, remain evident in his subsequent writings, despite *Anti-Oedipus*'s rejection of the theatre in favour of the factory as a figure for the desiring-production of thought. This, then, is

Deleuze's notion of philosophy *as* theatre – a thought-theatre of movement, 'vibrations, rotations, whirlings, gravitations, dances or leaps which directly touch the mind/spirit [*esprit*]', 'pure forces, dynamic lines in space', and paradoxical words before words, gestures before organised bodies, masks before faces, and phantoms before characters.

What of Deleuze's thought *about* theatre? The seminal text is 'One Manifesto Less', Deleuze's commentary on Carmelo Bene's *Richard III*, published in *Superpositions* (1979). Here Deleuze brings together several themes from *Kafka* and *A Thousand Plateaus*, including those of minor literature, language as subset of a general pragmatics, and speeds, intensities and affects as primary components of the arts. Bene's minor theatre sets in continuous variation not only all linguistic components ('phonological, syntactic, semantic or even stylistic') and sonic elements of speech, but also music, sound, gesture, costume and setting, thereby inducing 'a kind of generalized chromaticism'. This, adds Deleuze, is 'theater itself, or "spectacle"' (OML 209). Bene stages a theatre of 'difformation', a term Deleuze borrows from Nicholas Oresme, whose fourteenth-century geometry of forms and qualities was, in Deleuze's words, 'based on the distribution of speeds between different points of a moving object, or the distribution of intensities between different points of a subject' (OML 215). Such difformation involves both *deformation* of the conventions of theatre and *transformation* of the remaining elements into something new. In this regard, Bene is for Deleuze an exemplary artist, since, he says, 'the subordination of form to speed, to variation in speed, the subordination of the subject to intensity or affect, to the intensive variation of affects: these are, it seems to us, two essential goals to achieve in the arts' (OML 215).

Deleuze's thought *as* theatre and thought *about* theatre, then, stress movement, force, speed, intensity, affect, direct contact with the mind/spirit, and the difformation of words, bodies, faces, characters, sounds and sights in the comprehensive 'spectacle' of a 'generalized chromaticism'.

And now to the Eastern side of my stage. Let me stress first the fundamental difference between Bene and Deleuze's minor theatre and the theatres of Beijing opera, Kathakali and Nō. Minor theatre is a continuation of avant-garde movements in its creative subversion of traditional dramatic conventions, whereas the Asian theatres I cite are steeped in traditions maintained through centuries of training, theorisation and performance. Nonetheless, if we take *difformation* in Nicolas Oresme's sense as simply the continuous change of forms and qualities at varying velocities, we may see within these Asian theatrical traditions the difformations of a generalised chromaticism. Further, I argue that the traditional nature of these dramas *itself* generates the high levels of stylisation that differentiate them from the Western theatre and make them worth considering from a Deleuzian perspective.

Beijing Opera

First, Beijing opera, many of whose characteristics will be paradigmatic of all the Asian theatres I consider. Unlike Kathakali and Nō, Beijing opera has no central texts that detail its practices and theories, its traditions being conveyed directly through training and performance (something that is also true of Kathakali and Nō). Hence, I will base my remarks on Elizabeth Wichmann's *Listening to Theatre*, which offers a formal and theoretical analysis of the genre drawn from her years of study and training in a Beijing opera company. More so even than Western opera, Beijing opera is a *Gesamtkunstwerk*, a 'total artwork', integrating dance, music, sound, speech, song, costume and make-up in a single 'spectacle'. (The only theatrical element missing in Beijing opera, as in Kathakali and Nō, is that of elaborate sets.) Wichmann identifies the fundamental aesthetic principles of Beijing opera as those of synthesis, stylisation and conventions, all guided by a pursuit of the beautiful (*méi*). Synthesis entails a constant assimilation of various modalities with one another, such that sound, sight and body are never considered in isolation. Stylisation informs all aspects of the drama, in each case involving a modification of the mundane – hence the elaborate costumes, mask-like make-up (as well as the use of actual masks), rhymed speech, delivery in song, choreography of all bodily movement, and so on. Notable especially is the pervasive 'presentation of a three-dimensional network of circles, arcs, and curved lines' (Wichmann 1991: 4), every movement, individual and collective, and every linguistic and melodic line, being conceived in terms of curves. Such stylisation heightens and idealises the real world, but also separates the performance world from the outside. Through its conventions, which have no iconic or indexical relation to the mundane world, the existential quiddity of the theatrical realm of Beijing opera is further stressed.

Beijing operas generally enact a corpus of well-known stories, enumerated at 1,389 plots in a 1980 compilation of all the genre's recorded synopses. According to the scholar Hwang Mei-shu, one-third of the plots come from just thirteen novels, the remainder having sources in '"history, true stories, sketches, notebooks, legends, [other] novels, and earlier plays"' (cited in Wichmann 1991: 12–13). Plot, however, is not the central focus of the genre. Rather, it is emotion. Each song, each scene and each sequence of scenes is shaped by the progression of 'a series of emotional states, each the reaction of the major character(s) to developments in the basic situation' (Wichmann 1991: 20). Music plays a leading role in conveying emotions, for which reason it is central to the art form itself, as is evident in the fact that 'attending a Beijing opera performance is traditionally referred to as "listening to theatre" (*tingxi*) and acting in a play is termed "singing theatre" (*changxi*)' (Wichmann 1991: 1). Performers are admired for their virtuosic mastery of various skills in speech and song, but 'the major aim of the display of skill [. . .] is the expression of emotion' (Wichmann 1991: 269).

The musical system of Beijing opera, known as *pihuang*, renders audible subtle emotional states through conventions inaccessible to untrained ears. The basic units of the system are melodic-phrases (*qiang*), metrical types (*banshi*), modes (*diaoshi*) and modal systems (*shengqiang xitong*) (Wichmann 1991: 53). The specific emotions of individual melodic-phrases, the smallest unit of the musical system, are shaped by tendencies in meters and modes. The basic meters and their emotional correlatives are as follows: primary-meter (*yuanban*): relatively unemotional presentation of facts and narration; slow-meter (*manban*): peaceful, introspective situations; fast-meter (*kuaiban*): situations of excitement or anticipation; fast-three-eyes (*kuaisanyan*): introspective, relatively unemotional, but in males it 'often gives the impression of strength' (Wichmann 1991: 63); two-six-meter: straightforward situations but with 'a sense of excitement or anticipation' (Wichmann 1991: 65); flowing-water-meter (*liushuiban*): 'excitement or anticipation approaching (but not quite reaching)' (Wichmann 1991: 65); dispersed-meter (*sanban*): gentle emotions; lead-in meter (*daoban*), often followed by undulating-dragon meter (*huilong*): 'sudden grief, extreme unhappy surprise, and other intense, unexpected emotions' (Wichmann 1991: 69); and shaking-meter (*yaoban*): 'exterior calm and interior tension' (Wichmann 1991: 70). Modes and modal systems constitute the largest unit of the musical system. Each mode has its 'mode nature' (*diaoshixing*) and its characteristic atmosphere (*qifen*). The primary modes are *xipi* and *erhuang*, *xipi*'s atmosphere being 'sprightly, bright and clear, energetic, forceful, and purposeful', and *erhuang*'s 'relatively dark, deep and profound, heavy and meticulous' (Wichmann 1991: 85). The *nanbangzi* mode, used only for female melodic-passages, expresses 'smooth and exquisite or happy sentiments, as well as meditation and silent thought' (Wichmann 1991: 116). The *sipingdiao* mode, related to *erhuang*, is flexible in atmosphere, expressing emotions associated with 'relaxed lightness, remembrance, impelling indignation, and sorrowful desolation' (Wichmann 1991: 121). The *gaobozi* mode, developed in other musical forms and only recently adopted by Beijing opera, expresses 'indignant grief' (Wichmann 1991: 128).

The specific nuances of emotion arise from a conjunction of song and text within dramatic situations, but what I want to stress is that Beijing opera, besides being a multimodal spectacle of stylised and conventionally coded visual, sonic and corporeal movement, is above all a theatre of musical affect, in which each melodic phrase is shaped by flexible yet emotionally appropriate meters and the broad atmospheric qualities of the modes. Text and plot mediate emotion, but the conventions of the musical system render those emotions both *immediate*, directly touching the mind/spirit/body below the level of linguistic cognition, and *abstract*, in that they are generated within a self-enclosed musical system. What music does, in short, is to convert ordinary emotions into *affects*, in the strictly Deleuzian sense of the term.

Kathakali Dance Drama

Something similar occurs in Kathakali drama, although the emphasis in this theatre is on dance rather than music. Like Beijing opera, Kathakali is a multimodal 'spectacle', involving a synthesis of word, sound, music, costume, make-up, gesture and dance, high stylisation of the realm of mundane experience and conventions specific to the artworld of Kathakali. Its plots and texts are traditional, but the focus of Kathakali, like that of Beijing opera, is on emotion. Kathakali is a descendent of traditional Sanskrit drama, and its practice is informed by Sanskrit drama's central theoretical text, the 850-page *Nātyaśātra* (c. 200 CE), traditionally attributed to Barata Muni. Barata Muni treats all aspects of performance, paying special attention to the drama's evocation of emotions. He distinguishes states (*bhāvas*) from sentiments (*rasas*), the latter being the ultimate object of the performance's evocation and the audience's reception. *Bhāvas* are of three kinds: dominant, transitory and temperamental (or involuntary). The eight dominant *bhāvas* are love, mirth, sorrow, anger, energy, terror, disgust and astonishment. The thirty-three transitory *bhāvas* are discouragement, weakness, apprehension, envy, intoxication, weariness, indolence, depression, anxiety, distraction, recollection, contentment, shame, inconstancy, joy, agitation, stupor, arrogance, despair, impatience, sleep, epilepsy, dreaming, awakening, indignation, dissimulation, cruelty, assurance, sickness, insanity, death, fright and deliberation. The eight temperamental *bhāvas* are paralysis, perspiration, horripilation, change of voice, trembling, change of colour, weeping and fainting. The eight *rasas* are the erotic, the comic, the furious, the pathetic, the heroic, the terrible, the odious and the marvellous. Of these *rasas*, four are original and four derivative, the erotic giving rise to the comic, the furious to the pathetic, the heroic to the marvellous, and the odious to the terrible.

In Kathakali performance practice, the *bhāvas* and their related *rasas* are represented in various ways, including the nine basic facial expressions (*navarasas*) and the twenty-four basic hand gestures (*mudras*). The nine facial expressions correspond to the eight traditional *rasas* and a ninth *rasa* of peace or at-onement. These I would classify as stylised elements. The hand gestures, by contrast, are strictly conventional. Although they serve multiple purposes (signing words, miming objects, providing asymbolic ornaments in the dance), they cluster in fields associated with the *bhāvas* and their corresponding *rasas*.

Rasa literally means 'taste', and Barata Muni repeatedly explains the relationship between *bhāvas* and *rasas* in terms of cooked food (*bhāvas*) and its taste (*rasas*). 'Just as a combination of spices and vegetables imparts good taste to the food cooked, so the States [*bhāvas*] and the Sentiments [*rasas*] cause one another to originate' (Ghosh 1951: 107). *Bhāvas* produce *rasas*, and hence there can be no *rasas* prior to *bhāvas*, but there are no *bhāvas* devoid of *rasas*. The *rasas* are generated by the actors and consumed by the audience, providing a common medium for the production and reception of the drama. In this theory of *bhāvas* and *rasas* I find a lucid analysis of the relationship between affections and affects in Deleuze. *Rasas* form an olfactory, gustatory, tactile, and nonverbal atmosphere, a *haecceity*, common to performers and audience. The *rasas* emerge in the performance event and attain an impersonal existence. Their stylised and conventional presentation emphasises their autonomous mode of existence within the performance event as a world distinct from, yet connected to, the outside world.

Ultimately, its devotees see the aesthetic experience of the *rasas* as one that extends into the realm of the mystical. In their book on Kathakali drama, Nair and Paniker argue that Kathakali, more so than any of the performing arts in Indian, 'and perhaps, even the world', is one that is 'farthest from earthly reality and humanism. There is no attempt at representing the mundane world in any manner – whether by imitation or otherwise. Only epic, non-human beings are chosen for the re-creation of a story for presentation on the stage' (Nair and Paniker 1993: x). As a result, for the enlightened connoisseur of Kathakali, the drama 'takes the connoisseur away from the transient worldly experience of pleasure to one of transcendental entrancement', thereby allowing the connoisseur to 'experience bliss which is non-dual, at which level there is no difference between beauty and ugliness', a bliss that 'is also the level of divine art – that is, art beyond art' (Nair and Paniker 1993: 4). It is only through a painstaking process of spiritual discipline that the spectator may eventually attain the status of true connoisseurship. As a neophyte, the would-be connoisseur attends only to the most basic physical and emotional elements of the drama, but through repeated exposure to performances, coupled with education and training under the supervision of advanced connoisseurs of the art form, the individual is able to reach an elevated level of awareness beyond that of simple absorption of plot, movement and spectacle. And it is only the rare individual, 'only a *tattwabhinivesi* (philosophically-oriented person)', who will be able to savour the essence of a Kathakali performance. Ultimately, such a philosophically oriented individual, claim Nair and Paniker, will exhibit a sensibility above that of the performer. 'While the actor puts to conscious use his innate skill which is enhanced by constant practice, the connoisseur engages in the super-conscious act of receiving and appreciating every single aspect of the performance. He is therefore superior to the performing artiste' (Nair and Paniker 1993: 16–17). When, for example, the phenomenon of *eklochana*, the expression of two different *rasas* in two eyes that appears to be simultaneous, is made manifest on the stage, it is the connoisseur alone who brings full realisation to the phenomenon.

> The artiste, with continuous movements and regular practice, makes such an action possible, but it requires the supreme imagination of the spectator to visualize these eye movements as simultaneous. The *Kathakali eklochana* is thus meaningful only when its reach extends to the learned connoisseur. (Nair and Paniker 1993: 17)

Nō Drama

Much of what I have said about Beijing opera and Kathakali also pertains to Nō drama – a multimodal spectacle that synthesises textual, sonic, visual and corporeal elements within a stylised and convention-laden artworld, with emphasis not on its traditional plots but its lyrical elements, both poetic and musical, its affective dimensions, its displays of performance virtuosity and its elicitation of enlightened responses among the cognoscenti.

The extraordinary treatises of Zeami Motokiyo (1363–1443), a master actor and leader of his family's Nō company, offer insight into the world of Nō in all these regards, but what I want to stress is the extent to which Zeami's teachings about the theory and practice of Nō reflect a general mental and spiritual discipline and worldview.

Zeami identifies the fundamentals of Nō acting as the Two Basic Arts of chant and dance and the Three Role Types (*santai*) of old person, woman and warrior. Proper training in these basics allows the actor to 'create the specifics of any particular role' (Rimer and Masakazu 1984: 65). The actor's implementation of these skills produces what Zeami calls the actor's 'Flower', and mastery of these skills eventuates in the attainment of the supreme goal of Grace (*yūgen*). Zeami differentiates nine levels in the advancement of the actor's development, the last three being the Flower of Tranquillity, the Flower of Profundity, and the highest, the Flower of Peerless Charm (*myō*). Peerless Charm, says Zeami, is summed up in the Zen phrase 'In Silla, in the dead of night, the sun shines brightly.' Peerless Charm 'surpasses any explanation in words and lies beyond the workings of consciousness [. . .] in a realm beyond logical explanation' (Rimer and Masakazu 1984: 120). It manifests Perfect Freedom (*taketaru kurai*) and Perfect Fluency (*yasuki kurai*), which transcend consciousness, skill or intention (Rimer and Masakazu 1984: 136). When an actor exhibits Peerless Charm in a performance, the audience reacts with a gasp of astonishment, experiencing the Fascination (*omoshiroki*) of Feeling that Transcends Consciousness (*mushinkan*) (Rimer and Masakazu 1984: 138, 133). To explain the Fulfilment (*jōju*) of an ideal performance, Zeami refers to a tale in which the goddess Amaterasu 'had shut the great stone door', bringing darkness to the world, and then opened the door such that 'light suddenly appeared', bringing 'unreflecting joy' to all creatures. In an ideal performance, he says, 'Peerless Charm that transcends words' corresponds to the moment when 'the world was plunged into darkness'; the 'sudden brightness' to the actor's Flower; and the experience of that brightness to the audience's Fascination of Feeling that Transcends Consciousness (Rimer and Masakazu 1984: 133).

This reference to cosmic events is not ancillary to Zeami's thought, but indicative of the conceptual framework informing his remarks. Peerless Charm is represented by darkness because it is invisible. Its essence is 'spirit' and 'a true enlightenment established through art' (Rimer and Masakazu 1984: 90). Audiences often remark that the highest moment in a performance comes when the actor does nothing, in an 'interval which exists between two physical actions'. In such a moment, the actor

> must rise to a selfless level of art, imbued with a concentration that transcends his own consciousness, so that he can bind together the moments before and after that instant when 'nothing happens'. Such a process constitutes that inner force that can be termed 'connecting all the arts through one intensity of mind'. (Rimer and Masakazu 1984: 96–7)

Zeami relates Peerless Charm to the Buddhist doctrine of Being and Non-Being, remarking that

> Being might be said to represent an external manifestation that can be seen with the eyes. Non-Being can be said to represent the hidden fundamental readiness of mind that signifies the vessel of all art [since a vessel is empty]. It is the fundamental Non-Being that gives rise to the outward sense of Being [in the *nō*].

The actor's vessel of Non-Being is one with the cosmos, for

> The world of nature is the vessel that gives birth to all things, alive and inert alike [. . .] To make this multitude of things an adornment for our art, an actor must become one in spirit with the vessel of nature and achieve in the depths of the art of the *nō* an ease of spirit that can be compared to the boundlessness of that nature itself, thus to achieve at last the Art of the Flower of Peerless Charm. (Rimer and Masakazu 1984: 118–19)

In a similar vein, after detailing the three principles of *jo* (gentle beginning) *ha* (dramatic development) and *kyū* (rapid finish), which should shape every element of Nō, from the smallest bodily movement, poetic phrase or melodic line, to individual scenes, entire plays and sequence of plays, Zeami adds, 'in thinking over the matter carefully, it may be said that all things in the universe, good and bad, large and small, with life and without, all partake of the process of *jo*, *ha*, and *kyū*' (Rimer and Masakazu 1984: 137).

In Nō drama, then, we find all the features of Beijing opera and Kathakali – the multimodal synthesis of the arts, stylisation and convention, the evocation of affect and creation of an atmospheric haecceity common to performers and audience – but also a theory of dramatic performance and reception that emphasises emotional, mental and spiritual experience beyond cognition. That theory is grounded in the thought and practice of Buddhism, from which Zeami draws many of his terms, and it is evident that, for Zeami, Nō is a corporeal, mental and spiritual discipline whose aim is to attain and promote enlightenment in performers and audience alike. Zeami's frequent allusions to Zen make it clear that Nō is a 'way' (*do* in Japanese, *dao* in Chinese), and hence like the art of archery (*kyudo*), the art of writing (*shodo*) or the art of tea (*chado*), one of the many means whereby one may reach enlightenment and thereby grasp the fundamentals of cosmic truth. Thus, his theatre is finally a way of living, focused on dramatic performance, but grounded in an all-encompassing worldview.

Conclusions

What may be gained from this juxtaposition of Deleuze and Asian theatre? First, Deleuze's theatre as thought, with its 'vibrations, rotations, whirlings, gravitations, dances or leaps which directly touch the mind/spirit [*esprit*]', 'pure forces, dynamic lines in space', and paradoxical words before words, gestures before organised bodies, masks before faces, and phantoms before characters, finds a much more congenial dramatic analogue in Beijing opera, Kathakali and Nō than in most forms of Western drama. The Western theatrical tradition, as many commentators on Eastern drama note, has been dominated by Aristotle's *Poetics*, directly in tragedy and indirectly in comedy. Although ancient Greek tragedy involved singing and dancing, Aristotle subordinated these elements to action, character, thought and diction, calling action 'the soul of a tragedy' (Aristotle 1902: 29), since 'the incidents and the plot are the end of a tragedy; and the end is the chief thing of all' (Aristotle 1902: 27). He deemed music an 'embellishment', and he dismissed 'spectacle' as 'the least artistic' of the elements of tragedy because it is 'connected least with the art of poetry' (Aristotle 1902: 29). When Deleuze says of Bene's 'generalized chromaticism', which sets all the elements of drama in 'continuous variation', that 'This is theater itself, or "spectacle"' (OML 209), he is deliberately opposing Bene's avant-garde practice to the norms of conventional Western drama. Had Deleuze been addressing the audiences of Bejing opera, Kathakali and Nō, such a statement would have been received as unexceptional. His anti-mimetic approach to the theatre would likewise have met with general assent, since plot is subordinate to emotion and thought in these Eastern dramatic forms, as would his enthusiasm for dance, movement, dynamic forces and a direct, nonrational connection between the spectacle and the *esprit*.

Second, the fact that Deleuze's characterisation of minor theatre's 'generalized chromaticism' aptly describes many features of Beijing opera, Kathakali and Nō suggests that traditional as well as avant-garde dramatic practices may fulfil the aims of a deterritorialising difformation that generates differential speeds and intensive affects. The highly stylised elements of Beijing opera, Kathakali and Nō (the predominance of the curve, circle and arc in Beijing opera, the exaggerated facial expressions of Kathakali, the ceremonial chant of Nō, for example) and their purely conventional elements (Beijing opera's musical modal system, Kathakali's complex of hand gestures, Nō's interplay between chant and percussive punctuation) all defamiliarise the mimetic elements of the dramas and thereby open the theatrical spectacle to the evocation and reception of modes of experience independent of plot. The stylisations and conventions of Beijing opera, Kathakali and Nō do not lead to an empty formalism, but instead make possible a theatre of affect and thought, one removed from ordinary reality but simultaneously intensely engaged with the non-rational dimensions of corporeal and mental life. The implications of this isomorphism between Western avant-garde theatre, as represented by Bene, and the traditional Eastern dramatic forms of Beijing opera, Kathakali and Nō might well guide an exploration of the broad differences in Western and Eastern traditions and mentalities, something Deleuze and Guattari attempt in a rough, schematic fashion in their opposition of Western arborescence and Eastern rhizomatics in the opening plateau of *A Thousand Plateaus*.

Third, Beijing opera's *pihuang* musical system and the *Nātyaśātra*'s theory of *bhāvas* and *rasas* offer a much more detailed analysis of emotions, affects and their interrelationship than we find in Deleuze, and ones whose taxonomies of feeling delineate intriguing associations (at least to a Westerner, such as me). The *pihuang* meters have a certain intuitive logic – a calm meter for narration (*yuanban*), one for introspection (*manban*), one for excitement or anticipation (*erliuban*) and one for intense emotions (*huilong*) – but why should there be two meters for introspection (*manban* and *kuaisanyan*), one of which in males 'often gives the impression of strength' (*kuaisanyan*), and why three meters for excitement or anticipation (*kuaiban*, *erliuban* and *liushuiban*), one of which involves 'straightforward situations' (*erliuban*) and another 'excitement or anticipation approaching (but not quite reaching)' (*liushuiban*)? The basic modes likewise seem to conform to commonsense categories – one for positive emotions (*xipi*), one for negative (*erhuang*) – but why should *erhuang* be described as 'heavy and *meticulous*', and why would the flexible *sipingdiao* mode bring together 'relaxed lightness, remembrance, impelling indignation, and sorrowful desolation'? It would seem that each meter and each mode invokes an atmosphere (*qifen*) that defies ready verbal articulation, and that the *pihuang* system as a whole is a means of producing haecceities that remap the common-sense coordinates of the emotions.

The *Nātyaśātra*'s taxonomy of *bhāvas* and *rasas* makes much finer distinctions among feelings than does that of Beijing opera, enumerating forty-nine *bhāvas* and eight *rasas*, but, like Beijing opera's *pihuang* musical system, Kathakali's system of *bhāvas* and *rasas* invites rethinking of (at least Western) categories of emotion, first in the specifics of the differentiation and identification of dominant, transitory and temperamental (or involuntary) emotions, and then in the discrimination of thirty-three transitory states, which not only subdivides emotions into minute categories but also conjoins them with states of consciousness and their attendant physiological causes (intoxication, stupor, sickness, sleep, epilepsy, dreaming, awakening, insanity and death). Most important, however, is that the distinction between *bhāvas* and *rasas* parallels the Deleuzian differentiation of emotions from affects, providing not only a classification of affects into the categories of four primary and four secondary *rasas*, but also a metaphorical basis for conceptualising emotions and affects (foods and tastes) and a metaphysical framework for relating emotions to affects (the spiritual discipline that leads connoisseurs from crude corporeal appreciation to enlightened comprehension).

Fourth, Barata Muni's and Zeami's theories of drama provide a means of understanding the nature of audience response in a theatre of affect, something that Deleuze does not directly address. The *Nātyaśātra*'s differentiation of *bhāvas* and *rasas* not only separates common emotions from affects but also identifies affects as the atmospheric medium in which performers and audience undergo a collective theatrical event. The Kathakali tradition of connoisseurship as a spiritual discipline with finely articulated nuances of appreciation (the simultaneity of two *rasas* expressed in the eyes of the performer, for example) suggests the possibility of developing a taxonomy of affective reception that would enrich the Deleuzian concepts of aesthetic affects and percept. And Zeami's treatment of actors, audiences and emotional, mental and spiritual states beyond cognition provides an extended meditation on the questions raised by Deleuze's brief remarks about thought and theatre's direct, unmediated contact with the mind/spirit, a meditation that might be extended to Deleuze's remarks on other arts (such as painting, which in the case of Francis Bacon, according to Deleuze, attempts to bypass the brain and directly touch the nerves).

Finally, in Zeami's theory and practice of Nō, I believe we have a means of bringing thought and theatre together in a suggestive zone of indiscernibility. For Zeami, Nō is a Buddhist way of living, the *do* of Nō, we might say, and as such the theatre of Nō is both practice and thought. That thought-practice itself is informed by a comprehensive view of the cosmos. For Deleuze, philosophy, too, is a way of living, something he and Guattari make explicit in *What is Philosophy?* when they stress the importance of inventing new possibilities of life and new modes of existence, 'a possibility of life' being 'evaluated in itself in the movements it lays out and the intensities it creates on a plane of immanence', and 'a mode of existence' being measured solely by the criteria of 'the tenor of existence, the intensification of life' (WP 74). The cosmic dimension of such thought is evident when Deleuze and Guattari speak of absolute deterritorialisation in philosophy as the moment 'when the earth passes into the pure plane of immanence of a Being-thought, of a Nature-thought of infinite diagrammatic movements', which in turn reterritorialises itself 'as the creation of a future new earth' (WP 88). In Deleuze, then, we may say that the exoteric aspect of philosophy as a way of living is its textual, expository form, and its esoteric dimension is that of the broader range of practices within the cosmic theatre of life. Conversely, the exoteric manifestation of Nō is its theatrical performance, and its esoteric element is the invisible thought-practice of Buddhism that informs every element of the drama. (Zeami's descendants preserved his writings as a closely guarded secret, the first full publication of his writings appearing only in the 1940s.) One would never mistake a text of Deleuze for a Nō drama, but perhaps we might find a means of thinking them together as different ways of living that meet on 'the pure plane of immanence of a Being-thought, of a Nature-thought of infinite diagrammatic movements' (WP 88).

V. Sight, Sound and Language

13

The Landscape of Sensation

What is the relationship between texts and images in Deleuze's conception of the arts? One means of initiating a response to this question is to examine the figure of the 'landscape', which has a certain prominence in *A Thousand Plateaus*, appears briefly in *Cinema 1*, and then resumes a position of some importance in *What is Philosophy?* and *Essays Critical and Clinical*. To call the landscape a full-blown 'concept', in the terms set out in *What is Philosophy?*, is perhaps excessive. Rather, it seems more accurate to describe the landscape as a 'conceptual motif', a recurring element that participates in the functioning of several key concepts – faciality, the reflection-image, sensation, percepts, affects, fabulation. Although the motif is introduced initially in *A Thousand Plateaus* as part of a discussion of the face–landscape complex and painting, when Deleuze elaborates on the theme later in that book and in subsequent texts, the landscape proves to be germane to his treatment of several other arts as well – notably, architecture, sculpture, cinema, music and literature. It is in his discussion of the landscape and literature that this conceptual motif becomes especially interesting, for here we see clearly the tensions between speaking and seeing, between texts and images, tensions that suggest a decidedly non-linguistic dimension to Deleuze's conception of literature.

The Landscape and the Face

According to the *Robert dictionnaire historique*, the word *paysage* first appears in French in 1549, initially as 'a term of painting designating the representation of a generally rural site, then the painting itself'. The word's history roughly parallels that of its English counterpart, 'landscape', a rendition of the Dutch *landschap* imported in 1602 to designate a painting of natural inland scenery. Interestingly, the first reference in English to the natural world itself as a 'landscape' does not appear until 1642 (here in the simple sense of 'a bird's-eye view'), which suggests that art precedes nature in this instance and that painters taught people to see aesthetic landscapes in the world. It is not surprising, then, that in Plateau Seven of *A Thousand Plateaus*, 'Year Zero: Faciality', Deleuze and Guattari associate the *paysage* with painting, nor that they approach it as a culturally constructed object. In Deleuze and Guattari's analysis, the landscape functions in coordination with the face as part of a process that 'facialises' reality. When individuals speak, they make facial expressions – smiles, grimaces, sneers, frowns – that 'define zones of frequency or probability' (ATP 168) whereby speech-acts are sorted, regulated and normalised in accordance with dominant systems of signification. At the same time, facial expressions 'form loci of resonance that select the sensed or mental reality and make it conform in advance to a dominant reality' (ATP 168), that reality enforcing the positions of the interlocutors as subjects. Far from being a natural entity, the face is a constructed object, which operates in conjunction with two regimes of signs: the signifying, despotic regime, in which every signifier refers to another signifier in an endless play of signification controlled by a central, despotic power; and the post-signifying, passional regime, in which a point of obsessional fixation determines a dominant reality and constructs a subject. The dual processes of signification and subjectivation, then, govern the mixed semiotic of the despotic and passional regimes of signs, and the face channels those processes through signification-related 'zones of frequency' and subjectivation-oriented 'loci of resonance'.

The face functions in tandem with the mixed semiotic of the

despotic and passional regimes to enforce networks of signification and subjectivation, and since the goal of that mixed semiotic is to subsume everything within its order, faciality extends from the face per se to other body parts, to neighbouring objects, and to the surrounding milieu. Fetishisation (foot fetish, hair fetish, shoe fetish) is a symptom of the facialisation of the body and its associated objects, one that proceeds not via resemblance (the foot resembling a face) but via a coordination of forces of discipline passing through faces and the body. That passage of forces may then radiate to include an entire landscape. Indeed, Deleuze and Guattari claim, 'All faces envelop an unknown, unexplored landscape; all landscapes are populated by a loved or dreamed-of face, develop a face to come or already past' (ATP 172–3). This interplay of forces through landscapes and faces shapes both architecture and painting: 'Architecture positions its ensembles – houses, towns or cities, monuments or factories – to function like faces in the landscape they transform. Painting takes up the same movement but also reverses it, positioning a landscape as a face, treating one like the other' (ATP 172).

The face of faciality is created through a process of decoding and overcoding. The head as polysemic body part is first decoded, and then it is overcoded as functional extension of the despotic–passional regimes of signs. In turn, the facialisation of the body entails a decoding of the body as a site of multiple semiotic circuits and a subsequent overcoding of that site as the corporeal surface of a single system of signs. The facialisation of the landscape merely amplifies this process of decoding and overcoding. It is important to note, however, that the overcoding of facialisation is not a textualisation of the visual. To speak is not to see. Although the face works in conjunction with language to enforce the disciplinary networks of the despotic–passional regimes of signs, the face is distinct from the verbal signs it channels, modulates and regulates. The face, the facialised body and the facialised landscape may be associated with various discourses and vocabularies, but they have their own mode of organisation. They constitute a general schema of visibility, a kind of vectorial gridding of the visual as a component co-functioning with language in the maintenance of a field of forces. In this regard, the facialised world resembles the domain of 'visibilities' that Deleuze sees as a central feature of Foucault's work. Foucault's 'visibilities' take form within what Deleuze calls a 'regime of light', a structure of scintillations, shadows, glares and reflections, a given regime of light serving as the condition of possibility that determines what can be seen and what cannot. Each historically specific regime of light is in a dynamic relationship with a discursive formation, but visibilities are not reducible to statements. Rather, visibilities and statements intervene in one another, interconnect while remaining heterogeneous and incommensurable. The face–landscape complex of faciality may then be seen as a specific regime of light, one coordinated with the mixed linguistic semiotic of the despotic and passional regimes of signs.

The Musical Landscape

In *A Thousand Plateaus* Deleuze and Guattari assert that 'the "problem" within which painting is inscribed is that of the *face-landscape*', whereas the problem of music 'is entirely different: it is the problem of the *refrain*' (ATP 301). Despite this strict separation of the two arts, however, in their analysis of the refrain Deleuze and Guattari discover a musical aspect of the landscape. Refrains may be loosely defined as the rhythmic patterns through which organisms and their surroundings co-produce and maintain diverse ecological systems. Differences in the structuring patterns of various creature–habitat complexes, such as those that delimit milieu organisms from territorial animals, arise from the relative degrees to which refrains are deterritorialised in one context and reterritorialised in another. Music's task is to deterritorialise natural refrains in general and reterritorialise them within sonic compositions. Deleuze and Guattari find indications of this relationship between nature and music in the juxtaposition of Jakob von Uexküll's ecological writings and Olivier Messiaen's musical compositions. Von Uexküll treats nature as a grand symphony of interconnected activities and processes, each organism and its surroundings interrelated as point to counterpoint in a giant Baroque fugue. Messiaen for his part appropriates birdsong and natural sounds as compositional elements in much of his music.

In their account of the degrees to which refrains become deterritorialised in natural systems, Deleuze and Guattari state that at a certain stage in the emergence of territoriality (in the ethological sense of the term), refrains take on an autonomy of their own, at which point 'territorial motifs form *rhythmic faces or characters*, and [. . .] territorial counterpoints form *melodic landscapes*' (ATP 318). The term 'rhythmic characters' (*personnages rhythmiques*) comes from Messiaen, who explains that his conception of rhythm is dramatic, rhythms interacting with one another like characters in a play, one active, another passive, yet a third serving as a witness to the active–passive couple. Although Messiaen does not articulate the complementary concept of 'melodic landscapes' per se, he does indicate that in his birdsong-oriented compositions he situates the various bird motifs within an appropriate sonic landscape. For example, in the *Catalogue d'oiseaux* (1958), a massive series of pieces for solo piano, he features the song of a single bird in each piece but includes as well motifs from other birds and sounds corresponding to a given setting. He also prefaces each piece with a brief prose description of the natural scene he is rendering. 'Le merle bleu' (The Blue Rock Thrush, Book I, 3), for instance, presents a seascape in June near Banyuls-sur-Mer, with waves and cliffs providing the background against which the blue rock thrush, theckla lark, swifts and herring gulls issue their cries and songs. The first twenty measures of the score bear the following sequence of motif labels: cliffs, swifts, cliffs, swifts, water, swifts, water, blue rock thrush, water, swifts, water, theckla lark, water. This interweaving of birdsongs and seascape sounds continues throughout the piece, its composite texture suggesting how in both nature and music, to cite Deleuze and Guattari once again, 'territorial motifs form *rhythmic faces or characters*, and [. . .] territorial counterpoints form *melodic landscapes*' (ATP 318).

The Cinematic Landscape

Faciality's visual concepts of face and landscape, then, have aural counterparts in the concepts of the rhythmic character and melodic landscape, yet Deleuze and Guattari insist in *A Thousand Plateaus* that painting's central problem is that of the face–landscape. Hence, when in 1981 Deleuze speaks at length about painting in

Francis Bacon: The Logic of Sensation, one might expect further discussion of the face–landscape pair, but instead the face is treated only as a minor consideration and the landscape is not mentioned at all. In 1983, however, the landscape does appear briefly as part of Deleuze's exposition of the action-image and reflection-image in *Cinema 1*.[1] To contrast the Large Form and Small Form species of the action-image, Deleuze differentiates a 'respiration-space' from a 'skeleton-space' (*espace-ossature*) (C1 168). He derives the terms from Henri Maldiney's analysis of Chinese painting theory, which focuses on Hsieh Ho's sixth-century recommendation that the painter first 'reflect the vital breath; that is, create movement', and then 'seek the skeleton; that is, know how to use the brush' (Maldiney 1973: 167). (*Ossature* is Maldiney's French rendering of 'skeleton', the word *ossature* meaning both 'the disposition of the skeleton's bones' and 'any framework of elements structuring a whole'.) The unity of the cosmos arises from the vital breath (*chi* in Chinese) of the primordial void that permeates all things in a systolic and diastolic respiration, and the painter's task is to manifest this vital breath's movement as it 'appears' and 'comes into presence'. But the painter must also render individual details with discrete brush strokes, thereby demarcating the structuring *ossature* of the world and revealing the 'disappearing' of things, like the dragon whose tail disappears behind a cloud. Ultimately, the movement of the vital breath subsumes the *ossature* of the world within a single, unifying cosmic process, but Deleuze sees in this '*notion of the landscape*' (C1 187) two tendencies worth distinguishing, even if they are finally inseparable. The respiration-space is one in which the landscape is an all-encompassing milieu within which individual actions emerge and take their relative position. The landscape of the skeleton-space, by contrast, is one that is constructed piece by piece, from action to action – not, however, in a random fashion, but following a vector that reveals a 'line of the universe', a cosmic zigzag of vital energy. On the basis of this distinction Deleuze categorises various film plots, contrasting for example the respiration-space of John Ford's Westerns, in which a dominant landscape summons forth the characters' actions as responses to their surrounding situation, with the skeleton-space of Anthony Mann's Westerns, in which heterogeneous spaces are interconnected via the explosive actions of the protagonists as their movement-images fashion a 'line of the universe'. Deleuze likewise contrasts Kurosawa's respiration-space and Mizoguchi's skeleton-space, each of these directors pushing the action-image to its limit and thereby creating a reflection-image in which mental relations permeate physical relations.

What this cinematic treatment of the landscape adds to the previous landscapes of painting and music is a narrative dimension of sorts. If painting's deterritorialisation of the face–landscape is primarily spatial, and music's deterritorialisation of rhythmic characters and melodic landscapes is primarily temporal, cinema's respiration-space and skeleton-space are spatiotemporal, images in movement that are tied to narratives, at least in the classic cinema. We must note, however, that for Deleuze conventional narratives are a secondary product of movement-images, which generate stories through the unfolding of trajectories regulated by the sensory-motor schema. Films are not visual translations of discursive narratives, but non-discursive images that are incommensurable with the verbal terms that may be used to describe them.

The Landscape and Sensation

In *What is Philosophy?* the landscape is associated with the 'percept', which, along with the 'affect', is one of the two constituents of 'sensation', sensation itself delineating the domain proper to the arts. Deleuze and Guattari derive their sense of the landscape from Henri Maldiney, whose account of the operation of form and rhythm in visual art is based on a phenomenological reading of Cézanne's comments on painting. (We might note that Maldiney sees in Hsieh Ho's observations about Chinese painting simply another version of the insights articulated by Cézanne.) Maldiney's guide to his understanding of Cézanne's art is Erwin Straus, who in *The Primary World of the Senses* (1935) argues that we must distinguish the world of perception, in which subject and object are clearly distinguished and situated within common-sense spatiotemporal coordinates, from the world of sensation, a primary, preverbal world we share with animals, in which subject and object are indistinguishable and space-time moves with us in a perpetual Here-Now. In Straus's terms, the space of perception is a space of *geography*, whereas sensation's space is that of the *landscape*. Maldiney argues that this Strausian primary space of sensation is what Cézanne is describing when he remarks that as he begins to paint, he is one with the world that surrounds him: 'We are an iridescent chaos. I come before my motif, I lose myself there [. . .] We germinate' (cited in Maldiney 1973: 150). At this moment, says Cézanne, man is 'absent, but entirely within the landscape' (cited in Maldiney 1973: 185).

Clearly, a version of the Strausian opposition of the geography of perception and the landscape of sensation is at play in Deleuze and Guattari's statements that 'the aim of art is to wrest the percept from perceptions of objects and the states of a perceiving subject' (WP 167), and that 'the percept is the landscape before man, in the absence of man' (WIP 169). This Strausian landscape, it would seem, is quite different from the landscape of *A Thousand Plateaus*, and indeed the earlier landscape was a facialised landscape – that is, a landscape territorialised by forces of facialisation. But as Deleuze and Guattari insist repeatedly, immanent within any stratified power structure are forces of deterritorialisation, and this new landscape is a deterritorialising domain of haecceities and becomings. Understandably, then, in *What is Philosophy?* the landscape is most frequently paired not with faces but with becomings, 'Becoming animal, plant, molecular, becoming zero' (WP 169), becomings constituting the realm of affects, in which humans become non-human. Sensation, then, consists of affects and percepts, and in the words of Deleuze and Guattari's aphoristic summation, '*Affects are precisely these nonhuman becomings of man*, just as percepts – including the town – are *nonhuman landscapes of nature*' (WP 169). This coupling of becomings and landscapes may be seen as a version of the dyad of rhythmic characters and melodic landscapes, in that both pairs delineate actors within an environment, the actors in one pair being humans engaged in becomings, and in the other pair rhythms interacting with one another. And, in fact, Deleuze and Guattari make use of the *rhythmic character–melodic landscape* pair at several points in *What is Philosophy?* We must observe, however, that in *What is*

Philosophy? the primary sense of the landscape is not melodic but visual. 'The landscape *sees*' (WP 169), say Deleuze and Guattari. And when they invoke percepts and affects, they most often speak of percepts as 'visions' and the artist as creator of landscapes as a 'seer' (*un voyant*). Just a few examples: 'Everything is vision, becoming' (WP 169); 'The artist is a seer, a becomer' (WP 171); 'the artist is the presenter of affects, inventor of affects, creator of affects, in relation with the percepts or visions that the artist gives us' (WP 174; trans. modified). Aesthetic figures 'are sensations: percepts and affects, landscapes and faces, visions and becomings' (WP 177). (Note that this last citation provides the only pairing of landscapes and faces in *What is Philosophy?*)

This pairing of percept–landscapes and affect–becomings, however, is further complicated as Deleuze and Guattari refine their speculation on the 'incarnation' of sensation in the arts. 'We spoke too quickly when we said that sensation embodies [*incarne*]' (WP 178), they remark. Percepts and affects do not unite in a single phenomenological 'flesh of the world'. Rather, the embodiment of becomings presupposes 'not so much bone or skeletal structure [*ossature*] as house or framework [*armature*]' (WP 179). The house, we might say, is a third element, between landscapes and those who are undergoing a becoming-animal. The house is a kind of scaffolding, a structuring schema of planes, its walls, roof, floor, doors and windows functioning as so many 'frames' (WP 179), in both the pictorial and the cinematic sense, within which forces are delineated and through which forces intercommunicate. The surfaces and openings of the house serve as membranes and conduits for the interaction of forces outside and inside its scaffolding of planes and frames. 'In fact,' say Deleuze and Guattari, 'the house does not shelter us from cosmic forces; at most it filters and selects them' (WP 182).

In the course of articulating the concept of the house, Deleuze and Guattari expand the notion of the 'landscape' to include the universe as a whole. If affective becomings constitute one element of sensation, and the house a second, 'the third element', they say, 'is the universe, the cosmos. Not only does the open house communicate with the landscape, through a window or a mirror, but the most shut-up house opens onto a universe' (WP 180).

The house is a scaffolding that delimits and frames forces, but the landscape is ultimately unframed and without limits, a plane that extends into infinity. 'The flesh, or rather the figure, is no longer the inhabitant of the place, of the house, but of the universe that supports the house (becoming). *It is like a passage from the finite to the infinite*, but also from territory to deterritorialization' (WP 180). In an initial formulation, then, Deleuze and Guattari state that sensation consists of percepts and affects, '*nonhuman landscapes of nature*' and '*nonhuman becomings of man*' (WP 169). In their final formulation, however, the concept of the house is added and the term 'landscape' is replaced by the word 'cosmos': 'In short,' they say, 'the being of sensation is not the flesh but the compound of nonhuman forces of the cosmos, of man's nonhuman becomings, and of the ambiguous house that exchanges and adjusts them, makes them whirl around like winds' (WP 183). At this point it is worth observing that in this triad of universe–house–becomings, we have a version of the three elements that Deleuze argues are basic to Bacon's paintings: the infinite plane of a monochrome field; the isolating structure of a cube, circle or frame of some sort; and the figure undergoing a metamorphosis as forces from the monochrome plane compress and deform it and as the figure's internal forces seek escape through the body and across the structure's isolating membrane to the monochrome field. Hence, though Deleuze seems in *Francis Bacon* to abandon *A Thousand Plateau*'s problematic of landscape and face, in reality he is simply exploring it in different terms, the landscape articulated as monochrome field, the face as figure.

As we will recall, in *What is Philosophy?* the movement from the house to the universe is said to be '*like a passage from the finite to the infinite*, but also from territory to deterritorialization' (WP 180). Through this association of the house with territory and the cosmos with deterritorialisation, Deleuze and Guattari initiate a recapitulation of their analysis of the interconnection of art and nature conducted in the Refrain section of *A Thousand Plateaus*. Indeed, they assert in *What is Philosophy?* that 'the whole of the refrain is the being of sensation' (WP 184). The refrain has three inseparable components, or moments: a point of emergent order; a circumference of delimited structure; and a line of flight towards the infinite. In nature, territorial animals build a habitat by extending the rhythms of an emergent point of order to the circumference of a specific territory, but that territory always is open to the cosmos. The refrain is a force of both territorialisation and deterritorialisation, and the 'territory-house system' (WP 183) communicates directly with the universe. Thus 'if nature is like art, this is always because it combines these two living elements in every way: House and Universe, *Heimlich* and *Unheimlich*, territory and deterritorialization, finite melodic compounds and the great infinite plane of composition, the small and large refrain' (WP 186).[2]

We may thus construct the final composite model: (1) landscape, melodic landscape, respiration-space and skeleton-space, universe, cosmos, monochromatic field, deterritorialisation; (2) house, structure, territory; and (3) face, rhythmic characters, non-human becomings, figure. How might the various arts be situated in regard to this model, if we consider it in its most literal, physical sense? Architecture would seem to be the art most directly related to the model, in that an inhabited building in an open space would be a material manifestation of the triad of landscape-house-becomings. For this reason, Deleuze and Guattari assert that 'architecture is the first of the arts' (WP 186) and that animals, in constructing habitats, are artists. Next would come sculpture, whose three-dimensional objects occupy a physical space, and often an actual landscape. The alliance of architecture and sculpture as modellings of spatial relations, in fact, is such that one might (with considerable caution) regard architecture as a utilitarian form of sculpture. Third would come iconic figurations of the model, such as cinema and painting, in that both arts frequently offer visual analogues of actual landscapes, habitats and inhabitants. (Theatre might be included here, though primarily as performance practice rather than written text.) Music would seem more removed from the model than the preceding arts, Messiaen's creative 'transcriptions' of sonic landscapes and birdsongs providing the most immediate instances of music's deterritorialisation of natural refrains, with most musical compositions much less clearly related to physical landscapes and habitats. And the art most distant from the model, I would argue, is literature, especially prose fiction, in that literature's rendering of actual landscapes, habitats and inhabitants takes place not through iconic but through symbolic figuration.

The Literary Landscape

It is in their remarks on literature in *What is Philosophy?* that Deleuze and Guattari's tripartite model becomes most provocative, especially as regards the landscape. 'The novel has often risen to the percept' (WP 168), they say, evoking various landscapes – 'oceanic percepts in Melville, urban percepts [. . .] in Virginia Woolf' (WP 168–9), 'the moor as percept' (WP 168) in Hardy, 'Faulkner's hills, Tolstoy's or Chekhov's steppes' (WP 169). It would seem that Deleuze and Guattari are situating these authors within the ekphrastic tradition, treating them as practitioners of a kind of 'word painting'. And, in fact, Deleuze elsewhere explicitly makes this link between literature and painting, in *Foucault* calling Faulkner 'literature's greatest "luminist"' (F 81), and in *Essays Critical and Clinical* first describing Whitman's corpus as 'one of the most coloristic of literatures that could ever have existed' (CC 59), and then labelling T. E. Lawrence 'one of the greatest landscape painters [*paysagistes*] in literature', as well as 'one of the great portraitists', since in his work 'faces correspond to the landscapes' (CC 116). Readers might concede that all these authors are particularly successful at evoking landscapes, but few would see such evocations as central to these writers' works, let alone to all literature. In most fiction, landscapes are secondary elements that merely provide the setting within which actions transpire. Fictions involve stories, linear sequences of action, whereas settings, especially landscapes, generally manifest a static or cyclical temporality. As Deleuze and Guattari say, the landscapes of Hardy, Melville, Woolf, and others create 'beings of sensation, which preserve in themselves the hour of a day, a moment's degree of warmth' (WP 169). Such landscapes are clearly instances of what Deleuze and Guattari in *A Thousand Plateaus* call haecceities, 'a season, a winter, a summer, an hour, a date' (ATP 261), whose temporality is that of Aion, 'a floating, "nonpulsed time', 'the indefinite time of the event' (ATP 262).

Of course, percepts, '*the nonhuman landscapes of nature*', are inseparable from affects, '*the nonhuman becomings of man*' (WP 169), and in such non-human becomings we have actions. Yet Deleuze and Guattari's literary examples of non-human becoming, such as Ahab's becoming-whale or Mrs Dalloway's becoming-city, isolate only a portion of the actions of their respective novels, and not necessarily the central aspects of those fictions. Nor is there much of a plot in Ahab's obsession with Moby-Dick or Mrs Dalloway's dissolution within the London cityscape. Deleuze and Guattari associate the creation of percepts and affects with what they call 'fabulation' (WP 168, 171), but they do not indicate what *fabulas* might be generated by fabulation. As Deleuze explains in *Cinema 2* and *Essays Critical and Clinical*, fabulation is the process whereby artists invent 'a people to come', a future collectivity not yet in existence. Fabulation is a matter of 'legending *in flagrante delicto*' (C2 150; trans. modified), but Deleuze does not specify what legends might result from fabulation.

In his essay on T. E. Lawrence's *Seven Pillars of Wisdom*, Deleuze treats Lawrence as a *paysagiste* and fabulator, his landscapes and fabulations, according to Deleuze, being 'images projected into the real' (CC 119). 'The finest writers', says Deleuze, 'have singular conditions of perception that allow them to draw on or shape aesthetic percepts like veritable visions' (CC 116), and Lawrence's landscapes are such visions, images 'abstracted' from perception, projected on to the external world, and fashioned with such intensity that the image takes on a life of its own. Lawrence also fabulates, in that he evokes the collective identity of an Arab 'people to come', but such fabulation involves again the projection of images rather than the narration of stories. Lawrence's fabulations reveal 'a profound desire, a tendency to project – into things, into reality, into the future, and even into the sky – an image of himself and others so intense that *it has a life of its own*' (CC 117–18). Lawrence's use of 'what Bergson called a fabulatory function', says Deleuze, 'is a machine for manufacturing giants', an image 'projection machine' that 'is inseparable from the movement of the [Arab] Revolt itself: it is subjective, but it refers to the subjectivity of the revolutionary group' (CC 118).[3]

If, then, we pair percepts and affects with landscapes and

fabulation, both are manifest in literature as visions, as images projected into the real and imbued with a life of their own, and such images would seem to have no necessary relation to narratives, even if some of them are 'fabulations'. There is, in fact, an explicit opposition of images to narratives that one can find in Deleuze. In *Francis Bacon*, Deleuze asserts that 'painting has neither a model to represent nor a story to narrate' (FB 6), which is why Bacon isolates the figures in his paintings. The clichéd images of the world are mere illustrations of conventional stories, and Bacon's isolation of the figure 'is thus the simplest means [. . .] to break with representation, to disrupt narration, to escape illustration, to liberate the Figure' (FB 6). The whole of Deleuze's analysis of cinema aims to displace language and narration as the conceptual framework for understanding film. Narratives exist in film, but only as secondary derivations of images. 'Narration is never an evident [*apparent*] given of images, or the effect of a structure which underlies them; it is a consequence of the visible [*apparent*] images themselves, of the perceptible images in themselves, as they are initially defined for themselves' (C2 27). But most telling is Deleuze's study of Beckett's television plays, in which he treats Beckett as a writer attempting to 'bore holes in language' and create pure images. In order to fashion pure images, Beckett must silence the incessant 'voices and their stories' (CC 157) that haunt language. Only when 'there is no longer any possibility or any story' (CC 158) can an image arise, one 'freed from the chains in which it was bound' by conventional language and its narratives.

Beckett's impatience with narrative belies a basic distrust of language, and in Beckett's efforts to go beyond words Deleuze finds one of literature's fundamental aims. In *Essays Critical and Clinical* Deleuze says that writing's goal is to create

> visions and auditions that are not of language, but which language alone makes possible [. . .] It is through words, between words, that one sees and hears. Beckett spoke of 'drilling holes' in language in order to see or hear 'what was lurking behind'. One must say of every writer: he is a seer, a hearer, 'ill seen ill said', she is a colorist, a musician. (CC lv)

Writers push words to their limits, evoking images while at the same time forcing language itself to stutter and stammer and thereby produce an asignifying music. Implicit in this valorisation of visions and auditions is an opposition of the discursive and the non-discursive, with non-discursive visions and auditions arising at the limits of the discursive. Why privilege the non-discursive dimension of literature? The answer, I believe, lies in Deleuze's *Foucault*, a book that is as much a presentation of Deleuze's thought as Foucault's. Deleuze praises Foucault for recognising within power relations the incommensurable strata of visibilities and statements. Regimes of light bring forth what may be seen, whereas regimes of signs determine what may be said. The two strata are separate, yet there is also a primacy of statements over visibilities. 'The statement has primacy by virtue of the spontaneity of its condition (language) which gives it a determining form, while the visible element, by virtue of the receptivity of its condition (light), merely has the form of the determinable. Therefore, we can assume that determination always comes from the statement, although the two forms differ in nature' (F 67; trans. modified). The implication of this analysis is that language has an inherent tendency to dominate the visible and the non-discursive as a whole. The facialised landscape, coded and coordinated in its operation with the despotic–passional regimes, then, is but one manifestation of this tendency. And the most effective linguistic means of overcoming this tendency is to reverse the asymmetrical relationship between the discursive and the non-discursive, to push language to its limits and produce images and sounds, visions and auditions, which escape the hold of regimes of signs and take on a life of their own.

Deleuze remarks that Foucault's approach to visibilities and statements 'is singularly close to the contemporary cinema' (F 65; trans. modified), in that both treat sound and sight as separate strata, 'a visible element that can only be seen, an articulable element that can only be spoken' (F 65). Deleuze's approach to literature, I would argue, is equally cinematic, the language of writers like Beckett giving rise to audiovisual strata, asignifying sounds and pure images. And in this cinematic affinity we might find a means of accounting for literary narrative such that it is no longer the mere manifestation of linguistic codes and cultural conventions. The landscapes of the action-image in *Cinema 1* are composites of situations and actions, action-spaces that generate different sequences of images, some in accordance with an englobing 'respiration space', others with a 'skeleton space', unfolding along a 'line of the universe'. Perhaps one could treat literary stories like cinematic narratives, as secondary products of movement-images and time-images, temporal effects of the visions and auditions that arise as authors 'bore holes in language'. But a reading of *Cinema 1* and *Cinema 2* as guides to literary narrative will have to wait another day.

The Landscape of Sensation

The landscape of faciality is a landscape of stratification, part of a face–landscape complex co-functioning with the mixed semiotic of the despotic and passional regimes of signs. The landscape of sensation is a landscape of destratification, of percepts which are intimately related to affects. The 'nonhuman landscapes of nature' and the 'nonhuman becomings of man' (WP 169) form part of a triad of cosmos–house–becomings, the 'being of sensation' consisting of 'the compound of nonhuman forces of the cosmos, of man's nonhuman becomings, and of the ambiguous house that exchanges and adjusts them' (WP 183). The house may be part of a territorial habitat, but it always communicates with a plane of deterritorialisation. In the deterritorialising landscape, images take on a life of their own, one that is visual, or perhaps sonic (as in Messiaen's 'melodic landscapes'), but never textual. Literature, like the other arts, creates 'nonhuman landscapes of nature', hallucinatory images at the limits of language, visions interconnected with sonic auditions. Deleuze sees painting, music and cinema as arts that seek to transcend their limits – painting, by rendering visible invisible forces, music by capturing silent forces within sounds, cinema by fashioning a stratum of 'the unspeakable and what can only be spoken' and a stratum of what is 'at once invisible and yet can only be seen' (C2 260). But perhaps no art is more devoted to overcoming itself than literature, which aspires to create 'visions and auditions that are not of language, but which language alone makes possible', such that the writer becomes 'a seer, a hearer', 'a colorist, a musician' (CC lv).

Notes

1. In *A Thousand Plateaus*, Deleuze and Guattari remark on the close relationship between the face and the cinematic close-up. In *Cinema 1*, Deleuze discusses the face and the close-up at length, as part of his treatment of the affection-image, but he does not directly mention the landscape in that context. Nevertheless, he does argue that various objects may be 'facialized' through the close-up, and that ultimately the *espace quelconque* ('any-space-whatever') and the 'emptied space' are the genetic signs pertaining to the affection-image (C1 120). It would seem, then, that the association of the face and the landscape is in effect here, despite the absence of the word 'landscape' itself.
2. We should note here that the 'territory–house system' includes the habitat and its inhabitants, and hence the dyad of territory–deterritorialisation must be regarded as shorthand for the triad of becomings–house–universe.
3. In *What is Philosophy?*, Deleuze and Guattari remark that 'Bergson analyzes fabulation as a visionary faculty very different from the imagination and that consists in creating gods and giants' (WP 230, n. 8).

14

Deleuze and Roxy: The Time of the Intolerable and Godard's *Adieu au langage*

For Deleuze, the modern cinema is signalled by a crisis in the action-image and a concomitant confrontation with the intolerable, or that which exceeds absorption within the sensory-motor schema. In *Cinema 2*, Deleuze presents Jean-Luc Godard as one of the primary practitioners of the modern cinema, citing his films frequently to explicate various aspects of the time-image. Had Deleuze lived long enough to see Godard's 2014 3D film, *Adieu au langage*, he most certainly would have praised it as an exemplary exploitation and expansion of the possibilities of the time-image. He would also have seen in it a form of resistance to the intolerable brought forth through a becoming-animal, a becoming-dog that might well have surprised and amused him.

The Intolerable

The time-image, for Deleuze, is an image steeped in crisis. In the closing chapter of *Cinema 1*, 'The Crisis of the Action-Image', Deleuze identifies five elements in post-war American cinema that signal a collapse of the common-sense spatio-temporal coordinates of the sensory-motor schema: the emergence of dispersive situations that replace the globalising or synthesising situations of the action-image; the deliberate weakening of linkages, connections and relations that provide continuity from one situation to another; the substitution of aimless wanderings, strolls and continual back-and-forth journeys for the goal-oriented plotlines of action-image films; the disenchantment of quotidian reality induced by an acute awareness of the world as a mere circulation of clichés; and the sense of the cliché-ridden image-world as an impenetrable conspiracy of control and manipulation (see especially C1 205–11).

These symptoms of crisis in American film mark a partial collapse of the sensory-motor schema, but Deleuze finds the advent of its full collapse, and its positive exploitation, only in Italian Neorealism, the French New Wave and the films of Yasujiro Ozu. Here, amid the breakdown of the sensory-motor schema, new images arise: opsigns and sonsigns, signs of pure optic and sonic situations. Such signs emerge when characters suddenly experience their situation as intolerable. Deleuze explains that the intolerable is not defined by some quantum of suffering, terror or violence, but solely by the characters' inability to react to their situation within the structure of the sensory-motor schema.

> It is a matter of something too powerful, or too unjust, but sometimes also too beautiful, and which henceforth outstrips our sensory-motor capacities. [. . .] It can be a limit-situation, the eruption of a volcano, but also the most banal, a plain factory, a wasteland. (C2 18)

In such moments of crisis, when a coherent reaction to a situation becomes impossible, 'the character or the viewer, and the two together, become visionaries' (C2 19). A 'seeing function' arises (C2 19), *une fonction de voyance*, which makes 'pure vision a means of knowledge and action' (C2 18; trans. modified). The clichéd images of the sensory-motor schema are shattered and opsigns and sonsigns reveal things in themselves, 'literally, not metaphorically' (C2 20).

The vision of the intolerable is inherently political, in that the clichés of the sensory-motor schema are shaped by 'our economic interests, ideological beliefs and psychological demands' (C2 20). To see the intolerable is to protest that too much is tolerated, too much violence, cruelty, ugliness and stupidity is assimilated within the quotidian sensory-motor schema. Foucault, says Deleuze, 'saw what was intolerable in things' (N 103), and throughout his philosophy he 'never stopped being a *voyant*' (F 50). Likewise, 'the modern political cinema', Deleuze argues, is 'no longer constituted on the basis of a possibility of evolution and revolution, like the classical cinema, but on impossibilities, in the style of Kafka: *the intolerable*' (C2 249).

The opsigns and sonsigns of the intolerable give rise to direct images of time, as well as new relations between sight and sound and between thought and image. The forces of opsigns and sonsigns 'enter into relation with yet other forces [. . .] those of the time-image, of the readable image and the thinking image [. . .] "chronosigns", "lectosigns" and "noosigns"' (C2 23). Chronosigns manifest themselves as time-crystals, peaks of the present, sheets of the past, and the powers of the false, which reveal 'temporality as a state of *permanent crisis*' (C2 112), a pure form or force of time that puts 'the notion of truth into crisis' (C2 130). With lectosigns, 'as the eye takes up a clairvoyant function [*une fonction de voyance*], the sound as well as visual elements of the image enter into internal relations which means that the whole image has to be "read", no less than seen, readable as well as visible' (C2 22). And with noosigns, 'a camera-consciousness' emerges, one that is 'no longer defined by the movements it is able to follow or make, but by the mental connections it is able to enter into' (C2 23).

Adieu au langage

Godard's *Adieu au langage* could well serve as a textbook (or text-film) of the possibilities of chronosigns, lectosigns and noosigns.[1] For those who haven't seen the film, no synopsis can adequately convey a sense of the work. Perhaps best described as an essay collage, the seventy-minute film consists of roughly 370 shots, a few lasting from two to five minutes, most on the screen for less than half a minute, many for only a few seconds. If there is a central plot among the multiple scraps of incipient narrative (too numerous to detail here), it involves two couples, Josette–Gédéon and Ivitch–Marcus (played by actors remarkably similar in appearance), in both cases a married female and a male lover, who walk around naked or minimally clothed in what appears to be the same apartment. In separate scenes outside the apartment, a third man – presumably the husband – issues threats in German to each of the women, who in both cases respond, 'Ça m'est égal!' ('I don't care!'). The first couple picks up a stray dog at a gas station, and later they apparently leave the dog on a lakeside dock. The dog subsequently appears in the apartment of the second couple. But this parallel mirror-plot of the two couples and the dog and irate husband they have in common occupies only a small portion of the film, the action fragmented and intercut with diverse images and sounds that function as visual and sonic motifs rather than story elements. Well over half the script consists of citations from sociological, literary and philosophical works; the score is a collage of fragments from Alfredo Bandelli, Ludwig van Beethoven, Giya Kanchelli, Arnold Schœnberg, Jean Sibelius, Valentin Silvestrov, Dobrinka Tabakova and Pyotr Tchaikovsky; and clips from various films are intercut or shown on a background TV screen in the couples' apartment: Alexandre Aja's *Piranha 3D*, Artur Aristakisyan's *Ladoni*, Boris Barnet's *By the Bluest of Seas*, Howard Hawks's *Only Angels Have Wings*, Henry King's *The Snows of Kilimanjaro*, Fritz Lang's *Metropolis*, Rouben Mamoulian's *Dr. Jekyll and Mr. Hyde*, Jean-Pierre Melville's *Les Enfants terribles* and Robert Siodmak's *Menschen am Sonntag*.[2] The film also includes archival footage of Hitler, Nazi parades, World War II bombers and bombs, helicopters, battle scenes and the Tour de France. Title cards and black screens punctuate the film, as do repeated shots of a ferry arriving and departing from a pier, shots of streets, houses, trees, rivers, lakes and clouds, and multiple clips of the dog Roxy.

The time of *Adieu au langage* defies any assimilation within a chronometric sensory-motor schema. Markers of the seasons – snow, autumn leaves, mature crops, early-spring foliage – recur in random patterns. The central plot of the two couples implies the existence of parallel durations, unattached to any goal-driven narrative, and interconnected in ways that suggest numerous temporal bifurcations, loops and reiterations. The film's sonic and visual components possess the characteristic autonomy of lectosigns, each component exploring variations within its medium while intervening in the other. Voices overlap, shift from right to left channel, from live-action stereo to full studio surround sound. Musical passages are cut at arbitrary places in the phrase and repeated in fragments of varying lengths. Off-camera sounds of gulls and a car crash have no visual justification, and off-camera gunfire is followed by images that only minimally integrate the sounds within an embryonic proto-narrative. The visual elements vary in texture from grainy cell phone footage to high-definition video, with a wide range of colour saturation, and the camera's presence is constantly asserted, through stuttered slow motion, handheld camera jerks, diagonal and rotating framings, and so on. But perhaps most importantly the film is in 3D, which Godard handles in a decidedly unconventional way. And if irrational cuts characterise noosigns, one could say that *Adieu au langage* is one giant noosign, each cut demanding that viewers puzzle out the mental relations that interconnect the film's images.

These chronosigns, lectosigns and noosigns are not mere formal inventions, but responses to the intolerable, both as articulated by the characters and as enunciated in the voice-overs. What is the intolerable in *Adieu au langage*? The list is long: consumerism, capitalism, colonialism, totalitarianism, the state, the society of the spectacle, Hitler, fascism, the Holocaust and war in general. All these themes are addressed in Godard's preceding films, but here they are framed in terms of an additional intolerable element: what Primo Levi called the 'shame of being human' (a phrase Deleuze comments on in *Negotiations* [N 172]). Many critics argue that the film's star is Godard's dog, Roxy. And Roxy's function is to put into question human animality – to explore what humans and other animals have and don't have in common. In the film, humans are separated from animals by language, self-consciousness and war; what they share are sight, sound and bodies.

Roxy and Humans

Images of war are scattered throughout the film: battle scenes, explosions, bombers, bombs falling in slow motion and helicopters. From the onset, war and Roxy are juxtaposed. The film opens with six seconds of low-resolution, square-pixel war footage in saturated reds, blues, purples, oranges and yellows. Sounds of explosions, machine gun fire and shouting voices accompany these arresting images. After a twelve-second clip from Hawks's *Only Angels Have*

Wings, we see Roxy in close-up. The proximity of war and dog seems arbitrary at first, but gradually the significance of the association becomes clear. In one sequence, a male voice-over cites a passage from Cesare Pavese's *The House on the Hill*: 'Now that I have seen war, I know that if it ended everyone would ask, "What do we do with the bodies?" Perhaps only for them is the war over.' On the screen we see Roxy defecating, and then shots of Roxy calmly walking along the shore of Lake Geneva. The scene suggests that the dog, unlike the humans of Pavese's narrative, is free of the burden of endless war and at peace with the world around him. In another sequence, archival footage of a helicopter in a grey sky is followed by shots of a dark-green low-resolution close-up of a helicopter touching down, an explosion in the violent colours of the opening battle scene, and a close-up of a dog's head in a flaming pile of debris, moving only when two concussive blasts jolt the body. Here, war engulfs the dog; human violence brings death to the animal that throughout the film has been presented as serene and benign. Implicit in this juxtaposition of images is an animal indictment of human cruelty and brutality. At another point in the film, as the camera pans across an urban parking lot to a distant cityscape, a voice-over cites a passage from Clifford Simak's sci-fi tale of a post-human world in which genetically enhanced dogs tell ancient tales of a vanished reality: 'The family makes a circle around the fire. The young pups listen without saying a word. And when the story is over, they ask many questions. What is man? Or, what is a city? Or, again, what is war?' In Simak's story, the pups have never seen humans, cities or wars, and they are mystified by the traditional legends of such creatures and their history. In the film, by contrast, the pups give voice to a larger question. What is it that connects Man, City and War? Why is human civilisation inextricably linked to war and violence? The answer comes in a shot of Josette in close-up, telling Gédéon an anecdote of the Nazi concentration camps. 'When he entered the gas chamber, a child asked, "Why" to his mother. And an SS shouted, "Hier ist kein Warum!" Pas de pourquoi.' Why war? Why cruelty and savagery? There is no reason. In the face of humble animals, we stand shamed. As Ivitch says at one point, God could not, or would not make us humble. 'So he made us humiliated'.

Only self-conscious beings can be humiliated, since their shame arises from awareness of themselves in the eyes of others. Animal humility, by contrast, stems from an absence of self-consciousness, and at several points in the film Godard explores the ramifications of human self-consciousness and its relation to canine consciousness. 'There is no nudity in nature', a voice intones over an image of Roxy. 'And the animal, therefore, is not nude because he is nude.' Josette, Gédéon, Ivitch and Marcus wander nude in their apartment, briefly don a robe or a raincoat, then strip naked again, without any particular motive for their actions. Gédéon sits on the toilet, comparing his posture to that of Rodin's *Thinker*, and as he defecates in Josette's presence he says that his position is that of true human equality and that here thought finds its place 'dans le caca'. Roxy also defecates on camera, but his act is no more remarkable than his nudity. What some critics label Godard's scatology is actually an inquiry into the problematic status of human animality, which Godard presents through images of the couple's unselfconscious nudity accompanied by intellectual commentary on art, social class, thought and shit. A zone of indiscernibility is opened in which the differences between humans and animals such as dogs are blurred. The gratuitous, desexualised treatment of clothing and the transgression of excretory proprieties force awareness of the corporeal realities humans share with other animals as well as the cultural norms that set humans apart.

Godard offers a more philosophical reflection on this theme when a male voice-over cites Paul Valéry: 'No one could think freely if his eyes were locked in another's gaze. As soon as gazes lock, there are no longer exactly two of us. It is difficult to remain alone.' At the beginning of these lines, Roxy's head appears in black-and-white profile against the background of a rushing stream. With the word 'freely' this shot is replaced by a colour stop-action image of Roxy's face in frontal view. Seven stop-frames of Roxy's face ensue, each closer to the camera, each focusing more fully on Roxy's gaze. When the voice-over completes the phrase 'As soon as gazes lock', Godard cuts to a twilight shot of Roxy in mid-distance walking in the shallow water of a lake, and then strolling on the shore. With this idyllic image before us we hear that 'It is difficult to remain alone.' Two minutes later a male voice repeats the phrase: 'It is difficult to remain alone.' This time we see Roxy standing in snow beside a rushing stream. In neither case does Roxy seem to find solitude difficult. When the camera fixes its gaze on Roxy's eyes, there is no question of Roxy losing his freedom when looking at the Other. His animal gaze at the camera (and audience) is steady, alert and unperturbed.

The relation of human to animal freedom is framed in more complex terms in another sequence when a male voice-over cites Levinas: 'Only free beings can be strangers to each other. They have a shared freedom but that is precisely what separates them.' A shot of Roxy resting in a car precedes the quote. A black screen appears, the voice begins to speak, and a white dot forms in the middle of the screen. At the word 'precisely' Godard cuts to a mid-shot of Roxy against a background of grass, the footage overexposed with blue bands pulsing across the image. Over this image the voice-over stops. This overexposed image is then followed by a shot of Roxy walking a rock path beside a lake, the bulrushes tinted bright orange, red and green, the rocks a watery blue, and then a second shot of a vibrant harlequin green field of long grass, with Roxy barely visible in the distance, only his head and shoulders occasionally rising from the greenery. The lakeside shot is accompanied by the sound of wind gusts and Roxy's footsteps, the grass field by the sound of chirping birds. All the images suggest that Roxy is a free being, but nothing indicates that he is a stranger to others, nor that his freedom is predicated on a shared freedom that separates him from the Other. Roxy's freedom is untroubled by the paradoxes of self-consciousness, which only knows freedom as a shared separation. Roxy's freedom is presented as an unrestrained movement through a vital and pulsating land- and soundscape, hyperreal in its chromatic intensity.

Roxy and Vision

But more important is the animal's unselfconscious gaze as a challenge to human vision. With Roxy's head in close-up, a voice says, 'It is not the animal that is blind, but man, blinded by consciousness, and incapable of seeing the world. What is outside, wrote Rilke, can be known only via an animal's gaze.' Godard's response to intolerable visual clichés has always been to create new ways of seeing, but in *Adieu au langage* that response is situated in a becoming-animal that seeks images outside canine or standard human perception. Godard frames the problem in a voice-over citation of a passage on painting from Marcel Proust's *Jean Santeuil* (mistakenly attributed to Claude Monet by the narrator):

> When – the sun already setting – the river still sleeps in the dreams of fog, we do not see it anymore than it sees itself. Here it is already the river, and the eye is arrested, one no longer sees anything but a void, a fog which prevents one from seeing further. In that part of the canvas, one must paint neither what one sees, since one sees nothing, nor what one doesn't see, since one must paint only what one sees, but one must paint that one doesn't see.

In these sentences, we find a visual version of the literary paradox faced by Kafka – which, for Deleuze, is central to understanding Kafka's art – the 'impossibility of not writing, the impossibility of writing in German, the impossibility of writing otherwise' (K 16). And, we recall, Deleuze sees this paradox of impossibilities as central to political cinema, which is 'no longer constituted on the basis of a possibility of evolution and revolution, like the classical cinema, but on impossibilities, in the style of Kafka: *the intolerable*' (C2 249).

Godard's response to this problem is not simply to show us that we do not see – that clichés keep us from directly viewing the world – but to invent a mode of vision that has never existed before. And it is in 3D that Godard finds such a genuinely new way of seeing.[3] In his 3D images, Godard creates a different kind of lectosign, one that brings the crisis of the intolerable within the sign. What must be read in each sign is not its relation to other signs, but the relation of its parts to one another. This reading has its own undetermined time – that of the eye's movement within the shot, as it shifts focus from one element to another.

Conventional 3D films, as many have remarked, are initially arresting, but soon the eye adjusts and the 3D effect almost disappears. Godard's use of the medium is such that the eye is never allowed to normalise the images. From time to time, Godard offers images that are easy to assimilate, such as a shot of a woman's hands in a leaf-strewn fountain. Framed in the shot are the woman's arms in the left foreground, the water surface delineated by the floating leaves, and the hands moving below the surface to the right. Here, 3D simply adds a conventional sense of depth, with arms, water-surface and hands forming a diagonal spatial continuum from the closest to the furthest elements of the image. But more often Godard imposes conflicting demands on the eye. In a shot of blood being splashed into a bathtub, for example, a foreground scrub brush in the upper-right corner of the frame is a distraction, its sharp, focused delineation pulling the eye away from the primary event of splashes of blood striking the tub surface and running down the drain. A visual irritant, the too-present brush eventually forces the eye to shift its focus from the tub to the brush and back again. In several shots through a car windscreen (a common motif in Godard), the foreground windscreen is a more insistent irritant, making the images much more difficult to negotiate than the bathtub shot. In most of these shots, it is raining or snowing, and the water or snow on the windscreen is in sharp focus, as are the wipers sweeping the screen. The eye tries to see through the glass, but the surface has detail and precision that are compatible only with a foreground focus. As the eye strains to process the moving images beyond the windscreen, the glass surface relentlessly impedes the gaze and forces a stuttering shift of focus from foreground to background. The difficulties of negotiating the image are further compounded in a spinning handheld shot of autumn-leaved tree branches against a purple-and-blue sky. The multiple planes of the leaves at various distances allow no stable focal point and force the eye to wander haphazardly within the image until, at the close of the shot, leaves come into extreme close-up and give one the sensation of being poked in the eye.

And then there's what Calum Marsh called 'the shot of the year' (Marsh 2014), the shot that brought spontaneous applause when the film was premiered at Cannes. In 2D, the shot is innocuous, but in 3D it is painful to watch. 3D movies are usually shot with two cameras side by side, a fixed distance apart. 'The shot of the year' opens with Davidson [an older professor and friend of Ivitch's] and Ivitch in the frame, but as Ivitch is dragged away from Davidson by her husband, the cameras separate from one another. The left camera remains stationary and focused on Davidson, while the right camera tracks the movements of Ivitch and her husband to the right. When Ivitch finally returns to Davidson, the right camera assumes its original position in alignment with the left camera. What one sees are superimposed, irreconcilable images. As Jacob Kastrenakes observes, 'At first, you have no idea what's going on – your eyes twist in pain, you lift your 3D glasses up in confusion'. He discovers that if you close one eye, 'you see 2D action of the character on the left; close the other eye, and you see 2D action of the character on the right' (Kastrenakes 2014). But while this viewing strategy reveals the components of the image, it provides no means of reconciling the conflicting, superimposed images with both eyes open. In the shots of the bathtub, windscreen and spinning leaves, the eye traverses the image, negotiating the conflicting levels of attention, following an undetermined time as the gaze moves from one element to another. In this shot, however, there is no negotiation. One sees a smear of time, an astonishing, exhilarating but almost unendurable stretch of temporal crisis. It is as if the film's new way of seeing, brought forth by the intolerable, were itself a nearly unbearable vision at the limits of the human capacity to see.

There is nothing specifically canine about Godard's 3D images. Rather, they are animal-induced images fashioned in an effort to follow Rilke's challenge to know the outside 'via an animal's gaze'. Geoffrey O'Brien observes that

> in Roxy, Godard finds a more heroic figure than has yet appeared in his films, a figure whose movements through the natural world, to the edge of the water, through the underbrush, do indeed reinvent a primal cinema at one with the world it represents. At some point the 3-D process becomes a metaphor for an animal perception of the world that we can only guess at. (O'Brien 2014)

O'Brien rightly senses the connection between Roxy and the 3D process, but the 3D image, far from being a metaphor, is itself an animal perception, albeit the perception of an indeterminate animal, neither human nor canine, a perception in passage between the two and towards something 'that we can only guess at'.

Vision and Language

This animal-induced vision is non-linguistic, and at a very simple level it may be regarded as a vision in opposition to language. These title cards appear twice – 1 Nature; 2 Métaphore – and one might posit the 3D becoming-animal vision as Nature and the language-mediated gaze as Metaphor, thereby recalling Deleuze's remark that the time-image is literal, not metaphorical. As we recall, humans are 'incapable of seeing the world', and hence in need of an animal's gaze, because they are 'blinded by consciousness', and Godard makes clear that self-consciousness and language are inextricable. Marcus indicates as much when he entertains the hypothesis that 'the face-to-face invents language', and later he ties language to humans' troubled relationship with the Other. During the film's second disorienting split-camera blur shot, in which the left camera stays focused on Ivitch as the right camera tracks Marcus, Marcus says that 'With language, something's happening . . . There's something troubling our relation to the world . . . It acts against pure freedom.' And as he moves away from Ivitch, he adds, 'I speak – subject . . . I listen – object.' Ivitch responds, 'We need to get an interpreter . . . Soon, everyone will need an interpreter to understand the words coming from their own mouths.'

It would seem that the 3D seeing-via-Roxy requires an adieu to language. A male voice suggests as much when he cites Blanchot, 'I seek poverty in language', as does Josette when she exclaims, 'Words! Words! I don't want to hear them spoken anymore!' One way beyond language is through sound. When Marcus speaks of the 'face-to-face' of language, he slowly intones the phrase 'si le face-à-face invente le langage', and then repeats the first word: 'si . . . si . . .' Ivitch responds, 'do re mi fa sol si', to which Marcus replies, 'la . . . la . . .'. Here, a conjunction gives rise to linguistic signs of musical sounds outside language. And then there are the two title cards that rewrite the film's title – AH DIEUX, OH LANGAGE. In the 'AH' and 'OH', both of which appear on separate title cards, language reaches its limits. This is no Fort-Da but an Ah-Oh of intensities, sonic expressions of affects beyond linguistic articulation. At this point, in this Ah-Oh of intensities, human and animal enter a zone of indiscernibility.

In the closing moments of the film, Godard evokes this sonic zone of indiscernibility, but in a complex sequence of sounds and images that requires further contextualisation to be fully appreciated. So, before examining the film's ending, a brief digression.

Metaphor, Apaches, Dogs and Children

The title card '2 Métaphore' clearly points to the essentially metaphorical nature of language, but a second reading of the title is obliquely insinuated when Davidson responds to Ivitch's question, 'What difference is there between an idea and a metaphor?' His answer, 'Ask the Athenians when they take the tram', may seem a feeble etymological joke, but the film's images suggest otherwise. Metaphor comes from the Greek *metapherein*, 'to transfer, carry over', from *meta-*, 'over, across', plus *pherein*, 'to carry, bear'. Nothing in the Greek suggests a literal mode of transport, but Davidson's wordplay invites speculation about the significance of the many images of vehicles in the film. Six shots of a ferry on Lake Geneva appear at regular intervals. Seven shots through a car windscreen punctuate the film, one shot lasting over a minute, the others between ten and thirty seconds. There are several shots of passing cars and parked cars, planes, helicopters and even four shots of bicycles. But most significant is a twenty-one-second section that juxtaposes Roxy and a train entering a Metro stop. At one-second intervals, the approach of the train towards the camera in three-quarter view is intercut with four shots of Roxy's head against a speckled-black asphalt background. The fourth shot of Roxy is followed by a perpendicular view of Metro carriages passing in a succession of three stuttered blurs. After a brief black screen, the blurred succession of carriages continues for eight seconds, but this time with a black silhouette of Roxy's head and shoulders superimposed on the image, as if he were calmly contemplating the train from some unspecified outside location. The slow, meditative strains of the second movement of Beethoven's Seventh Symphony play throughout the sequence, reinforcing the sense that Roxy and the train belong to separate worlds.

Roxy's world is outside language, but also in some respects outside the entirety of urban civilisation, represented by the Metro and all the other images of 'metaphoric' modes of transport. Roxy passes through the modern human world, but he belongs to a natural world with which humans have lost touch. Early in the film, Godard calls attention to the difference between contemporary and traditional societies. The student Marie rails against the law: 'In fact, the law cheats. The law that denies its own violence, cheats. The law that denies what turns it into a state apparatus, cheats. And the law that deems itself self-legitimizing, cheats twice.' Her friend Alain counters, 'I think that in primitive societies, this was not the case.' When Marie objects, 'And when one had a war?', Alain responds, 'It is a war, but of society against the State' (an allusion to Pierre Clastres familiar to any reader of Deleuze and Guattari).[4] Such traditional societies not only ward off the State, but also remain in close contact with nature, as Godard indicates when a male voice-over says, 'The Apache Indians, the Chiricahua tribe, they call the world: the forest.' The film is filled with images of the forest, but no humans are shown in that space – only Roxy. Clearly, the world of law and the State apparatus, of cities and Metros, is far removed from the forest, the animal world that Roxy inhabits.

Midway through the film, the Apaches are mentioned a second time when Marcus says to Ivitch, 'I don't know about you, but when I was a kid, we played Indians. The Apaches were my favourite. To say "the world", they said "the forest".' Implicit in this remark is a connection between children, the Apaches and the forest – and thereby a connection with Roxy. At the close of a sequence of Marcus and Ivitch conversing in their apartment, Marcus says, 'We will have children.' Ivitch responds, 'No, not yet. A dog, if you want.' As this scene closes, the pensive opening measures of Schœnberg's *Transfigured Night* begin. A fifteen-second shot of four hands playing a piano is then followed by a scene of a young boy and young girl walking through an orchard in early spring, the colours of the landscape and the children's clothing in enhanced, vibrant hues. In voice-over, Ivitch says softly and slowly, 'Imagine that you are still a little boy.' The film cuts to an image of clouds in a deep blue sky as Ivitch says, 'We looked at cloud shapes.' Two more shots of the boy and girl ensue as *Transfigured Night* continues to play. Over these images, Ivitch says, 'As a girl, I saw dogs everywhere.' Marcus asks, 'In the blue or the white?' to which she responds, 'We are together, both.' Marcus then says, 'We need to have children.' The idyllic images of the children stop and a black screen appears as Ivitch answers, 'Not certain.' The music ends, and she adds, 'A dog, yes!'

In this playful sequence, a choice between child and dog frames images of children in an orchard, a cultivated forest midway between the wild and civilisation. Ivitch evokes a consciousness that finds dogs in clouds – indeed, dogs everywhere. The dogs are in the blue and the white, inseparably together, as are the young boy and girl. Ivitch invites Marcus to participate in the enchanted childhood realm of imaginative interaction with nature, but he breaks the spell by reiterating adult concerns: 'We need to have children.'

The End of *Adieu au langage*

And now to the conclusion of *Adieu au langage*. The last shot before the credits shows a foreground close-up of two bright-red poppies, rustling in the wind, and a car passing in the background. A black screen follows with sounds of a crying baby and a howling dog. These sounds stop after the first credit title card appears. With the second title card, we hear a reprise of a song that accompanied the film's opening credits, 'La caccia alle streghe' ('The Witch Hunt'), a song celebrating worker/student solidarity and their fight for revolution. As the final title card of the credits appears, the song is replaced by a din of crowd noises, amid which a voice shouts the opening lines of a French nursery song (sung to the tune of 'For he's a jolly good fellow') that dates to the eighteenth century: 'Marlbrough s'en va-t-en guerre, / Marlbrough s'en va-t-en guerre, / Marlbrough s'en va-t-en guerre' ('Marlborough is going to war, / Marlborough is going to war, / Marlborough is going to war'). During the final shout of the sentence, the credits' black screen is succeeded by an image of Roxy walking a magenta path into a forest of green and blue leaves and black and orange-red trunks and branches. The sound stops, then four seconds later, in a startling high-volume blast, the shouting voice screams the closing line of the nursery song chorus: 'Ne sait quand reviendra' ('Doesn't know when he'll return'). Silence again, then a final image of Roxy running towards the camera along the same forest path.

First, then, we see nature (the poppies) in the foreground, the human *tekhnē* of a mode of transport in the background, the juxtaposition of the two emphasising the unresolved conflicts inherent in their coexistence. This is followed by the non-linguistic sounds of the dog mingled with the pre-linguistic sounds of the infant. This sonic zone of indiscernibility signals a becoming-dog and a becoming-child, an opening to intensities outside language and the human institutions and practices that modify nature. These sounds give way to a song of resistance and potential revolution, suggesting that the *fonction de voyance* engaged through a confrontation with the intolerable opens up possibilities of transformative thought, sensation and action. In the final images and sounds, however, we are reminded of the two divergent destinies that await baby humans and canines: that of the infant, who will soon sing nursery songs of war with no foreseeable end, and that of the dog, who will live among humans, but will be able to run back and forth through the forest, which is what the Apaches called 'the world'.

Roxy the Seer

In *A Thousand Plateaus*, Deleuze and Guattari say, '*anyone who likes cats or dogs is a fool*' (ATP 240; emphasis in original). Donna Haraway especially has taken exception to this statement, devoting several pages of *When Species Meet* to a vituperative screed against Deleuze and Guattari's mocking remarks about doting dog owners.[5] But Haraway ignores Deleuze and Guattari's assertion that, even if one must distinguish pets from 'pack or affect animals that form a multiplicity', it is also possible 'for any animal to be treated in the mode of the pack or swarm [. . .] Even the cat, even the dog' (ATP 241). Dogs were the first animals to be domesticated by humans, and they have been selectively bred to prefer human company to the company of other dogs – something Godard reminds us of in *Adieu au langage* when a voice-over says, 'And Darwin, citing Buffon, affirms that the dog is the only being on earth that loves you more than it loves itself.'[6] Hence, there is an inbred tendency for human–canine bonds to reinforce cultural norms that subordinate dogs to humans and valorise the human over the animal. But the domestication of dogs represents a long process of co-evolution involving both dogs and humans, one that opens an area of proximity between humans and another life form that is unparalleled in human relations with any other species. The dog is itself a zone of indiscernibility, living both inside and outside the human world, inviting the most infantilising of human attachments, but also affording a means of engaging human animality and thereby undoing the category of the human.

For the most part, Godard shows Roxy in landscapes unmarked by human presence: amid forests, beside rivers and lakes, in fields of grass and snow. At one point, Roxy walks through a gateway to a human habitation; at another, he stands on a railroad trestle; and in a few shots he paces the couples' apartment floor or rests on their couch. But nowhere is Roxy shown with a human being. His status as pet is virtually ignored. Throughout the film he is presented as an autonomous being, a self-contained creature unselfconsciously moving within his surroundings. Only once does Godard anthropomorphise Roxy. While various images of Roxy by a river occupy the screen, a voice-over cites a passage from Clifford D. Simak's *Time and Again*, substituting the name Roxy for that of the novel's protagonist, Sutton:

> The water spoke to him in a deep and serious voice. Roxy began to think. It's trying to talk to me as it has always tried to talk to people through the ages. Dialoguing with itself when there is no one to listen. But trying. Trying always to communicate to people the news that it has to give them. Some of them have taken from the river a certain truth. But none of them . . .

This is Roxy, the Cynic dog-philosopher living according to nature, in Heraclitean contemplation of water and the flow of all things. The sounds of a choir singing Valentin Silvestrov's liturgical chant 'Lord God' play before, during and after this sequence, situating Roxy and the river in an aural realm that aspires to render sonorous the ineffable. The effect is not to humanise Roxy, but to derive from human thought a mode of contemplation that belongs neither to humans nor to dogs. The result is the evocation of 'a certain truth', but one that trails off into silence before it can be enunciated.

The implicit opposition of nature and culture, and the association of pristine wilderness with traditional peoples, children and animals, might suggest that Godard is simply reviving the clichés of Romanticism and repackaging them in a jumbled collection of disconnected fragments. Such is not the case, however. The film's seemingly Romantic elements have a polemical function. Roxy, children and the Apaches serve as vantages from which to confront the intolerable, as points of resistance to war, violence, cliché and the malaise of contemporary quotidian existence. Traditional peoples are invoked solely to indict State violence and the degradation of human relations with the environment. The brief images of the carefree children in a landscape of pulsating colour are in sharp contrast to the dark browns and blacks of Marcus and Ivitch's apartment, with the perpetual glow of the large-screen TV in the background, the two of them speaking in flat, inexpressive tones. Like Gédéon and Josette, Marcus and Ivitch show no joy or vitality, simply an anesthetised numbness. Hence, beneath Ivitch's amusing suggestion that they have a dog instead of children is an implicit refusal to perpetuate the melancholy world she inhabits. And as for Roxy, he has a certain nobility, yet not that of a canine noble savage, but that of a self-possessed, autonomous and inscrutable being whose mere presence brings into sharp relief the contours of human consciousness and behaviour.

Roxy initiates a becoming-dog, a becoming-other that seeks something beyond human words, thoughts and vision. This becoming-other, however, is not in service of a Romantic primitivism or the restoration of some lost paradise. Although Godard sees much that is intolerable in the modern technological world, he promotes no return to the past but seeks a future-oriented transformation of our world through a creative use of its potentials. The Nature Godard invokes in his title cards is a new nature, one that has never existed before. The film's images of the natural world are decidedly unnatural – the colours constantly altered, enhanced and distorted, the visual textures varying in clarity and resolution, and all within a 3D format that defamiliarises object relations and makes palpable an alien dimension within conventional space. Godard exploits all the technological possibilities of cinema – that most machinic of arts – to invent new ways of seeing, hearing and thinking that blur the lines between nature and artifice, the human and the non-human. Just as the film attempts to move beyond language through language, via citation after citation of sociological, anthropological, historical, philosophical and literary texts, so it seeks a vision beyond contemporary mediated vision through the media that now limit our seeing.

The Intolerable and Belief in This World

The modern cinema begins with the intolerable, with images that cannot be processed within the sensory-motor schema. The intolerable activates a *fonction de voyance*, a power of seeing that promotes the invention of new cinematic signs: chronosigns, lectosigns and noosigns. The modern cinema's aim is to create new ways of seeing and hearing, but its ultimate goal is to restore belief in this world. 'Only belief in this world can reconnect man to what he sees and hears [. . .] Restoring our belief in the world – this is the power of modern cinema' (C2 172). The characters in *Adieu au langage* have lost faith in this world, as is so pointedly demonstrated when Ivitch opts to have a dog instead of children. But Godard's becoming-dog attempts to reconnect humans to what they see and hear by inventing a visual and sonic world beyond the grasp of our common-sense senses.

God is mentioned in several texts Godard cites in the film, but never gods. And yet he chooses to rewrite 'adieu' as 'AH DIEUX' ('OH GODS'). If AH DIEUX is opposed to OH LANGAGE as NATURE is opposed to MÉTAPHORE, then it is Nature that is the realm of the gods. What gods? Not transcendent deities, but the animistic, immanent powers of the natural world that Roxy contemplates by the riverside, when '[t]he water spoke to him in a deep and serious voice'. That nature, however, is a new nature, one that has never existed before. Late in the film, Godard in voice-over cites Dostoyevsky's *The Possessed*: 'It's what Kiriloff said: "Two questions, a big one and a small one".' A female voice asks, 'The small one?' to which Godard responds, 'Suffering.' 'And the big one?' she inquires. 'The other world, the other world.' The world of suffering: the world of the intolerable. And the other world? Not an afterlife, but this world made new, a world we can believe in.

Notes

1. A number of insightful commentaries on *Adieu au langage* have appeared. Especially helpful are Bordwell (2014a) and Bordwell (2014b). Also of interest are Brody (2014), Ehrlich (2014), Foundas (2014), Kastrenakes (2014) and Williams (2014).
2. Ted Fendt (2014) provides an invaluable resource for study of the film, cataloguing most of the film's textual references, with citations of the film passage in French and in English translation, as well as citations of the original passage, with translations when necessary. All my citations of Godard's textual references are taken from Fendt's catalogue.
3. For insight into the technical aspects of Godard's use of 3D, see Rizov (2014), in which Rizov talks with Godard's director of photography, Fabrice Aragno, about the conventions of 3D cinema and the deviations from those conventions that he and Godard employ.
4. For discussions of Clastres, see AO 148, 190 and ATP 357–61.
5. See Haraway (2008: 27–30) for her critique of Deleuze and Guattari. For a detailed response to her attack, see Chapter 19.
6. For evidence of canine preference of human to canine company, see Tuber et al. (1996).

15

Visions and Auditions: The Image in the Late Thought of Deleuze

In 'Literature and Life', the opening essay of his last book, *Essays Critical and Clinical* (1993), Deleuze says that great literature has three features: it produces 'a decomposition or destruction of the maternal language'; it creates 'a kind of foreign language within language'; and it brings forth 'Visions and Auditions that no longer belong to any language' (CC 5). The motifs of the decomposition of the maternal tongue and the invention of a foreign language within language are long-standing elements of Deleuze's approach to literature, but the concepts of Visions and Auditions are new, and determining precisely what he means by these terms is difficult, given the fact that he did not live long enough to elaborate on them further. It is possible, however, to suggest something of the direction Deleuze was exploring through these concepts by examining Deleuze's commentary on Beckett's television plays, 'The Exhausted' (1992), and key essays in *Essays Critical and Clinical.* What such an examination reveals is that the concepts of Visions and Auditions are inseparable from Deleuze's reflections on the image in his final writings. While the concepts of Visions and Auditions remain tied to literature, that of the image pertains to all the arts, whose general vocation is to make possible the event of a pure image. At times, Deleuze seems to celebrate a form of aestheticism in this embrace of the pure image, but at others he makes it clear that there is a political dimension to the image, and specifically to those images labelled Visions and Auditions, which are the inventions of great writers. That political dimension is part of Deleuze's proposal 'to take up

Bergson's notion of fabulation and give it a political meaning' (N 174).

From Cinema to Television

To understand what Deleuze means by Visions and Auditions, we must first trace the development of his concept of the image in his late work. Before the appearance of *Cinema 1: The Movement-Image* (1983) and *Cinema 2: The Time-Image* (1985), the concept of the image plays a relatively minor role in Deleuze's thought. Of necessity, he speaks frequently of the imagination and mental images in his first book, *Empiricism and Subjectivity: An Essay on Hume's Theory of Human Nature* (1953), since these are terms central to Hume's philosophy. Likewise, in *Bergsonism* (1966) Deleuze provides a detailed exposition of Bergson's theory of images. But when he turns from his treatment of other philosophers and writers to articulate his own philosophy in *Difference and Repetition* (1968) and *The Logic of Sense* (1969), the concept of the image is given no particular importance.[1] In the third chapter of *Difference and Repetition*, Deleuze does expound at length on the 'dogmatic image of thought' (DR 148) – a topic addressed earlier in *Proust and Signs* (PS 94–102) – but he provides little clarification of his motive for naming it an 'image' of thought. In his speculations on the infant's accession to language in *The Logic of Sense*, Deleuze adopts a psychoanalytic use of the term, employing the notion of the *imago* to characterise one component of the psychic apparatus, while incorporating into his analysis some elements of his earlier commentary on the fetish as image in *Masochism: Coldness and Cruelty* (1967). Yet here, too, the image retains its marginal status within Deleuze's conceptual schema. One might expect the image to feature prominently in Deleuze's most extended treatment of painting, *Francis Bacon: The Logic of Sensation* (1981), but the concept's function in this work is primarily to stress the importance of the 'figure' and the 'figural'. 'Images' in this book denote 'conventional representational images', whereas 'the figural' is that element of Bacon's painting that disturbs and undermines the images of conventional representation and makes possible the disclosure of forces and intensities immanent within such images.

With the cinema books, however, all this changes, and the image takes centre stage. Not only is cinema discussed entirely in terms of images, but those images are also situated within an ontology of images that embraces the entire cosmos. Seeking a metaphysics adequate to the cinema, Deleuze adopts Bergson's suggestion at the beginning of *Matter and Memory* (1896) that matter be treated simply as 'a collection of images' (Bergson 1959: 161). As Bergson sees it, idealism and realism are 'two equally excessive theses' (Bergson 1959: 161). The idealist regards the object as a mere mental representation with no necessary correlation with external reality, whereas the realist views the object as a thing whose qualities are without proven relation to those apprehended by the perceiver. In treating matter as a collection of images, Bergson offers a conception of the image that is something more than what the idealist calls a 'representation' and something less than what the realist calls a 'thing'. The object, says Bergson, 'exists in itself and, on the other hand, the object is, in itself, pictorial [*pittoresque*], as we perceive it: it is an image, but an image which exists in itself' (Bergson 1959: 162). Hence, through the concept of the image, Bergson is able to consider 'matter before the dissociation that idealism and realism have brought about between matter's existence and its appearance' (Bergson 1959: 162).

On the basis of this ontology of the image, Deleuze develops a taxonomy of cinematic images and their related signs, grouping them into the two large categories of movement-images (typical of the classic cinema) and time-images (characteristic of the modern cinema). The prominence of the image in this analysis is noteworthy, but Deleuze's commitment to this ontology of images does not continue in writings subsequent to the cinema books, at least in these terms. Indeed, far from treating everything as image in his later works, Deleuze comes to speak of the image as something rare and difficult to create. In the general ontology of the cinema books, then, we find little to clarify the concept of the image Deleuze articulates at the close of his life. Yet in the final chapter of *Cinema 2: The Time-Image*, Deleuze does offer a significant characterisation of the modern cinema that bears directly on his exposition of the image in 'The Exhausted' and *Essays*

Critical and Clinical – that of a cinema in which the visual and the sonic components of film become autonomous. In such films, speech 'turns in on itself; it is no longer a dependent or something which is part of the visual image; it becomes a completely separate sound image; it takes on a cinematographic autonomy and cinema becomes truly autonomous' (C2 243). In the films of Marguerite Duras and others, the division between sight and sound is even more pronounced: 'There are no longer even two autonomous components of a single audio-visual image, as in Rossellini, but two "heautonomous" images, one visual and one sound, with a fault, an interstice, an irrational cut between them' (C2 251).

This opposition of the visual image (*image visuelle*) and sound image (*image sonore*) is striking, given the common association of images with visual pictures. Of course, if everything is an image, then a sound image is no more unusual than a visual image, but in Deleuze's late thought on the image, although he abandons Bergson's vocabulary of a general ontology of images, he continues to conceive of the domain of the image as one that is both visual and sonic. In *Cinema 2*, Deleuze focuses on language in his discussion of the sound image, but he also recognises the existence of 'a single sound continuum' (C2 234), which includes speech, music and various sound effects, all of which may be regarded as diverse sound images. This qualification is essential, since the sound images Deleuze later calls 'Auditions' in *Essays Critical and Clinical* are those of a music that is produced in language but that is neither strictly linguistic nor non-linguistic, but that forms 'the outside *of* language' (CC lv).

In *Cinema 2*, Deleuze parenthetically remarks that the films of Duras and others 'would never have arisen without television' (C2 251), even if television by and large has not fulfilled its potential. It is no surprise, then, that in 'The Exhausted', Deleuze's essay on Samuel Beckett's television plays, he focuses on the medium's separation of sight and sound in his analysis of these works. Deleuze identifies a common goal throughout Beckett's career – that of going beyond language, 'of "boring holes" in the surface of language so that "what lurks behind it" might at last appear' (CC 172). Beckett pursues this goal, according to Deleuze, by exhausting language's possibilities, first, by fashioning a restricted set of terms that are combined in all possible permutations (what Deleuze calls language I, a language of nouns); then by eliminating all possible personal and cultural stories, memories, desires and so on from the voices that enunciate words (language II, a language of voices); and, finally, by creating an any-space-whatever in which pure images may appear (language III, 'a language of images, resounding and coloring images' [CC 159]). Language I is especially evident in Beckett's novels; language II in his novels, theatre and radio pieces; and language III in his television plays.

Language III 'no longer relates language to enumerable or combinable objects, nor to transmitting voices, but to immanent limits that are ceaselessly displaced – hiatuses, holes or tears', to 'something from the outside or from elsewhere'. This 'something from the outside', this gap or hole in language, 'is called Image, a visual or aural Image'. It appears only when language is freed from language I and language II. To create 'a pure and unsullied image, one that is nothing but an image', is to reveal the image 'in all its singularity, retaining nothing of the personal or the rational' (CC 138). Images come to us overlaid with all our cultural codes, our individual experiences, expectations, prejudices and assumptions. To perceive the image beneath its personal, cultural and rational covering requires the elimination of what is not really there, what is superadded by unconscious and conscious presuppositions, and the revelation of what *is* really there – an appearance without a specified percipient. The image is indefinite, 'A woman, *a* hand, *a* mouth, *some* eyes' (CC 158), not vague or imprecise, but impersonal and acontextual, neither a functioning component of a world of action (*this* woman, *this* hand) nor a Platonic Idea (*the* woman, *the* hand). 'To *make* an image from time to time' is 'extremely difficult', but, Deleuze asks, 'can art, painting, and music have any other goal?' (CC 158).

What is important about the image is not its content, but its form, which Deleuze characterises as 'its "internal tension", [. . .] the force it mobilizes to create a void or bore holes, to loosen the grip of words, to dry up the oozing of voices, so as to free itself from memory and reason: a small, alogical, amnesiac, and almost aphasic image' (CC 159). The image is an event, a process rather than a thing, an emergence imbued with 'a fantastic potential energy, which it detonates by dissipating itself' (CC 160). The image appears as an explosion that disappears just as it is appearing. Given the image's instability and evanescence, it is not only difficult to create, but also difficult to tell whether its creation has taken place at all: 'even painters, even musicians, are never sure they have succeeded in making an image. What great painter has not said to himself, on his deathbed, that he had failed to make an image, even a small or simple one?' (CC 161).

In his analysis of Beckett's television plays, Deleuze shows how Beckett systematically engages the difficult task of creating images, each of the four plays under Deleuze's consideration marking a stage in their fashioning. The first play, *Quad*, presents a closed, anonymous 'any-space-whatever' (*espace quelconque*), within which four cloaked figures exhaust the permutations of movement along the peripheries of a featureless square space and the X of the diagonals that connect the square's four corners. There are no words, no voices and no sounds other than the swishing of robes and the shuffling of feet. The play does not create images but instead explores the space within which images may appear.

Ghost Trio offers another any-space-whatever, a room with a door, window, mirror and pallet. Close-ups of the elements of the room eventually give way to a shot of a man in silhouette who is hunched over a tape recorder. A female voice-over intones the names of the objects that appear on camera, and then the voice is replaced with brief passages from Beethoven's Piano Trio Opus 70, no. 1 (the so-called 'Ghost Trio'), played while the male figure is bent over the tape recorder. At the close of the play, the figure's face is seen in the mirror, and then a small boy appears in the doorway. Here, the sound of words yields to music, and the any-space-whatever gives rise to two visual images, the man's face and the small boy.

Deleuze argues that though '*Trio* goes from the space to the image', this movement does not fully attain its goal, for 'The *Trio* leads us from space to the thresholds of the image' (CC 168, 169). The third play, . . .*but the clouds*. . ., however, does produce images within an any-space-whatever. A male voice-over describes a male figure's movements within a featureless circle of light, calling the shadows to the East 'the roads', the shadows to the West 'the closet', and the North space in front of the camera 'sanctum'. Midway through the play, the voice tries to summon up the memory image of a woman reciting lines from Yeats's 'The Tower'. As the man is shown in the sanctum, the voice speaks of the chances of the memory image appearing, which are one or two in a thousand. The voice recites fragments from 'The Tower' ('but the clouds', 'of the sky') and briefly an image of a woman's eyes and mouth emerges and then fades at the top of the dark screen, once for two seconds, then twice for five seconds. At the play's conclusion, the voice recites the poem's complete line: '. . . but the clouds of the sky . . . when the horizon fades . . . or a bird's sleepy cry . . . among the deepening shades . . .' (Beckett 1986: 422). What the play offers, in Deleuze's analysis, is the difficult production of a brief visual image (a depersonalised face), accompanied by poetic images that point beyond words, towards the visual image of 'the clouds of the sky / When the horizon fades' and the sound image of 'a bird's sleepy cry / Among the deepening shades'.

Nacht und Träume, the last of the television plays, takes its name from Schubert's late lied, the closing lines of which are briefly hummed without accompaniment and then sung by a male voice-over. The play opens with a fade-in, lower left corner of the screen, of a man's upper torso and head in silhouette, leaning over a table. The Schubert fragment is heard as the man, labelled 'the dreamer' in the script, slowly lowers his head to rest on the table. The voice stops, and in the upper right corner of the screen, a left-right inverted image of the man resting his head on the table appears (the dream). A hand emerges and touches his head. He raises his head; a hand appears with a chalice and raises it to his lips. He drinks, then a hand appears with a cloth and wipes the man's brow. The hand and cloth retreat into the darkness, the man raises his hand, and a hand emerges from the darkness and grasps the man's hand. The upper right image fades. The dreamer in the lower left area raises his head as the voice sings and then hums the same phrase from Schubert. The upper right area fades in again, and the camera slowly moves towards that image until it fills the screen. The preceding action in this area is repeated. The camera pulls back, the upper right area fades out, and then the lower left image slowly disappears in silence.

Beckett calls the lower left figure 'dreamer' and the upper right area 'his dreamt self', but Deleuze insists this is not an invocation of the Romantic notion of an ideal or fantasised dream, but an instance of the insomniac dream, in which one does not dream *in* sleep, but '*alongside* insomnia' (CC 171) (and, in fact, on screen we see dreamer and dream alongside one another). What Beckett shows is the production of an evanescent visual image, the waking dream of insomnia, which belongs neither to daylight wakefulness nor nocturnal sleep, but to a state and space in between, indeterminately mental and physical. This visual image is inaugurated both times by the phrase 'Soft dreams come again', but these words are sung, and only after the tune has been hummed without words. Language and music coalesce, and once the dream image appears they both fall into silence, the sound image produced in the play being a continuum of words, music and silence.

Ideas and the Virtual

In the television plays, Beckett 'bores holes' in language to reveal 'something from the outside or elsewhere'. This something from the outside Deleuze labels language III, yet it is not strictly language itself, but visual images and sound images in an autonomous relation of co-presence or back-and-forth oscillation between one another. In these plays, Beckett literally goes beyond language to fashion non-linguistic visual images and sound images. For writers, however, there is no television screen or audio track where the something from the outside may be physically produced. The beyond of language must emerge within language. It must belong to language and yet tend towards language's outside, towards its limit.

> The limit is not outside language, it is the outside *of* language. It is made up of visions and auditions that are not of language, but which language alone makes possible. There is also a painting and a music characteristic of writing, like the effects of colors and sonorities that rise up above words [. . .] One must say of every writer: he is a seer, a hearer, 'ill seen ill said,' she is a colorist, a musician. (CC lv)

These visions and auditions are part of a delirium of language, something like the visual and sonic hallucinations of schizophrenics. And yet they

> are not fantasies, but veritable Ideas that the writer sees and hears in the interstices of language, in its intervals. They are not interruptions of the process, but breaks that form part of it, like an eternity that can only be revealed in a becoming, or a landscape that only appears in movement [. . .] The writer as seer and hearer, the aim of literature: it is the passage of life within language that constitutes Ideas. (CC 5)

Clearly, Deleuze is not referring to Platonic Ideas when he speaks of visions and auditions as 'veritable Ideas'. Rather, he is invoking the concept of the virtual, which appears early in his writings and continues to the end of his career. It is helpful to review select moments in Deleuze's life-long meditation on the virtual, for only then can we understand why Deleuze says Visions and Auditions are 'like an eternity' and that 'the passage of life within language' is what 'constitutes Ideas'.

An early exposition of the virtual and its relation to Ideas may be found in *Proust and Signs* (1964), where the virtual is associated with Proust's notion of essences. For Proust, Deleuze argues, art reveals essences, which, like Bergson's 'past in itself', are virtual. In Proust's words, which Deleuze cites frequently in his writings, essences are 'Real without being actual, ideal without being abstract' (PS 58; trans. modified). Essences are like the Combray of Marcel's involuntary memory in the *Recherche*, not the actual Combray or Marcel's actual personal memory of it invoked by the taste of the madeleine, but a virtual Combray that only exists in itself as an impersonal essence. Essences are like the theme of the Vinteuil sonata, immanent within but irreducible to the actual sounds of its performance. Essences are enfolded or implicated differences that unfold or explicate themselves in the actual, all essences coexisting in an ultimate 'perplication' of differences. One may speak of 'essences or Ideas apropos of Vinteuil's little phrase' (PS 100), but only if such Ideas are conceived of in terms of this perplication and implication of difference.

Deleuze elaborates on this concept of the virtual as perplicated and implicated difference in *Difference and Repetition* (1968), where he characterises Ideas as 'problematic or "perplexed" virtual multiplicities, made up of relations between differential elements'. Such Ideas are engaged in a 'flow of exchange' with intensities, which are 'implicated multiplicities, "implexes", made up of relations between asymmetrical elements which direct the course of the actualisation of Ideas and determine the case of solution for problems' (DR 244). Ideas are virtual, real yet not actual, and intensities mark the point at which the virtual is actualised. One may say, then, that the Ideas and intensities of *Difference and Repetition* together correspond to the essences of *Proust and Signs*.

In *The Logic of Sense* (1969), Deleuze shifts vocabulary, largely using the term 'Idea' to refer to Platonic Ideas and designating the virtual by diverse terms, including that of 'the event'. Nonetheless, Deleuze does state that 'events are ideal' and that 'the mode of the event is the problematic' (LS 53–4), thereby keeping alive the notion of the Idea put forward in *Difference and Repetition*. It would seem, however, that, at this point in Deleuze's thinking, the word 'Idea' itself is too contaminated by its Platonic associations to play a prominent role in his effort to 'reverse Platonism', which he sees as one of philosophy's main tasks. 'To reverse Platonism', he says, 'is first and foremost to remove essences and to substitute events in their place' (LS 53). When Deleuze says that the event 'is ideal by nature', and must be distinguished from 'its spatio-temporal realization in a state of affairs' (LS 53), he is stressing the difference between the virtual event and its actualisations. 'Events are the only idealities', Deleuze concludes, not Platonic essences.

Deleuze specifies further that

> Events are ideational singularities which communicate in one and the same Event. They have therefore an eternal truth, and their time is never the present which realizes them and makes them exist. Rather, it is the unlimited Aion, the infinitive in which they subsist and insist. (LS 53)

This notion of the event's virtual time of Aion, as opposed to the actual time of Chronos, appears again in Deleuze and Guattari's exposition of the concept of 'becomings' in *A Thousand Plateaus* (1980). Chronos, they state, is 'the time of measure that situates things and persons, develops a form, and determines a subject', whereas Aion is

> the indefinite time of the event, the floating line that knows only speeds and continually divides that which transpires into an already-there that is at the same time not-yet-here, a simultaneous too-late and too-early, a something that is both going to happen and has just happened. (ATP 262)

The floating time of Aion is that of an infinitive – 'to run', for example, which enfolds within itself all actualizations in chronological time: I run, they had run, we will have run, and so on. It is an eternity (*aion* means 'eternity' in Greek), yet not a transcendent but an immanent eternity of an elusive 'between-time' of delirious 'becomings', in which the common-sense coordinates of space, time and individual identity are suspended. Becomings have an identity, but it is that of an indefinite article, 'a day, a season, a year, *a life* (regardless of its duration) – a climate, a wind, a fog, a swarm, a pack (regardless of its regularity)' (ATP 262). When *the* wolf, *the* horse or *the* child enters into a becoming, they become *a* wolf, *a* horse, *a* child and 'cease to be subjects to become events, in assemblages that are inseparable from an hour, a season, an atmosphere, an air, a life' (ATP 262).

In his last essay, 'Immanence, A Life . . .' (1995), Deleuze brings together the notions of the event, the time of Aion, the identity of the indefinite article and the virtual in his remarks on immanence and 'a life'. Ever the champion of a philosophy of immanence, Deleuze reiterates in these final, brief pages that immanence is never immanent *to* anything, but is, in itself, a pure transcendental field, prepersonal and pre-individual, in which there is no differentiation of subject and object. This transcendental field is 'pure immanence', which Deleuze defines as 'A LIFE, and nothing else' (PI 27). To explain this notion of 'a life', Deleuze cites an episode from Dickens's *Our Mutual Friend*, in which a deservedly despised man is found dying, and yet, despite his wickedness, those who find him take care of him. What they respond to is 'a life', one that emerges between the evil man's life and death. At this point, 'the life of the individual gives way to an impersonal and yet singular life that releases a pure event freed from the accidents of internal and external life, that is, from the subjectivity and objectivity of what happens' (PI 28). It is an indefinite life, *a* life, which does not itself have moments, 'but only between-times, between-moments'. It exists in the time of Aion, 'the immensity of an empty time where one sees the event yet to come and already happened' (PI 29). This impersonal and yet singular life is 'the index of a multiplicity: an event, a singularity, a life' (PI 30). That multiplicity is the transcendental field, pure immanence, which we may speak of as life *in toto*, but only if we qualify that this 'life as a whole' is an irreducible multiplicity, one that is only ever manifest in singular events, each of which is *a* life. Hence Deleuze's statement that pure immanence is 'A LIFE, and nothing more'. And such 'A LIFE' is one with the virtual:

> A life contains only virtuals. It is made up of virtualities, events, singularities. What we call virtual is not something that lacks reality but something that is engaged in a process of actualization following the plane of its particular reality. The immanent event is actualized in a state of things and in a lived state that make it happen. (PI 31; trans. modified)

Auditions and Visions

At this point, it should be clear what Deleuze means when he says that Visions and Auditions are 'veritable Ideas', which are 'like an eternity' constituted by 'the passage of life within language'. Visions and Auditions are virtual events, whose time is the eternity of Aion, whose identity is that of the indefinite article, and whose appearance is an index of the multiplicity of pure immanence, 'A LIFE'. We must now delve more deeply into the specifics of Visions and Auditions as they are presented in *Essays Critical and Clinical*, considering sounds first and then sights.

The notion of 'a music characteristic of writing' (CC lv) might at first glance seem pedestrian, given that there is a sonic dimension to language and that literary critics speak often of the musical dimension of style, especially in poetry. But the music of Auditions has little to do with the sonorous beauty of a mellifluous style. Rather, Auditions mark the end point of a process of dismantling language and creating a foreign language within it, a process whereby writers make language itself stutter and stammer. In 'He Stuttered', Deleuze offers several examples of stuttering in one's own tongue, many of which he touches on in earlier writings. He references the ascetic intensity of Kafka's minor use of German induced through a deliberate impoverishment of vocabulary and syntax; the stylistic peculiarities of T. E. Lawrence and Kleist; Raymond Roussel's progressive expansion of parentheses within parentheses; and Céline's 'exclamatory sentences and suspensions that do away with all syntax in favor of a pure dance of words' (CC 112). He cites Gherasim Luca's poem 'Passionnément', in which Luca fragments the phrase 'je t'aime passionnément' into the lines 'Passionné nez passionnem je / je t'ai je t'aime je / je je jet je t'ai jetez / je t'aime passionem t'aime'; e e cummings's asyntactic 'he danced his did'; and Beckett's lines that make 'the sentence grow out from the middle, adding particle upon particle (*que de ce, ce ceci-ce, loin là là-bas à peine quoi* . . .) so as to pilot the block of a single expiring breath (*voulais croire entrevoir quoi* . . .)' (CC 110–12). All these writers set language in disequilibrium and push it towards a limit 'that is no longer either syntactic or grammatical'. This thrust towards a limit finds 'its raw state in Artaud's breath-words', 'inarticulate words, blocks of a single breath' (CC 112). One might think that such sonic blocks of a single breath are Auditions, but in fact Auditions are, paradoxically, beyond sound.

> Words paint and sing, but only at the limit of the path they trace through their divisions and combinations. Words create silence [. . .] *When a language is so strained* that it starts to stutter, or to murmur or stammer . . . *then language in its entirety reaches the limit* that marks its outside and makes it confront silence. (CC 113)

The music of Auditions is thus a virtual music, wrested from the sounds of language as it stammers towards its limit. Its sonorities 'rise up above words', appear 'through words, between words' (CC lv), in the gaps and holes of language, the in-between that is immanent within language, but virtual rather than actual, always about to be or already having been actualised.

Is the music of Auditions a silent music, or a music emergent within the silence at language's limit? Deleuze offers little clarification of this question, but it seems he is not proposing that Auditions are like John Cage's composition *4'33*, the music of a pianist sitting with folded hands at an untouched piano. Rather, he hints that Auditions are hallucinatory sounds evoked through 'an atmospheric quality, a milieu that acts as the conductor of words' (CC 108). In his comments on stuttering in Melville's *Pierre, or the Ambiguities*, Deleuze says that Isabelle's 'murmurings, and her soft, "foreign intonations"' become stammerings when situated within the milieu of 'the hum of the forest and caves, the silence of the house, and the presence of the guitar'. Likewise, Deleuze remarks that the stutterings of Masoch's characters are doubled by 'the heavy suspense of the boudoir, the hum of the village, or the vibrations of the steppe' (CC 108). What this suggests is that the verbal evocation of sounds creates an atmospheric milieu in which a music beyond language arises, one that 'reverberate[s] through the words' (CC108). Hence, Auditions are not the actual sounds of spoken language, nor are they mere silence conceived of as music, but instead hallucinatory sounds reverberating through an atmospheric milieu that emerges from language.

These are admittedly vague speculations, but their general thrust is confirmed by Deleuze's comments on Visions, which are considerably more detailed than those on Auditions. The atmospheric milieu Deleuze speaks of is not solely auditory but also visual, and it is within such a milieu that Visions emerge, and they do so as virtual images.

In 'What Children Say', Deleuze characterises Visions as virtual images in the course of his treatment of the unconscious, which is misunderstood if it is conceived of as imaginary rather than real. Unconscious libido, he asserts, must be viewed in terms of a cartography of 'world-historical trajectories', where 'it does not seem that the real and the imaginary form a pertinent distinction'

(CC 62). In Freud's analysis of Little Hans, Freud restricts all desire to the nuclear family and ignores Hans's movements across the space of his environment and his connections with people and things within and outside the family apartment, including the girl next door, the street and the horse that falls one day as it is beaten. His desire is immanent to the milieu he inhabits, and within it the imaginary and the real are 'like two juxtaposable or superimposable parts of a single trajectory, two faces that ceaselessly interchange with one another, a mobile mirror'. At the limit, 'the imaginary is a virtual image that is interfused with the real object, and vice versa, thereby constituting a crystal of the unconscious' (CC 63). Here Deleuze is reviving a concept he developed in *Cinema 2*, that of the 'crystal-image', a cinematic image in which the actual and the virtual coexist in an indeterminable oscillation between the two (C2 68–97). Certain film-makers, he argued, such as Ophuls, Renoir, Fellini and Visconti, are able to fashion images that are like mirrors, in which reflections and what is reflected cannot be definitively distinguished. The cartographic unconscious of 'What Children Say' functions in a similar fashion. For a crystal of the unconscious to form,

> it is not enough for the real object or the real landscape to evoke similar or related images; it must disengage *its own* virtual image at the same time that the latter, as an imaginary landscape, makes its entry into the real, following a circuit where each of the two terms pursues the other, is interchanged with the other. (CC 63)

When this interpenetration of virtual and actual images takes place, a Vision is created: '"Vision" is the product of this doubling or splitting in two [*doublement ou dédoublement*], this coalescence' (CC 63).

Deleuze adds that this map of virtual/actual images is accompanied by another map of intensities, which are becomings that subtend the trajectories of images: 'The image is not only a trajectory, but also a becoming. Becoming is what subtends the trajectory, just as intensive forces subtend motor forces.' The libido's investment of such intensive becomings

> presents itself with an indefinite article [. . .]: *an* animal as the qualification of a becoming or the specification of a trajectory (*a* horse, *a* chicken); a body or an organ as the power to affect and to be affected (*a* stomach, *some* eyes . . .); and even the characters that obstruct a pathway and inhibit affects, or on the contrary that further them (*a* father, *some* people . . .). (CC 65)

The Visions of the unconscious, then, are images, which are paradoxical doubling/splitting coalescences of the virtual and the actual, and at the same time intensive powers of affecting and being affected whose mode of expression is the indefinite article.

In 'What Children Say', Deleuze's interest is in challenging the traditional psychoanalytic conception of the unconscious, and it is within this context that he describes Visions as coalescences of virtual and actual images. To see what bearing this characterisation has on literature, we must turn to his essay on T. E. Lawrence's *Seven Pillars of Wisdom*, 'The Shame and the Glory: T. E. Lawrence'. The best writers, Deleuze argues, 'have singular conditions of perception that allow them to draw on or shape aesthetic percepts like veritable visions' (CC 116). Melville perceives the ocean, Lawrence perceives the desert, but each possesses a singular '*subjective condition*' that is sensitive to the subtleties of the objective milieu of water or sand, but that creates a subjective double of the outside, 'a private ocean' in Melville's case, and in Lawrence's, 'a private desert that drives him to the Arabian deserts, among the Arabs, and that coincides on many points with their own perceptions and conceptions, but that retains an unmasterable difference that inserts them into a completely different and secret Figure'. Melville and Lawrence convert perceptions into impersonal, asubjective percepts and thereby 'transmute' perception and '"abstract" a Vision from it' (CC 116–17). In each writer, this abstraction of a Vision is one with 'a profound desire, a tendency to project – into things, into reality, into the future, and even into the sky – an image of himself and others so intense that *it has a life of its own*' (CC 117–18).

The desiring unconscious described in 'What Children Say' engages 'the real landscape to evoke similar or related images', but also disengages '*its own* virtual image', 'an imaginary landscape', and then brings about a coalescence of the real and the imaginary, the virtual and the actual that remains 'a doubling or splitting in two' (CC 63). In a similar fashion, Melville and Lawrence double the outside landscape of ocean or desert with an abstracted, depersonalised virtual landscape that is projected on to the world. That projected landscape is an image, and when fashioned with sufficient skill and power, the image takes on a life of its own and lives that life interfused with the real. It is this ability to create such a doubled landscape within a concrete entity that sets the writer apart from the desiring subject, for the writer (like all artists) not only desires, but also produces an artwork that makes that desire manifest.

In Lawrence, the projection of images into the real is accompanied by an embrace of the Idea, which for Lawrence is not a transcendent god or ideal, Deleuze argues, but the immanent force of light: 'the Idea, or the abstract, has no transcendence. The Idea is extended throughout space, it is like the Open [. . .] Light is the opening that creates space.' Light is the invisible spacing of space, the perplicated, differential matrix from which space unfolds and opens up. Ideas, conceived of as light, 'are forces that are exerted on space following certain directions of movement: entities or hypostases, not transcendences'. And such Ideas have political ramifications. The rebellion of Bedouin tribes that Lawrence leads

> is light because it is space (it is a question of extending it in space, of opening up as much space as possible) and it is an Idea (what is essential is predication [that is, the prophetic enunciation of the abstract concept of the rebellion]). (CC 115)

The images of Visions, then, are interfused with the invisible force of the light of Ideas. Lawrence's world is one of entities, images and Ideas. Lawrence fashions 'at the limit of language, the apparition of great visual and sonorous images' and evokes entities that 'populate a private desert that is applied to the external desert, and projects fabulous images onto it through the bodies of men, beasts and rocks. Entities and Images, Abstractions and Visions combine to make of Lawrence another William Blake' (CC 124).

Fabulation and the People to Come

In his Preface to *Essays Critical and Clinical*, Deleuze cites Beckett's project of boring holes in language when introducing the concept of Visions and Auditions, and much of what Deleuze says about Visions and Auditions in *Essays Critical and Clinical* is consonant with his analyses of visual images and sound images in 'The Exhausted'. But if Visions and Auditions may be equated with Beckett's visual and sound images, what Deleuze does not stress in 'The Exhausted' is the political dimension of Visions and Auditions. That dimension is most evident in Deleuze's essays on T. E. Lawrence and on Walt Whitman.

When Deleuze says that Lawrence projects 'an image of himself and others so intense that *it has a life of its own*', he adds that such an image 'is always stitched together, patched up, continually growing along the way, to the point where it becomes fabulous. It is a machine for manufacturing giants, what Bergson called a fabulatory function' (CC 118). What Deleuze is referencing here is Bergson's concept of 'fabulation', which he develops in *The Two Sources of Morality and Religion* (1932). Bergson argues that humans have an inherent tendency to personify natural forces and then, via a faculty of 'fabulation', to create 'fantasmatic representations' of natural forces in the form of spirits and gods. Ultimately, such fabulations may become so 'vivid and haunting' that they 'may precisely imitate perception' (Bergson 1959: 1066–7). Bergson sees fabulation as a negative function, whose primary object is to induce obedience in a closed society of 'us versus them', but Deleuze argues that Bergsonian fabulation may be reconceived in such a way that it has a positive sense, one bound up with the project of inventing a people to come. Activist artists aspire to create art for the people, but the problem is that 'a people isn't something already there. A people, in a way, is what's missing' (N 126). In the absence of a genuine collectivity, artists have no option other than to invent a 'people to come', a future collectivity projected into the real as an image so intense that it takes on a life of its own.

Lawrence is often accused of mythomania, but Deleuze argues that Lawrence's effort in his book is not to aggrandise his own actions and seek personal glory. Rather, it is to imagine a collectivity and project images of that collectivity into the real.

> In short, it is not some sort of contemptible individual mythomania that compels Lawrence to project grandiose images on his path, beyond his often modest undertakings. The projection machine is inseparable from the movement of the Revolt itself: it is subjective, but it refers to the subjectivity of the revolutionary group. (CC 118)

What Lawrence fashions through his writings are images of himself and his Arab troops as a future collectivity, a people not yet in existence but in the process of coming to be. Deleuze draws a parallel between Lawrence's fabulation and that of the Palestinian rebels and the Black Panthers Jean Genet writes about in *Prisoner of Love* (1986). Genet asserts that there is a desire 'more or less conscious in every man, to produce an image of himself and propagate it beyond his death' (Genet 1992: 261). Individuals and groups invent multiple self-images, adopt poses, develop characteristic gestures, movements, and facial expressions, and then project them into the world. 'From Greece to the [Black] Panthers, history has been made out of man's need to detach and project fabulous images, to send them as delegates into the future.' A mythomaniac, Genet asserts, is simply someone 'who can't project his image of himself properly', who does not know how to make the image 'live a life of its own' (Genet 1992: 262).

Deleuze offers another example of the political dimension of Visions and Auditions in his essay 'Whitman', in this case such projected images serving as fabulations not of a warring revolutionary movement but of a democratic ideal in harmony with nature. Deleuze says that Whitman views 'the world as a collection of heterogeneous parts' whose 'law is that of fragmentation' (CC 57). The law of the fragment 'is as valid for Nature as it is for History', and Whitman's project is to construct a whole from these fragments, 'a whole that is all the more paradoxical in that it only comes *after* the fragments and leaves them intact, making no attempt to totalize them' (CC 58). Whitman fabricates this whole by inventing relations between fragments. In his poetic portrayal of nature, 'the relations between colors are made up of contrasts and complementarities, never given but always new', and 'the relations between sounds or bird songs, which Whitman describes in marvelous ways, are made up of counterpoints and responses, constantly renewed and invented'. The visual and sonic whole of nature that he creates is 'a polyphony: it is not a totality but an assembly, a "conclave", a "plenary session"' (CC 59). The nature he envisions 'is inseparable from processes of companionship and conviviality' (CC 59), and those same processes inform his conception of optimal relations between humans and nature and among humans. 'Camaraderie' is the word Whitman uses to designate the harmonious being-together he finds in nature and seeks to promote among people in their relations with one another and with the natural world. This camaraderie is not a given, but something produced, a process 'that implies an encounter with the Outside, a march of souls in the open air, on the "Open Road"' (CC 60). The society of comrades 'is the revolutionary American dream', one in which 'Democracy and Art themselves form a whole only in their relationship with Nature'. The society of camaraderie is a people to come, one made up of visions and auditions projected into the future. Whitman starts with 'spontaneity or the innate feeling for the fragmentary', and then moves to 'the reflection of living relations that are constantly acquired and created'. The spontaneous fragments constitute 'the element through which, or in the intervals of which, we attain the great, reflected visions and auditions of Nature and of History' (CC 60; trans. modified).

Conclusion

What, then, are Visions and Auditions? They are images. They are coalescences of the virtual and the actual. They are events, movements, trajectories, processes, becomings and intensities. Their time is the floating time of Aion, their mode of individuation that of the indefinite article. They are problematic Ideas that are immanent forces of A LIFE. They are a painting and a music at the limits of language, revealed above words, through words, in the gaps between words. And what writers see and hear in their

Visions and Auditions are visual and sound images of a people to come, a revolutionary future collectivity whose images are given such intensity that they take on a life of their own.

Note

1. A notable exception is the essay 'Michel Tournier and the World without Others', first published in 1967 and then reprinted in a modified form as an appendix to *The Logic of Sense* (LS 301–21). There, Deleuze equates images with simulacra and phantasms (LS 315). In *Difference and Repetition* and *The Logic of Sense*, Deleuze advocates the reign of simulacra, entities that escape the logic of Platonic Ideas and faithful copies, and the concept of the simulacrum plays a central role in those works. Only in the Tournier essay, however, does Deleuze use image as a synonym of simulacrum, and only in the 1969 version of the essay. The focus on images in the Tournier essay is motivated by Tournier's text, which thematises the image, and it is only after writing *Difference and Repetition* and *The Logic of Sense* that Deleuze revises the Tournier essay to assimilate his earlier discussion of images within the conceptual framework of simulacra. It is telling that the image–simulacrum equation occurs only in this essay, not in *Difference and Repetition* or in any other section of *The Logic of Sense*.

VI. Nature

16

A Thousand Ecologies

It is evident from the title alone of Guattari's *The Three Ecologies* (1989) that his thought had taken an ecological turn in his later writings, but what of his works jointly authored with Deleuze, especially the earlier *Anti-Oedipus: Capitalism and Schizophrenia, I* (1972) and *A Thousand Plateaus: Capitalism and Schizophrenia, II* (1980)? Are those texts ecological, or at least eco-friendly? They are, I believe, though in a sense that requires careful specification, in part due to the contested nature of many concepts and models in ecology studies, but in part as well due to Deleuze and Guattari's idiosyncratic terminology and the ends to which it is addressed in their writings – ends that are not incompatible with those of an ecological philosophy, but that subordinate such ends to other concerns. Deleuze and Guattari's primary goal in the two volumes of *Capitalism and Schizophrenia*, as well as *What is Philosophy?* (1991), is to develop and practise a mode of thought, and in the process engage issues in a wide range of fields, some of which have an obvious bearing on the sciences of ecology (biology, chemistry, genetics, ethology), others of which would seem far removed from that domain (aesthetics, sociology, political theory, history). In a 1988 interview, Deleuze said that he planned to write a book titled 'What is Philosophy?', but he added that he and Guattari also wanted 'to get back to our joint work and produce a sort of philosophy of Nature, now that any distinction between nature and artifice is becoming blurred' (N 155). Deleuze and Guattari never completed this projected exposition of a 'philosophy of Nature', but the outlines of that philosophy may be discerned in the works they did produce, and those outlines may be regarded as ecological in many respects.

At the beginning of *Ecology, Community and Lifestyle* (1989), Arne Naess helpfully distinguishes ecology from what he calls 'ecophilosophy' and 'ecosophy'.[1] Ecology he defines as 'the interdisciplinary scientific study of the living conditions of organisms in interaction with each other and with the surroundings, organic as well as inorganic' (Naess 1989: 36). He characterises the methodology inherent in the study of ecology as one 'suggested by the simple maxim "all things hang together"'. The field of 'ecophilosophy' he describes as the study of 'problems common to ecology and philosophy'. Ecophilosophy is 'a descriptive study' that 'does not make a choice between fundamental value priorities, but merely seeks to examine a particular kind of problem' at the juncture of ecology and philosophy. Unlike ecophilosophy, 'ecosophy' addresses questions concerning humans and nature from the perspective of 'one's own personal code of values and a view of the world which guides one's own decisions' (36). Clearly, Deleuze and Guattari are not ecologists engaged in the interdisciplinary scientific study of organisms and their surroundings, but their thought about nature is decidedly ecophilosophical. And, as we shall see, that thought is ecosophical – that is, value-laden and value-directed – although in a way that Naess himself, with his commitment to deep ecology, would no doubt find unacceptable.

The Ecological Refrain

Deleuze and Guattari's most focused consideration of organisms and their surroundings is Plateau Eleven of *A Thousand Plateaus*, which is devoted to the concept of the refrain. Using song in territorial birds as a paradigmatic instance of a natural refrain, Deleuze and Guattari expand the sense of the refrain to include any organising rhythmic pattern that brings together heterogeneous entities that function in concert within the natural world. Their chief inspiration for this musical model of nature is the pioneering ecologist Jakob von Uexküll, who speaks of a grand symphony of nature, in which relations of point and counterpoint structure organisms and their milieus.[2] In von Uexküll's analysis, each organism traces a developmental melody in its gestation, growth and eventual demise. Its form unfolds in counterpoint to diverse elements of its surroundings, the gutter-like contour of the oak leaf in counterpoint to falling rain, the octopus's muscular pocket in counterpoint to the incompressible water it squeezes in order to propel itself. Relations among conspecifics (in sexual organisms, for example, between male and female, between parents and progeny, among territorial competitors, and so on), between predators and prey (spider and fly), among symbionts of various sorts (orchid and wasp, liver fluke and sheep, termite and intestinal parasite), all are so many contrapuntal arrangements of mutually corresponding melodies, the totality of such motifs forming the symphony of nature.

Deleuze and Guattari's concept of the refrain is essentially an elaboration on von Uexküll's notion of the contrapuntal melody. Like von Uexküll, they stress the interconnections among developmental, ethological and environmental processes, treating the growth trajectories of individual organisms, the regular patterns of their behaviour, and the configurations of their interactions with their organic and inorganic surroundings as intertwined and interdependent refrains. Hence, when they consider the song of the brown stagemaker bird, they regard the sonic refrain as but one component of 'a veritable *machinic opera* tying together orders, species, and heterogeneous qualities' (ATP 330). The male stagemaker sings while perched within its territory on a stick selected as the stage of its performance. The male delineates its territory by sawing leaves from surrounding trees and distributing them bottom side up on the periphery of its staked area. It fluffs its throat feathers while signalling through song its presence to other males and to prospective mates. The sonic refrain of the bird's song, then, is only one of a multitude of refrains – the refrain of its development from egg to adult, the refrains of its behavioural patterns (feather display, leaf gathering, stick perching), the refrains of interaction among other males and with female stagemakers, and so on.

Implicit as well in Deleuze and Guattari's treatment of the refrain is a specific approach to evolutionary theory, something that is less evident in von Uexküll's work. In their discussion of birdsong and territoriality, Deleuze and Guattari insist that the formation of territories is not a secondary product of basic drives (as Lorenz and others posit), but instead is its own explanation. They recognise that various functions (sexual, alimentary, aggressive, predatory) are organised within a territory, but no single function causes the territory to come into existence. Various functions

> are organized or created only because they are *territorialized*, and not the other way around. The T factor, the territorializing factor, must be sought elsewhere: precisely in the becoming-expressive of rhythm or melody, in other words, in the emergence of proper qualities (colour, odour, sound, silhouette . . .). (ATP 316)

In the case of the stagemaker, the plucking of a leaf and its inverted placement on the ground mark the emergence of a quality proper to the bird (the bird's action serving to extract the leaf from the natural surround and make the colour of its inverted surface a territorial quality), and that leaf is a component of a rhythm that expresses the territory. One might see this analysis as a circular explanation, in that the bird's territorialising activities explain the formation of the territory. Deleuze and Guattari's point, however, is (1) that the territory is not some inert stretch of ground staked out by a bird, but instead the complex of patterns and rhythms involving the bird, other birds, other animals, trees, plants, earth, water, air in a territorial ensemble – in short, the territory is the ecosystem of bird-environment; and (2) that the emergence of a territorial animal in evolutionary history is the manifestation of a particular configuration of organism-environment that results simply from a non-teleological process of creative experimentation exhibited throughout the world.

In this regard, I see Deleuze and Guattari as promoting a view of nature similar to that put forward by Varela, Thompson and Rausch in *The Embodied Mind* (1991).[3] Varela et al. argue at length against any separation of organism and environment in evolutionary theory, asserting that organisms and their milieus are dynamic entities involved in an interactive process of co-evolution. Organisms and environments are 'mutually unfolded and enfolded structures' (Varela et al. 1991: 199) that together bring forth a world. This process of reciprocal co-evolution Varela et al. refer to as a 'structural coupling' (Varela et al. 1991: 151) of organism and environment. Varela et al. also oppose the standard neo-Darwinian notion of the survival of the fittest, claiming that natural selection does not produce the best organism for a given environment, but instead merely eliminates those organisms that are not viable. Nature affords a wide range of possibilities for viable organism–environment structural couplings, and all that is required is that an organism be good enough for survival in its milieu, not that it be the milieu's optimal inhabitant (whatever that might be). In their terms, the evolutionary process 'is *satisficing*, (taking a suboptimal solution that is satisfactory) rather than optimizing', and it proceeds via '*bricolage*, the putting together of parts and items in complicated arrays, not because they fulfil some ideal design but simply because they are possible' (Varela et al. 1991: 196).

Eco-Machinism

This notion of Nature as *bricoleur* is widespread in *A Thousand Plateaus*, evident not only in the concept of the refrain, but also in that of the 'assemblage' as collection of heterogeneous entities that somehow function together, and that of the interpenetrating 'strata' of inorganic, organic and anthropological forms (developed in Plateau Three). A world of *bricolage* is evident as well in *Anti-Oedipus*, where the cosmos is described as a realm of universal desiring-production, in which ubiquitous desiring-machines are connected in circuits through which pass diverse flows and fluxes. Such circuits of desiring-production may include what we normally think of as machines (referred to as 'technical machines' by Deleuze and Guattari), but they may also connect human organs, diverse organisms and inorganic entities and processes in make-shift, variable relations, and the flows may consist of matter, energy, information, sensations, thoughts, fantasies, and so on. Unlike 'technical machines', desiring-machines do not aspire to a maximum efficiency, but instead 'work only when they break down, and by continually breaking down' (AO 8). Desiring production is 'satisficing', in the language of Varela et al., good enough to function but only in a way that makes room for glitches, pauses, divagations and impromptu variations. Perhaps the best images of desiring production are those of the Rube Goldberg cartoons included in the appendix of the second edition of *Anti-Oedipus*, each of which presents a comically improbable sequence of human, animal and inorganic entities linked in diverse causal relations (perceptual, behavioural, mechanical, chemical and so on), the assemblage of entities forming a complex machine of decided inefficiency dedicated to the performance of the simplest of tasks (eating less, remembering to mail a letter). The satisficing Nature of desiring production is likewise filled with shifting circuits of heterogeneous elements connected in multiple, unexpected combinations that function with varying degrees of efficiency.

Throughout *Anti-Oedipus* Deleuze and Guattari use the figure of the machine to describe the world, and although machine imagery is somewhat less prevalent in *A Thousand Plateaus*, it is still present. In *Anti-Oedipus*, Deleuze and Guattari wish to counter psychological models that stress interpretation, replacing a psychoanalysis that uncovers the meaning of the unconscious with a schizoanalysis that simply charts its functioning. A machine does not express any meaning as it operates but simply does what it does, and in this regard the unconscious may be regarded as a machine. But Deleuze and Guattari adopt the machine model not simply to undo psychoanalytic presuppositions but also to subvert all distinctions between the natural and the artificial, between the non-human world and the social, cultural and technological world constructed by humans. As they assert early in *Anti-Oedipus*,

> we make no distinction between man and nature: the human essence of nature and the natural essence of man become one within nature in the form of production or industry, just as they do within the life of man as a species [. . .] man and nature are not like two opposite terms confronting each other – not even in the sense of bipolar opposites within a relationship of causation, ideation, or expression (cause and effect, subject and object, etc.); rather, they are one and the same essential reality, the producer-product. (AO 4–5)

All the elements of culture and nature, of the human and the non-human world, are desiring-machines engaged in desiring production. 'Everything is a machine. [. . .] Producing-machines, desiring-machines, everywhere, schizophrenic machines, all of species life: the self and the non-self, outside and inside, no longer have any meaning whatsoever' (AO 2). The nature-machine model, of course, goes back at least to La Mettrie, but Deleuze and Guattari insist that their desiring machines are not mere mechanical devices. They propose their 'machinism' as an alternative to both mechanism and vitalism, rejecting paradigms that reduce everything to a rudimentary physics as well as those that spiritualise matter with a separate life force. Their machinism instead posits the existence of an 'anorganic life' (ATP 503) that spans the human, non-human, organic and inorganic in a single process of interfused co-functioning.

Such a machinism should not be construed as an anti-nature or anti-ecology stance, though it does suggest opposition to any conception of environmentalism as a means of restoring a corrupted nature to its prelapsarian, non-human purity. One might see such a stance as merely a realistic response to present circumstances. As the conservation biologist Michael Soulé argues,

> Soon, the distinctions between preservation, reintroduction, and restoration will vanish. In 2100, entire biotas will have been assembled from (1) remnant and reintroduced natives, (2) partly or completely engineered species, and (3) introduced (exotic) species. The term *natural* will disappear from our working vocabulary. This term is already meaningless in most parts of the world because anthropogenic fire, chemicals, and weather, not to mention deforestation, grazing, and farming, have been changing the physical and biological environment for centuries, if not millennia. (Soulé 1989: 301)

But Deleuze and Guattari's machinism is less a concession to an unfortunate reality than a commitment to exploring the possibilities of human invention. Their language of machines and desiring production seeks to avoid the extremes of either technophobia or technophilia, of either a Rousseauistic return to nature or a science-driven construction of an artificial paradise. Their position in this regard seems close to that of Donna Haraway, whose 'A Cyborg Manifesto' echoes Deleuze and Guattari's machinic thematics at several points. For her, as for Deleuze and Guattari, the natural–artificial distinction is untenable, and the figure of the cyborg, like that of the desiring-machine, serves to counter any conception of humans and their relationship to the world in terms of a stable, unproblematic nature (whether human or non-human). The cyborg appears 'precisely where the boundary between human and animal is transgressed', and hence 'far from signaling a walling off of people from other living beings, cyborgs signal disturbingly and pleasurably tight coupling' (Haraway 1991: 152). Haraway does not minimise the dangers emergent in our increasingly technological world, but, like Deleuze and Guattari, she finds in that world potential for new ways of configuring social and environmental relations in terms that blur clear distinctions among humans, machines and nature.

The Eco-Whole

Deleuze and Guattari's focus on interconnecting flows of desiring-production, on interfolded refrains that constitute organism–environment complexes, and on the cosmos as the domain of a single anorganic life might suggest that they advocate a kind of ecological holism, and in a limited sense this is true. They certainly oppose any atomistic analysis of nature that ignores the constitutive relations of living systems, and often their treatment of circuits of flows and refrains reinforces the basic insight that '"all things hang together"' (Naess 1989: 36). But they repeatedly assert as well that all circuits of desiring-production are irreducible multiplicities that cannot be subsumed within the traditional logic of the one and the many, or the whole and its parts. In *Anti-Oedipus*, they observe that

> the problem of the relationships between parts and the whole continues to be rather awkwardly formulated by classic mechanism and vitalism, so long as the whole is considered as a totality derived from the parts, or as an original totality from

> which the parts emanate, or as a dialectical totalization. (AO 44)

If there is a whole, they claim, it is 'a totality alongside various separate parts, it is a whole *of* these particular parts but does not totalize them, it is added to them as a new part fabricated separately' (AO 42).

Deleuze himself, however, does not categorically reject all reference to the 'whole' (*le tout*), for in *Cinema 1* he assigns the concept of the whole a prominent place in his film theory, positing the existence of a whole immanent within every film shot that 'is like thread which traverses [the shot] and gives each one the possibility, which is necessarily realized, of communicating with another, to infinity' (C1 16–17). But this whole is not a closed totality. Rather, 'the whole is the Open', by which 'every closed system opens to a duration which is immanent to the whole universe' (C1 17). Deleuze and Guattari make similar use of the notion of an open whole in *What is Philosophy?* when they describe philosophy's plane of immanence as 'a powerful Whole that, while remaining open, is not fragmented: an unlimited One-All, an "Omnitudo"' (WP 34). And though they nowhere refer explicitly to the cosmos as an open whole, their speculations about the existence of an ultimate cosmic 'totality of all BwO's [Bodies without Organs], a pure multiplicity of immanence [. . .] the plane of consistency (*Omnitudo*, sometimes called the BwO)' (ATP 155–6) suggests that they would not object to such an appellation.

In one sense, this stress on the openness of the whole may be seen as a reminder of the basic fact of any real-world systems analysis, including an ecological analysis, that no system is finally self-contained. In Anthony Wilden's terms, context is always a function of 'punctuation', of a provisional closure of a system and its components (see Wilden 1980: 111–13). If one studies a specific ecosystem, say an Australian coral reef, one delimits the area, the life forms and processes one wishes to study, ignoring the larger context of the Pacific Ocean as a whole, of which the coral reef is a part, and the even larger context of the earth's ocean system, that of the solar system as movement-energy source, that of the galaxy, and so on. At every scale of analysis, what counts as a system is a function of its punctuation, the determination of a provisional closure in a theoretically unlimited and always open totality (especially if the universe is indeed expanding).

Yet Deleuze and Guattari also advocate not simply a spatial, methodological openness but also a temporal openness, and in this regard their thought runs counter to some tendencies in discussions of ecology, especially those regarding questions of conservation and habitat restoration. Throughout his career Deleuze remains a proponent of the Bergsonian intuition that time matters and that the future is genuinely new. Bergson observes that the dominant conception of time in Western philosophy is essentially spatial, one in which time functions merely as a measure of successions of static slices of space. As a result, the dynamic thrust of the world's becoming is ignored and time adds nothing significant to our accounts of reality. Bergson objects as well to deterministic models of the universe, arguing that in them 'the whole' is already 'given', that is, already knowable and hence closed. Such is the view of classical science, summed up in the Laplacean conception of the universe as one in which linear causal relations govern all phenomena and any future state of the world may be predicted from a complete knowledge of past and present configurations of matter and energy. Bergson argues that the whole is never given, for the future is unpredictable and unknowable. The movement of becoming is fundamental to any conception of the universe, as is its thrust into an undetermined future.[4] This Bergsonian view of becoming and the openness of the future is evident throughout Deleuze and Guattari's writings, especially in the section on 'becomings' in *A Thousand Plateaus* (ATP 232–309).

Speed and the Imbalance of Nature

Such a stress on becoming and indeterminate wholes may not be incompatible with ecological thought, but it does call into question tacit assumptions common in public discussions of environmental issues. Chief among these is the postulate of a 'balance of nature' that humans have disrupted and that conservation efforts must restore. Though ecosystems analyses include a temporal dimension, the postulate of a balance of nature suggests that in natural (that is, non-human) ecosystems the interaction of elements is essentially homeostatic – regular, stable and unchanging overall. In such a conception, time ultimately makes no difference, the future is but a repetition of the present system of kinetic relations, and the whole is closed. Obviously, Deleuze and Guattari would find unacceptable any postulated balance of nature, but in this they are not alone, for many ecologists have also questioned this hypothesis. Stuart Pimm, for example, in *The Balance of Nature?* argues at length that natural systems seldom operate in equilibrium, and indeed often function in states far from equilibrium. Stability in the strict sense is rare in ecosystems, Pimm shows, and if there is a degree of regularity in natural systems, it must be analysed in terms of the system's response to variables – in terms of resilience (the speed with which a variable within the system is returned to equilibrium), persistence (the rate at which a variable is changed to a new value within the system), resistance (the ability of the system to absorb a permanently changed variable) and variability (the degree to which its variables vary over time).[5] Yet, despite such regularity within variability, says Pimm, ultimately all natural systems change over time, and if ecological models are to be adequate, they must include a historical, evolutionary dimension in their analyses.

> Species are added to and lost from communities, at rates that depend on features of the species themselves and also on the features of the community's food web structure and on how that structure developed. [. . .] Community structure changes, and as it changes it alters the framework against which population changes take place. (Pimm 1991: 4)

What Pimm's work makes clear is that environmental issues are less about natural stability and human-induced instability than about rates of change and kinds of change. The question is not whether humans have induced change in ecosystems, but whether they have inordinately accelerated or inhibited change and in such ways that are deleterious, whether to humans specifically or to terrestrial life forms in general. I would argue that Deleuze and Guattari's concept of the body as a configuration of speeds and affects is germane to the issues of both rates of change and kinds of change. In *A Thousand Plateaus*, Deleuze and Guattari state that

> on the plane of consistency, *a body is defined only by a longitude and a latitude*: in other words the sum total of the material elements belonging to it under given relations of movement and rest, speed and slowness (longitude); the sum total of the intensive affects it is capable of at a given power or degree of potential (latitude). (ATP 260)

What constitutes a body may vary from subinidividual configurations of speed and affect (individual organs, the circulatory system, digestive system and so on), through the entities that we commonly refer to as bodies (organisms), to supraindividual configurations of speed and affect (male–female, predatory–prey, species communities, ecosystems as a whole). In Plateau Six, 'How Do You Make Yourself a Body without Organs?', Deleuze and Guattari formulate a diagnostics and an ethics of speeds, asserting that, in producing a Body without Organs (that is, a body on the plane of consistency), one always runs the danger of entering into a suicidal black hole or of fostering a fascistic, cancerous Body without Organs. In the case of the black hole, a precipitous speed induces self-destruction; in that of the cancerous Body without Organs, accelerated components engulf and eventually destroy other components, supplanting them and rendering the whole diseased and pathogenic. Although Deleuze and Guattari frame their discussion largely in sociopolitical terms, it is not difficult to extend the concepts of the black hole and the cancerous Body without Organs to a treatment of ecological issues, especially given their opposition to any definitive separation of the social, cultural and technological world of humans from the non-human world. If ecosystems are construed as bodies, clearly such phenomena as global warming may be regarded as black holes of accelerated self-destructive speeds; and systems in exacerbated disequilibrium, such as those induced by the introduction of rabbits in Australia or kudzu in the American South, may be seen as cancerous bodies, each possessed of pathogenic differential speeds among its components.

Deleuze and Guattari's concept of corporeal affect, in addition to that of speed, may also be brought to bear on an ecological diagnostics and ethics, but before addressing this point I must return briefly to Deleuze and Guattari's qualified holism. Besides the concepts of a spatially open whole of ever-expanding contexts and that of a temporally open whole of becoming and an undetermined future, one may also discern in Deleuze and Guattari what might be called an epistemologically and methodologically open whole. In Plateaus Twelve and Fourteen, Deleuze and Guattari distinguish striated from smooth space, describing the one as a 'relative global' and the other as a 'local absolute'. The striated space of the relative global 'is limited in its parts, which are assigned constant directions, are oriented in relation to one another, divisible by boundaries, and can interlink', whereas the smooth space of the local absolute is 'an absolute that is manifested locally, and engendered in a series of local operations of varying orientations' (ATP 382). A striated space is a discretely bounded space, and hence a totalising, 'global' space, and within its borders all points may be charted in a fixed coordinate system – hence each interior component has a 'relative' existence in relation to the global totality. A smooth space, by contrast, has no demarcated boundaries. It is an area of ever-expanding horizons, an open whole, and as such, a whole that can never be grasped and mastered in its totality. It can only be experienced and conceived from within, from a 'local' perspective. Yet when it becomes manifest, it does so as an 'absolute', as an unqualified, perpetually expanding whole-in-becoming.

Striated and smooth spaces are inseparable from the processes that take place within them. They are produced by their inhabitants, and in this sense they are functions of modes of being and relations of power. One produces a striated space when one striates it, when one delimits an area and charts it in a coordinate system. Conversely, one produces smooth space when one follows flows of becoming, when one smooths over boundaries and engenders a metamorphic movement towards an ever-unfolding horizon. Although Deleuze and Guattari discuss striated and smooth space primarily in human terms, their treatment of territoriality and the refrain suggests that other organisms produce and inhabit striated and smooth spaces, and it is evident as well that priority must be granted to smooth over striated space. Humans, like all other life forms, seek to master their ambient space-time, to organise it, control it and render it a habitable milieu, territory, social sphere and so on. Yet they also participate in flows that unsettle organisational patterns and thereby open up mutative lines of potential development. When they do so, organisms produce the smooth space of an open whole, one in which the organisms' actions coalesce with the becoming of the world in its thrust towards an undetermined future.

Speciesism and the Open Whole

If the cosmos is an open whole, and if that whole presents itself only as a smooth 'local absolute', the methodological implication is that the whole cannot be conceived from the outside, but must always be understood from a perspective within the whole. Deleuze and Guattari's valorisation of smooth space, then, implies a commitment to a kind of Nietzschean perspectivism (hardly a surprise, given Deleuze's long-standing Nietzschean proclivities) and a rejection of the notion that there is any 'view from nowhere'. In this regard, Deleuze and Guattari's position is consonant with that of Varela and his frequent collaborator Humberto Maturana, whose collective work on natural systems Cary Wolfe aptly situates within what is sometimes called 'second-order cybernetics', which may be characterised as a disciplinary matrix within which the study of the organisation of complex systems (cybernetics) includes a meta-level recognising the existence of the observer-scientist as a complex system within the observed system itself. As Wolfe notes, Maturana and Varela's second-order cybernetics avoids any simplistic relativism, for it 'does not dispense with systematic description altogether', but instead 'recasts the relationship between a system and its elements [. . .] as open-ended and yet not random, fundamental and yet not foundational in the usual ontological sense' (Wolfe 1995: 55). This second-order cybernetics does, however, require that all knowledge claims be situated within an emergent context.

Wolfe sees Maturana and Varela's second-order cybernetics as providing a means of moving beyond the traditional humanistic dualism of mind and body and its related representational model of cognition, in that Maturana and Varela's approach commits them to a notion of cognition as embodied action. But later in his analysis Wolfe reproaches Maturana and Varela for engaging in 'speciesism' (Wolfe 1995: 66), or a valorisation of *Homo sapiens* over other species, an activity that he regards as inimical to second-order cybernetics. I find this critique puzzling, if Wolfe is using 'speciesism' as many deep ecologists do – that is, as a label for a bias that denies the intrinsic value and equal rights of all species. The hard-line position on equal rights and equal value for all species, I would argue, entails precisely the 'view from nowhere' that second-order cybernetics makes untenable. If the observer is always part of what is observed, and if the observer is a human being, it is difficult to see how the embodied action of that observer can be anything but observer-centered, and hence 'species-centric'.

In this characterisation of second-order cybernetics and the ethics of deep ecology I have perhaps moved too swiftly from observation to valorisation, from 'is' to 'ought', but, though I would not conflate epistemology and ethics, I would argue that they are not unrelated. Both knowledge and values are perspectival, even if the relationship between the two is not fixed. Maturana and Varela's second-order cybernetics, like Deleuze and Guattari's perspectivism, does indeed problematise the assumptions of traditional representational realism, but so also does it call into question the postulate of non-situated, transcendent values. As Sahotra Sarkar demonstrates at some length, deep ecology's attribution of intrinsic value to every species implies such a postulate, and I find convincing his argument that this postulate is incoherent.[6] Whatever one's stance on biodiversity, conservation, habitat restoration and so on, he argues, the values one promotes must be 'anthropocentric', at least in the sense that they cannot be entirely divorced from our existence as members of the species *Homo sapiens*. In this regard, then, Deleuze and Guattari's perspectivism, like Maturana and Varela's second-order cybernetics, must be seen as anthropocentric.

Becoming and the Human

Yet it is precisely at this juncture that Deleuze and Guattari's thought might help us reconfigure this issue. In *What is Philosophy?* Deleuze and Guattari assert that the goal of thought is to create 'possibilities of life or modes of existence' (WP 73) and thereby help constitute a 'people to come' and a 'new earth' (WP 109). No genuine, viably functioning human collectivity exists at present, they argue, and hence the formation of such a collectivity must involve a future people, a 'people to come'. But the formation of such a people is inseparable from the creation of a new earth, for there is no ultimate distinction between humans and nature, and hence no means of transforming humans without simultaneously transforming the world they inhabit. The only means of fashioning a new people and a new earth is to engage in 'becomings', or processes of 'becoming-other' – becoming-woman, becoming-child, becoming-animal, becoming-molecular. Such processes undo hierarchical binaries that privilege male over female, adult over child, human over non-human, and the macro over the micro, not by simply inverting them, but by inducing a passage *between* boundaries such that both poles of a binary opposition dissolve in zones of indiscernibility as something new and uncharted emerges.

> To think is to experiment, but experimentation is always that which is in the process of coming about – the new, remarkable and interesting [. . .] The new, the interesting, are the actual. The actual is not what we are but, rather, what we become, what we are in the process of becoming – that is to say, the Other, our becoming-other. (WP 111–12; trans. modified)

Most significant for our purposes are processes of becoming-animal (and perhaps also those of becoming-plant or becoming-mineral), for such processes call into question our species identity. Hence, to say that Deleuze and Guattari's perspectivism is necessarily anthropocentric is not to presume that we know what 'anthropos' is or can become. The future of the human in becomings is other-than-human, whatever that may be, and one of its trajectories passes through a becoming-animal. 'We become animal so that the animal also becomes something else. The agony of a rat or the slaughter of a calf remains present in thought not through pity but as the zone of exchange between man and animal in which something of one passes into the other' (WP 109). Thus, Deleuze and Guattari's perspectivism, rather than reinforcing an opposition of the human and the non-human, instead calls for a dissolution of that divide.

And it is here that we may return to the question of corporeal affects and their valorisation. In processes of becoming, bodies are defined by their speeds and their affects, the latter characterised by the given body's powers of affecting and being affected. Important to note is that this affectivity is not unidirectional – a capability not simply of affecting but also of being affected. Some organisms have limited ranges of affectivity, capable of perceiving, acting on and reacting to their surroundings in only a few ways, whereas others have more expanded channels of interaction with their world. Humans seem to have multiple modes of affectivity, yet, as Deleuze is wont to remark in a phrase he adopts from Spinoza, we do not yet know what a body is capable of.[7] Only through an experimentation on the body do we discover what a body is – that is, what its powers of affecting and being affected might become. Nor is it even obvious what constitutes a body, for in processes of becoming, a configuration of speeds and affects might form a body within an organism (an organ, a metabolic system) or a collective body (multiple organisms, communities, ecosystems). The creative movement of thought involves a process of becoming-other, and such a becoming-other is inseparable from an experimentation of bodies, a process of formation and transformation of configurations of speeds and affects that opens up new possibilities of interaction.

Biodiversity, Ecosophy and Possibilities of Life

If the object of thought is to invent 'possibilities of life or modes of existence' and thereby help constitute a 'people to come' and a 'new earth', and if such invention must proceed through a becoming-other, including a becoming-animal (or plant, bacterium and so on), then a general reduction in the number of organisms available for such becomings would constitute a reduction in the possibilities of life. For this reason, I would argue that Deleuze and Guattari's ethics of inventing a people to come and a new earth is compatible with the promotion of biodiversity. Modes of existence that destroy habitats, induce pandemics or foster pathogenic disequilibrium inhibit a creative exploration of the possibilities of bodies and decrease the options for a reconfiguration of humans and the earth. The fewer the life forms available for becoming-other, the fewer the trajectories available for creative transformation.[8]

If, then, we return to Naess's categories of ecology, ecophilosophy and ecosophy, we may say first that, although Deleuze and Guattari are obviously not ecologists, that is, scientists engaged in empirical ecological research, their thought about nature has a decidedly ecological orientation, in that their machinism promotes the view of nature as a complex of interactive organism–environment systems. Second, though they do not directly examine the relationship between the disciplines of philosophy and ecology, and hence they are perhaps not ecophilosophers in the strict sense Naess gives the term, their treatment of nature invites a reconceptualisation of fundamental philosophical issues, especially those of the relationship between the human and the non-human, the natural and the artificial, organism and environment, observer and context, parts and the whole. And, third, although they do not engage directly in the construction of an ecological ethics, they are ecosophers in that the ethics of their thought informs their views of the relationship of humans to the world. Their machinism calls into question any blanket condemnation of technology, any unqualified valorisation of a pristine, non-human wilderness, and any promotion of the intrinsic value of all organisms. Their qualified holism posits a whole that is open, both spatially and temporally, and hence one that undermines any conception of nature as fundamentally balanced and stable in its functioning. And that whole is only manifest as a 'local absolute', and thus it can only be conceived and experienced from a specific perspective within the whole. As a result, their perspectivism commits them to an anthropocentric ethics, yet one that subverts received notions of the human and calls for the creation of a new collectivity and a new earth. Finally, that perspectivism implies that their holism is a pluralism, in that the open whole revealed in each perspectival view is ultimately irreducible to any 'perspective of all perspectives' that might unify the plurality of perspectives that may emerge from that whole. In this sense, if thought may unfold across a thousand plateaus, there are a thousand ecologies that would unfold within those plateaus, a thousand ways of attempting to create a new collectivity and a new earth.

Notes

1. Ecosophy, of course, is a key term in Guattari's late work. He describes his thought as an ecosophy in *The Three Ecologies* and in *Chaosmosis*, and the posthumous collection of essays *Qu'est-ce que l'écosophie* takes its title from one of its entries. Guattari does not mention Naess, nor need he have heard of Naess to have adopted the term 'ecosophy', since its use had become widespread in the 1980s. My concern here is not to compare Guattari's use of the term with that of others in ecological studies, but to situate Deleuze and Guattari's collaborative writings in relation to deep ecology via the taxonomy of ecology, ecophilosophy and ecosophy proposed by Naess, one of deep ecology's most prominent exponents.
2. Deleuze and Guattari rely primarily on von Uexküll (1956) for their account of his symphony of nature. See Bogue (2003: 58–62) for a more extended discussion of von Uexküll and Deleuze and Guattari.
3. For a more detailed examination of the relevance of Varela et al. (1991) for Deleuze and Guattari's thought, see Bogue (2003: 66–9).
4. See B 96–8 for a presentation of Bergson's critique of the whole as 'given' in deterministic models.
5. See Pimm (1991: 13–14) for an exposition of these terms; see also Sarkar (2005: 118–19) for an expansion of Pimm's taxonomy.
6. See Sarkar (2005), esp. pp. 45–74.
7. For an exposition of this Spinozistic conception of the body, see SPP 122–30.
8. It should be noted, however, that such a commitment to biodiversity need not imply a commitment to wilderness restoration, as is sometimes assumed. Not only is the concept of wilderness as 'territory devoid of human presence' suspect in its implicit opposition of humans and nature, but the goal of wilderness restoration may at times be in conflict with that of the maintenance of biodiversity. Sarkar offers an instance of such a conflict in India, where the creation of a wilderness

area through the removal of human herders and their cattle from a marshland led to a catastrophic growth of grasses that made the area uninhabitable by migrating birds and many other species (see Sarkar 2005: 42–3). For this and many other reasons, Sarkar argues that conservation biology, with its focus on biodiversity, be recognised as a discipline distinct from that of general ecology.

17

Nature, Law and Chaosmopolitanism

In a fascinating essay, John Sellars compares what he calls 'Deleuze's Cosmopolitanism' to the cosmopolitanism of the early Stoics. Sellars argues that Deleuze's politics is decidedly cosmopolitan, but in a manner that departs at certain key points from ancient cosmopolitanism. The primary difference between Deleuze and the Stoics, he argues, lies in their understanding of the cosmos. Sellars finds an especially stark presentation of that difference in Deleuze and Guattari's *A Thousand Plateaus*, in which they contrast the State and the war machine. For the Stoics, the cosmos is a *polis* or cosmic state, whereas for Deleuze and Guattari, argues Sellars, the cosmos is an essentially chaotic realm of unbridled metamorphosis. Sellars ultimately views Deleuze's politics as 'utopian' and unable to 'offer a model for collective political action'. In Sellars's reading of Deleuze, 'the political transformation that the cosmopolitan tradition envisages can only be brought about one person at a time' (Sellars 2007: 36). I believe that Sellars is fundamentally misguided in this reading and that Deleuze and Guattari in fact promote a 'chaosmopolitanism' that combines macro- and micropolitical action and embraces utopianism only in a limited and non-idealistic way. Their chaosmopolitanism also revives and reconfigures the correlation of nature and the sociopolitical fundamental to Cynic and early Stoic cosmopolitanism. And, finally, such a chaosmopolitanism provides a useful context for considering Deleuze and Guattari's views on nature, law, norms and normativity.

Ancient Cosmopolitanism

Before addressing Sellars's analysis of Deleuze's cosmopolitanism, I must first trace in some detail the development of the concept in ancient Greece and Rome. Diogenes of Sinope (c. 412/403–324/321 BCE), often referred to as Diogenes the Cynic, is generally credited with inventing the word 'cosmopolitan'. When asked where he came from, Diogenes responded, 'I am "a citizen of the cosmos"' (*kosmopolitēs*, D.L. 6.63). Most scholars have taken this remark to be entirely negative, but John Moles argues that 'Diogenes' cosmopolitanism unites a negative, rejection of the conventional city and *ta politika* ("politics"), with a positive, assertion of the primacy of the "state in the *kosmos*"' (Moles 1995: 137). As Moles characterises the traditional position, when Diogenes declared himself a cosmopolitan,

> and when he wrote, 'The only good government is that in the cosmos' (*monēn . . . orthēn politeian tēn en kosmōi*, D.L. 6.72), he meant only what he expressed elsewhere in tragic verses (D.L. 6.38): 'Without a city, without a house, without a fatherland, / A beggar, a wanderer with a single day's bread' – namely, that he had no polis and rejected the polis as 'against nature' (*para phusin*). (Moles 1996: 107)

Yet Moles points out that saying, 'I am without a polis' (*apolis eimi*) is a negative statement, whereas saying, 'I am "a citizen of the cosmos"' (*kosmopolitēs*) is a positive assertion, one in keeping with the Cynic ideal of living 'according to nature'. Nature, in the Cynic view, 'provides an ethical norm observable in animals and inferable by cross-cultural comparisons' (Branham and Goulet-Cazé 1996: 8). This norm ignores all the human class, gender, racial and national distinctions that institutions such as the *polis* enforce. Living according to this norm facilitates harmonious relations among humans, animals and the gods, and promotes the Cynic pursuit of freedom (*eleutheria*) and self-sufficiency (*autarkeia*), whereas living according to the laws of the *polis* limits freedom, imposes distinctions among humans, and impedes proper relations with the natural world. True sages are at home anywhere, and their moral attunement to nature gives them the autonomy of kings or gods. Their *politeia*, their 'state', Moles argues, 'is nothing other than a *moral* "state": that is, the "state" of being a Cynic', and in claiming to be a *kosmopolitēs* the Cynic 'expresses a positive allegiance to the whole earth' (Moles 1996: 111). Although the wisdom of the sage is rare, sages together form an ideal *politeia*, and through their teachings they seek to extend their wisdom to all humankind and thereby point the way towards a universal cosmic *politeia*, one that has no need of law courts, currency, temples and so on.

Cynic and Stoic conceptions of cosmopolitanism are often contrasted, but Moles concludes that Cynic cosmopolitanism 'already contained all the essential positive qualities that the Stoics endowed with a fuller exposition, and that they integrated into a fully developed physical system' (Moles 1996: 119). What differentiates Cynics from Stoics is that, although both advocated living according to nature, the Cynics

> gave greater weight to animalistic primitivism and individual self-sufficiency, because these ideas contributed to the simplicity and attractiveness of their message: What could be more natural than to live the life of animals? What more comforting than the conviction that self-sufficiency leads to happiness? (Moles 1996: 120)

In Moles's view, Cynic cosmopolitanism, in rejecting the city and advocating life according to universal nature, 'provided the impetus for a crucial move in ancient political thought: that between theories based on the polis and those based on natural law' (Moles 2000: 434). Yet though the Cynics provided the impetus for such a move, they themselves did not identify 'law' as the central principle governing nature. The Stoics made this connection, for which reason, says Katja Maria Vogt, 'the early Stoics may justly be counted among the ancestors of natural law theory' (Vogt 2008: 3). Early Stoics refer to the law as the 'common law' (*koinos nomos*), which Vogt sees as 'an ancestor of what has later come to be called the *natural* law'. Stoic law is common in that it is 'common to all human beings, and exists independently from the actual laws and customs in actual cities', and in this regard it resembles natural law. What differentiates Stoic common law from later conceptions of natural law is that Stoic law, unlike natural law, is *physical* as well as ethical, a law that 'pervades the cosmos, and is identified with a corporeal god' (Vogt 2008: 161). For the Stoics, law and reason are identical. 'It is a core claim of Stoic *physics* that law, or reason, pervades and regulates the cosmos, and is identical with Zeus. It is a core *ethical* claim that law and reason are prescriptive' (Vogt 2008: 162). The cosmos is the dwelling place of the gods and humans, and hence the cosmos is their *polis*, a cosmic city already governed by law and reason, even if no actual *polis*, in the conventional sense of the term, fully manifests this cosmic order. The cosmic *polis* of Stoic cosmopolitanism, then, in one regard, is not a utopian ideal since

> the cosmos *as a city* exists, will not deteriorate, and could not be instituted through any human effort. The cosmos is the common 'home' to all its inhabitants, and it is regulated by the law. Since no city other than the cosmos is regulated by the *common* law [. . .] the cosmos is the *only* city. (Vogt 2008: 67)

The goal of the Stoic sage is to live according to the common law, which means to become a fully reasonable being whose actions are completely at one with the cosmic order. The sage seeks always to engage in 'appropriate action' (*kathêkonta*) suited to the given situation, and, in so doing, to follow the law of perfect reason, a law that is not a set of specific rules but a single guiding principle of cosmic order. As practitioner of appropriate action, the Stoic sage becomes a genuine citizen of the cosmic city, not a mere inhabitant, like other humans, who are rational creatures – that is, creatures capable of reason – but not yet fully reasonable beings. The collectivity of Stoic sages and gods forms the citizenry of the cosmic *polis*, and among this human citizenry the kinship of reason and law establishes a bond that makes the individual sages fellow-citizens in a genuine community. But what of the unenlightened inhabitants of the cosmic city? Are they of concern to the Stoic sage? Some scholars have said no, that the Stoic conception of the cosmic city is exclusively that of a community of sages, and that the bonds that unite them are simply a product of their individual attainment of perfect reason. Vogt and others, however, have argued persuasively that the Stoic principle of *oikeiôsis*, or 'belonging to us', dictates that the sage consider all humans as potential fellow-citizens, towards whom kindness, warmth, generosity and affection should be extended. According to this reading, then, Stoic virtue involves not simply personal enlightenment, but a beneficent engagement with all humanity, and thus the Stoic concept of cosmopolitanism has as an essential component the notion of a bond of kinship among all humankind.

By articulating the notion of cosmopolitanism in terms of the cosmic law of reason, the Stoics transformed Cynic cosmopolitanism as a practice into a philosophical concept. Two important consequences arose from this concept of cosmic law. First, it separated humans from other animals in a decisive way. Cynics such as Diogenes scorned intellectual abstraction, and, though adept at syllogistic reasoning, they stressed the importance of action in accordance with nature. Their model for human behaviour was not that of logicians but animals, whose simplicity showed the way towards happiness. Admittedly, the Stoics did include all of creation in their conception of a law-governed cosmos, but they distinguished clearly between the human soul and the souls of other animals. Humans alone possess a 'governing principle' (*hêgemonikon*), which allows them to perform ethical actions and which makes them, according to Chrysippus, the only 'animals whose nature is political' (*On Law*, cited in Vogt 2008: 186). Hence, Stoic cosmopolitanism, while embracing a broad cosmic law, pertains primarily to human beings, the only political animals.

The second consequence of framing cosmopolitanism in terms of cosmic law was that it facilitated an extension of the concept of cosmopolitanism to include questions of practical governance and the establishment of laws in actual political entities. Pivotal in this development was Cicero. Though not a Stoic himself, Cicero embraced the Stoic concept of cosmopolitanism. In the *De legibus*, Cicero argues that reason is what is most divine in man and the cosmos; that perfected reason is wisdom; that reason exists in both humans and gods; and that if they have reason in common, humans and gods must also have right reason in common.

> And since right reason is Law, we must believe that men have Law also in common with the gods. Further, those who share Law must also share Justice; and those who share these are to be regarded as members of the same commonwealth [. . .] Hence we must now conceive of this whole universe as one commonwealth [*civitas*] of which both gods and humans are members. (*Leg.* 1.23; trans. modified)

Yet Cicero's basic interest, he says in *De republica*, is not to use these concepts to 'follow the example of Socrates in Plato's work, and myself invent an ideal State of my own' (*Rep.* 2.3), but to apply them to issues of governance in the actual Roman state. Cicero shares the Stoic belief that all humans are capable of reason, but, unlike the Stoics, he tends to minimise the differences between the sage and the unenlightened, suggesting that adherence to right reason and true justice is within the capacities of all people. He admits that human laws are not always just – indeed such laws are not really laws at all (*Leg.* 2.12) – and he concedes that his reflections on law must accommodate certain limitations in the masses: 'But since our whole discussion has to do with the reasoning of the populace, it will sometimes be necessary to speak in the popular manner, and give the name of law to that which in written form decrees whatever it wishes, either by command or prohibition' (*Leg.* 1.19). Nonetheless, Cicero entertains the possibility of creating an actual just State whose citizens observe laws that are formulated in accordance with right reason. Such laws would fulfil law's fundamental aim of ensuring 'the safety of citizens, the preservation of States, and the tranquility and happiness of human life' (*Leg.* 2.11), and the citizens' virtue would consist of obeying these State laws.

From Diogenes to Cicero, then, we may trace a dramatic change in the relationship between the concepts of cosmopolitanism and the State. For Diogenes, the actual *polis* is against nature, and the only true *polis* is the cosmos. Being a citizen of the cosmos means pursuing the virtues of freedom and self-sufficiency by living, as other animals do, in accordance with nature. For early Stoics such as Zeno and Chrysippus, the cosmos is a *polis* in that it is regulated by perfect reason and common law. To be virtuous is to engage in appropriate action, thereby following a single governing principle – *the* law – rather than observing specific rules. Although the Stoic concept of *oikeiôsis*, or 'belonging to us', suggests that the sage has concern for all humankind, the Stoic vision of an eventual worldwide *polis* accommodates no compromise in the standard of virtue as perfect reason but requires the full enlightenment of all citizens. In such a future *polis*, there would no longer be any need for political or legal institutions. Hence, as Schofield argues, the Stoic idea of the city 'is *not* a conception of the *state*: if we take it that there have to be further conditions satisfied (e.g. the centralization of authority, the division of powers) for a community to form a state' (Schofield 1999: 73). The citizens of such a universal cosmopolitan community would be the gods and all humans (but only humans, since other animals do not possess a rational soul). Finally, in Cicero the cosmos is most decidedly a State ruled by rational laws, and human communities may aspire to be embodiments of that cosmic order. Law is not an inner guiding principle, but a set of precepts that ensure the safety, tranquility and happiness of citizens and the preservation of the State. Virtue is less a matter of practising appropriate action than of obeying rules and fulfilling civic duties.

Sellars's Critique and Its Problems

Let us turn now to Sellars's appraisal of what he calls Deleuze's cosmopolitanism. If the Ciceronian version of the concept is in question, then Deleuze is decidedly anti-cosmopolitan, in that he consistently rejects the State apparatus as an oppressive structure. This is nowhere more evident than in the Nomadology section of *A Thousand Plateaus*, where the nomadic war machine is contrasted with the State apparatus. As Sellars correctly observes, in *A Thousand Plateaus* Deleuze and Guattari tie nomadism to the concept of smooth space, an unmarked domain of nomadic movement, which they oppose to striated space, a geometrically graphed and charted area of fixed positions and stable identities. Striated space is quintessentially *polis*-space, whereas smooth space is the pasturage and wilds of the nomads, outside the city (see ATP 380; 557 n. 51). The nomads are a turbulent metamorphic force, and to ward off the constant threat of the State they invent the war machine, which is less an instrument of destruction than a practice of transformation and revolutionary change. Deleuze and Guattari clearly valorise smooth space, the nomadic and the war machine over striated space, sedentarism and the State. In smooth space, individuals roam freely over the open land; in striated space, a transcendent authority allocates demarcated real estate to individuals. Hence, Sellars argues,

> What we are offered is a political ethic in which individuals distribute themselves across a territory rather than distribute territory to themselves. It is, fundamentally, a cosmopolitan ethic, a rejection of political ties to particular locations, and a reorientation of the way in which one relates to social and political space. (Sellars 2007: 34)

Sellars sees the primary difference between the Stoics' and Deleuze and Guattari's cosmopolitanism in their conception of the cosmos. The Stoic cosmos is a *polis* governed by reason (*logos*) and law (*nomos*); whereas, for Deleuze and Guattari, the cosmos is a 'chaosmos', in which, according to Sellars, 'everything is in a continual state of flux at various levels of speed and slowness' (Sellars 2007: 35), and such a 'chaosmos', Sellars argues, is governed neither by reason nor by law. Despite this fundamental difference, however, Sellars sees both the Stoics and Deleuze and Guattari as advocates of a utopian politics inspired by 'a personal ethical project of self-transformation in which each individual alters their own relation to space and traditional political states' (Sellars 2007: 36).

There are several problems with Sellars's analysis. First, Deleuze and Guattari always stress the collective over the individual in political action. In *Anti-Oedipus*, Deleuze and Guattari's critique of psychoanalysis is precisely that it is 'personological', familial and apolitical, and one of their fundamental theses is that desiring-production is immediately social and political. In *Kafka: Toward a Minor Literature*, Deleuze and Guattari define minor literature in terms of 'the deterritorialisation of language, the connection of the individual to a political immediacy, and the collective assemblage of enunciation'. In minor literature 'everything [. . .] is political', and 'everything takes on a collective value' (K 17–18). And throughout *A Thousand Plateaus* and *What is Philosophy?*, whenever topics of a political nature are addressed (especially the plateaus on Micropolitics and Segmentarity, Nomadology, and the Apparatus of Capture, and in the 'Geophilosophy' chapter of *What is Philosophy?*), the collective and social are given priority over the personal. Deleuze and Guattari consistently conceive of political action in terms of what they label in *Anti-Oedipus* 'subjected groups', those who are defined and controlled by external forces of subjectivation and domination, and 'subject groups', those who assume agency as a self-defining collectivity (see especially AO 348–50). Although Deleuze does articulate a Stoic-inspired ethics of the event in *The Logic of Sense* – an ethics of being 'worthy of the event' – and though this ethics is incorporated into Deleuze and Guattari's texts, this ethics is more than the single person's affirmation of chance, multiplicity and becoming. It is always an ethics that is at once individual and collective, and, in fact, one that cannot realise its potential in the absence of collective action.

Second, even though Deleuze and Guattari identify the essence of their transformative politics as 'molecular', and oppose it to the 'molar' politics of conventional institutions, such as governments, political parties, NGOs and so on, by no means do they ignore the necessity of pursuing both a molecular and a molar politics at the same time. In distinguishing the molecular and the molar, the micropolitical and macropolitical, Deleuze and Guattari are not speaking about actual physical scale, but about qualitatively different processes that take place at all levels of social interaction. Any political change necessarily involves a becoming-other whereby the status quo is set in disequilibrium. Deleuze and Guattari label such change 'molecular' to emphasise its decentred, multivalent character, and, if successful, this molecular becoming-other undermines the fixed, solid 'molar' dimension of established institutions and practices. But a molecular politics cannot ignore the domain of molar institutions. Hence, when they advocate a micropolitical 'becoming-woman' within feminism, through which the coordinates of the standard opposition of male–female are destabilised, they add, 'It is, of course, indispensable for women to conduct a molar politics, with a view to winning back their own organism, their own history, their own subjectivity' (ATP 276).

This theoretical orientation towards collective action at the level of micro- and macropolitical intervention is confirmed in the political commitments and actions of Deleuze and Guattari. Deleuze himself engaged only in limited political activism during his career, but he did support various collective projects (most notably Foucault's *Groupe d'information sur les prisons*) and political causes (such as the Palestinian movement). Guattari, by contrast, was a dedicated and frenetically engaged activist throughout his life. He attempted to put into practice his political philosophy in various institutional settings, including political parties per se, but also trade unions, media collectives, research groups and psychiatric institutions. And whether Guattari's efforts may be judged successful or not, he never shied away from implementing the theoretical tenets of micropolitics and macropolitics in concrete situations involving groups of varying dimensions, ranging from intimate research groups to international alliances, such as the coalition of ecologically oriented political parties in France, Germany and Italy.

Third, it is not at all certain that Deleuze and Guattari's opposition to the State is also an opposition to the city. In ancient Greece, two usages of the term *polis* may be distinguished: *polis* versus hinterlands (roughly city versus country) and *polis* versus surrounding State territory. In the former, *polis* designates a demographic/geographic concept; in the latter, a political concept. At first glance, the two concepts of the *polis* seem identical in Deleuze and Guattari – the city and the State appear to be the same thing. The City of Ur is the Urstaat (ATP 217); the war machine's enemy is 'the State, the city [*ville*], state and urban phenomenon [*le phénomène étatique et urbain*]' (ATP 417); the war machine destroys 'the State-form and the city-form with which it collides' (ATP 418); the city and the State are 'in reciprocal presupposition' (ATP 434). And yet the distinction between the sedentary and the nomadic is not absolute: there are distinctions among the 'transhumant, semisedentary, sedentary [and] nomadic' (ATP 430–1). It is possible to create a smooth space within the city and 'live in the city as a nomad, or as a cave dweller' (ATP

500). Paris at times is a 'city haunted by nomads' (ATP 558 n. 61), and Amsterdam is said to be a 'rhizome-city' (ATP 15). Most decisively, in an extended passage on the difference between towns (*villes*) and States, the town

> is defined by entries and exits; something must enter it and exit from it. It imposes a frequency. [. . .]. It is a phenomenon of *transconsistency*, a *network*, because it is fundamentally in contact with other towns. It represents a threshold of deterritorialization, because whatever the material involved, it must be deterritorialized enough to enter the network, to submit to the polarization, to follow the circuit of urban and road recoding. The maximum deterritorialization appears in the tendency of maritime and commercial towns to separate off from the back-country, from the countryside (Athens, Carthage, Venice). [. . .] Towns are circuit-points of every kind, which enter into counterpoint along horizontal lines; they effect a complete but local, town-by-town integration. (ATP 432)

In every regard, the State is the town's opposite. The State is a 'phenomenon of *intraconsistency*. [. . .] It makes the town resonate with the countryside. It operates by stratification; in other words, it forms a vertical, hierarchized aggregate that spans a dimension of depth' (ATP 433).

In *What is Philosophy?*, this same contrast of the horizontal and the vertical, of transconsistency and intraconsistency, is framed in terms of the horizontal *city* versus the vertical State. The State assimilates the surrounding territory within 'a higher arithmetical Unity', whereas the city 'adapts the territory to a geometrical extensiveness that can be continued in commercial circuits' (WP 86). Both the State and the city 'deterritorialise' the unmarked earth and impose a reterritorialisation on it, but the State does so through transcendence, whereas the city does so through immanence. In ancient Greece, the city functioned as a '*milieu of immanence*' (WP 87), Athens being the paradigmatic example of such a milieu: 'For a fairly short period the deepest bond existed between the democratic city, colonization, and a new imperialism that no longer saw the sea as a limit of its territory or an obstacle to its endeavour but as a wider bath of immanence' (WP 88). The development of such a milieu of immanence was what made possible the invention of philosophy, since the milieu of immanence allowed for a pure sociability, the friendship and rivalry of citizens, and the exchange of opinions, all of which were inhibited in the stratified, hierarchical State. Ancient philosophy, then, was intimately linked to the horizontal, immanent deterritorialisation of the city, and in a similar fashion philosophy was revived in early modern Europe with the advent of capitalism and the emergence of commercial cities (such as Venice), which provided a similar milieu of immanence outside the control of the State. The ancient city and the early modern city, then, served as the contingent condition for the development of philosophy. 'Modern philosophy's link with capitalism, therefore, is of the same kind as that of ancient philosophy with Greece: *the composition of an absolute plane of immanence with a relative social milieu that also functions through immanence*' (WP 98). Given this valorisation of the city in opposition to the State, it seems clear that the contrast of nomads and the city/State does not sum up Deleuze and Guattari's political philosophy and that the dual meaning of *polis* as city and State is one they exploit in an effort to articulate a more nuanced differentiation of the State from other forms of social organisation than that framed in the simple war machine–State opposition. This positive assessment of the city is important to note, since it counters any temptation to see Deleuze and Guattari's remarks on nomadism as an anti-urban primitivism. And the connection of philosophy with the city and capitalism suggests that among the problems facing philosophy and political action today is that of exploiting the city's milieu of immanence as a means of escaping the oppressive grip of capitalism.

Fourth, Sellars's analysis simplifies and distorts the concept of 'chaosmos'. Deleuze and Guattari's point is not that the cosmos is chaotic, but that it combines forces of formation and deformation within a process of constant transformation. Only at a certain level of analysis is 'everything in a continual state of flux at various levels of speed and slowness', and only as a *virtual* dimension that coexists with and is immanent within an *actual* dimension of individuated entities, regulated processes, and relatively stable power relations. In Deleuze and Guattari's terms, forces of deterritorialisation and reterritorialisation are omnipresent in the cosmos, and, although these forces are qualitatively different, they are only tendencies that are always manifest in mixtures and inextricable combinations of multivalent interaction: 'the territory itself is inseparable from vectors of deterritorialization working it from within'; and deterritorialisation 'is in turn inseparable from correlative reterritorializations' (ATP 509). These forces pervade the cosmos, from quantum, atomic and molecular elements, to inorganic and organic forms at various scales of composition, to social, cultural and political modes of organisation and practice. The chaosmos is replete with mutative, metamorphic forces that dissolve structures, undo relations and send elements in random trajectories and velocities. But the same forces connect elements in new combinations, form assemblages of heterogeneous elements that function together, and establish provisional, relatively homeostatic processes of organisation that shape the specific environments of individual life forms, including humans, with their complex creations of machines, institutions, customs, laws, artworks and so on. Deleuze, after all, calls his philosophy a 'constructionism' or 'constructivism' (N 147; 158), but nowhere a 'deconstructionism' or 'destructivism', and philosophy's goal is the *invention* of concepts whereby new connections may be forged, new assemblages of relations that cohere and co-function. These same principles of construction, creation and connection are at play throughout the cosmos. As *A Thousand Plateaus*' 'Geology of Morals' plateau makes clear, such principles are present in geological, biological and human strata, and they are inseparable from the 'anorganic life' (ATP 503) that courses through the universe. In the plateau on the *ritournelle*, or refrain, these principles are fundamental to Deleuze and Guattari's analysis of the common features of animal and human territories. The refrain, which pervades the construction and functioning of territories, is always a pattern that simultaneously territorialises and deterritorialises, forming points of order and areas of control, but also lines of flight towards new zones of potential invention and construction.

Finally, if Deleuze and Guattari's politics can be described as 'utopian', it is only in a very limited sense of the word, and certainly not that which informs Sellars's uses of the term. Deleuze and Guattari reject the utopian strain of political thought that orients social action in terms of a pre-established plan, blueprint or model of a desirable future. Such utopian visions are by their nature projections of the limitations of the present, and they are generally the creations of individuals, which are later adopted by groups. Most schemas are transcendent impositions of preconstructed concepts developed by an individual who has risen above the fray, in no way immanent productions of the groups directly engaged in struggles for social transformation. Given the frequent identification of such transcendent schemes as 'utopian', it is not surprising that in *What is Philosophy?* Deleuze and Guattari cast doubt on the usefulness of the term, saying at one point that, 'in view of the mutilated meaning public opinion has given to it, perhaps *utopia* is not the best word' (WP 100), and at another that 'utopia is not a good concept' (WP 110). They also caution that 'in utopia (as in philosophy) there is always the risk of a restoration, and sometimes a proud affirmation, of transcendence, so that we need to distinguish between authoritarian utopias or utopias of transcendence, and immanent, revolutionary, libertarian utopias' (WP 100). In their immanent, revolutionary and libertarian sense of the term, '*utopia is what links* philosophy with its own epoch' (WP 99). The word 'utopia' designates '*that conjunction of philosophy, or of the concept, with the present milieu*' (WP 100). Philosophy's task is to engage the forces of relative deterritorialisation present in the milieus of immanence that give rise to philosophy and sustain it (such as ancient Athens, early modern European cities, or, let us hope, our contemporary world) and push them to the level of absolute deterritorialisation. By creating concepts, philosophy surpasses the limit internal to relative deterritorialisation and, in so doing, turns that limit '*back against itself so as to summon forth a new earth, a new people*' (WP 99). The new earth and new people do not exist at present; they are 'to come', *à venir*, 'a future new earth' (*une nouvelle terre à venir*) (WP 88), 'the people to come' (*le peuple à venir*) (WP 109). And, we should note, although philosophy summons forth a new earth and new people via absolute deterritorialisation, the future earth and people are sites of reterritorialisation: 'Deterritorialization of such a plane [the milieu of immanence's plane of relative deterritorialisation] does not preclude reterritorialization but posits it as the creation of a future new earth' (WP 88). If Deleuze and Guattari's political philosophy is utopian, then, it is only in this very specific sense: their project is to identify elements of relative deterritorialisation in a given social milieu and push them beyond their internal limits to the level of absolute deterritorialisation, with the goal of facilitating a reterritorialisation of forces in a new earth and a new people. And it is precisely this utopian project that may be described as 'chaosmopolitan'.

Chaosmopolitanism, Politics, Law and Democracy

Deleuze and Guattari focus their attention on strategies for initiating social change, and hence on processes of deterritorialisation that make possible the invention of something new. This orientation no doubt arises from their sense that developing such strategies is the most pressing task philosophy faces today. 'We do not lack communication', they say. 'On the contrary, we have too much of it. We lack creation. *We lack resistance to the present*' (WP 108). Resistance to the present is the necessary condition for the invention of a new earth and a new people, but resistance only initiates such a creative project. Deleuze and Guattari say little about subsequent stages of utopian creation beyond inaugural deterritorialisation, yet there are indications in Deleuze's late thought that certain principles, if not specific institutions, might be brought to bear in the constructive phase of creating a new earth and people, and that these principles are normative and compatible with democracy and the rule of law. These principles concern what Deleuze calls jurisprudence, becoming-democratic, and becoming-imperceptible.

In his insightful study of law in Deleuze, Laurent de Sutter distinguishes a critical and a clinical approach to law, the critical exposing the absurdities and fundamental injustices of various traditional conceptions of law, the clinical providing a positive, curative model of law as jurisprudence. Deleuze sees Sade and Sacher-Masoch, for example, as carrying out a critique of law, Sade through the invention of institutions of implacably logical cruelty and ironic defiance of law, Masoch via the masochist's contract, which assents to law, but in such a way as to parody law and expose its emptiness as pure form. The clinical conception of law as jurisprudence rejects the model of law as restriction, prohibition and limitation, and argues for a positive, creative practice of law that extends human relations. Deleuze finds inspiration for this notion of law in Hume, who envisions institutions as means of inventing ever-expanding and increasingly inclusive relations among humans. Jurisprudence for Deleuze is essentially case law, and its positive function is similar to that of Hume's institutions. Jurisprudence is not a foundational body of fixed laws, but an open practice of assessing singular situations and inventing ways of promoting rights, equality and freedom. As Deleuze says in a 1988 interview, 'Rights aren't created by codes and pronouncements but by jurisprudence. Jurisprudence is the philosophy of law, and deals with singularities, it advances by working out from singularities' (N 153). This valorisation of jurisprudence clearly indicates that Deleuze's critique of law (and Deleuze and Guattari's critique of the State) does not reject notions of law and governance as a whole, but makes room for a positive practice of law, and one may assume that such jurisprudence would be an important part of any future collectivity.

Paul Patton also notes the importance of jurisprudence in Deleuze's late thought, commenting that 'Deleuze's endorsement of rights and jurisprudence clearly commits him to the existence of law and the kind of constitutional state that this implies' (Patton 2010: 153). Patton counters the claim that Deleuze's thought is elitist and anti-democratic, arguing that Deleuze's disparaging remarks about democracy are directed at democracies as they now exist, which, in Deleuze's analysis, are far from democratic, for which reason the new 'people and earth will not be found in our democracies' (WP 108). Far from rejecting democracy as a form of governance, Deleuze advocates a 'becoming-democratic that is not the same as what States of law are' (WP 113). As Patton convincingly shows, this endorsement of democracy does not represent a radical break from Deleuze's earlier work; rather, it 'is not only consistent with but draws on elements of the earlier work' (Patton 2010: 140). Deleuze puts forward what Patton calls a 'pragmatic and relativized ontology' (Patton 2010: 142) in which all aspects of the world are governed by processes of deterritorialisation and reterritorialisation. Although the two processes are inextricable, deterritorialisation is the more important and the more valuable of the two, for which reason the two processes of this pragmatic ontology are normative, 'in the sense that they provide a framework within which to evaluate the character of particular events and processes' (Patton 2010: 144–5). Patton then shows that, when Deleuze critiques democracies, he simply applies this ontological normativity to the evaluation of political institutions. Implicit in Deleuze's critique, Patton demonstrates, is a deep-seated commitment to principles of justice, equality and freedom. Patton concludes that Deleuze's political thought is utopian, but only in a sense loosely akin to Rawls's 'realistic utopianism', in that it is firmly grounded in the sociopolitical context of the real world, which it engages in an initial absolute deterritorialisation of contextual elements and has as its endpoint a reterritorialisation of elements in a new earth and people – not an ideal world, but, it is hoped, one that is better than the present world. And essential components of this utopianism are the normative principles of justice, equality and freedom. Hence, although Deleuze does not address questions of how one might go about creating a political order that ensures these values, his normative commitments in no way preclude their application to the task of fashioning a genuinely democratic political order.

Hume guides Deleuze's thought about jurisprudence, but also about the political dimension of 'becoming-imperceptible', which Tim Clark aptly names a 'politics of sympathy'. For Hume, the problem facing society is to enlarge individuals' concerns beyond their immediate sphere, to invent institutions that enable individuals to have sympathy for family, community, nation and, eventually, all humankind. In *Dialogues*, Deleuze says that becoming-other proceeds via assemblages, an assemblage being 'a co-functioning, it is "sympathy", symbiosis' (D 52). Becoming-imperceptible is the end point of becoming-other, the most deterritorialised form of becoming. To become-imperceptible is 'to world (*faire monde*), to make a world (*faire un monde*). By a process of elimination, one is no longer anything more than an abstract line.' One acts as does the camouflage fish when it blends in with its surroundings: 'this fish is crisscrossed by abstract lines that resemble nothing, that do not even follow its organic divisions; but thus disorganized, disarticulated, it worlds with the lines of a rock, sand and plants, becoming imperceptible' (ATP 280). To become-imperceptible is also to become like everyone else (*comme tout le monde*), and it is in this regard that becoming-imperceptible takes on its political sense.

In 'Immanence: A Life', Deleuze comments on a scene in Dickens's *Our Mutual Friend*, in which Riderhood, a thoroughly despicable character, seems to be dying, and those around him momentarily suspend their hostility towards him and sympathise with him, not as an individual, but as *homo tantum*, as a concrete manifestation of an impersonal yet singular life, *a* life. As Deleuze suggests in 'Bartleby; or, the Formula', sympathy directed towards such an impersonal yet singular life may form the basis of a renewed social order. In this essay, Deleuze identifies a utopian strain in Melville that is the American, democratic counterpart of the nineteenth-century communist ideal of the society of comrades, one 'that has no other determination than that of being man, *Homo tantum*' (CC 86). Melville envisions America as a nation inclusive of all nationalities, 'a universe, a society of brothers, a federation of men and goods', in which the individual 'has no consciousness of himself apart from the proprieties of a "democratic dignity" that considers all particularities as so many ignominious stains that arouse anguish or pity' (CC 85). The community Melville imagines fights on two fronts: 'against the particularities that pit man against man and nourish an irremediable mistrust; but also against the Universal or the Whole, the fusion of souls in the name of great love or charity' (CC 87). That which brings coherence to a truly democratic society is the impersonal singularities of individuals which make possible a sympathy that is not a sentimental condescending charity or pity *for* others, but a feeling *with* them. Citing D. H. Lawrence, Deleuze says of Melville's democracy of impersonal singularities that it is held together by '"all the subtle sympathizings of the incalculable soul, from the bitterest hate to passionate love"' (CC 87).

Deleuze finds in Whitman a similar democratic ideal. For

Whitman, the world 'is a collection of heterogeneous parts: an infinite patchwork or an endless wall of dry stones' (CC 57). The world is thus not a Whole, but a shifting configuration of relations among parts.

> Nature is not a form, but rather the process of establishing relations. It invents a polyphony; it is not a totality but an assembly, a 'conclave', a 'plenary session'. Nature is inseparable from processes of companionship and conviviality, which are not preexistent givens but are elaborated between heterogeneous living beings in such a way that they create a tissue of shifting relations, in which the melody of one part intervenes as a motif in the melody of another (the bee and the flower). (CC 59)

The poet's task is to extract fragments from the world and invent new relations, such that humans may form life-enhancing bonds with nature and among one another. Whitman calls such life-enhancing bonds among humans 'camaraderie', which, says Deleuze, 'is the variability that implies an encounter with the Outside, a march of souls in the open air, on the "Open Road"'. Whitman's ideal is the 'maximum extension and density' of relations of camaraderie leading to the formation of

> a political and national character – not a totalism or a totalitarianism but, as Whitman says, a "Unionism". Democracy and Art themselves form a whole only in their relationship with Nature (the open air, light, colors, sounds, the night . . .); lacking these, art collapses into morbidity, and democracy, into deception. (CC 60)

Clearly, Deleuze's characterisations of Melville's and Whitman's conceptions of democracy reflect his own views: a Unionism, a federation of individuals, each a *homo tantum*, each defined by singularities, bound together through an impersonal sympathy, a becoming-imperceptible in which each individual becomes *tout le monde*, 'everyone else', but also, in the literal sense of *tout le monde*, 'all the world'. Such a federation is consonant with the principles governing Deleuzian jurisprudence and the process of 'becoming-democratic', and, as Patton points out, those principles are one with Deleuze's pragmatic ontology of deterritorialisation and reterritorialisation. Hence, Deleuze's politics is chaosmopolitan in a fundamental sense. For Deleuze, and not simply for Whitman, democracy and art – and, we must add, philosophy – form a whole 'only in their relationship with Nature'. Nature is polyphonic, 'a tissue of shifting relations, in which the melody of one part intervenes as a motif in the melody of another' (CC 60). Processes of deterritorialisation continually play through the chaosmos, including the domains specific to human interactions, and Deleuzian politics valorises such deterritorialisation, finding in this process the means of inventing something new. But the chaosmos simultaneously reterritorialises, constructs new forms, new relations, new modes of existence. Likewise, Deleuze's politics calls for the reterritorialisation of deterritorialised philosophical thought in the creation of a new earth and a new people. This chaosmopolitanism is a broad ecology and ethology of shifting relations that form an entangled network (a rhizome) of heterogeneous assemblages, within which politics proper finds its place. Neither technophilic nor technophobic, this chaosmopolitan ecology undermines any distinction between the natural and the artificial, wilderness and civilisation, *tekhnē* and *physis*, valorising instead the anorganic life that informs the functioning of the chaosmos' rhizomic tangle of assemblages. To become-imperceptible within this rhizomic tangle is politically to become *tout le monde* and cosmically 'to world (*faire monde*), to make a world (*faire un monde*)' (ATP 280).

Normativity

Deleuze's ontology provides a basis for normative evaluation, and implicit in Deleuze's conception of democracy and the rule of law is a normative assessment of the extent to which given institutions further genuine justice, equality and freedom. But one may call Deleuze's ontology and politics normative in another sense. Georges Canguilhem, whose pioneering work in the philosophy and history of biology brought to light the conceptual dynamics in biological thought of norm and deviation, the normal and the pathological, also developed a notion of normativity that has a bearing on the concept of chaosmopolitanism. Canguilhem argues that

> there is no such thing as *abnormal*, if by the term we mean merely the absence of a previous positive condition or state. From the biological, social and psychological points of view, a pathological state is never a state without norms – such a thing is impossible. Wherever there is *life* there are norms. Life is a polarized activity, a dynamic polarity, and that in itself is enough to establish norms. (Canguilhem 1994: 351)

Each life form is normative, in the sense that it establishes the values that delimit the parameters of the normal and the pathological and determine the norms which inform its actions. 'There is no fact that is normal or pathological in itself.' The normality and norms of a given life form 'will come to them through their normativity' (Canguilhem 1994: 354). The health of a life form is determined by its normativity – by the norms and the domain of normality it produces for itself.

> Any normality open to possible future correction is authentic normativity, or health. Any normality limited to maintaining itself, hostile to any variation in the themes that express it, and incapable of adapting to new situations is a normality devoid of normative intention. When confronted with any apparently normal situation, it is therefore important to ask whether the norms that it embodies are creative norms, norms with a forward thrust, or, on the contrary, conservative norms, norms whose thrust is toward the past. (Canguilhem 1994: 352)

If authentic normativity is a creative, flexible, future-oriented health, then one may say that Deleuze's political philosophy is authentically normative. Although Deleuze is speaking of literature when he says that health 'consists in inventing a people who are missing [. . .] a possibility of life' (CC 4), the same may be said of philosophy, whose goal is the creation of a new earth and people. But one may also say that Deleuze's thought as a whole is authentically normative. His thought is not only a 'constructionism' or a 'constructivism' but also a 'vitalism' (N 143), a thought that seeks 'to free life from what imprisons it', to invent 'possibilities of existence' through the creation of concepts. Canguilhem's notion of normativity, while much broader than that of a political normativity of principled evaluation, is consonant with the political concept, in that both may be derived from what Patton calls Deleuze's normative, machinic, 'pragmatic and relativized ontology', an ontology that 'is also an ethics or an ethology' (Patton 2010: 142).

Chaosmopolitanism

What, then, is the relationship between Deleuze's chaosmopolitanism and the cosmopolitanism of the Cynics and Stoics? It resembles Diogenes' cosmopolitanism in its recognition of the bonds that connect humans to the non-human world, but it departs in its 'machinic' conception of nature, which is antithetical to Diogenes' primitivism and his rejection of the *polis* as constitutively 'against nature'. In its conception of humans' relationship to nature, chaosmopolitanism is also unlike early Stoic cosmopolitanism, which separates humans from other animals and conceives of the cosmic city primarily in terms of human relations. The Stoic conception of cosmic law as reason obviously has no place in chaosmopolitanism, which views the chaosmos as neither rational nor purely chaotic, but as constituted by processes of deterritorialisation and reterritorialisation, the dissolution of forms and creation of new forms. But the Stoic notion of law as a single principle leading to 'appropriate action' (*kathêkonta*) is not entirely foreign to the chaosmopolitan concept of jurisprudence, in that appropriate action, like jurisprudence, is always contextual, never reducible to fixed and unchanging rules. And the Stoic principle of *oikeiôsis*, or 'belonging to us', which leads Stoic sages to embrace all humankind within a single community of concern, has a loose kinship with chaosmopolitan 'sympathy', which makes possible a federation of *homines tanti*, individuals connected through their singularities and the impersonal anorganic life that passes through them. Unlike Stoic *oikeiôsis*, however, chaosmopolitan sympathy extends beyond humans to the chaosmos as a whole. Chaosmopolitanism resembles Ciceronian cosmopolitanism, which envisions the implementation of cosmic law within actual cities, but only in that chaosmopolitanism's 'realistic utopianism' connects deterritorialised thought to the pragmatic realm of sociopolitical action. The Stoic figure of the cosmos as city has no counterpart in chaosmopolitanism, save in the very loose sense that the chaosmos is the common habitat of all life forms, and hence the *polis* of which all life forms are 'citizens'. The *polis* does have a place in chaosmopolitanism, however, as the locus of politics within the chaosmos, a site distinct from, but inextricably connected to, the world as a whole. Here, the normativity of jurisprudence and 'becoming-democratic' guides political action while at the same time embodying the broader normativity of health that fosters 'creative norms [. . .] with a forward thrust' (Canguilhem 1994: 352). Chaosmopolitanism does indeed posit a different concept of the cosmos than that of Cynic or Stoic cosmopolitanism, and its sense of the *polis* is at odds with the notion of a cosmic city, but chaosmopolitanism is not chaotic and anarchic, nor is it utopian in an idealistic sense. Rather, it is a complex of thought and practice that brings the chaosmos and politics together in a single concern.

Appendix I

We might note that Sellars's choice of nomadism as the political model with which to juxtapose Deleuze and the Stoics is no doubt motivated by an intriguing passage from Plutarch's *De fortuna Alexandri* (*On the Fortunes of Alexander*, 329 A–B), which Sellers cites and glosses. Plutarch comments as follows on Zeno's now-lost treatise *Republic*:

> The much admired *Republic* of Zeno, who founded the Stoic sect, is aimed at this one main point, that our arrangement for habitations should not be based on cities or peoples, each one distinguished by its own special system of justice, but we should regard all men as citizens and members of the populace, and there should be one way of life and one order, like that of a

> herd grazing together and nurtured by a common law/pasturing (*nomos*). This Zeno wrote, picturing as it were a dream or image of a philosopher's well-regulated republic, but it was Alexander who gave effect to the theory. (Cited in Schofield 1999: 104)

Sellars points out that *nomos* may mean either 'law' or 'pasture', depending on whether the accent falls on the first or second omicron, and that, although modern Greek employs a diacritical mark to signify this distinction, Zeno wrote before the introduction of such marks and hence the sense of 'a common *nomos*' is inherently ambiguous. In *Difference and Repetition*, Deleuze makes reference to the ancient Greek meaning of *nomos* as pasturing in his exposition of the concept of a 'nomadic distribution' (DR 36), and it is from the seed of this concept that Deleuze later develops his broad concept of nomadism. As we have seen, for Zeno and the early Stoics 'a common *nomos*' would definitely mean 'a common law', and possibly 'a common pasturing', whereas for Deleuze, in Sellars's opinion, 'a common pasturing' would be the only sense of *nomos* which could be assimilated within Deleuze's concept of nomadism.

Appendix II

It seems likely that this practical conception of the cosmic State is what Marcus Aurelius had in mind when he wrote roughly 200 years after Cicero:

> If the intellectual capacity [*noeron*, mind] is common to us all, common too is reason [*logos*], which makes us rational creatures [*logikoi*]. If so, that reason also is common which tells us to do or not to do. If so, law [*nomos*] also is common. If so, we are citizens [*politai*]. If so, we are fellow-members [*politeumatos*] of an organized community [*metechomen*] [Farquharson: 'we are partakers in one constitution'; Hicks and Hicks: 'we are [. . .] subject to one unwritten constitution']. If so, the Universe [*kosmos*] is as it were a state [*polis*] – for of what other single polity can the whole race of mankind be said to be fellow-members? – and from it, this common State [*poleos*], we get the intellectual

> [*noeron*], the rational [*logikon*], and the legal instinct [*nomikon*], or whence do we get them? (*Med.* 4.4 [trans. Haines])

In Cicero and Marcus, then, the cosmos is a State. Before proceeding, however, we should pause to consider a terminological difficulty raised by Stoic political texts. Marcus uses the word *polis* to speak of the cosmic state, and Zeno employs the same word in his *Republic*. *Polis*, of course, means 'city', although it may also be used to mean 'commonwealth' or 'State', and *polis* can be rendered in Latin either as *civitas* or *res publica*. Schofield observes that in *De legibus* Cicero speaks of a common *civitas*, or State, not a *res publica*, or commonwealth (Schofield 1999: 68). Seneca, by contrast, uses the words *res publica* to oppose the ideal community of humanity and the actual community of a given governmental unit [*De otio* 4.1]). Schofield also concludes that

> the Stoic idea of a city is nothing but an idea of a community founded on common acceptance of social norms. It is *not* a conception of the *state*: if we take it that there have to be further conditions satisfied (e.g. the centralization of authority, the division of powers) for a community to form a state. (Schofield 1999: 73)

This terminological problem is especially evident in translations of the passage from Marcus cited above: Haines translates *polis* as 'state', Farquharson as 'Commonwealth' first, and then as 'city', and Hicks and Hicks as 'city' throughout the passage.

18

The Companion Cyborg: Technics and Domestication

Donna Haraway's 'A Cyborg Manifesto: Science, Technology, and Socialist-Feminism in the Late Twentieth Century', first published in the *Socialist Review* in 1985, is by far her best-known work.[1] Her proposal to displace the feminist myth of the goddess with that of the cyborg, 'a hybrid of machine and organism, a creature of social reality as well as a creature of fiction' (Haraway 1991: 149), signalled her commitment to a socialist-feminism that is neither technophilic nor technophobic but fully engaged with the problematics of the interpenetration of nature and culture in such diverse realms as biology, ecology, cybernetics, economics, politics and ethics. In *Simians, Cyborgs and Women: The Reinvention of Nature* (1991), which included a revised version of 'A Cyborg Manifesto', and in *Modest_Witness@Second_Millennium. FemaleMan© Meets_OncoMouse™: Feminism and Technoscience* (1997), Haraway continued her exploration of these issues in rhetorical terms largely consonant with those of the 'Cyborg Manifesto'. In 2003, however, she adopted a new master trope and discursive idiom in *The Companion Species Manifesto: Dogs, People, and Significant Otherness*, upon which she expanded in her 2008 study *When Species Meet*. In these last two books, her focus is not on cyborgs but on dogs, and specifically her passionate participation in 'the dog–human sport called agility' (Haraway 2008: 26). Haraway claims that there is continuity in her work, saying in her 2003 manifesto, 'I have come to see cyborgs as junior siblings in the much bigger queer family of companion species' (Haraway 2003: 11), but the later work's incessant doggy-talk reports from dogland often make it hard to retain awareness of the cyborg connection. My object here is to put Haraway's cyborg and companion species tropes in relation to Deleuze and Guattari's concept of 'becoming', and thereby explore the contours of Deleuze and Guattari's conception of the non-human.

Becoming and Becoming-with

Upon a first reading of Haraway's 'A Cyborg Manifesto', those familiar with Deleuze and Guattari might well surmise that Haraway herself had been aware of their work when she composed the essay, given how similar her positions in 'A Cyborg Manifesto' are to those of Deleuze and Guattari, especially as articulated in *Anti-Oedipus* and *A Thousand Plateaus*. It would hardly be surprising, for example, to find this sentence in *Capitalism and Schizophrenia*: 'The cyborg is a creature in a post-gender world; it has no truck with bisexuality, pre-oedipal symbiosis, unalienated labor, or other seductions to organic wholeness' (Haraway 1991: 150). When Haraway says that 'the cyborg has no origin story' (150), one cannot help but recall Deleuze and Guattari's repeated insistence that 'a line of becoming has neither beginning nor end, departure nor arrival, origin nor destination [. . .] A line of becoming has only a middle' (ATP 293). In the cyborg, says Haraway, 'the boundary between human and animal is thoroughly breached' (151), a remark that echoes Deleuze and Guattari's lengthy treatment of the boundary-breaching process of 'becoming animal' in *Kafka: Toward and Minor Literature* and in Plateau Ten of *A Thousand Plateaus*. Haraway's declaration that the cyborg undoes the distinction 'between animal-human (organism) and machine' (152) is fully compatible with the 'machinic' alternative to vitalism and mechanism that informs both volumes of *Capitalism and Schizophrenia*. When reading that the cyborg blurs 'the boundary between physical and non-physical' (153), one might think specifically of Plateau Four's 'incorporeal transformations', but in general of Deleuze and Guattari's exploration of the nuances attendant on the immanence of the virtual and the actual. That the cyborg's identity 'is fully political' (155) seems a reiteration of Deleuze and Guattari's assertion throughout *Anti-Oedipus* that all desiring-production is immediately social and political; and that cyborg identity is constructed out of 'otherness, difference, and specificity' (155) sounds like a variation on themes in all of Deleuze and Guattari's works, both those jointly and those separately written.

These striking parallels, however, are apparently coincidental. In a 2006 interview, Haraway said that she had not read Deleuze and Guattari before 2005 (Gane 2006: 156).[2] And when she did so, she was enraged by their approach to animals in Plateau Ten of *A Thousand Plateaus*. After pointing out the limitations of Derrida's thought about animals, Haraway remarks that

> Deleuze and Guattari are much, much worse. I think their becoming-animal chapter (Deleuze and Guattari, 1987: 232–309) is an insult because they don't give a flying damn about animals – critters are an excuse for their anti-oedipal project. Watch the way they excoriate old women and their dogs as they glorify the wolf pack in their 'horizon of becoming' and lines of flight. Deleuze and Guattari make me furious with their utter lack of curiosity about actual relations among animals and between animals and people, and the way they despise the figure of the domestic in their glorification of the wild in their monomaniacal anti-oedipal project. And people pick them up as if they were helpful in figuring sociality beyond the human. Nonsense! (Gane 2006: 143)

In *When Species Meet* (2008), Haraway expands on these sentiments in a four-page critique that maintains the same tone of outrage and anger (an attack, to my knowledge, unequalled in intensity elsewhere in her writings). Haraway does claim that 'there is much that I love in other work of Deleuze' (what work she does not specify), and she says she 'is indebted to Deleuze and Guattari, among others, for the ability to think in "assemblages"' (Haraway 2008: 314) – a concession muted in its generosity, given that Deleuze and Guattari *invented* the concept of the assemblage. But in the Becomings plateau she finds

> little but the two writers' scorn for all that is mundane and ordinary and the profound absence of curiosity about or respect

> for and with actual animals, even as innumerable references to diverse animals are invoked to figure the authors' anti-Oedipal and anticapitalist project. (Haraway 2008: 27)

The Becomings plateau articulates 'a philosophy of the sublime, not the earthly, not the mud' (28). She finds offensive Deleuze and Guattari's assertion that '*anyone who likes cats or dogs is a fool*' (ATP 240), but their most egregious statement is that 'Ahab's Moby Dick is not like the little cat or dog owned by an elderly woman who honors and cherishes it' (ATP 244). Haraway comments,

> The old, female, small, dog- and cat-loving: these are who and what must be vomited out by those who will become-animal. Despite the keen competition, I am not sure I can find in philosophy a clearer display of misogyny, fear of aging, incuriosity about animals, and horror at the ordinariness of the flesh, here covered by the alibi of an anti-Oedipal and anticapitalist project. (Haraway 2008: 30)

Haraway reads a lot into one sentence. Misogyny? Agreed, Deleuze and Guattari at times lapse into inadvertent sexism, and this reference to the *vieille dame* and her pet is a particularly insensitive instance of it. But the aims of their project are hardly misogynistic. They privilege 'becoming-woman', saying 'all becomings begin with and pass through becoming-woman. It is the key to all other becomings' (ATP 277). And whatever one makes of this controversial concept, the motivation behind the concept is scarcely misogynistic. Ageism? The dog-loving 'vieille dame' is opposed to Captain Ahab, who at age fifty-eight and a veteran of forty years at sea (and an amputee, let us remember) is hardly young, especially by the standards of the nineteenth century. *Fear* of ageing and *horror* at the ordinariness of the flesh? It's hard to know how to respond, since there are no signs of fear or horror in the sentence that so offends Haraway, and I find no such fear or horror anywhere in the works of Deleuze or Guattari. Contempt for cat and dog lovers? It is interesting that Haraway quotes Deleuze and Guattari's dismissal of this group as fools, but not the ensuing passages in which they argue that 'There is always the possibility that a given animal, a louse, a cheetah or an elephant, will be treated as a pet, my little beast. And at the other extreme, it is also possible for any animal to be treated in the mode of the pack or swarm [. . .] Even the cat, even the dog' (ATP 241). Cleary, Deleuze and Guattari's target is the sentimental infantilisation of animals, something Haraway herself castigates as 'the neurosis of caninophiliac narcissism' (Haraway 2003: 33). Incuriosity about animals and scorn for the ordinary? I cannot agree, but I will return to these questions in a bit.

Besides what she sees as 'the systematic nausea D&G let loose in their chapter in response to all that is ordinary', Haraway is concerned by the incessant talk of multiplicities, metamorphoses and lines of flight. Real animals are individuals, she insists, and her effort is to 'own up to the fraught tangle of relatings called "individuals"'. What she calls 'becoming-with animals' is not the same as becoming-animal.

> I think of all the conversations among humans watching their canine buddies at an ordinary dog park that lead them to a larger civic and artistic world, as well as exchanges about poop bags and dog diets. These are not becoming-animal, but they are about ordinary, daily becoming-with that does not seem very Oedipal to me. (Haraway 2008: 314–15)

Haraway is correct that her becoming-with animals is not the same as Deleuze and Guattari's becoming-animal, but the difference is subtle. Most often when Haraway discusses becoming-with animals, she focuses on human–dog partners who live together and change one another through their ongoing daily interactions. This is the domain of the ordinary, the mundane, the earthly, the mud, which, according to Haraway, Deleuze and Guattari scorn. And indeed, Deleuze and Guattari show no interest in detailing the dynamics of such human–animal interactions. (Whether this stems from scorn for domesticated animals I will address later.) But in the broadest sense, Haraway's becoming-with denotes symbiotic, co-evolving relations of otherness that bring multiple species together in complex combinations. Deleuze and Guattari in fact make reference in the Becomings plateau to several instances of such becoming-with that Haraway would recognise: orchid–wasp, cat–baboon–C virus, roots–microorganisms (ATP 238), truffle–tree–fly–pig (ATP 242), tick–mammal (ATP 278). She derides the ecstatic sublimity of Deleuze and Guattari's description of becoming's proliferation via 'contagions, epidemics, battlefields and catastrophes' (ATP 241), but Deleuze and Guattari also forgo such rhetorical flourishes at times and simply speak of alliances (ATP 233, 238, 243–4, 246–9, 278, 291) and symbiosis (ATP 242, 249–50, 258), terms Haraway herself uses. To my mind, Deleuze and Guattari's references to various symbiotic relations hardly suggest an 'incuriosity about animals', and their talk of orchids, tics, pigs, plant roots and viruses is scarcely symptomatic of 'a philosophy of the sublime, not the earthly, not the mud' (Haraway 2008: 28).[3]

What sets 'becoming with animals' apart from becoming-animal is that in Haraway there is no distinction between the virtual and the actual, between de- and reterritorialisation, whereas in Deleuze and Guattari the distinction is fundamental. Misreadings of Deleuze and Guattari, such as Haraway's, arise because the concept of 'becoming-other' (a term I will use to cover the gamut of specific becomings) is mistaken for 'becoming' as it is construed in the traditional opposition of being and becoming. Haraway, Deleuze and Guattari all embrace a general ontology of becoming, but for Deleuze and Guattari that sense of 'becoming' characterises the real, both actual and virtual, whereas 'becoming-other' pertains to the virtual alone. Deleuze and Guattari are fascinated by the *noce contre nature* of orchid and wasp, the strange alliances of truffle–tree–fly–pig and tic–mammal, but their focus is on the becomings immanent within these assemblages, the zones of indiscernibility that make possible the relatively stable relations among species in long-term alliances. Not all aspects of a given species-alliance are becomings, although becomings are always immanent within every alliance.

The concept of 'becoming-other' identifies something extracted from the real, a dimension with a different time and different identities and modes of relation. Deleuze and Guattari's attention is directed to moments of transition, mutation and metamorphosis – not so much moments within the general flow of common-sense time (becoming writ large) as moments 'between time', in a floating time of the infinitive, whose real-world extension may be as fleeting as a nanosecond or as prolonged as an hour, a season, a life or an epoch. The identity of a becoming-other is that of an atmosphere, an aura, a 'thisness' ('haecceity'), and this identity is constitutively multiple. What Haraway derides as Deleuze and Guattari's ecstatic sublime is rather a rhetoric designed to evoke a qualitatively 'other' world, one that indeed is dramatically figured in Ahab's becoming-whale, but that is also evoked in the quiet of Mrs Dalloway's walk through the streets of London (ATP 263) or the subtleties of James's becoming-woman in *What Maisie Knew* and *Daisy Miller* (ATP 290). If a genuine becoming-other were to transpire in what Haraway terms a becoming-with, say between her and her dog, Haraway and dog would enter a zone of indiscernibility in which, immanent within the dog, would be both a pack and an anomalous individual (and a pack and anomalous individual immanent within Haraway). In no way does this virtual becoming-other ignore the actual individuality of Haraway and her dog. It simply names something else, a mode of existence that at its highest level of deterritorialisation may be characterised only in terms of configurations of speeds and intensities on a plane of consistency.

At the species level, Haraway's 'becoming-with' comes closer to Deleuze and Guattari's 'becoming-other'. Companion species, she says, 'is a permanently undecidable category [. . .] that does not predetermine the status of the species as artifact, machine, landscape, organism or human being', that has 'the relation as the smallest unit of being and of analysis' and that is at once singular and plural, for 'every species is a multispecies crowd' (Haraway 2008: 165). But there is also a moment in *When Species Meet* when Haraway describes an experience with her dog that Deleuze and Guattari would label a genuine becoming-dog. Haraway describes this moment in terms of the joy of purposeless play, a moment that only emerges fully in such rare performance-events as a flawless agility-run in a competition.

> Unexpected conjunctions and coordination of creatively moving partners in play take hold of both and put them into an

> open that feels something like an eternal present or suspension of time, a high of 'getting it' together in action, or what I am calling joy. (Haraway 2008: 241)

It is only in this unfolding continuum of floating time, differential speeds and intensive affects that Haraway sets forth on a genuine becoming-dog.

Domestication

Despite Haraway's objections, I find complementarity in her becoming-with and Deleuze and Guattari's becoming-other. There is no inherent conflict between her concern with interspecies symbiosis and the quotidian relations between humans and animals, on one hand, and Deleuze and Guattari's interest in the creative becomings of art that emerge in human–animal zones of indiscernibility, on the other. Haraway claims that Deleuze and Guattari despise the domestic and glorify the wild, and hence that her becoming-with is antithetical to their becoming-other, but even this distinction is not so certain. For Haraway, a supposed valorisation of wolves over dogs in *A Thousand Plateaus* is paradigmatic of Deleuze and Guattari's scorn for the domestic, but dogs, Deleuze and Guattari assert, may be partners in a becoming-other, and indeed they speak at several points of a process of becoming-dog (ATP 29, 34, 36, 244, 249, 258–9, 268, 274–5, 278). Sometimes they stress the wild side of dogs (Penthesilea's joining her hunting dogs in devouring Achilles, for example), but sometimes not. True, Deleuze and Guattari consistently use the words 'domestic', 'domesticated' and 'domestication' to denote negative processes of control, restriction, repression and limitation, but domestication may be construed in a way that Deleuze and Guattari could affirm as a positive process. And such a construal, surprisingly, is that of domestication as a process of 'becoming-with'.

Haraway says that she adapts the term 'becoming-with' from Vinciane Despret (Haraway 2008: 308), who develops a new definition of domestication in her article 'The Body We Care For: Figures of Anthropo-zoo-genesis' (2004). Despret opens her essay with a reflection on the famous case of 'Clever Hans', the horse who supposedly could perform mathematical calculations and signal his answers by tapping his right hoof on the floor. Oskar Pfungst, who published the results of his careful study of Hans in 1911, concluded that the horse was not a gifted mathematician but a discerning reader of human movements. Pfungst discovered that humans who elicited correct responses from Hans involuntarily bent their heads and trunks towards Hans the moment Hans's tapping reached the correct answer. Despret remarks that 'the horse could not count, but he could do something more interesting: not only could he read bodies, but he could make human bodies be moved and be affected, and move and affect other beings and perform things without their owners' knowledge' (Despret 2004: 113). From Pfungst's account of his experiments, Despret deduces further that Hans not only could respond to involuntary human movements, but also could teach humans how to respond to his tapping. Humans who initially could not elicit correct responses from Hans, but who persisted in working with Hans, eventually became successful partners by learning via Hans's cues to nod in the appropriate manner. Hans 'made them move otherwise, he changed the habits of their bodies and made them talk another language. He taught them how to be affected differently in order to affect differently' (Despret 2004: 116).

The relationship between Hans and his partners, Despret argues, is a specialised version of the relationship between horse and rider that emerges over time as the two become attuned to one another. Citing the work of the ethologist Jean-Claude Barrey, Despret notes that skilled riders unconsciously develop movements that are analogues of their horses' movements, such that 'talented riders behave and move like horses'. When humans and horses have reached mutual attunement, 'human bodies have been transformed by and into a horse's body'. Who influences and who is influenced, however, is undecidable. 'Both, human and horse, are cause and effect of each other's movements. Both induce and are induced, affect and are affected' (Despret 2004: 115). What distinguishes Hans from other horses is that he 'was able to switch from one sense (the sense of kinaesthesia) to another: the visual. Talented horses generally read through their skin and their muscles. Hans could read all these signals visually. Hans was truly talented' (Despret 2004: 115).

The case of Clever Hans is usually cited to caution researchers against unconscious bias in experimentation with animals, but Despret argues that the ideal of pure objectivity in such experimentation misconstrues the relationship between researchers and their animal subjects, in which both parties affect, and are affected by, one another, even in the laboratory. To support this claim, Despret reviews Rosenthal's 1966 experiment with rats designed to confirm the existence of the 'Clever Hans effect', whereby animal researchers unconsciously influence experimental results. Rosenthal divided a class of students into two groups, giving each student a rat whose task was to learn to negotiate a maze. One student group was told that their rats were selectively bred to be especially intelligent, the other group that their rats were especially dull. In fact, the rats had been bred under identical conditions. As Rosenthal expected, the 'bright' rats performed well, the 'dull' rats poorly. The object of Rosenthal's study, however, was not simply to confirm the Clever Hans effect, but to determine the causes of the result, and in this, Despret finds Rosenthal wanting. Rosenthal's ideal experimenter, he said, would be an automaton – someone incapable of being affected, and hence able to test rats without personally affecting them – and his assumption was that students alone produced the results. But Despret sees evidence in Rosenthal's own report that students and rats together participated in a process of mutual attunement. The students 'put their trust in their rats, emotional trust, trust that is conveyed in gestures, in students' bodies, in all these rats' bodies that were manipulated, caressed, handled, fed and encouraged'. The result was that 'the students succeeding in attuning their rats to their beliefs', and 'these beliefs brought into existence new identities for the students and for the rats' (Despret 2004: 122).

The emotional relations between students and rats, 'made of expectations, faith, belief, trust' (Despret 2004: 122), are representative constituents of the practice that Despret calls 'domestication'. Domestication, she says, is 'an "anthropo-zoo-genetic practice", a practice that constructs animal and human'. In the case of Rosenthal's experiment, 'the rat proposes to the student, while the student proposes to the rat, a new manner of becoming together, which provides new identities' and opportunities 'to disclose new forms of "being together"' (Despret 2004: 122). Crucial to this 'becoming together', says Despret, is belief, which she defines as 'what makes entities "available" to events' (Despret 2004: 122). What Rosenthal's experiment showed was 'how an affected and affecting student makes himself available to the "becoming" of the rat, as well as how the rat makes itself available to the "becoming" of the student' (Despret 2004: 123). Despret cautions, however, that 'becoming available' is not the same as 'being docile'. Becoming available entails the possibility of resistance, whereas being docile does not. Becoming available is the process Despret labels domestication. Despret does not name the process that creates docile beings, but it seems to conform to the common notion of domestication as subjugation. I would argue, then, that the distinction between becoming available and being docile invites us to differentiate between positive and negative domestication, the one grounded in mutuality and freedom, the other in domination and subservience.

The similarities between Despret's domestication and Deleuze and Guattari's becoming-animal are striking. First is the obvious Spinozistic orientation that Despret shares with Deleuze and Guattari. All three define bodies in terms of their affects – their powers of affecting and being affected. Clever Hans possessed an unusual power of being affected by humans, but he in turn 'taught them how to be affected differently in order to affect differently' (Despret 2004: 116). Likewise, Deleuze and Guattari look at various animals in terms of 'the active and passive affects of which the animal is capable in the individuated assemblage of which it is a part' (ATP 257). Second is the authors' close association of affects with becoming. For Deleuze and Guattari, of course, affects are central to becoming – indeed, 'Affects are becomings', they say, and 'the reality of a becoming-animal [. . .] is affect in itself' (ATP 256, 259). In the case of Despret, the process of mutual becoming between animals and humans pervades her analysis, as when she discerns in Rosenthal's experiment 'how an affected and affecting student makes himself available to the "becoming" of the rat, as well as how the rat makes itself available to the "becoming" of the student' (Despret 2004: 123). Third is the emphasis the authors place on the event. For Despret, domestication requires belief, which she defines as being available to events. For Deleuze and Guattari, becoming-other discloses *Aion*, 'the indefinite time of the event', 'the time of the pure event or of becoming', 'something that is of the order of the event, of becoming or of the haecceity' (ATP 262–4).[4] Finally, Despret's domestication and Deleuze and Guattari's becoming-animal open possibilities for alternative modes of existence. For Despret, domestication discloses 'a new manner of becoming together, [. . .] provides new identities [. . .] new forms of "being together"' Despret 2004: 122). In Deleuze and Guattari, implicit throughout the Becomings plateau is a valorisation of becoming-other as a means of inventing new possibilities for life, something they make explicit later in *What is Philosophy?*, where they associate becoming with the creation of a 'new earth' and a 'new people' (WP 99, 101, 108–10, 112).

Clearly, the range of phenomena included within Deleuze and Guattari's concept of becoming-animal is much broader than that encompassed in Despret's notion of domestication, but the similarities suggest that the investigations of Despret, and those of Haraway, complement rather than clash with those of Deleuze and Guattari. The work of Despret and Haraway explores in detail aspects of human–animal relations that Deleuze and Guattari ignore and that deserve consideration within their category of becoming-animal. Despret's positive characterisation of domestication invites us to consider human relations with what are commonly called domesticated species as alliances and symbiotic relations equally demonstrative of a becoming-animal as those between orchid and wasp, or humans and wolves. Despret's and Haraway's attention to the gentle affects attendant on the care, trust, belief and availability of 'becoming-with' offers a necessary corrective to the assumption that Deleuze and Guattari's becoming-animal is inherently violent – something their rhetoric at times invites, as when they speak of becoming-animal as proliferating through 'contagion, epidemics, battlefields, and catastrophes' (ATP 241). And Despret's distinction between 'becoming available' and 'being docile' offers a useful means of understanding Deleuze and Guattari's statement that any animal may be treated as a pet, and any pet may give rise to a genuine becoming. In Despret's terms, the question for Deleuze and Guattari would not be whether an animal is wild or domestic, but whether it is engaged by humans in a process of mutual becoming-available, or one of subjugating the animal and making it docile.

Cyborgs and Technics

In her 2003 manifesto, Haraway says, 'I have come to see cyborgs as junior siblings in the much bigger queer family of companion species' (Haraway 2003: 11). Before considering the implications of this reclassification, I would like to return to Haraway's concept of the cyborg and use it to explore another dimension of Deleuze and Guattari's approach to the non-human. As noted above, one may find echoes of all the cyborg's primary characteristics in Deleuze and Guattari, but Haraway's object of analysis differs greatly from that of Deleuze and Guattari. Her interest is in the human–machine–organism interface of what she calls 'technoscience', a sociocultural coalescence of technology and science that emerges in the nineteenth century and becomes dominant in the late twentieth century. Deleuze and Guattari, by contrast, are focused on machines in the broadest sense of the term, especially in *Anti-Oedipus*, where everything is treated as a machine. Desiring machines are what interest Deleuze and Guattari, not machines in the ordinary sense of the term, whether high-tech or primitive, which they label 'technical machines' (AO 141). As a result, the specifics of modern technology per se are seldom addressed in *Capitalism and Schizophrenia*. For those who study Deleuze and Guattari, then, Haraway's work on cyborgs and technoscience maps territory they never explored and that deserves further consideration from a Deleuze–Guattarian perspective. It also points to a larger topic that Deleuze and Guattari scarcely address, and one that Haraway herself shies away from – that of technology in the broadest sense of *tekhnē*, or 'technics'. Haraway's 'cyborg story', she says, 'is a fairly historically limited one' (Gane 2006: 146), and she resists subsuming the cyborg within a general account of humans' relationship to technics. Yet that relationship, I believe, is one that needs further elaboration, both in Haraway and in Deleuze and Guattari.

Here, Bernard Stiegler's philosophy of technics offers a useful means of connecting the ubiquitous desiring-machines of *Anti-Oedipus* and the historically delimited cyborgs of technoscience. For Stiegler, the evolution of *Homo sapiens* and the development of *tekhnē* are inseparable, and in that sense technics are constitutive of human being. Stiegler calls technics 'tertiary retention', a concept he derives from Husserl. Husserl identifies primary retention as the synthesis of time that establishes the present as a flow, and secondary retention as memory in the common sense of the term. Husserl insists that the secondary retention of memory is internal to consciousness and in no way dependent on anything external to it, but Stiegler argues that all memory requires some external support, some element outside consciousness that functions as a tool, a prosthesis that humans create and that simultaneously creates them. Such an external support is a 'tertiary retention', an external collective memory whose fundamental components are tools and language. 'A tool is, before anything else, memory' (Stiegler 1998: 254), the simplest, most primitive flint shard retaining the memory of its social construction. Likewise, language is a tool, in that it, too, retains in its signs the memory of its social, cultural and historical construction. *Logos* and *tekhnē*, far from being opposed, are simply different modes of tertiary retention. Humans and their tools form a single evolutionary complex, and it is via collective memory and its socio-material supports that humans are able to evolve in a fashion unlike that of other species.

Stiegler identifies three periods in the history of technics and society: artisanal culture, industrial culture and hyperindustrial culture (Stiegler 2011a: 4). In artisanal cultures, the tool is a material retention of its invention, construction and previous implementation, but its use is dependent on the artisan's know-how, which is developed through a social memory passed on from artisan to artisan. In industrial cultures, artisanal tools give way to industrial machines, which incorporate in their workings the know-how that formerly belonged exclusively to the artisan. Artisans are 'proletarianised', de-skilled, deprived of their *savoir-faire* and reduced to being ancillary operators of tools rather than active users (Stiegler 2010: 37). In hyperindustrial cultures, the proletarianisation of machine operators continues, but a new form of proletarianisation emerges as well, a universal de-skilling that induces a loss of both *savoir-faire* and *savoir-vivre*, the knowledge of how to live (Stiegler 2010: 27). Central to the formation of hyper-industrial culture is the thorough integration of consumption with capitalist production and the emergence of what Stiegler calls the 'consciousness market' or the 'programming industry' (Stiegler 2011b: 73–4). Through mass media, saturated with the values of consumerism manufactured by the programming industry, the collective tertiary retention of social memory is synchronised, standardised and made a functional component of capitalist production.

There is no clear conceptual counterpart to Stiegler's tertiary retention in Deleuze and Guattari, but Stiegler's history of technics does resonate with passages in *A Thousand Plateaus*. Stiegler relies on Henri Leroi-Gourhan's account of hominin evolution to support his argument that technics are constitutive components of human evolution, and Deleuze and Guattari make use of the same account in their description of the 'alloplastic' stratum of human culture (ATP 60). Leroi-Gourhan argues that bipedalism freed human hands from their locomotive function and thereby made possible the invention and manipulation of tools, while simultaneously freeing the mouth from its grasping function to allow the development of language. For Stiegler, Deleuze and Guattari, the emergence of the hand–tool and face–language couples is decisive in human evolution. Stiegler's distinction between artisanal and industrial culture is also echoed in Deleuze and Guattari's differentiation of 'machinic enslavement' and 'social subjection'. In pre-industrial cultures, humans are components of social machines and hence subject to 'machinic enslavement'. With the advent of industrial culture, however, humans become adjuncts to the machine, 'no longer a component of the machine but a worker, a user [. . .] subjected *to* the machine and no longer enslaved *by* the machine' (ATP 457). In the contemporary age of 'cybernetic and informational machines' (ATP 457), a new order emerges in which machinic enslavement and social subject coexist, as media and markets subsume humans within a general culture of 'processes of normalization, modification, modeling and information' (ATP 458).

Deleuze and Guattari's account of industrial social subjection and the cybernetic and informational conjunction of social subjection and machinic enslavement is complementary with Stiegler's characterisation of technics in industrial and hyperindustrial cultures. And Deleuze, Guattari and Stiegler all view the emergence of the hand–tool and face–language couples as constitutive of human beings as a species. This suggests, I would argue, that through Stiegler's philosophy of technics we may expand upon the implications of Deleuze and Guattari's approach to 'technical machines' within their general machinics. And via Stiegler's technics we may situate Haraway's cyborg as a specific configuration of human and non-human elements within the species-constitutive process of prosthetic tertiary retention.

Cyborg or Dog?

Haraway's treatment of the cyborg, then, when situated within Stiegler's philosophy of technics, may be used to determine the specific ways in which technics and technoscience might function as means of becoming-other within Deleuze and Guattari's conceptual framework. And her work on human–dog relations, when filtered through Despret's notion of domestication, helps suggest dimensions of becoming-animal in Deleuze and Guattari that were never developed in their writings. But Haraway proposes to collapse the distinction between cyborgs and human–dog couples by including 'cyborgs as junior siblings in the much bigger queer family of companion species' (Haraway 2003: 11). What makes this subsumption possible is the adoption of a very broad definition of 'species': 'By species I mean, with thanks to Karen Barad's theory of agential realism and intra-action, a kind of intra-ontics/intra-antics that does not predetermine the status of the species as artifact, machine, landscape, organism, or human being' (Haraway 2008: 165). Haraway's dominant focus in *When Species Meet* is on human–dog relations, and hence the implications of this broad definition of species are not always apparent. But in a chapter devoted to her father and the prostheses that enabled him to lead a full life, the wide range of Haraway's category of 'companion species' is made evident. As a child, Haraway's father developed tuberculosis, which calcified his hip joints and permanently limited his mobility. Nonetheless, with the aid of a wheelchair he was able to play baseball as a boy, and with crutches he was able to become a successful sports writer as a man. When he was young, the 'wheelchair was in a companion-species relation to the boy; the whole body was organic flesh as well as wood and metal; the player was on wheels, grinning' (Haraway 2008: 167). For her father,

> To be in a companion-species relationship was the viable way of life. He was lucky to have a concatenated series of partners, including the wheelchair, the crutches, and the attention and resources of his parents and friends. (Haraway 2008: 170–1)

According to Haraway's earlier terminology, her father clearly would have qualified as a cyborg, and I question whether his relation to his wheelchair and crutches should be included within his relation to parents and friends as so many configurations of companion species. Better, I would argue, would be to view the conjunction of boy–wheelchair–crutches–parents–friends as an assemblage, and to preserve the figures of both the cyborg and companion species as potential constituents of various assemblages. The concepts of cyborgs and companion species each serve important functions. The notion of companion species is grounded in the human–dog relation, and that relation, when properly enacted, may give rise to an ethics of care, respect and responsibility for otherness that entails the same responsiveness towards every species, whether 'artifact, machine, landscape, organism or human being' (Haraway 2008: 165). The cyborg, by contrast, emphasises the interpenetration of humans, machines and natural systems and an attendant oppositional politics of 'otherness, difference and specificity' (Haraway 1991: 155). The two models reinforce one another, but each does a different kind of work, and in very different rhetorical terms. Both the conceptual movement from dogs to cyborgs and the movement from cyborgs to dogs strain in the middle, and that tension is valuable. Becoming-machine and becoming-animal may interpenetrate, but their specificity should be maintained.

The question, finally, is whether any master trope should be used to characterise all cosmic processes of becoming. I believe not, and for that reason I would reject Haraway's companion species model as well as the machine model that Deleuze and Guattari adopt in *Anti-Oedipus*. It is better to employ multiple figures and discursive registers to describe the cosmos. This is precisely what Deleuze and Guattari do in *A Thousand Plateaus*, and the terms and language they use, in my judgement, are more advantageous for a comprehensive philosophy of the real than those of cyborgs and companion species. The language of *A Thousand Plateaus* is insistently abstract yet figural – planes of consistency, speeds and intensities, abstract machines and assemblages, haecceities, lines of flight, refrains, rhizomes, strata, smooth and striated space, and so on – and such language opens a conceptual space within which thought may traverse received categories in ways that are not afforded by the concepts of cyborgs and companion species. Within this space, various becomings may be traced, each of which opens a zone of indiscernibility between the human and non-human, between the animal and machine, the vegetable and mineral, the organic and inorganic.

Haraway's extended meditations on cyborgs and companion species suggest significant ways in which Deleuze and Guattari's thought might be extended into areas they left largely unexamined, specifically the dynamics of becoming-other in technoscientific culture and animal domestication. Haraway's concept of the cyborg, when conjoined with Stiegler's philosophy of technics, offers a means of mapping a becoming-machine specific to what Deleuze and Guattari call 'technical machines'. And her concept of companion species, when combined with Despret's notion of domestication as 'anthropo-zoo-genesis', helps chart a becoming-animal midway between the wild and the docile. It is unfortunate that Haraway so thoroughly misreads Deleuze and Guattari and hence never genuinely encounters their work. But that should not prevent students of Deleuze and Guattari from reading Haraway, for she has much to offer in exploring the paths of becoming-other in Deleuze and Guattari that lead from the human to multiple domains of the non-human.

Notes

1. Grebowicz and Merrick (2013) have shown in great detail the extent to which the influence of 'A Cyborg Manifesto' has overshadowed that of the rest of Haraway's work. See esp. pp. 147–64.
2. Haraway's reasons for not reading Deleuze and Guattari are curious. Late in the interview, after having lambasted Deleuze and Guattari's concept of 'becoming animal', she remarks: 'I refused to read Deleuze and Guattari until last year. I'm a very recent reader, and now I know why I refused to read them. Everyone kept saying I'm a Deleuzian, and I kept saying "no way". This is one of the ways women thinkers are made to seem derivative of male philosophers, who are often their contemporaries – made to seem derivative and the same, when we are neither' (Gane 2006: 156). Apparently, she knew she was not Deleuzian without having read Deleuze, and she refused to read Deleuze and Guattari for reasons only revealed after she had read them ('and now I know why I refused to read them'). It is hard to avoid the conclusion that Haraway was far from a sympathetic reader when she finally examined their texts.
3. Had Haraway continued reading beyond the Becomings plateau, she would have found in Plateau Eleven, 'Of the Refrain', substantial evidence that Deleuze and Guattari are very much interested in animals, with passages devoted to the relationship between spiders and flies and between bumblebees and snapdragons (ATP 314), the mating dance of the stickleback fish (ATP 317), the function of the grass stem in several species of Australian grass finches (ATP 324–5), the migratory behaviour of salmon, locusts, chaffinches and lobsters (ATP 326), and the complex assemblage of territorial components of the stagemaker bird (ATP 315–16, 331, 336).
4. Despret's notion of 'being available to events' also resonates with remarks Deleuze made in the first section of the film interview *L'Abécédaire de Gilles Deleuze*, 'A is for Animal'. There Deleuze spoke of always being 'on the lookout' (*aux aguets*) for encounters, and he associated this process of being 'aux aguets' with animals. See Beaulieu (2011: 71, 83) and Stivale (2014: 69–71, 78–80).

19

Vitalism and the Force That Is But Does Not Act: Ruyer, Leibniz and Deleuze

In an essay on Leibniz and Deleuze, Daniel W. Smith aptly observes, 'In the end, Deleuze does with Leibniz what he does with every figure in the history of philosophy: through an extraordinarily careful conceptual reading, Deleuze ultimately makes *use* of Leibniz's philosophy and Leibniz's concepts in the pursuit of his own philosophical aims' (Smith 2010: 151). The same may be said of Raymond Ruyer, whose philosophy of biology plays an important though often unrecognised role in Deleuze's thought.[1] In Ruyer's case, however, Deleuze executes a double appropriation – that of using Ruyer to assist in his use of Leibniz. A helpful way of approaching this double appropriation is to reflect on Deleuze and Guattari's statement in *What is Philosophy?* that

> Vitalism has always had two possible interpretations: that of an Idea that acts, but is not – that acts therefore only from the point of view of an external cerebral knowledge (from Kant to Claude Bernard); or that of a force that is but does not act – that is therefore a pure internal Awareness [*Sentir*] (from Liebniz to Ruyer). (WP 213)

Deleuze and Guattari's characterisation of the first type of vitalism clearly draws on Chapter 18 of Raymond Ruyer's *Néo-finalisme* (Ruyer 1952: 205–27; 2012: 225–48),[2] in which Ruyer critiques Kant and Bernard for separating a directing 'idea' from physical forces, thereby rendering inexplicable the efficacy of the idea within the material world. That characterisation of Kant and

Bernard is defensible, but describing the second form of vitalism as 'that of a force that is but does not act', while perhaps valid for Leibniz, seems difficult to sustain in the case of Ruyer. To determine the significance of this characterisation of Ruyer's vitalism requires a detailed account of Ruyer's thought in relation to Kant and Bernard, a close examination of Deleuze's presentation of Ruyer in *The Fold* as 'the latest of Leibniz's great disciples' (TF 102), and a final assessment of this characterisation within the context of *What is Philosophy?*

Kant, Bernard and Organicism

In Chapter 18 of *Néo-finalisme* Ruyer examines several biological theories that he groups under the broad category of 'organicism'. Organicism, he says, 'wants neither to reduce the organism to physico-chemical phenomena, nor to explicate organic specificity through a distinct principle, whether vital principle or soul [*âme*], that would intervene *dynamically* in the unfolding of physical phenomena' (Ruyer 1952: 205; 2012: 225). Organicists claim to avoid the extremes of mechanistic determinism and vitalistic finalism by treating the organism as a totality or whole rather than a mere collection of parts. Ruyer observes that organicism has the advantage of accommodating positivistic scientific experimentation while resisting reductivist accounts of organisms as mere physico-chemical processes, yet without any appeal to a force that intervenes in the formation of biological entities. 'Unfortunately,' Ruyer adds, 'this advantageous doctrine has the weakness of only existing verbally. Organicism is an empty concept that designates nothing real; it is a "square circle"' (Ruyer 1952: 206; 2012: 226). Without some dynamic self-forming force of its own, the organicists' 'whole' can only be left unexplained, or be explained as a product of mechanical forces; its supposed irreducibility to its constituent elements in either case proves to be a mere fiction.

Ruyer finds the roots of the organicist position in Kant. While affirming the universal validity of the mechanistic and deterministic laws of causality in the physical world, Kant maintains that the teleological judgement is also legitimate, though only through reflective judgement. Kant admits that purposiveness is visibly evident in nature, but he deems illegitimate any assertion of purposiveness as a cause in the formation or behaviour of specific living beings. The only means of bringing determinism and purposiveness together is through God, who simultaneously establishes the laws of nature and the final purpose of the universe. The faculty of understanding regards nature as deterministic, the faculty of reason sees nature as purposive, and the faculty of judgement harmonises the two faculties, but only by rising to the supersensible and by uniting understanding and reason in an unknown manner. The final cause, then, 'is not a force, but only a point of view, legitimate moreover and indispensable, not only for living beings but also for the entire world' (Ruyer 1952: 208; 2012: 228).

Ruyer sees in the biologist Claude Bernard (1813–78) a position similar to that of Kant. In his *Lessons on the Phenomena of Life Common to Animals and Plants* (1878), Bernard argues that a guiding idea presides over the growth of every organism, and that this idea, 'and this idea alone, creates and directs' (cited in Ruyer 1952: 208; 2012: 228). Yet the idea does not directly participate in the physical world: 'The vital force directs the phenomena it does not produce; the physical agents produce the phenomena they do not direct' (cited in Ruyer 1952: 208; 2012: 228). The idea is a metaphysical entity, and Bernard deems it a great error 'to believe that this metaphysical force is active' (cited in Ruyer 1952: 208; 2012: 228). But Bernard never specifies precisely how the metaphysical idea and physical phenomena interact. Instead, like Kant, Bernard posits the unity of the two levels as mysteriously arising out of the creation of the universe, from an 'initial impulse', both biological and cosmic, that serves the same function as God in Kant's system.

Perhaps the vitalism of Kant and Bernard may be construed as 'that of an Idea that acts, but is not', in that the Idea has no physical existence, and yet mysteriously manages to direct the formation of physical phenomena. In the case of Kant especially one may say that the Idea acts 'only from the point of view of an external cerebral knowledge', given that the purposiveness of nature is evident only through a reflective judgement. But one might just as well describe this vitalism as that of an idea 'that is but does not act', especially in the case of Bernard, who explicitly denies that the metaphysical directive force is active. And indeed, Deleuze himself characterises the vitalism of Kant and Bernard in such terms in *The Fold*, noting that their vitalism 'breaks with animism, all the while keeping two levels, the one being mechanical and the other only regulative or directive, in a word, "ideal" without being active' (TF 160). For Ruyer, either characterisation would be acceptable, since both point to the fundamental problem of maintaining the existence of purposive ideas or directive forces and mechanical, deterministic physical phenomena without explaining how the two levels interact. Ruyer's solution is to argue that the forces of directive, purposive ideas and those of deterministic physical phenomena are the same forces, simply manifest in two different ways.

Forms, Aggregates, Auto-Overflight and Absolute Surfaces

Ruyer makes a basic distinction between forms and aggregates. Forms are self-structuring and self-sustaining entities whose components are connected through non-localisable relations of forces. All true forms are living forms, and the simplest of such forms is the atom. Crucial for Ruyer are the discoveries of quantum physics, according to which atomic particles are less things than activities, zones of forces sustaining a given form. A carbon atom 'is not a structure; it represents a *structuring activity*' (Ruyer 1958: 58), one that 'acts as a systemic unity and not as a summation of elementary actions' (Ruyer 1952: 218; 2012: 239). The force of the atom and of all living forms cannot be understood in terms of the laws of traditional physics because those laws pertain only to aggregates and the interactions among discretely differentiated forms. Aggregates are collections of disconnected forms devoid of any intrinsic self-structuring unity. A bucket of sand is an aggregate, as is a cloud, a mountain or a planet. They are mere accretions of atoms and molecules that take on various shapes according to mechanical laws of adhesion, erosion and so on. Aggregates are interrelated by simple contiguity, not by a non-localisable self-structuring unity. Traditional mechanics accounts for the regularities of contiguous relations, such as those among billiard balls on a table, but not for the workings of living forms. Such forms can only be understood when each living form is identified as a consciousness with agency.

This association of living forms with consciousness is not some type of anthropomorphic animism. Ruyer's object is not to attribute all aspects of human consciousness to other living forms, but instead to situate human consciousness within a continuum of living forms from atoms to humans, such that human consciousness is seen as a complex, highly specialised self-aware version of the consciousness evident in varying degrees of complexity throughout the world of living forms. An amoeba, for example, has no central nervous system, but it exhibits basic characteristics of consciousness – perception, self-generated and goal-directed activity, memory, learning, adaptation and invention. An atom has fewer powers than an amoeba, but it too is a consciousness, displaying what Ruyer regards as the fundamental attribute of consciousness – that of a self-forming form that sustains its organisational configuration through time.

Although human consciousness as a whole is not an apt model for consciousness in general, it does provide us with direct evidence of a basic element of all consciousness as the auto-overflight (*auto-survol*) of an absolute surface.[3] Ruyer explains these concepts by considering the example of Ruyer himself seated at a chequerboard-surfaced table. Ruyer points out that analyses of consciousness typically presume the necessity of an external observer in order to understand consciousness, which leads to an infinite regress, each observing consciousness requiring another behind it ad infinitum. He counters that consciousness does not operate this way. The seated Ruyer regarding the chequerboard table is in immediate possession of the table surface of his perception. There is no distinction between perceiver and perceived, between having the perception and being the perception. His consciousness is in '*self-enjoyment*' (Ruyer 1952: 81; 2012: 93)[4] of the table surface, everywhere present on that surface as if in a non-localisable 'auto-overflight' across the surface. That surface is 'absolute', in that the mechanistic laws of time and space do not apply to it. Consciousness is present everywhere and nowhere, passing at an infinite speed across the surface. It perceives all the squares of the chequerboard design at once, sensing them as a whole while maintaining their separate identities. The squares, if considered from the vantage of a single square, are related by mere contiguity, or in Ruyer's favourite phrases, *partes extra partes* (Latin, 'parts outside parts'), or *de proche en proche* (French, literally, 'from close to close', idiomatically 'by degrees', 'closer and closer' or 'step by step'). If so considered, however, the squares would be a simple aggregate, with no genuine form. But consciousness does not function *partes extra partes*, *de proche en proche*; instead, it seizes all the parts as a single system of relations.

Themes and the Trans-spatial

This example helps explain the concepts of auto-overflight and absolute surface, but it does not sufficiently emphasise the dynamic nature of self-forming forms. Consciousness is 'essentially a *force de liaison*' (Ruyer 1952: 113; 2012: 126), a force of joining, binding or connection (all possible translations of *liaison*, a fundamental term in Ruyer's vocabulary). Its ubiquitous overflight of an absolute surface is an active making and sustaining of *liaisons*. A living form is a self-sustaining activity in which there is no distinction between shape and force, between what it is and what it does. Consciousness is a material 'consciousness-force' (Ruyer 1946: 293) inseparable from the *liaison*-organised form it enacts.

Ruyer's rationale for identifying consciousness and self-forming form becomes clearer when one considers the process of morphogenesis. Grasping the functioning of an already formed organism is relatively easy, its morphology lending itself to the usual reductive, mechanistic explanation of its operation – the heart, lungs, brain, nerves, muscles, bones and so on of an adult mammal working together as so many machines in complex circuits of interaction. But living organisms are machines that build themselves, and, while doing so, manage to function without the organs necessary for their survival once fully formed. They are, in fact, not machines at all, but coordinated, unified, goal-directed activities guided by memory. Morphogenesis proceeds according to a theme, which is like a musical melody that unfolds in time but that has coherence as a melody only when conceived of as a whole. The theme is 'trans-spatial' (Ruyer 1952: 132; 2012: 145), both in the sense that it is a non-localisable auto-overflight of an absolute surface, and in the sense that it exists outside the ordinary chronometric time-space in which it develops and grows. For this reason, Ruyer speaks of the trans-spatial theme as a vertical theme, which plays itself out along the horizontal axis of chronometric time. Each self-forming form capable of self-replication, from viruses and bacteria to human beings, inherits the memory of the theme that will guide it in its morphogenesis.

That memory, however, is not like a fully detailed blueprint, program or code. Ruyer rejects all versions of preformationism, arguing instead for a kind of guided epigenesis. A mouse embryo, for example, possesses the memory of its 'mouseness', a knowledge of how to make itself as a mouse, but the process of its self-formation is a task that entails invention, adaptation, adjustment and constant re-equilibration. The embryo begins with a rough sketch of its architecture, and then builds itself through progressive differentiations – first the axes of front–back, top–bottom and bilateral symmetry, then more specific differentiations, such as the bud of a limb, a right limb, a right front limb and so on. At each stage, the mouse plays out its developmental theme, but as a guided ad-hoc variation on the theme that grows increasingly detailed as it progresses. Hence, says Ruyer, 'the organism forms itself with risks and perils; it is not formed. [. . .] The living being forms itself directly according to the theme, without the theme having first to become idea-image and represented model' (Ruyer 1958: 261-2).

The developmental theme of unicellular organisms is relatively simple compared to those of complex organisms – such as mice, cats and humans – for such organisms are themselves hierarchies of self-forming forms. The organs of the mouse, for example, are self-forming forms brought under the dominance of the 'mouse form'. The mouse, then, is a colony of forms, a coordinated group project involving a hierarchy of agents. Yet the difference between 'organ' and 'individual' is not always clear. Indeed, 'the hesitation between "being an individual" and "being the organ of an individual" is found throughout the organic domain' (Ruyer 1958: 95). Since every self-forming form is a consciousness, which we may call an 'I', we may thus say of every human being, as of every complex organism, '"I" am made of all the other I's that I have already produced as if through a sort of cellular division of internal and dominated reproduction. I am a colony, both psychological and biological' (Ruyer 1958: 97).

It is important to note that Ruyer's concept of the developmental theme does not imply a conventional idealism, for the theme, though 'trans-spatial', is always immanent within the material world. The theme 'never loses contact with the spatio-temporal plane', even though it 'is not constrained to actualise in space, at every moment, the totality of the structure which it is capable of constructing' (Ruyer 1946: 13). At a mouse embryo's conception, for example, its developmental theme exists mostly as a virtual potential, but as the mouse grows, the theme becomes increasingly 'embodied' in the spatio-temporal world. If the mouse dies without offspring, the developmental theme dies with it. Should it reproduce, the developmental theme continues in its progeny, but at no point does the theme become separate from the organisms in which it is actualised.[5]

For Ruyer, then, there is no such thing as inert matter. All matter is living. 'The world is nothing but a gigantic heap of organisms, some small, some large, and the so-called "material" world is opposed to the so-called "living" world only because the former is a heap of the smallest organisms [that is, atoms]' (Ruyer 1958: 68). Every organism is a consciousness, and every consciousness is an active force, a 'formative activity' (Ruyer 1958: 238) with a trans-spatial theme. Atoms are 'pure activities' (Ruyer 1952: 162; 2012: 178), less forms than 'form-activities', whose theme is simply the continuance of the form-activity specific to each atom. At this level, the spatio-temporal and the trans-spatial are indistinguishable. Molecules, like atoms, have as their theme the mere continuance of their form, but their form-activity involves a primary colonisation of other forms, each molecule being 'a domain where energies interchange, where energy structures itself, where a structural state "chooses itself", among an essential multiplicity of possible states' (Ruyer 1958: 59). With viruses and bacteria, the developmental themes include self-replication as well as self-continuation, and with organisms of increasing complexity the themes unfold over expanding stretches of time and involve larger and larger colonisations of subordinate forms.

Ruyer and Deleuze's Leibniz

In *The Fold*, Deleuze opens Chapter 8, 'The Two Floors', by framing Leibniz's opposition of monads and bodies as one between 'distributive unities' and 'collectives, flocks or aggregates' (TF 100; trans. modified). A few pages later, he presents Ruyer as one of the 'great disciples' of Leibniz, associating Ruyer's self-forming forms with monads and his aggregates with bodies. Deleuze ingeniously extracts from Ruyer's account of forms those elements that align with Leibniz's concept of monads, while introducing the slightest deviations from Ruyer to mask Ruyer's differences with Leibniz. Tellingly, Deleuze bases his portrayal of Ruyer's living forms primarily on Ruyer's description of human perception – specifically, that of Ruyer seated at the chequerboard-surfaced table – rather than Ruyer's many accounts of living forms as dynamic processes of development. Deleuze accurately describes Ruyer's living forms as 'absolute surfaces or volumes, unitary domains of "overflight"' (TF 102; trans. modified), vertical rather than horizontal. But he adds that they are 'absolute vertical positions', which suggests that the vertical, trans-spatial theme of living forms is detached from its horizontal unfolding in time. Deleuze repeats Ruyer's assertion that there is no distinction between subject and object in consciousness' overflight of an absolute surface, but he also says that living forms are

> absolute interiorities that take hold of themselves and everything that fills them, in a process of 'self-enjoyment', by drawing from themselves all perceptions with which they are co-present on this one-sided surface, independently of receptive organs and physical excitations that do not intervene at this level. (TF 102–3)

Ruyer's forms are unities, and hence 'interiorities', but not 'absolute', if by this it is meant that they are without relation to anything outside themselves. That they draw 'from themselves all perceptions' suggests that they are not simply 'co-present' with their perceptions but generative of the perceptions, which is something Ruyer does not claim. And saying that they occur 'independently of receptive organs' only makes sense in Ruyer's terms if 'at this level' is taken to mean 'at this abstract level of analysis'.

The passage is fully coherent, however, if 'at this level' means 'at the level of Leibnizian monads "without doors or windows"'. Monads, indeed, are absolute interiorities, and their perceptions are drawn from within, in that each monad expresses the entire world and its clear perceptions emerge from the world's infinite, obscure unconscious microperceptions that it folds within itself. Those perceptions are also independent of receptive organs since the monads are souls, not bodies. But for Ruyer, living forms are inseparable from physical matter. 'The organic world makes manifest only the one great fact: form is not separable from matter. Living matter never presents itself except as formed' (Ruyer 1958: 52). Quantum physics is so important for Ruyer because, at the level of atoms, there is no distinction between form and force, being and doing, or consciousness and matter. When he differentiates living forms from aggregates, he is not opposing forms to bodies, but living bodies to aggregates of living bodies. An organism's theme is trans-spatial, and hence vertical, but it is inseparable from its temporal unfolding as matter-form, and hence not an 'absolute vertical position'.

At the end of his discussion of Ruyer, Deleuze seems to recognise something of the material dynamism of Ruyer's self-forming forms: 'genuine or absolute forms are primitive forces, essentially individual and active unities, that actualise a virtual or a potential, and that harmonise themselves one with another [*qui s'accordent les unes aux autres*] without determining themselves by contiguity [*de proche en proche*]' (TF 103; trans. modified). Once again, however, the sentence adequately describes only Leibnizian monads, not Ruyer's forms. As Deleuze explains later in the chapter, primitive forces are monadic forces, not corporeal forces, which are derivative forces. He also argues that monads actualise the virtual, whereas bodies realise the possible – hence, what Ruyer takes to be the material enactment of the trans-spatial theme is presented here as the incorporeal unfolding of the virtual within the non-material dimension of monads. Ruyer does indeed say that genuine forms do not determine themselves *partes extra partes*, but his self-forming forms interact with one another, affect one another during the course of their development, occasionally work in concert, but often conflict with one another. In his philosophy, there is no room for the pre-established harmony of monads. His forms are bodies in contact with other bodies, not forms 'that harmonise themselves with one another'.

The *Vinculum Substantiale*

There is one point at which the thought of Deleuze's Leibniz and that of Ruyer almost coincide, and that is during Deleuze's explication of Leibniz's concept of the *vinculum substantiale*.[6] Developed late in his life during his correspondence with Father Des Bosses (1706–16), the *vinculum substantiale*, or substantial bond, was introduced by Leibniz to account for the unity of composite substances. Each monad is a substance, and a body belongs to each monad. There is a real distinction between the monad and its body, but the two are inseparably united through divine pre-established harmony. Each monad is a one, complete in itself. Yet my human body has multiple components, and hence multiple corresponding monads, which somehow are unified as the single monad 'me', and the single monad 'me' possesses a single unified body, not a mere aggregation of body parts. How is it, then, that self-sufficient monads can become unified parts of another monad? Leibniz's answer is, through a *vinculum substantiale*, a relation between a dominant monad and multiple dominated monads that 'substantiates' the composed substances of the dominated monads and dominant monad as a single substance. Through the vinculum, an aggregate of dominated monads is transformed into an organised unity under the domination of a single monad. The relation between dominant and dominated monads is asymmetrical, in that the dominant monad is a constant whereas the dominated monads are variables that change over time. Just as my body remains the same even though its cells die and regenerate at various speeds, so the dominant monad maintains its oneness even as various dominated monads enter into and out of relation with the dominant monad.

The vinculum, as Christiane Frémont explains, 'is nothing but a relation', one that 'is superadded by God: not *additum*, as when one adds something, but *superadditum*, as when something is superposed or superimposed on an ensemble of elements' (Frémont 1981: 36). It is also 'a principle of action' (Frémont 1981: 37), but deprived of perception, and hence a paradoxical element, since for Leibniz the principle of action is perception. It is a pure relation and principle of action that 'belongs' to the dominant monad without being a part of that monad, and that unifies the dominated monads without being a part of them either. From Ruyer's perspective, the vinculum is precisely what is missing in Leibniz's monadology. For Ruyer, however, the vinculum, as pure relation and principle of action, is not something superadded to the world by God, but itself the fundamental principle immanent within all living forms. For him, consciousness is nothing other than the '*force de liaison*' (Ruyer 1952: 113; 2012: 126) that unifies every living form. As Ruyer's son, Bernard Ruyer, says of his father's metaphysics, it is 'in many regards a monadology, in which the monads are nothing but doors and windows' (Ruyer, B. 1995: 48).

The vinculum also provides a connection between monads and bodies that almost makes them indiscernible, and hence similar to Ruyer's living forms, which are indistinguishably mental and material. Every monad, or soul, has a body, but bodies belong to dominated monads in two different ways. Using Whitehead's opposition of public and private, Deleuze says that what is public in dominated monads is their status as constituents of an aggregate, 'their derivative state'. What is private in each monad, by contrast, is its 'in-itself by-itself' (TF 118), that is, its status as an autonomous monad. As constituents of the body of a dominant monad, each monad belongs to that body. But at the same time, each dominated monad has its own body (since for every monad there is a corresponding body). Hence, for dominated monads, there is a double belonging to two bodies, a public belonging to the body of the dominant monad, and a private belonging to the dominated monad's own body. The vinculum 'only binds souls to souls', but the vinculum

> is what inaugurates the inverse double belonging by which it ties them together. It links to a soul that possesses a body to other souls that this body possesses. Operating only on souls, the vinculum nonetheless puts into effect a back-and-forth movement from soul to body and from bodies to souls. (TF 120; trans. modified)

Souls do not act on bodies, and the belonging of a body to a soul does not constitute an action.

> But the belonging makes us enter into a strangely intermediate, or rather, original, zone, in which every body acquires the individuality of a possessive insofar as it belongs to a private soul, and souls accede to a public status; that is, they are taken in a crowd or in a heap, inasmuch as they belong to a collective body. Is it not in this zone, in this depth or this material fabric between the two levels [of monads and bodies], that the upper is folded over the lower, such that we can no longer tell where one ends and the other begins, or where the sensible ends and the intelligible begins? (TF 119; trans. modified)

Were this zone of indiscernibility to efface entirely the division between the sensible and the intelligible, we would have the universe of Ruyer's living forms. But in Deleuze's Leibniz, however complexly interfolded, monads and bodies remain distinct.

Finally, the vinculum offers a way of seeing Leibniz's primitive forces and derivative forces as a single force, which would seem to accord with Ruyer's understanding of force. One of Ruyer's constant themes is that the force of consciousness is not different from physical force – indeed, he sees the attribution of a separate force to consciousness as the central problem of traditional vitalism. There is no separate conscious force or energy: 'What appears to the physicist as a bond [*liaison*] through an energy of exchange, is nothing other than an elementary field of consciousness' (Ruyer 1958: 243). Usually, Leibnizian primitive forces are associated with monads and derivative forces with the phenomena of bodies (see Lodge 2001), a view that suggests the existence of two discrete forces. But Deleuze argues that Leibniz's primitive forces and derivative forces are the same force, simply configured differently via the vinculum.

Deleuze remarks that Leibniz often distinguishes three classes of monads: 'bare entelechies or substantial forms that only have perceptions; animal souls that have memory, feeling and attention; and, finally, reasonable souls' (TF 118). When analysed in terms of the vinculum, one may say that reasonable souls, or rational monads, are always dominant; animal monads are those that may either be dominated by a dominant vinculum or themselves dominate other monads (animal monads); and bare entelechies are those monads that do not come under the control of a vinculum. Bare entelechies, unlike the other monads, exist only as masses in constant perturbation. They are mere tendencies, whose unity of movement has to be 'recreated or reconstituted at each and every instant' (TF 117). Primitive and derivative forces are commonly divided between monads and bodies, but via the vinculum Deleuze argues that they are the same force:

> *Derivative forces are none other than primitive forces*, but they differ from them in status or aspect. Primitive forces are monads or substances in themselves and by themselves. Derivative forces are *the same*, but under a vinculum or in the flash of an instant. In one case, they are taken in multitudes [*en foules*] [. . .] while in the other they are taken in a mass [*en amas*]. (TF 117; trans. modified)

This unification of forces, however, does not bring Leibniz closer to Ruyer, since the unification takes place exclusively in the domain of monads. If derivative forces may be called mechanical or material forces, it is only 'because they belong to a body, they are present to a body, an organism or an aggregate' (TF 117). Derivative forces 'are no less really distinct from this body, and they do not act upon it any more than they act upon one another' (TF 118). It is simply the relationship of belonging that connects derivative forces to bodies. Hence, Deleuze concludes that the two floors of monads and bodies

> are really distinct and yet inseparable by dint of a presence of the upper in the lower. The upper floor is folded over the lower

> floor. There is no action of the one on the other, only belonging, double belonging. The soul is the principle of life through its presence and not through its action. *Force is presence and not action.* (TF 119; trans. modified)

Brains, Vibrations and Contemplation

The Fold, then, offers one explanation of how Leibniz's vitalism may be described as 'that of a force that is but does not act' (WP 213). But in *What is Philosophy?*, Deleuze and Guattari give the phrase another sense, one that is associated with micro-brains, the contraction of vibrations, and contemplation.

In their summary of the relationship among philosophy, art and science, Deleuze and Guattari state that '*The brain is the junction* – not the unity – *of the three planes*' (WP 208) of philosophy, art and science – the plane of immanence, the plane of composition and the plane of reference.[7] Deleuze and Guattari insist that the brain is not to be considered in terms of a map of connections among various specialised sites, nor in terms of a Gestalt of forces in relations of tension and equilibrium, since both models resort to a logic of *partes extra partes*, *de proche en proche*: 'Ready-made paths that are followed step by step [*de proche en proche*] imply a preestablished track, but trajectories constituted within a field of forces proceed through resolution of tensions also acting step by step [*de proche en proche*]' (WP 209). Instead, the brain must be seen as an 'auto-overflight', 'a "true form", primary, as Ruyer defined it: neither a Gestalt nor a perceived point of view but a *form in itself*'. Such a form 'remains copresent to all its determinations without proximity or distance, traverses them at infinite speed', and 'makes of them so many *inseparable variations* on which it confers an equipotentiality without confusion' (WP 210; trans. modified)

This account of the brain relies heavily on Ruyer, who himself speaks at length about the brain as a self-forming form. Ruyer approaches the topic via the concept of 'equipotentiality', a characteristic exhibited by embryos and, Ruyer argues, by brains as well. Embryonic cells initially are unspecified in their function, equipotential in their ability to assume various forms during the process of differentiation. (Today we speak of pluripotent stem cells.) Such equipotentiality, he argues, 'is not, properly speaking, a "property" of material tissues and their chemistry' (Ruyer 1952: 59; 2012: 66), but the characteristic of an absolute domain in auto-overflight. Experiments demonstrating the non-localisable functions of the brain lead Ruyer to conclude that the brain, too, is an absolute surface in auto-overflight, and hence equipotential. 'The brain, in the adult organism, is an area that remains embryonic.' Hence, 'the brain is an embryo that has not completed its growth', whereas 'the embryo is a brain, which begins to organise itself before it organises the external world' (Ruyer 1952: 73; 2012: 82).

Deleuze and Guattari associate the brain's auto-overflight with philosophy. In their analysis of the arts, by contrast, they identify a second function of the brain – that of contracting sensations. Something of Ruyer remains in this analysis when Deleuze and Guattari posit the existence of 'microbrains', arguing that 'not every organism has a brain, and not all life is organic, but everywhere there are forces that constitute microbrains, or an inorganic life of things' (TF 213). Ruyer could assent to this observation, since in his terms, the human brain is a self-forming form, and self-forming forms exist at all levels of the material world, not simply at the level of vertebrates but also at the level of amoebas, bacteria, molecules and atoms; and since self-forming forms are living forms, life is present in both organic and inorganic matter. But otherwise, Deleuze and Guattari's brain of sensation has no counterpart in Ruyer.

The description of the artistic brain as a contraction of vibrations is a variation on Deleuze's characterisation in *Difference and Repetition* of the first passive synthesis of time as contraction. This synthesis is the synthesis of habit, which is a contraction of instants within a present and a conservation of them in a contemplative soul. 'We are contemplations', and 'a soul must be attributed to the heart, to the muscles, nerves and cells, but a contemplative soul whose entire function is to contract a habit' (DR 74). Contraction is also evident at an organic level, in that every organism is made of 'contemplated and contracted water, nitrogen, carbon, chlorides and sulphates, thereby intertwining all of the habits of which it is composed' (DR 75). Contraction 'is both a contemplation and the auto-satisfaction of that contemplation', a 'beatitude' like that described by Plotinus in the third *Ennead*, where 'all is contemplation!' (DR 74, 75).

Deleuze returns to this theme in *The Fold*, characterising perception as a parallel process involving the contraction of vibrations by physical organs and the differential emergence within monads of a conscious perception from unconscious minute perceptions. Organs contract vibrations, whereas the monad, or soul, 'alone conserves and distinguishes the minute components' (TF 98; trans. modified). Deleuze also describes the event in terms of contraction and contemplation, offering a modified version of *Difference and Repetition*'s Plotinian vision of the world as contemplation in his characterisation of Whitehead's 'prehensions', which Deleuze regards as similar to Leibniz's monads. When a prehension achieves 'satisfaction as a final phase', it is 'filled with itself' and experiences '*self-enjoyment*' (TF 78). This concept of self-enjoyment is 'biblical' and 'neo-Platonic', says Deleuze. 'The plant sings of the glory of God, and while being filled all the more with itself it contemplates and intensely contracts the elements whence it proceeds. It feels in this prehension the *self-enjoyment* of its own becoming' (TF 78).

In their remarks on the brain of art, Deleuze and Guattari provide another variation on the themes introduced in *Difference and Repetition* and *The Fold*. The brain of art exists on a plane of composition that is possible, whereas philosophy's plane of immanence is virtual. Clearly, the Leibnizian association of monads with the virtual-actual, and bodies with the possible-real, is here reconfigured to differentiate philosophy and the arts, suggesting a more markedly corporeal dimension to the arts than philosophy. And, indeed, art's fundamental characteristic is that of Leibnizian bodies – the contraction of vibrations. The brain of art is one of sensation. 'Sensation contracts vibrations', and 'sensation itself vibrates because it contracts vibrations'. The 'brain-subject' of sensation is a '*soul* or *force*, since only the soul preserves by contracting that which matter dissipates, or radiates, furthers, reflects, refracts, or converts' (WP 211). Such contraction 'is pure contemplation, for it is through contemplation that one contracts, contemplating oneself to the extent that one contemplates the elements from which one originates' (WP 212). Citing Plotinus, Deleuze and Guattari evoke a world in which all is contemplation, each entity being a contracting contemplation that experiences self-enjoyment. Each contemplative contraction is a brain-soul, each brain or microbrain, each soul or microsoul, contracting and contemplating vibrations. The 'brain-subject' of sensation is force, but 'as Leibniz said', force 'does nothing or does not act, but is only present; it preserves' (WP 212). Sensation 'is on a plane that is different from mechanisms, dynamisms, and finalities'. On sensation's plane of composition, 'contemplating is creating, the mystery of passive creation, sensation' (WP 212).

It is during their discussion of this second brain of sensation that Deleuze and Guattari identify the vitalism of Leibniz and Ruyer as 'that of a force that is but does not act'. Ruyer does describe nutritive processes that resemble the organic contractions of sensation, and he also speaks of the self-enjoyment of living forms from time to time. For Ruyer, however, organic processes are always active, and the self-enjoyment of living forms is never associated with beatitude or contemplation, but only with the autonomy and completeness of each living form. Ruyer would agree that living forms cannot be understood in terms of 'mechanisms', that is *partes extra partes*, but he would insist that they are inseparable from 'dynamisms and finalities'. Living forms are agents pursuing goals, whether they be atoms persisting in the maintenance of their form, or embryos enacting a developmental theme in their purposive self-construction as fully formed organisms. It is for this reason that Ruyer describes his philosophy of biology both as a psycho-biology and a neo-finalism. Hence, whether construed within the terms of *The Fold* or those of *What is Philosophy?*, Ruyer's vitalism cannot be described as that of a force that is but does not act.

Ultimately, it is Ruyer's finalism that sets him apart from Deleuze and from Deleuze and Guattari. Ruyer's trans-spatial is virtual, but it is never without a purposive developmental theme. A living form is a consciousness-agent working through memory and creativity towards a goal. For Ruyer, a philosophical concept or a work of art is only a continuation of the individual's morphogenesis, an activity with minimal memory and maximal creativity, but still directed towards an end, however indistinct and vague it may be. By contrast, Deleuze and Guattari's philosophy-brain is a superject mind/spirit (*esprit*) in absolute overflight at infinite speed, and their arts-brain is an inject soul (*âme*) of contraction and contemplation. Philosophy's plane of immanence is without direction or orientation, the plane of the event that 'neither begins nor ends [. . .] the immanent aternal [*l'internel*]' (WP 156–7). Art's plane of composition is one of pure possibility, of coexisting compossibilities and incompossibilities. The sensations of this plane are affects and percepts, contractions irreducible to corporeal affections and perceptions. Its contemplations unfold on a plane of unspecified possibilities, its force undetermined by any spatio-temporal coordinates, and hence free from the 'mechanisms, dynamisms, and finalities' (WP 212) of the world of action.

Conclusion

In the texts of Ruyer that Deleuze cites, there are many themes that resonate with Deleuze's philosophy, and hence there are grounds to hypothesise a broad influence of Ruyer on Deleuze's thought. But when Deleuze actually cites Ruyer, it is most often to invoke his concept of the auto-overflight of an absolute surface. To deploy this concept, Deleuze extracts it from its context and directs it to his own uses – chiefly, those of expanding on Leibniz's theory of monads and of characterising philosophy's plane of consistency. In both instances, he treats Ruyer as a disciple of Leibniz who advocates the vitalism of a force that is but does not act. But Ruyer, though inspired by Leibniz, formulates a much different monadology, one in which monads are nothing but doors and windows, nothing but *liaisons* actively forming themselves. His is a vitalism in which forces exist *and* act – indeed, their action is synonymous with their being. For him, there is only one force, always dynamic and goal-oriented. That force is consciousness-force, matter-form in sustained, non-localisable self-formation. Deleuze finds an ingenious and inventive use for the concept of auto-overflight, seizing on its trans-spatial nature and utilising it in his own thought within the domains of the virtual and the possible. But Deleuze's Ruyer is an other Ruyer, just as his Leibniz is an other Leibniz. Each is transformed and reconfigured, subsumed within Deleuze's ongoing philosophical project. It is important to specify the changes Deleuze imposes on Ruyer and Leibniz, not simply to differentiate Deleuze from Ruyer and Leibniz, and thereby recognise the autonomous ends each pursues in his respective philosophy, but also to appreciate the creative possibilities that Deleuze opens up through his appropriations and transmutations of their thought.

Notes

1. There is little secondary literature on Ruyer in French or English. Meslet (2005) provides a thorough examination of Ruyer's philosophy of nature. Several insightful essays may be found in Vax and Wunenburger (1995). For a brief synopsis of Ruyer's philosophy in English, see Wiklund (1960). For studies of Ruyer and Deleuze, see Bains (2002) and Bogue (2009).
2. In 2012 the Presses Universitaires de France published a reprinting of *Néo-finalisme*, with pagination different from that of the 1952 edition. In my citations of *Néo-finalisme*, I include references to both the 1952 and 2012 editions.
3. The word *survol* poses special problems for English translators. The verb *survoler* means literally 'to fly over', and a *survol* is a 'flight over' something. In *What is Philosophy?*, *survol* is translated as 'survey'. In *The Fold*, 'survol' is rendered as 'overview', and *en auto-survol* as 'self-surveiling'. To emphasise the literal sense of the word, I have chosen to translate *survol* as 'overflight', and *auto-survol* as 'auto-overflight'.
4. It is worth noting that Ruyer says he takes the term 'self-enjoyment' (which he always maintains in the original English) from Samuel Alexander's 1920 book *Space, Time and Deity* (Ruyer 1952: 81), not from Whitehead, who himself borrowed the term from Alexander. Ruyer shows sympathy for Whitehead throughout his works, but Ruyer's use of 'self-enjoyment' is distinct from that of Whitehead. For Ruyer, '*erlebt, enjoys, survole, pense*' (Ruyer 1946: 24) are synonyms.
5. Ruyer's theology does provide a context in which it may be said that themes exist beyond the living entities in which they are actualised. For Ruyer, all living forms are agents working towards ideals. He identifies God 'not with a being or a meaning or an activity that is transcendent to the world, but with the two poles [agent and ideal] of all finalist activities, which together make up the world. God is

thus the supreme Agent as well as the supreme Ideal, and "Creativity" cannot be distinguished from a God who is simultaneously and indissolubly Agent and Ideal' (Ruyer 1952: 261; 2012: 285). God exists as agent within all living forms and subsists within all the ideals towards which living forms work. All living forms are free activities, but 'there is only one free *being*, God in us, and we only exist in creating, that is, in working according to the order of the ideal, which is also God in all Ideals. [. . .] Our soul makes itself in making our bodies and those prolongations of our body that are our tools. But the soul of our soul, according to the expression of the mystics, never has to make itself, because it is eternal, and it creates time and everything else. Just as we survive the changes in objects on which we work, just as we can pass from one activity to another, [. . .] so God survives the changes of bodies and souls. Our soul dies with our body, but the soul of our soul changes in body and soul, as we can change the object of our activity. The metamorphoses of ancient Zeus are the symbols of this truth: God takes us and leaves us just as we are able to take up and leave an ongoing task, although we are not truly able to cease acting' (Ruyer 1952: 263; 2012: 287). In my judgement, the existence of an eternal God as the 'soul of the soul' of all living forms does not alter the fact that the developmental themes of all living forms *qua* living forms remain tied to their material existence. God 'cannot be isolated from the World. His finality is not added to the finalities [of living forms]; his finality is the Sense/Meaning [*Sens*] of those finalities' (Ruyer 1952: 266; 290). It should be noted that Ruyer rejects any notion of pre-established harmony in his conception of God. 'Finally, the idea of God as Ideal and as Agent is not in contradiction with our mediocre traits, our faults, our evils, our sufferings, which are also his. The objection to pantheism, positive mysticism and finalism has always been posed in terms of the existence of negative values: ugliness, falseness, injustice, weakness, hate, wickedness. But, just as one must not confuse vision of blackness with no vision at all, so one must not confuse negative value and the absence of any axiology. The philosophy that establishes the reality of finalism has no pretention to being a theodicy' (Ruyer 1952: 267; 2012: 291).

6. Deleuze cites as sources for his treatment of the *vinculum substantiale* Belaval (1952) and Frémont (1981). These are but two of a wide range of interpretations of this difficult concept that have been offered by Leibniz scholars. For a summary of the diverse positions that have been staked out in this contentious interpretative field, see Look and Rutherford (2007).

7. Deleuze and Guattari make reference to Ruyer in their discussion of the planes of immanence and composition, but not in their treatment of science's plane of reference. Although Ruyer has a great deal to say about the philosophy of science, his thought on the subject bears no relation to Deleuze and Guattari's discussion of science's plane of rereference, for which reason I restrict my comments to Ruyer's role in Deleuze and Guattari's formulation of the brain of philosophy and the brain of the arts.

20

Plateau Three: Who the Earth Thinks It Is

The title of the Plateau Three is not just a joke. If Nietzsche's *Genealogy of Morals* traces the lineage of forces that have transformed an active, affirmative evaluation of good and bad into a reactive, negative judgement of good and evil, Deleuze and Guattari's 'Geology of Morals' offers a terrestrial account of the processes of stratification that eventuate in the human strictures that enforce the judgement of God. 'The Geology of Morals', in this sense, is an extension of the Nietzschean critique of conventional morality. Nor is the plateau's subtitle insignificant. 'Who Does the Earth Think It Is?' ('Pour qui elle se prend, la terre?') has as its counterpart a parenthetic remark later in the plateau: 'who does man think he is?' ('pour qui il se prend, l'homme?') (ATP 63). The idiom *se prendre pour* is used to accuse someone of pretentious self-importance, such that *pour qui tu te prend?*, 'who do you think you are?', might also be rendered as 'what makes you so special?' *Pour qui elle se prend* is comic when addressed to the geological earth, at least if one regards the planet as the third, inert rock from the sun. But the phrase is very serious when addressed to human beings, especially as we move further into the anthropocene epoch and suffer the consequences of our species' arrogance. A central purpose of Plateau Three, then, is to put humans in their place, in the sense of both countering our collective pride and positioning us in relation to other earthly entities. Once so positioned, humans may take seriously the question posed to the earth and perhaps discern in its response the hints of what Manuel DeLanda calls 'the wisdom of the rocks' (DeLanda 1992: 160), not a geology of morals, but a geology of ethics, or terrestrial ethology. My focus in examining the geology of morals and terrestrial ethology will be on the role of language in the plateau, first as terminological point of departure, and eventually as object of analysis. In between, I will identify the problem addressed in the plateau, sketch the complex workings of the model of stratification, and then consider the position of the domain of the human in relation to those of the inorganic and the organic.[1]

The Problem

In both volumes of *Capitalism and Schizophrenia*, Deleuze and Guattari advocate a materialism of a special sort. In *Anti-Oedipus*, they review at length the traditional opposition of mechanism and vitalism, arguing that their concept of machinic desiring production escapes the limitations of that opposition (AO 283–90). In *A Thousand Plateaus*, they make essentially the same point, saying that their approach to bodies in terms of differential speeds and affective intensities 'is not animism, any more than it is mechanism; rather it is universal machinism' (ATP 256). Yet they also state that there 'is a life proper to matter, a vital state of matter as such, a material vitalism' (ATP 411). That life is 'inorganic, germinal and intensive' (ATP 499), 'anorganic' (ATP 503), 'nonorganic' (ATP 507).[2] Matter is not inert stuff, but 'matter-movement [. . .] matter-energy [. . .] matter-flow [. . .] matter in variation' (ATP 407), matter that has both dynamic properties of self-differentiation and self-organisation and capacities of mutation, transformation and creativity. The life immanent to all matter, whether inorganic, organic, natural or artificial, is that of the machinic processes of self-differentiation, self-organisation, de-differentiation, de-organisation, reconfiguration and creation at work in the morphogenesis and metamorphosis of everything in the world.

Deleuze and Guattari open Plateau Three by saying that 'the Earth [. . .] is permeated by unformed, unstable matters, by flows in all directions, by free intensities or nomadic singularities, by mad or transitory particles' (ATP 40). This is the earth as matter-movement, matter-energy and matter-flow, imbued with an anorganic life, but 'unformed' and 'unstable'. The problem Deleuze and Guattari address in this plateau is how such unformed matter becomes organised and stabilised in the relatively fixed forms of inorganic and organic entities, as well as the homeostatic configurations of their relations. Deleuze and Guattari identify the process of such stabilisations and organisations as stratification. The choice of this term is significant, given that 'stratification' has among its principal meanings that of a geological arrangement of sedimentary rocks in distinct layers, and that of a sociological organisation of people in hierarchies of class and status. What Deleuze and Guattari will show is that rocks and humans, the extremes of the traditional Great Chain of Being, are equally subject to the process of stratification, as are all formed entities in between.

From Semiology to Ontology

Deleuze and Guattari take the primary terms of their description of stratification from linguistics – André Martinet's concept of double articulation and Louis Hjelmslev's notions of matter, form, substance, content and expression. In the heyday of French structuralism in the 1960s, Martinet's double articulation figured prominently in efforts to extend linguistic concepts to construct a general semiology, such as Saussure had envisioned earlier in the century. Martinet's distinction between two fundamental levels in linguistic expression – a first articulation of morphemes (monemes, in Martinet's parlance), or the smallest units possessed of form and meaning; and a second articulation of phonemes, the smallest units that distinguish or contrast meaning, without themselves having any meaning but solely form – was seen by many semiologists as a guide to the analysis of non-linguistic sign systems, leading them to ask how the fundamental elements of a given sign system – art, architecture, music, genetics – might be construed in terms of a double articulation of meaning-bearing units and purely formal units of differentiation.

This line of reasoning is evident, for example, throughout Roland Barthes's influential *Elements of Semiology* (1964). In *Elements*, Barthes also recognises the potential of Hjelmslev's linguistics for a general semiology. After defining the sign in Saussurean terms as signifier and signified, Barthes states that 'the plane of the signifiers constitutes the *plane of expression* and that of the signifieds *the plane of content*', adding that Hjelmslev specifies that 'each plane comprises two *strata*: *form* and *substance*' (Barthes 1967: 39–40). Attention to the form and substance of both expression and content, he argues, provides an important tool for analysing the language-like regularities of non-linguistic semiological systems.

It is against this background that Deleuze and Guattari's use of Hjelmslev and Martinet may be seen as a playful appropriation of linguistics' schemas and redeployment of those terms to counter linguistics' imperialistic semiological ambitions. Decisive in their reconfiguration of Hjelmslev is their attention to 'matter', the one element involved in Hjelmslev's form/substance opposition that Barthes ignores. Hjelmslev entertains the possibility of extracting from the world's languages something 'common to all languages' (Hjelmslev 1961: 50), which he calls *mening* ('meaning' in Danish), an 'amorphous "thought-mass"' like a 'handful of sand' (Hjelmslev 1961: 52). This amorphous *mening*, translated as 'purport' in English, but serendipitously as '*matière*' in French, is the universal 'thought-mass' of meanings carved up in different ways by different languages. *Mening* is 'unformed', and hence 'in itself inaccessible to knowledge' (Hjelmslev 1961: 76). It can only be approached through the forms of a given language, which turn the amorphous thought-mass into formed substances – 'just as an open net casts its shadows down on an undivided surface' (Hjelmslev 1961: 57), the outline of each square of the net constituting a form, and the surface so delineated a substance.

By taking Hjelmslev's 'matière' not as 'thought-mass' but as matter per se, Deleuze and Guattari convert the schema of a general semiology into a component of a general ontology. This matter, however, is not inert, brute matter, but 'the plane of consistency or Body without Organs, in other words, the unformed, unorganized, nonstratified or destratified body and all its flows; subatomic and submolecular particles, pure intensities, prevital and preindividual free singularities' (ATP 48). It is from this matter that the process of double articulation produces the forms and substances of the strata of content and expression. This double articulation is so varied that 'we cannot begin with a general model, only a relatively simple case' (ATP 40) – that of the processes of sedimentation and cementation that form sedimentary rock.[3] In the first articulation of sedimentation (content), pebbles (substance) are extracted from a silt flow and then sorted into uniform layers (form). In the second articulation of cementation (expression), the statistically ordered layers are further organised through inter-pebble structuration (form), that structuration producing sedimentary rock (substance). Framed more abstractly, 'the first articulation chooses or deducts, from unstable particle-flows, metastable molecular or quasi-molecular units (*substances*) upon which it imposes a statistical order of connections and successions (*forms*)', whereas the second articulation 'establishes functional, compact stable structures (*forms*), and constructs the molar compounds in which these structures are simultaneously actualized (*substances*)' (ATP 40–1). Forms organise, or 'code', substances and thereby fix, or 'territorialise', substances. Hence, the substance of content is territorialised matter that is coded by the form of content; and the form of expression further codes, or 'overcodes', the stratum of content and thereby increases territorialisation in the substance of expression.

In Deleuze and Guattari's initial formulation of double articulation, then, a linguistic concept is once again transformed. The double articulation of morphemes and phonemes yields a meaning-bearing content and a meaningless vehicle for the expression of that content. In Deleuze and Guattari's double articulation, there is no vehicle for the conveyance of meaning, but two constituents in a relational process. Content is a coded territorialisation that is overcoded and further territorialised in expression, which produces 'phenomena of centering, unification, totalization, integration, hierarchization, and finalization' (ATP 41). Unlike the relation between morphemes and phonemes, this formulation of the content/expression relation 'is never correspondence or conformity between content and expression, only isomorphism with reciprocal presupposition' (ATP 44). And as we shall see, the isomorphisms of content and expression are subject to multiple variations at different levels of scale and organisation.

Strata, Epistrata and Parastrata

By analysing the formation of sedimentary rock in terms of double articulation, Deleuze and Guattari take what must seem the most mechanistic of phenomena – the mere aggregation and solidification of inert particles via brute forces – and transform it into an instance of a process of selection/coding and overcoding/integration that occurs throughout all natural systems. Double articulation is evident, for example, in the determination of the three-dimensional structure of certain globular proteins. As Jacques Monod observes, this process involves a '"primary" structure [. . .] constituted by a topologically linear sequence of amino acid residues linked by covalent bonds' (first articulation), which is then stabilised via non-covalent interactions such that 'the polypeptide fiber folds in a very complex way into a compact, pseudo-globular bundle' (second articulation) (Monod 1971: 90–2). The cellular chemistry of the bacterium *Escherichia coli* also involves a two-stage process, the first in which elements are combined to form a limited number of compounds, and a second in which these unstable small molecules are assembled to produce chains of macro-molecules (Jacob 1973: 217). On a much higher scale, the functioning of an animal's organ systems (circulatory, respiratory, digestive and so on) may be analysed in terms of double articulation (though not as a temporal sequence of articulations). The animal's organs constitute the substance of content, and their regulation the form of content; the homeostatic regulation of those flows is the overcoding form of expression, and the organism as emergent process is the substance of expression.[4]

Each double articulation constitutes a stratum, and the unity of composition of the stratum involves three components: 'molecular materials, substantial elements, and formal relations or traits' (ATP 49). The molecular materials are selected from unformed matter to constitute a substratum, or exterior milieu, for the stratum; further organisation of those materials creates substantial elements, which emerge as an interior milieu; and formal relations both separate and connect the exterior and interior milieus. A supersaturated solution of sulfur, for example, begins to crystallise with the introduction of a seed crystal. As crystallisation commences, the molecular materials of the metastable solution (external milieu) are organised as substantial elements within each new crystal (interior milieu), the crystal surface delineating outside and inside (formal relation). Similarly, catalysts in a prebiotic soup may be seen as seed crystals in a metastable medium, an emergent organism forming an interior milieu, its membrane constituting the formal relation that divides and connects interior and exterior milieus.

Deleuze and Guattari insist that the exterior milieu, interior milieu and surface/membrane are all components within the stratum. But no stratum comes alone or undivided. Intermediary states fragment each stratum, dividing it into *epistrata*. In the formation of a crystal, for example, the crystallisation of the metastable solution does not proceed in a single, continuous process, but by distinct and discontinuous intermediary metastable states, each state constituting an epistratum. In a complex organism, intermediaries are evident in the organism's interior milieu, which consists of topologically complex milieus of relative interiority and exteriority, such that one interior milieu may serve as the exterior milieu of another. In the process of digestion, for example, the digestive cavity is the exterior milieu for the blood that irrigates the intestinal wall, while the blood is the exterior milieu for the digestive glands that discharge the products of their activity into the blood. The diverse interiorities and exteriorities within the organism constitute so many epistrata, and together 'they regulate the degree of complexity or differentiation of an organism' (ATP 50). A stratum, then, 'exists only in its substantial epistrata, which shatter its continuity, fragment its ring, and break it down into gradations' (ATP 50–1).

Besides fragmenting into epistrata, strata divide into *parastrata*. Epistrata mark intermediate states within internal milieus, 'piled one atop the other', whereas parastrata fragment the strata 'into sides and "besides"' (ATP 52). On the inorganic level, parastrata are intermediary states within exterior milieus. In crystal formation, for example, parastrata are varying opportunities for expansion afforded by the surrounding supersaturated solution. On the organic level, however, the nature of parastrata changes, for there they are associated with a third kind of milieu, neither exterior nor interior, but an '*annexed or associated milieu*' (ATP 51). In physico-chemical systems the interior milieu's substantial elements are formed from its exterior milieu's molecular materials – a crystal's substantial elements from the molecular materials of a supersaturated solution, or a primitive anaerobic organism's substantial elements from the molecular materials of a prebiotic soup. Both processes of replication via a conversion of external materials into internal elements constitute a fundamental 'alimentation', but one that exhausts itself with the eventual internal assimilation of all of the exterior milieu's materials. With the evolution of aerobic bacteria, however, organisms emerge that are capable of appropriating 'sources of energy different from alimentary materials' (ATP 51), sources available outside the organism's immediate exterior milieu in an annexed, or associated milieu. Such primitive aerobic respiration, then, may be taken as representative of the basic process of energy annexation beyond alimentation common to all organic life forms. Deleuze and Guattari also argue that associated milieus entail perception and reaction as well as alimentation (and hence a certain degree of cognition). Thus, the associated milieu is

> defined by the capture of energy sources (respiration in the most general sense), by the discernment of materials, the sensing of their presence or absence (perception), and by the fabrication or nonfabrication of the corresponding compounds (response, reaction). (ATP 51)

In organic systems, then, parastrata are the fragmentations of strata via associated milieus.

Epistrata involve substances and processes of territorialisation and deterritorialisation, whereas parastrata involve forms and processes of coding and decoding. An interior milieu is a territorialisation (a crystal or a cell, for example, constituting a territory within an exterior milieu), and epistrata consist of varying numbers of interior milieus. In no way is an interior milieu absolutely territorialised, however. To some degree, it is always relatively territorialised and relatively deterritorialised, and the same is true of the relations among interior milieus within epistrata, where 'variations that are tolerated below a certain threshold of identity' (ATP 50) mark the fluctuations between territorialisation and deterritorialisation among interior milieus that may be maintained within a given system of epistrata without the system collapsing. Likewise, in parastrata there is no coding without decoding. In genetic codes, for example, there is 'an essential margin of decoding: not only does every code have supplements capable of free variation, but a single segment may be copied twice, the second copy left free for variation' (ATP 53). Viruses may also transfer fragments of codes from one species to another. And, on a population level, there is always 'genetic drift', variations in a species gene pool regulated by population sizes and degrees of habitat isolation.

The Plane of Consistency and the Abstract Machine

Stratification creates formed substances from unformed matter. The unformed matter of this global stratification is the earth, 'the Deterritorialized, the Glacial, the giant Molecule [. . .] a body without organs' (ATP 40). It is the '*Omnitudo*' as 'potential totality of all BwOs' (ATP 157), 'the plane of consistency of Nature' (ATP 254). The strata are relative de/territorialisations and de/codings, whereas the earth is the plane of consistency of absolute deterritorialisation and absolute decoding. The earth's matter is 'unformed, unstable' (ATP 40), but it is not 'a chaotic white night or an undifferentiated black night' (ATP 70). It is a virtual domain, real without being actual, with characteristics that are immanent within the actual domain of formed substances. It is matter before individuation has taken place, 'prevital and prephysical' (ATP 43). It is a Body without Organs in that it is not an organism, or an organised, individuated and regulated entity; it is, 'in other words, the unformed, unorganized, nonstratified or destratified body and all its flows' (ATP 43). It is the source of forces and processes of morphogenesis and self-organisation immanent within matter, which are made manifest in the actualisations of those forces and processes. Though its matter is unformed, the plane of consistency is permeated 'by flows in all directions, by free intensities or nomadic singularities, by mad or transitory particles'

(ATP 40) and filled with 'subatomic and submolecular particles, pure intensities, prevital and prephysical free singularities' (ATP 43).

The primary elements that occupy the plane of consistency, then, are singularities, intensities, particles and flows. Singularities mark thresholds between stable dynamical systems, points of bifurcation from one system to another. A given distribution of singularities determines a multiplicity's virtual space of potentialities or capacities, which then may be actualised in an unspecified number of ways. When considered on the plane of consistency, however, singularities are absolutely deterritorialised, unassigned to any particular distribution, free and nomadic. Intensities are nonmetric aspects of multiplicities, a given degree of heat being an intensity that changes quality with any increase or decrease in temperature and that cannot be attained through simple metric addition (a substance at 40 degrees added to another at 40 degrees does not generate a substance at 80 degrees). More generally, intensities are like Kant's 'intensive magnitudes', which may be 'apprehended only as unity, and in which multiplicity can be represented only through approximation to negation = 0' (Kant 1965: 203). In Deleuze and Guattari's appropriation of Kant, intensity = 0 is not negative, but positive, various intensities being measured by their relative distance from zero, and zero itself functioning as the matrix of relatively deterritorialised intensities, the zero degree being pure deterritorialised intensity. The plane of consistency, or Body without Organs, 'causes intensities to pass', but the Body without Organs itself 'is nonstratified, unformed, intense matter, the matrix of intensity, intensity = 0' (ATP 153). (Hence the characterisation of the earth as 'the Glacial' – intensity at absolute zero.) Particles, or particles-signs, are 'elements of molecular multiplicities' (ATP 32) undifferentiated by distinctions between the semiotic and nonsemiotic. The concept of particles-signs is derived from the science of subatomic particles, but like its antithesis, the concept of black holes, it is used in a broad sense, in this case to designate deterritorialised elements that have escaped the domination of any formed entity and become 'mad or transitory' (ATP 40) on the plane of consistency. Flows, finally, are passages of matter-energy of all sorts – fluids, money, people, ideas – continuities that strata separate, control and regulate, but that inherently resist organisation, becoming pure currents of matter-movement on the plane of consistency.

That which connects the singularities, intensities, point-signs and flows of the plane of consistency is the abstract machine. It composes itself and composes the plane of consistency (ATP 511). It 'develops alone and in its own right on the plane of consistency whose diagram it constitutes, the same machine at work in astrophysics and in microphysics, in the natural and in the artificial, piloting flows of absolute deterritorialization' (ATP 56). One might say, then, that it is (1) the active dimension of the plane of consistency's self-constitution; (2) the open system of connections that define the capacities of the plane of consistency for the distribution of singularities and disposition of intensities, particles-signs and flows; and (3) the agency that outlines or 'diagrams' the relations among singularities, intensities, particles-signs and flows.

But the abstract machine is also immanent within the strata, where machinic assemblages '*effectuate* the abstract machine' (ATP 71). Machinic assemblages coadapt content and expression, establish biunivocal relations between them, guide the formation of epistrata and parastrata, and relate strata to other strata. In the strata, singularities are actualised in discrete distributions, and intensities, particles-signs and flows are territorialised and coded: 'The only intensities known to the strata are discontinuous, bound up in forms and substances; the only particles are divided into particles of content and articles of expression; the only deterritorialized flows are disjointed and reterritorialized' (ATP 70). In short, the virtual potentialities of the plane of consistency are actualised in the specific, and hence necessarily limiting and restricting, forms and substances of the strata, and the abstract machine serves a piloting role in that actualisation, which the machinic assemblages effectuate. The abstract machine is enveloped in the strata, and it constitutes the unity of the strata. The enveloped abstract machine is 'the Ecumenon' (ATP 50), and its enveloped manifestation is the abstract machine of double articulation.

The abstract machine on the plane of consistency, by contrast, is 'the Planomenon' (ATP 50). This is the same abstract machine, no longer enveloped, but now developed on the plane of consistency (and, one might add, de-enveloped through interventions in the strata). The developed abstract machine '*constructs continuums of intensity*', '*emits and combines particles-signs*' and '*performs conjunctions of flows of deterritorialization*'. 'Continuum of intensities, combined emission of particles or signs-particles, conjunction of deterritorialized flows: these are the three factors proper to the plane of consistency; they are brought about by the abstract machine and are constitutive of destratification' (ATP 70). It is important to note that although the developed and enveloped abstract machines are the same machine, the developed has priority over the enveloped:

> In fact, what is primary is an absolute deterritorialization, an absolute line of flight, however complex or multiple – that of the plane of consistency or body without organs (the Earth, the absolutely deterritorialized). This absolute deterritorialization becomes relative only after stratification occurs on that plane or body: It is the strata that are always residue, not the opposite. (ATP 56)

The Inorganic, Organic and Alloplastic Strata

'The organization of epistrata moves in the direction of increasing deterritorialization' (ATP 53). The same may be said of the strata of the inorganic, the organic and the human. Decisive in Deleuze and Guattari's differentiation of these three strata is François Jacob's 1974 article 'Le modèle linguistique en biologie'. In this essay, Jacob notes the widespread adoption of a linguistic model for understanding the genetic code (a model he himself uses frequently in *The Logic of Life*), but argues that DNA sequences and languages differ in important ways. He sees two principles underlying the analogy between the genetic code and language: a 'combinatory of elements, phonemes or chemical radicals, which, in themselves, are devoid of meaning but which, grouped in certain ways, acquire a signification'; and 'a strict linearity of the message'. He observes, however, that a combinatory of elements need not entail linearity. Atoms constitute a combinatory of limited elements, and in inorganic systems, they combine to form countless complex molecules and compounds. 'But in this case, it's a matter of complex structures in three dimensions. By contrast, what is limited to heredity and language is the linearity of the structures they engender.' The sole question is whether 'in the two systems, this linearity resides in the same logic, if it is founded on the same constraints' (Jacob 1974: 201). His conclusion is that it is not. Linguistics studies messages transmitted from a sender to a receiver, but 'there is none of that in biology: neither sender nor receiver' (Jacob 1974: 200). The transfer of information in the gene sequence is unidirectional, from nucleic acids to proteins. The linearity of the gene sequence is fixed to a single temporal unfolding, one that is constrained by the needs of guiding the morphogenesis of the individual organism and passing the genetic information on to the next generation of organisms. The linearity of language, by contrast, is constrained by 'an apparatus, vocal and auditory, which preexists it' (Jacob 1974: 201). The nature of the vocal-auditory medium necessitates a sequential enunciation and reception of information, but communication proceeds in two directions in an open succession of messages, and the relation among messages is unconstrained by any predetermined, fixed temporality.

Jacob's differentiation of the three-dimensional, non-linear structuration of inorganic compounds, the fixed, unidirectional linearity of the genetic code, and the flexible, bidirectional linearity of language provides Deleuze and Guattari with the basic framework for their analysis of the inorganic, organic and human strata – with the proviso, of course, that their conception of the double articulation of content and expression dramatically reconfigures Jacob's schema.

On the inorganic stratum, the relationship between content and expression is that of the molecular to the molar. The crystal, for example, is the molar expression of the molecular content of the supersaturated solution within which it arises. The propagation of additional crystals takes place along the surfaces of the incipient crystals, and it proceeds in all directions. Hence, expression in crystallisation may be said to be 'voluminous or superficial' (ATP

59). Expression on the inorganic stratum in general, like that of crystallisation, is a process of 'induction', like the induction of an electrical current or magnetic field, 'from layer to layer and state to state, or at the limit' (ATP 60). The passage from molecular to molar is also one of a unidirectional territorialisation. Hence, one may say of the crystal that its 'subjugation to three-dimensionality, in other words its index of territoriality', makes 'the structure incapable of formally reproducing and expressing itself; only the accessible surface can reproduce itself, since it is the only deterritorializable part' (ATP 60).

Genuine reproduction, that exhibited by organic life forms, requires a qualitative increase in deterritorialisation, and that increase is provided by the linear genetic sequence. In the organic stratum, the relationship between expression and content is not solely that of the molar to the molecular, although the molar–molecular relation does pervade the process of morphogenesis, in that development proceeds via the formation of increasingly large-scale structures. In the genetic sequence, expression becomes molecular and '*independent in its own right, in other words, autonomous*'. Genetic expression involves 'nucleic acids of expression and proteins of content' (ATP 59). The nucleic acids and proteins are independent formed substances, their only specified connection being that each protein corresponds to a given sequence of three nucleotides. This deterritorialisation of expression in the linear genetic sequence makes possible multiple deterritorialisations of the organism as a whole. Unlike a crystal, which merely induces further replication within its exterior milieu, the organism reproduces itself independently of its immediate exterior milieu. In morphogenesis, the linear genetic sequence allows a further deterritorialisation, in that the multiple interior and exterior milieus within the organism are put in mutual topological contact with one another through the genetic sequence. On the inorganic stratum, epistrata and parastrata are mere inductions. On the organic stratum, by contrast, epistrata and parastrata are transductions, fragmentations of the strata that are both molecular and molar 'independently of order of magnitude' (ATP 60). The epistrata of substances within the organism are relatively deterritorialised through the topological mutual presence of systems to one another without regard to distance. And the parastrata of forms afford the establishment of associated milieus through mutative decodings, recodings and intercodings of the organism with other organisms.

What I have referred to as the human stratum to this point is actually named the alloplastic stratum by Deleuze and Guattari, and the difference between the two designations is significant. The human is not an essence, but a product of a distribution of content and expression that differs from those of the inorganic and organic strata. The human is a mere result of the universal process of double articulation, which in this stratum has attained a new level of deterritorialisation. The stratum is alloplastic (Greek *allo* = other) in that 'it brings about modifications in the external world' (ATP 60). Of course, all systems, inorganic and organic, mutually modify one another, but the modifications of the alloplastic stratum are brought about by tools and language, *tekhnē* and *logos*, which are components specific to the alloplastic stratum that intervene in the inorganic and organic strata as forces external to those strata.

The alloplastic stratum has a single exterior milieu, not a pre-physico-chemical soup (the inorganic stratum), nor a prebiotic soup (the organic stratum), but a prehuman soup: 'the cerebral-nervous system' (ATP 64). This brain-soup substratum tends towards two poles of differentiation – the hand and the face – and double articulation performs a 'manual articulation of content' and a 'facial articulation of expression' (ATP 64) that eventuates in the distinction between gestures–tools and speech–language. Although central to the unity of composition of the alloplastic stratum, the brain-soup does not have priority as a causal force in human evolution. Deleuze and Guattari follow André Leroi-Gourhan in arguing that cerebral development is not the motor of human evolution but instead a secondary phenomenon made possible by antecedent muscular-skeletal adaptations related to locomotion and an increased mastery of space and time. Leroi-Gourhan sees the emergence of an erect posture as the decisive event in the evolution of the hominins that led to *Homo sapiens*. Through major modifications of the feet and spine, hominins gained the ability to stand, walk and run, and as a result their hands were freed from the function of locomotion, and their mouths from the function of grasping. Hands could then invent and manipulate tools, and mouths could invent and articulate language. And concomitant with the development of the new capacities of the hands and mouth was an expansion of the cerebral cavity and increase in the size of the brain, only made possible by the structural modifications necessary for an upright posture and a reconfiguration of the face (the projecting mouth-snout suitable for grasping giving way to a flattened face, which provided more room for the cerebral cavity in the skull).

In Deleuze and Guattari's terms these evolutionary developments are so many deterritorialisations and reterritorialisations, which eventuate in a general increase in the deterritorialisation of humans. The deterritorialising reconfiguration of feet and spine deterritorialises the locomotive hands and grasping mouth, allowing the reterritorialisation of hands as gestural agents of tool-making and the mouth as an apparatus for producing speech. Deleuze and Guattari elaborate further on Leroi-Gourhan's analysis, linking the evolution of an erect posture to a deterritorialisation of primates from the forest to the steppe.[5] Locomotion within the trees of the forest was facilitated by four grasping limbs, but when hominins ventured to the steppe, the absence of trees favoured the development of an erect posture, locomotive feet, and hands capable of fine-motor manipulation. Through such an erect posture, hominins gained an increased freedom of movement, and hence a higher degree of deterritorialisation. The steppe also made possible modifications of the vocal apparatus. The noise of the forest favoured the development of large lungs and a larynx capable of producing loud cries and screams; the relative quiet of the steppe, by contrast, allowed the development of a suppler sound instrument, with lips, tongue and descended larynx capable of producing finer sonic distinctions. The arboreal voice, in short, was deterritorialised on the steppe and reterritorialised in a freer, more deterritorialised vocal apparatus.

The formation of the alloplastic stratum proceeds via deterritorialisations of the hands and mouth, eventuating in a double articulation of hand–tool content and mouth–language expression. But it is the linearity peculiar to language that separates the organic and alloplastic strata. Language is not linear, but superlinear, more deterritorialised than the genetic sequence, since the temporal succession of its phonation does not limit its ability to represent various time relations. Further, such superlinearity 'engenders a phenomenon unknown on the other strata: *translation* [*traduction*], translatability, as opposed to the previous inductions and transductions' (ATP 62). Such translation is to be conceived in the broadest terms as 'the ability of language [. . .] to represent all the other strata and thus achieve a scientific conception of the world' (ATP 62). It is this power of translation that fosters the semiological imperialism of using linguistic models to explain all systems. (Witness Jacob's presupposition that physico-chemical, genetic and linguistic phenomena should be seen fundamentally as a Martinetian 'combinatory of elements [. . .] which, in themselves, are devoid of meaning but which, grouped in certain ways, acquire a signification' [Jacob 1974: 201].)

Language, Power and the Geology of Morals

Content and expression on the alloplastic stratum, then, may be parsed into a 'technological content' and a 'semiotic or symbolic expression' (ATP 61). But Deleuze and Guattari make a crucial addition to this formulation:

> Content should be understood not simply as the hand and tools but as a technical social machine that preexists them and constitutes states of force or formations of power [*puissance*]. Expression should be understood not simply as the face and language, or individual languages, but as a semiotic collective machine that preexists them and constitutes regimes of signs. A formation of power [*puissance*] is much more than a tool; a regime of signs is much more than a language. (ATP 61)

Despite the assignment of power solely to the machine of content, both these machines – technical social and semiotic collective – are assemblages of power, or *pouvoir*, as Plateaus Four and Five's analyses of order-words and regimes of signs make clear. It is telling in this regard that Deleuze and Guattari's explanatory model of the alloplastic relations between content and expression comes from Foucault's *Discipline and Punish* (ATP 66–7). Besides providing a clear example of the autonomy of content and expression (the prison-form of content versus expression's discourse of delinquency), their relation respectively to technical social and semiotic collective machines, and their relation to the abstract machine, the panopticon, makes evident that alloplastic stratification not only codes, territorialises, controls, restricts and rigidifies, but also effectuates asymmetrical power relations, which, in a word Deleuze will use later in characterising Foucault's project, constitute the 'intolerable' (N 103).

Plateau Three's trajectory is from geological stratification to the asymmetrical power relations of social stratification. The process of double articulation pervades the earth, at every level of organisation. Humans are produced on the alloplastic stratum as emergent but contingent manifestations of powers of relative deterritorialisation. Through primate and hominin corporeal deterritorialisations, the hands and mouth gain new capacities. Out of unformed matter a substratum of molecular materials takes shape, a prehuman soup, which gives a unity of composition to the alloplastic stratum. This prehuman brain-soup 'is a population, a set of tribes tending toward two poles' (ATP 64), those of the hand and mouth, which undergo double articulation as content and expression; *tekhnē* and *logos*; hand–gesture–tool and mouth–speech–language. In this co-emergence of content and expression, the form of expression attains the autonomy of superlinearity, which makes possible the translation of all strata into linguistic representations. Subtending this articulation of content and expression are pre-existing relations of force: technical social machines, or formations of power; and semiotic collective machines, or regimes of signs. The emergence of the alloplastic stratum marks a qualitative increase in deterritorialisation, but by no means is this a sign of progress, no ascent from the biosphere to the noosphere, *à la* Teilhard de Chardin (ATP 69). Such notions of human superiority, in fact, are illusory products of the alloplastic stratum. Technological and semiotic machines emerge on this stratum and increasingly transform the world. Such machines are part of the stratum, 'but at the same time rear up and stretch their pincers out in all directions at all the other strata' (ATP 63).

Techno-semiotic machines seem to constitute an intermediary state between the enveloped and developed states of the abstract machine, fully a part of the alloplastic stratum, yet sufficiently autonomous and pervasive in the other strata to engender the belief that they constitute the abstract machine of all strata. 'This is the illusion constitutive of man', however, and 'this illusion derives from the overcoding immanent to language itself' (ATP 63).

In an allusion to Antonin Artaud's 1947 radio play, *To Have Done with the Judgement of God*, Deleuze and Guattari say that 'the strata are the judgments of God', and that 'the earth, or the body without organs, constantly eludes that judgment, flees and becomes destratified, decoded, deterritorialized' (AP 40). The God of stratification is the immanent abstract machine of double articulation ('God is a Lobster' [ATP 40]), and conventional human moral codes are but a few of the multiple epistrata and parastrata that proliferate on the alloplastic stratum. In this narrow sense, Plateau Three provides a geology of morals, but in the broadest sense the geology of morals is a geology of language, the superlinear element that differentiates the alloplastic from the organic and inorganic strata. What the geology of morals reveals is the constitutive illusion of man, the belief that *tekhnē* and *logos* have dominance over all strata, and the pernicious tendencies of the relations of forces that have arisen, and continue to arise, in the technical social machines of content and the semiotic collective machines of expression.

Beyond the Strata

As John Protevi aptly observes, the Lobster-God of double articulation is unlike Spinoza's God, in that the Lobster-God is not all of nature, *Deus sive Natura*, but only a part of it (Protevi 2000: 39). The other part is the absolute deterritorialisation of the plane of consistency, the Body without Organs whose singularities, intensities, points-signs and flows compose the anorganic life of the earth. Deterritorialisation is primary, whereas stratification is a secondary residue, yet neither appears without the other. There is no virtual without the actual. Hence, in the real of nature, absolute deterritorialisation and absolute stratification are tendencies, limits never fully reached, and we, like everything else, are always relatively stratified and relatively deterritorialised. The question posed by the geology of morals is which tendency we promote: that of a morality of stratification, or that of an alternative ethics of the earth, a terrestrial ethology that valorises a deterritorialising mode of existence. Plateau Three does not articulate such an ethology; that task is reserved for the other plateaus. But it does provide an ontology of terrestrial systems that makes the valorisation of deterritorialisation more than a human choice.

Paul Patton has argued that Deleuze and Guattari's ontology 'is not ontology in the strong philosophical sense of the term but a pragmatic and relativized ontology [. . .] normative in a specific and formal sense' (Patton 2012: 142) in that it grants systematic priority to movements of deterritorialisation in all its various guises. Hence, Deleuze and Guattari's ontology 'is also an ethics or an ethology', which Patton calls 'an ethics of becoming' (Patton 2012: 142). Patton rightly stresses the ethico-political priorities that guide Deleuze and Guattari's thought and that are evident in all the plateaus of *A Thousand Plateaus*. But Plateau Three suggests that their ontological commitments are more than pragmatic, that the primacy of deterritorialisation is fundamental to their view of all terrestrial systems. Given that associated milieus are defined by energy capture and the cognitive functions of perception and response/reaction, the emergence of associated milieus on the organic stratum suggests that Deleuze and Guattari do make room for normativity, but a normativity that reaches beyond the human to all organic life forms. In this sense, their thought follows lines delineated by Georges Canguilhem, who sees all life forms as normative, the health of a given life form being determined by its normativity – that is, by the norms and the domain of normality it produces for itself.

> Any normality open to possible future correction is authentic normativity, or health. Any normality limited to maintaining itself, hostile to any variation in the themes that express it, and incapable of adapting to new situations is a normality devoid of normative intention. When confronted with any apparently

> normal situation, it is therefore important to ask whether the norms that it embodies are creative norms, norms with a forward thrust, or, on the contrary, conservative norms, norms whose thrust is toward the past. (Canguilhem 1994: 352)

This opposition of the authentic normativity of a creative, flexible, future-oriented health and the inauthentic normality of a conservative, rigid, past-oriented pathology is clearly consonant with the opposition of a deterritorialising ethology of becoming and a territorialising geo-morality of stratification.

But the primacy of deterritorialisation extends beyond the organic to the inorganic stratum as well, and whether such primacy retains a normative dimension on that stratum is doubtful. In crystallisation, for example, individuation proceeds from a deterritorialised supersaturated solution, the incipient crystal's surface being its 'only deterritorializable part'. The crystal's structure is 'incapable of formally reproducing and expressing itself' (ATP 60) because it is insufficiently deterritorialised. Only on the organic stratum do entities arise with sufficient deterritorialisation to allow them to annex associated milieus and thereby make normative evaluations of health or pathology. The primacy of deterritorialisation in crystallization resides solely in the supersaturated solution, which is pre-individual and hence devoid of discrete agents capable of valorising deterritorialisation.

The absence of normative agents is even more striking in stratification, and this is one of the reasons that the organisation of unformed matter is framed in terms of stratification rather than crystallisation. Whereas crystallisation involves the individuation of a discrete entity, sedimentation-cementation involves the production of a cohesive plurality. A geological stratum is an aggregate of materials, a geological formation rather than an individuated form. There is no clear agent internal to the system of sedimentation-cementation, for which reason it lends itself so well to a mechanistic analysis. But if there are no agents, there are 'agencings', *agencements machiniques*, machinic assemblage-forming processes. Such machinic agencings are 'inter-strata', relations-forces between content and expression, between strata and across strata, but also 'metastrata', between the strata and the developed abstract machine. They '*effectuate* the abstract machine insofar as it is developed on the plane of consistency or enveloped in a stratum' (ATP 71). They are the agencings of deterritorialisation and reterritorialisation that play through all cohesive formations, individuated entities and agents, without belonging to any of them. They are the anonymous agencings of a universal machinism, a vital materialism of anorganic life. Thus, the primacy of deterritorialisation is ontological in a strong sense; it is the primacy of creation, metamorphosis and becoming in all terrestrial systems. And normative valorisations of deterritorialisation are emergent properties of the organic stratum, effectuations of machinic agencings specific to that stratum and, by extension, to the alloplastic stratum.

What Plateau Three offers us, I believe, is a means of understanding Deleuze and Guattari's geophilosophy as a chaosmopolitanism, a contemporary counterpart to the cosmopolitanism of the Cynics and early Stoics.[6] The Cynics and early Stoics viewed philosophy as a way of living, and their cosmopolitanism entailed living in accordance with nature – for the Cynics, in harmony with plant and animal life, for the early Stoics, in harmony with law and reason (which they saw as at once both *physical* and ethical principles). The ethics of chaosmopolitanism, by contrast, calls for living in immanent resonance with the chaosmos of nature, affirming and participating in the creative, mutagenic and metamorphic powers of anorganic life, working to transform the stratifications that constrict that life and to invent new modes of existence. The Planomenon, the abstract machine on the plane of consistency, constructs continuums of intensity, emits and combines particles-signs, and forms conjunctions of flows of deterritorialisation. Thus, a chaosmopolitan ethics calls for engagement with the Planomenon, for the construction intensive continuums, the emission of particles-signs, and the conjunction of flows of deterritorialisation.

Notes

1. Adkins (2015) and Holland (2013) offer outstanding introductions to *A Thousand Plateaus* and to the complexities of Plateau Three. I find

Holland's remarks on Plateau Three especially helpful – indeed, this essay is largely an elaboration of his reading (p. 62) of the 'constitutive illusion of man' (ATP 63). Invaluable as well is the glossary of Bonta and Protevi (2004).

2. On non-organic life, see DeLanda (1992) and Protevi (2012).
3. Deleuze and Guattari call the second articulation 'folding', but as DeLanda points out (DeLanda 2000: 290), they are actually describing cementation, folding being a subsequent process following cementation.
4. I take this last example from Bonta and Protevi (2004: 152).
5. Deleuze and Guattari draw on Devaux (1933) for the idiosyncratic association of homonisation with the steppe. The more widely accepted savanna theory of homonisation, however, establishes a forest–savanna opposition that is roughly correlative to the forest–steppe opposition of Devaux.
6. For an extended exposition of Deleuze and Guattari's chaosmopolitanism, see Chapter 18.

Bibliography

Adieu au langage, film, directed by Jean-Luc Godard, France/ Switzerland: Canal+, Centre national de la cinématographie, 2014.

Adkins, Brent (2015), *Deleuze and Guattari's* A Thousand Plateaus: *A Critical Introduction and Guide*, Edinburgh: Edinburgh University Press.

Aristotle, *Poetics* (1902), trans. S. H. Butcher, 3rd edn, London: Macmillan and Co.

Attinello, Paul (2007), 'Postmodern or Modern: A Different Approach to Darmstadt', *Contemporary Music Review*, 26:1, 25–37.

Ayfre, Amedée (1969), 'The Universe of Robert Bresson', trans. Elizabeth Kingsley-Rowe, in *The Films of Robert Bresson*, ed. Ian Cameron, London, Studio Vista, pp. 6–24.

Badiou, Alain (2000), *Deleuze: The Clamor of Being*, trans. Louise Burchill, Minneapolis: University of Minnesota Press.

Bains, Paul (2002), 'Subjectless Subjectivities', in *A Shock to Thought: Expression after Deleuze and Guattari*, ed. Brian Massumi, London and New York: Routledge, pp. 101–16.

Barthes, Roland (1967), *Elements of Semiology*, trans. Annette Lavers and Colin Smith, New York: Hill and Wang.

Barthes, Roland (1995), *Œuvres complètes*, ed. Éric Marty, Paris: Seuil.

Beal, Amy C. (2007), 'David Tudor in Darmstadt', *Contemporary Music Review*, 26:1, 77–88.

Beaulieu, Alain (2011), 'The Status of Animality in Deleuze's

Thought', *Journal for Critical Animal Studies*, 9:1–2, 69–88.

Beckett, Samuel (1986), *The Complete Dramatic Works*, London: Faber & Faber.

Belaval, Yvon (1952), *La Pensée de Leibniz*, Paris: Bordas.

Bell, Jeffrey A. (2006), *Philosophy at the Edge of Chaos: Gilles Deleuze and the Philosophy of Difference*, Toronto: University of Toronto Press.

Bergson, Henri (1959), *Œuvres*, Édition du Centenaire, ed. André Robinet, Paris: Presses Universitaires de France.

Bogue, Ronald (2003), *Deleuze on Music, Painting, and the Arts*, New York: Routledge.

Bogue, Ronald (2006), 'Fabulation, Narration and the People to Come', in *Deleuze and Philosophy*, ed. Constantin V. Boundas, Edinburgh: Edinburgh University Press, pp. 202–25.

Bogue, Ronald (2009), 'Raymond Ruyer', in *Deleuze's Philosophical Lineage*, ed. Graham Jones and Jon Roffe, Edinburgh: Edinburgh University Press, pp. 300–20.

Bonta, Mark and John Protevi (2004), *Deleuze and Geophilosophy*, Edinburgh: Edinburgh University Press.

Bordwell, David (2014a), 'Adieu au langage: 2 + 2 x 3', *Observations on film art*, 7 September, available at http://www.davidbordwell.net/blog/2014/09/07/adieu-au-langage-2-2-2-x-3d (accessed 25 March 2015).

Bordwell, David (2014b), 'Say Hello to Goodbye to Language', Davidbordwell.net, 2 November, available at http://www.davidbordwell.net/blog/2014/11/02/say-hello-to-goodby-to-language (accessed 25 March 2015).

Boulez, Pierre (1968), *Notes on an Apprenticeship*, trans. Herbert Weinstock, New York: Alfred A. Knopf.

Boundas, Constantin V. (2007), 'Review Essay: Gilles Deleuze and his Readers. A Touch of Voluntarism and an Excess of Out-Worldliness', *Deleuze Studies* 1:2, 167–94.

Bowden, Sean, Simone Bignall and Paul Patton (eds) (2015), *Deleuze and Pragmatism*, New York: Routledge.

Branham, R. Bracht and Marie-Odile Goulet-Cazé (eds) (1996), 'Introduction', *The Cynics: The Cynic Movement in Antiquity and Its Legacy*, ed. R. Bracht Branham and Marie-Odile

Goulet-Cazé, Berkeley: University of California Press, pp. 1–27.

Bresson, Robert (1986), *Notes of the Cinematograph*, trans. Jonathan Griffin, New York: New York Review Books.

Brody, Richard (2014), 'Godard's Revolutionary 3-D Film', *The New Yorker*, 29 October, available at http://www.newyorker.com/culture/richard-brody/jean-luc-godards-3-d-movie (accessed 1 April 2015).

Buchanan, Ian (2000), *Deleuzism: A Metacommentary*, Durham, NC: Duke University Press.

Buchanan, Ian (2008), *Deleuze and Guattari's* Anti-Oedipus: *A Reader's Guide*, London: Continuum.

Bukofzer, Manfred F. (1947), *Music in the Baroque Era: From Monteverdi to Bach*, New York: Norton.

Butler, Octavia (1978), *Survivor*, New York: Doubleday.

Butler, Octavia (1989), *Lilith's Brood*, New York: Aspect, 1989. [*Dawn* (1987), *Adulthood Rites*, (1988), *Imago*, (1989)]

Butler, Octavia (1993), *Seed to Harvest*, New York: Grand Central. [*Wild Seed* (1980), *Mind of My Mind* (1977), *Clay's Ark* (1984), *Patternmaster* (1976)]

Butler, Octavia (1995), *Parable of the Talents*, New York: Grand Central.

Butler, Octavia (1998), *Parable of the Sower*, New York: Grand Central.

Butler, Octavia (2005), *Fledgling*, New York: Seven Stories.

Butler, Octavia (2010), *Conversations with Octavia Butler*, ed. Consuela Francis, Jackson: University Press of Mississippi.

Cage, John (1960), *Aria: Voice (Any Range)*, New York: Henmar Press.

Cage, John (1961), *Silence. Lectures and Writings*, Middletown, CT: Wesleyan University Press.

Canetti, Elias (1984), *Crowds and Power*, trans. Carol Stewart, New York: Farrar, Straus and Giroux.

Canguilhem, Georges (1994), *A Vital Rationalist: Selected Writings from Georges Canguilhem*, trans. Arthur Goldhammer, ed. François Delaporte, New York: Zone Books.

Carnegy, Patrick (1973), *Faust as Musician: A Study of Thomas Mann's Novel* Doctor Faustus, London: Chatto & Windus.

Carrière, Mathieu (1981), *Für eine Literatur des Krieges, Kleist*, Basel: Stroemfeld/Roter Stein.

Carrière, Mathieu (1985), *Pour une littérature de guerre, Kleist*, Arles: Actes Sud.

Cicero, Marcus Tullius (1928), *De Re Publica / De Legibus*, trans. Clinton Walker Keyes. Loeb Classical Library, Cambridge, MA: Harvard University Press.

Clark, Tim (2008), 'Becoming Everyone: The Politics of Sympathy in Deleuze and Rorty', *Radical Philosophy* 147, 33–44.

Cobley, Evelyn (2002), *Temptations of Faust: The Logic of Fascism and Postmodern Archaeologies of Modernity*, Toronto: University of Toronto Press.

Coole, Diana and Samantha Frost (eds) (2010), *New Materialisms: Ontology, Agency, and Politics*, Durham, NC: Duke University Press.

Cope, David H (1989), *New Directions in Music*, 5th edn, Dubuque: Wm. C. Brown.

Criton, Pascale (2007), 'L'esthétique intensive ou le théâre des dynamismes', in *Deleuze et les écrivains*, ed. Bruno Gelas and Hervé Micolet, Lyon: Cécile Defaut, pp. 57–69.

DeLanda, Manuel (1992), 'Nonorganic Life', in *Incorporations*, ed. Jonathan Crary and Sanford Kwinter, New York: Zone, pp. 128–67.

DeLanda, Manuel (2000), *A Thousand Years of Nonlinear History*, New York: Swerve Editions.

Deledalle, Gérard (1983), *La Philosophie américaine*, Lausanne: L'Âge d'Homme.

Der Westen (2010), 'Warum Mathieu Carrière sich in Kleist verliebt hat', 3 May http://www.derwesten.de/staedte/unser-vest/ruhrfestspiele/Warum-Mathieu-Carri-re-sich-in-Kleist-verliebt-hat-id2937461.html (accessed 1 June 2009).

Despret, Vinciane (2004), 'The Body We Care For: Figures of Anthropo-zoo-genesis', *Body & Society*, 10:2–3, 111–34.

Devaux, Émile (1933), *Trois problèmes: l'espèce, l'instinct, l'homme*, Paris: Le François.

Dolphjin, Rick and Iris van der Tuin (eds) (2012), *New Materialsm: Interviews and Cartographies*, Ann Arbor: University of Michigan Press.

Dosse, François (2010), *Gilles Deleuze & Félix Guattari: Intersecting Lives*, trans. Deborah Glassman, New York: Columbia University Press.

Drouet, Dominique (2007), 'Index des références littéraires dans l'œuvre de Gilles Deleuze', in *Deleuze et les écrivains: littérature et philosophie*, ed. Bruno Gelas and Hervé Micolet, Nantes: Cécile Defaut, pp. 555–81.

Ehrlich, David (2014), 'Goodbye to Language', *The Dissolve*, 28 October, available at http://thedissolve.com/reviews/1177-goodbye-to-language (accessed 1 April 2014).

Fendt, Ted (2014), '"Adieu au langage" – "Goodbye to Language": A Works Cited', *MUBI*, 12 October, available at https://mubi.com/notebook/posts/adieu-au-langage-goodbye-to-language-a-works-cited (accessed 1 April 2015).

Ferry, Luc (1995), *The New Ecological Order*, trans. Carol Volk, Chicago: University of Chicago Press.

Fiedler, Leslie (1968), *The Return of the Vanishing American*, New York: Stein and Day.

Foucault, Michel (1977), 'Theatrum Philosophicum', *Language, Countery-Memory, Practice: Selected Essays and Interviews*, ed. and trans. Donald F. Bouchard, Ithaca: Cornell University Press, pp. 165–96.

Foundas, Scott (2014), 'Cannes Film Review: "Goodbye to Language"', *Variety*, 21 May, available at http://variety.com/2014/film/reviews/cannes-film-review-goodbye-to-language-1201199140 (accessed 25 March 2015).

Frank, Manfred (1989), *What is Neostructuralism?*, trans. Sabine Wilke and Richard Gray, Minneapolis: University of Minnesota Press.

Frémont, Christiane (1981), *L'Être et la relation*, Paris: Vrin.

Gane, Nicholas (2006), 'When We Have Never Been Human, What Is to Be Done? Interview with Donna Haraway', *Theory, Culture Society*, 23:7–8, 135–58.

Gardner, Colin, and Patricia MacCormack (eds) (2017), *Deleuze and the Animal*, Edinburgh: Edinburgh University Press.

Genet, Jean. *Prisoner of Love* (1992), trans. Barbara Bray, Hanover: Wesleyan University Press.

Ghosh, Manomhan (trans.) (1951), *The Nātraśātra ascribed*

to *Bharati-Muni*, vol. 1, Calcutta: Asiatic Society of Bengal.

Grebowicz, Margret and Helen Merrick (2013), *Beyond the Cyborg: Adventures with Donna Haraway*, New York: Columbia University Press.

Griffiths, Paul (1981), *Modern Music: The Avant Garde Since 1945*, London: J. M. Dent.

Guattari, Félix (1995 [1992]), *Chaosmosis: An Ethico-Aesthetic Paradigm*, trans. Paul Bains and Julian Pefanis, Bloomington: Indiana University Press.

Guattari, Félix (2008 [1989]), *The Three Ecologies*, trans. Ian Pindar and Paul Sutton, London: Continuum.

Guattari, Félix (2013), *Qu'est-ce que l'écosophie?*, Abbaye d'Ardenne: IMEC.

Hallward, Peter (2006), *Out of This World: Deleuze and the Philosophy of Creation*, London: Verso.

Hannay, Alistair (1982), *Kierkegaard*, London: Routledge & Kegan Paul.

Haraway, Donna (1985), 'A Cyborg Manifesto: Science, Technology and Socialist Feminism in the Late Twentieth Century', *Socialist Review*, 80, 65–108.

Haraway, Donna (1990), *Primate Visions: Gender, Race and Nature in the World of Modern Science*, New York: Routledge.

Haraway, Donna (1991), 'A Cyborg Manifesto: Science, Technology, and Socialist-Feminism in the Late Twentieth Century', in *Simians, Cyborgs, and Women: The Reinvention of Nature*, London: Free Association Books, pp. 149–81.

Haraway, Donna (1997), *Modest_Witness@Second_Millennium. FemaleMan©Meets_OncoMouse™: Feminism and Technoscience*, New York: Routledge.

Haraway, Donna (2003), *The Companion Species Manifesto: Dogs, People, and Significant Otherness*, Chicago: Prickly Paradigm Press.

Haraway, Donna J. (2008), *When Species Meet*, Minneapolis: University of Minnesota Press.

Harvey, David (2000), *Spaces of Hope*, Berkeley: University of California Press.

Herzongenrath, Bernd (ed.) (2008), *Deleuze/Guattari and Ecology*, London: Palgrave.

Hjelmslev, Louis (1961), *Prolegomena to a Theory of Language*, trans. Francis J. Whitfield, Madison: University of Wisconsin Press.

Holbraad, Martin and Morten Axel Pedersen (2017), *The Ontological Turn: An Anthropological Exposition*, Cambridge: Cambridge University Press.

Holland, Eugene W. (1999), *Deleuze and Guattari's* Anti-Oedipus. *Introduction to Schizoanalysis*, London: Routledge.

Holland, Eugene W. (2006), 'The Utopian Dimension of Thought in Deleuze and Guattari', in *Imagining the Future: Utopia and Dystopia*, ed. M. Ryan Milner and R. Savage, Melbourne: Arena Publications Association, pp. 217–42.

Holland, Eugene W. (2013), *Deleuze and Guattari's* A Thousand Plateaus: *A Reader's Guide*, London: Bloomsbury.

Jacob, François (1973), *The Logic of Life: A History of Heredity*, trans. Betty E. Spillman, New York: Pantheon.

Jacob, François (1974), 'Le modèle linguistique en biologie', *Critique* 30:322, 197–205.

Jardine, Alice (1984), 'Woman in Limbo: Deleuze and His Br(others)', *SubStance*, 44/45, 46–60.

Kant, Immanuel (1965), *Critique of Pure Reason*, trans. Norman Kemp Smith, New York: St. Martin's.

Kastrenakes, Jacob (2014), 'Somebody Finally Made a Truly 3D Movie', *The Verge*, 21 September, available athttp://www.theverge.com/2014/9/21/6563495/goodbye-to-language-godard-messes-with-3d-and-its-awesome (accessed 26 March 2014).

Kierkegaard, Søren (1949), *Traité du désespoir*, trans. Knud Fehlov and Jean-J. Gateau, Paris: Gallimard.

Kierkegaard, Søren (1980), *Sickness unto Death*, trans. Howard V. Hong and Edna H. Hong, Princeton: Princeton University Press.

Kierkegaard, Søren (1983a), *Fear and Trembling*, in *Fear and Trembling/Repetition*, ed. and trans. Howard V. Hong and Edna H. Hong, Princeton: Princeton University Press.

Kierkegaard, Søren (1983b), *Repetition*, in *Fear and Trembling/*

Repetition, ed. and trans. Howard V. Hong and Edna H. Hong, Princeton: Princeton University Press.

Kingston, Maxine Hong (1976), *The Woman Warrior: Memoirs of a Girlhood among Ghosts*, New York: Alfred A. Knopf.

Kingston, Maxine Hong (1980), *China Men*, New York: Alfred A. Knopf.

Kingston, Maxine Hong (1989), *Tripmaster Monkey: His Fake Book*, New York: Vintage.

Kleist, Heinrich von (1982), *An Abyss Deep Enough: Letters of Heinrich von Kleist with a Selection of Essays and Anecdotes*, ed. and trans. Philip B. Miller, New York: E. P. Dutton.

Kleist, Heinrich von (1998), *Penthesilea*, trans. Joel Agee, New York: HarperCollins.

Kleist, Heinrich von (2010), *Selected Prose of Heinrich von Kleist*, trans. Peter Wortsman, Brooklyn: Archipelago.

Kohn, Eduardo (2013), *How Forests Think: Toward an Anthropology Beyond the Human*, Berkeley: University of California Press.

Kushner, Kenneth (2000), *One Arrow, One Life: Zen, Archery, Enlightenment*, Boston: Tuttle.

Lawrence, D. H. (1981), *Studies in Classic American Literature*, Harmondsworth: Penguin.

Leggett, Trevor (1978), *Zen and the Ways*, London: Routledge and Kegan Paul.

Lin, Tao (2007), *Eeeee Eee Eeee*, Hoboken: Melville House.

Lin, Tao (2009), *Shoplifting from American Apparel*, Brooklyn: Melville House.

Lin, Tao (2010), *Richard Yates*, Brooklyn: Melville House.

Lodge, Paul (2001), 'Primitive and Derivative Forces in Leibnizian Bodies', in *Nihil Sine Ratione: Mensch, Natur und Technik im Wirken von G. W. Leibniz*, ed. H. Poser, pp. 720–7, available at https://www.academia.edu/177477/Primitive_and_Derivative_Forces_in_Leibnizian_Bodies (accessed 9 June 2015).

Look, Brand C. and Donald Rutherford (2007), 'Introduction', in *The Leibniz–Des Bosses Correspondence*, ed. Look and Rutherford, New Haven, CT: Yale University Press, pp. xix–lxxix.

Maldiney, Henri (1973), *Regard espace parole*, Lausanne: Éditions l'Age d'Homme.

Mann, Thomas (1997), *Doctor Faustus: The Life of the German*

Composer Adrian Leverkühn, trans. John E. Woods, New York: Vintage.

Marcus Aurelius Antoninus (1908), *The Communings with Himself of Marcus Aurelius Antoninus Emperor of Rome. Together with His Speeches and Sayings*, a revised text and a translation into English by C. R. Haines, Loeb Classical Library, Cambridge, MA: Harvard University Press.

Marcus Aurelius Antoninus (1989), *The Meditations of Marcus Aurelius Antoninus*, trans. A. S. L. Farquharson, and a *Selection from the Letters of Marcus and Fronto*, trans. R. B. Rutherford, with an introduction and notes by R. B. Rutherford, Oxford: Oxford University Press.

Marcus Aurelius (2002), *The Emperor's Handbook: A New Translation of The Meditations*, trans. C. Scot Hicks and David V. Hicks, New York: Scribners.

Marsh, Calum (2014), 'The Shot of the Year', *The Dissolve*, 14 December 2014, available at https://thedissolve.com/features/2014-in-review/866-the-shot-of-the-year/ (accessed 26 July 2018).

Massumi, Brian (1992), *A User's Guide to Capitalism and Schizophrena: Deviations from Deleuze and Guattari*, Cambridge, MA: MIT Press.

Mengue, Philippe (2000), 'En hommage à Gilles Deleuze: Vincennes, une voix, un personnage proustien . . .', in *Tombeau de Gilles Deleuze*, ed. Yannick Beaubatie, Tulle: Mille Sources, pp. 49–56.

Mengue, Philippe (2003), *Deleuze et la question de la démocratie*. Paris: L'Harmmatan.

Meslet, Laurent (2005), *Le Psychisme et la vie: la philosophie de la nature de Raymond Ruyer*, Paris: L'Harmattan.

Miller, Henry and Michael Fraenkel (1946), *Hamlet*, vols 1–2, New York: Carrefour.

Moles, John L. (1995), 'The Cynics and Politics', in *Justice and Generosity: Studies in Hellenistic Social and Political Philosophy*, ed. André Laks and Macolm Schofield, Cambridge: Cambridge University Press, pp. 129–58.

Moles, John L. (1996), 'Cynic Cosmopolitanism', in *The Cynics: The Cynic Movement in Antiquity and Its Legacy*, ed. R. Bracht

Branham and Marie-Odile Goulet-Cazé, Berkeley: University of California Press, pp. 105–20.

Moles, John L. (2000), 'The Cynics', in *The Cambridge History of Greek and Roman Political Thought*, ed. Christopher Rowe and Malcolm Schofield, Cambridge: Cambridge University Press, pp. 415–34.

Monod, Jacques (1971), *Chance and Necessity: An Essay on the Natural Philosophy of Modern Biology*, trans. Austryn Wainhouse, New York: Vintage.

Naess, Arne (1989), *Ecology, Community and Lifestyle*, trans. and ed. D. Rothenberg, Cambridge: Cambridge University Press.

Nair, D. Appukuttan, and K. Ayyappa Paniker (eds) (1993), *Kathakali: The Art of the Non-Worldly*, Bombay: Marg.

Nietzsche, Friedrich (1967), *On the Genealogy of Morals and Ecce Homo*, trans. Walter Kaufman and R. Hollingdale, New York: Vintage.

O'Brien, Geoffrey (2014). 'Tree! Fire! Water! Godard!', *The New York Review of Books*, 3 November, available at www.nybooks.com/daily/2014/11/03/tree-fire-water-godard/ (accessed 2 April 2015).

Ormond-Smith, David and Paul Attinello (2007). 'Gay Darmstadt: Flamboyance and Rigour at the Summer Courses for New Music', *Contemporary Music Review*, 26:1, 105–14.

Paris, Jean (1965), *L'Espace et le regard*, Paris: Seuil.

Patton, Paul (2000), *Deleuze and the Political*, London: Routledge.

Patton, Paul (2010), *Deleuzian Concepts: Philosophy, Colonization, Politics*, Stanford: Stanford University Press.

Pimm, Stuart L. (1991), *The Balance of Nature? Ecological Issues in the Conservation of Species and Communities*, Chicago: University of Chicago Press.

Poole, Roger (1993), *Kierkegaard: The Indirect Communication*, Charlottesville: University of Virginia Press.

Protevi, John (2000), 'The Organism as the Judgement of God: Aristotle, Kant and Deleuze on Nature (That Is, on Biology, Theology and Politics)', in *Deleuze and Religion*, ed. Mary Bryden, London and New York: Routledge, pp. 30-41.

Protevi, John (2006), 'Deleuze, Guattari and Emergence', *Paragraph*, 29:2, 19–39.

Protevi, John (2012), 'Deleuze and Life', in *The Cambridge Companion to Deleuze and Guattari*, ed. Daniel W. Smith and Henry Somers-Hall, pp. 239–64.

Reader, Keith (2000), *Robert Bresson*, Manchester: Manchester University Press.

Rizov, Vadim (2014), 'Goodbye to 3-D Rules', *Filmmaker*, 20 October, available at http://filmmakermagazine.com/87878-goodbye-to-3-d-rules/#.VVU5aWAk-- (accessed 2 April 2015).

Rimer, J. Thomas and Yamazaki Masakazu (trans.) (1984), *On the Art of the Nō Drama: The Treatises of Zeami*, Princeton: Princeton University Press.

Roffe, Jon and Hannah Stark (eds) (2015), *Deleuze and the Non/Human*, London: Palgrave.

Roger, Alain (2000), 'Gilles Deleuze et l'amitié', in *Tombeau de Gilles Deleuze*, ed. Yannick Beaubatie, Tulle: Mille Sources, pp. 35–48.

Rosenbaum, Jonathan (1998), 'The Last Filmmaker: A Local, Interim Report', in *Robert Bresson*, ed. James Quandt, Toronto: Toronto International Film Festival Group, pp. 17–24.

Ruyer, Bernard (1995), 'La notion de liaison', in *Raymond Ruyer, de la science à la théologie*, ed. Louis Vax and Jean-Jacques Wunenburger, Paris: Kimé, pp. 45–54.

Ruyer, Raymond (1946), *Éléments de psycho-biologie*, Paris: Presses Universitaires de France.

Ruyer, Raymond (1952), *Néo-finalisme*, Paris: Presses Universitaires de France.

Ruyer, Raymond (1958), *La Genèse des formes vivantes*, Paris: Flammarion.

Ruyer, Raymond (2012), *Néo-finalisme*, preface by Fabrice Colonna, Paris: Presses Universitaires de France.

Sarkar, Sahotra (2005), *Biodiversity and Environmental Philosophy: An Introduction*, Cambridge: Cambridge University Press.

Sasso, Robert and Arnaud Villani (eds) (2003), *Le Vocabulaire de Gilles Deleuze*, Paris: Les Cahiers de Noesis/CHRI.

Scaff, Susan von Rohr (1998), *History, Myth, and Music: Thomas Mann's Timely Fiction*, Columbia, SC: Camden House.

Schofield, Malcolm (1999), *The Stoic Idea of the City*, Chicago: University of Chicago Press.

Schrader, Paul (1972), *Transcendental Style in Film: Ozu, Bresson, Dreyer*, Berkeley: University of California Press.

Sellars, John (2007), 'Deleuze's Cosmopolitanism', *Radical Philosophy*, 142, 30–7.

Skenazy, Paul and Tera Martin (eds) (1998), *Conversations with Maxine Hong Kingston*, Jackson, MS: University Press of Mississippi.

Smith, Daniel W. (2010), 'Genesis and Difference: Deleuze, Maïmon, and the Post-Kantian Reading of Leibniz', in *Deleuze and* The Fold*: A Critical Reader*, ed. Sjoerd van Tuinen and Niamh McDonnell, London: Palgrave Macmillan, pp. 132–54.

Somers-Hall, Henry, Jeffrey A. Bell and James Williams (eds) (2018), A Thousand Plateaus *and Philosophy*, Edinburgh: Edinburgh University Press.

Soulé, Michael E. (1989), 'Conservation Biology in the Twenty-first Century: Summary and Outlook', in *Conservation for the Twenty-first Century*, ed. D. Western and M. Pearl, New York: Oxford University Press, pp. 297–303.

Stiegler, Bernard (1998), *Technics and Time, 1: The Fault of Epimetheus*, trans. Richard Beardsworth and George Collins, Stanford: Stanford University Press.

Stiegler, Bernard (2011a), *The Decadence of Industrial Democracies*, trans. Daniel Ross and Suzanne Arnold, Cambridge: Polity Press.

Stiegler, Bernard (2011b), *Technics and Time, 3: Cinematic Time and the Question of Malaise*, trans. Stephen Barker, Stanford: Stanford University Press.

Stivale, Charles (2000), *Synopsis of Deleuze's ABC's*, http://www.langlab.wayne.edu/CStivale/D-G/ABCs.html (accessed 1 September 2011).

Stivale, Charles J. (2008), *Gilles Deleuze's ABCs: The Folds of Friendship*, Baltimore: Johns Hopkins University Press.

Stivale, Charles J. (2014), '*Être aux aguets*: Deleuze, Creation and Territorialization', in *The Animal Catalyst towards Ahuman Theory*, ed. Patricia MacCormack, London: Bloomsbury, pp. 69–80.

Sutter, Laurent de (2009), *Deleuze: la pratique du droit*, Paris: Michalon.

Tournier, Michel (1969), *Friday, or the Limbo of the Pacific*, trans. Norman Denny, New York: Pantheon.

Tournier, Michel (1988), *The Spirit Wind*, trans. Arthur Goldhammer, Boston: Beacon Press.

Tournier, Michel (1991), *The Midnight Love Feast*, trans. Barbara Wright, London: Collins.

Tuber, David S., Michael B. Hennesey, Suzanne Sander and Julia A. Miller (1996), 'Behavioral and Glucocorticoid Responses of Adult Domestic Dogs (*Canis familiaris*) to Companionship and Social Separation', *Journal of Comparative Psychology*, 110:1, 103–8.

Uexküll, Jakob von (1956), *Mondes animaux et monde humain, suivi de Théorie de la signification*, trans. P. Muller, Paris: Gonthier.

Ulman, Erik (1996), 'The Music of Sylvano Bussotti', *Perspectives of New Music*, 34:2, 186–201.

Varela, Francisco, Thompson, Evan, and Rosch, E. (1991), *The Embodied Mind: Cognitive Science and Human Experience*, Cambridge, MA: MIT Press

Vax, Louis and Jean-Jacques Wunenburger (1995), *Raymond Ruyer, de la science à la théologie*, Paris: Kimé..

Viveiros de Castro, Eduardo (2014), *Cannibal Metaphysics: For a Non-structural Anthropology*, trans. Peter Skafish, Minneapolis: Univocal.

Vizzini, Ned (2007), 'An Interview with Tao Lin', *Bookslut*, May 2007, available at www. bookslut.com/features/2007_05_011092.php (accessed 26 April 2013).

Vogt, Katja Maria (2008), *Law, Reason, and the Cosmic City*, Oxford: Oxford University Press.

Wichmann, Elizabeth (1991), *Listening to Theatre: The Aural Dimension of Beijing Opera*, Honolulu: University of Hawaii Press.

Wiklund, Rolf A. (1960), 'A Short Introduction to the Neofinalist Philosophy of Raymond Ruyer', *Philosophy and Phenomenological Research*, 21:2, 187–98.

Wilden, Anthony (1980), *System and Structure: Essays in Communication and Exchange*, 2nd edn, London: Tavistock.

Williams, Blake (2014), 'Cannes 2014: Adieu au langage (Jean-Luc Godard, France)', *Cinema Scope*, available at http://

cinema-scope.com/spotlight/adieu-au-langage-jean-luc-godard-france (accessed 2 April 2015).

Williams, James (2010), *Gilles Deleuze's Philosophy of Time: A Critical Introduction and Guide*, Edinburgh: Edinburgh University Press.

Wolfe, Cary (1995), 'In Search of Post-Humanist Theory: The Second-Order Cybernetics of Maturana and Varela', *Cultural Critique*, 30, 33–70.

Zarrilli, Phillip B. (2000), *Kathakali Dance-Drama: Where Gods and Demons Come to Play*, London: Routledge.

Žižek, Slavoj (2003), *Organs without Bodies: Deleuze and Consequences*, London: Routledge.

Zola, Émile (1964), *The Experimental Novel and Other Essays*, trans. Belle M. Sherman, New York: Haskell House.

Index